The New Constellation

The New Constellation

The Ethical-Political Horizons of Modernity/Postmodernity

Richard J. Bernstein

The MIT Press
Cambridge, Massachusetts

Second printing, 1993
First MIT Press edition 1992
©1991 Richard J. Bernstein

This book was printed and bound in the United States of America.

Library of Congress Cataloging-in-Publication Data

Bernstein, Richard J.
    The new constellation : the ethical-political horizons of modernity/ postmodernity / Richard J. Bernstein.
        p.   cm.
    Includes bibliographical references and index.
    ISBN 0-262-02337-7. — ISBN 0-262-52166-0 (pbk.)
    1. Philosophy, Modern—20th century. 2. Heidegger, Martin, 1889–1976. 3. Philosophy, French—20th century. 4. Postmodernism. 5. Ethics, Modern—20th century. 6. Political science—Philosophy—History—20th century. I. Title.
B804.B46 1991
190'9.'04—dc20   91-676
                                                                    CIP

For Paul and Rosemary

Contents

Acknowledgments

The essays in this volume were written at three different institutions: Haverford College, Frankfurt University (where I was a visiting professor in the spring, 1988) and the Graduate Faculty of the New School for Social Research. I have been extremely fortunate to have had colleagues and students who challenged me at almost every point. The semester I taught at Frankfurt University was especially significant. In addition to teaching a seminar dealing with the themes of these essays, I also participated in a seminar with Jürgen Habermas and Karl-Otto Apel that dealt with "modernity/ postmodernity." Because we share so much in common, we could focus attention on our differences, especially our different readings and interpretations of Heidegger, Gadamer, Derrida, Foucault, and Rorty. Both Habermas and Apel are formidable opponents and our discussions were intense and productive. I want to acknowledge the gracious hospitality I received in Frankfurt and the intellectual stimulation of my students and colleagues.

The senior fellowship that I received (1985–6) from the National Endowment for Humanities provided the opportunity for the reading and meditating required for writing these essays. My research assistants at the New School, Eduardo Duarte, Rick Lee, and Aaron Garrett helped in numerous ways to prepare this manuscript. I have also been blessed with a cheerful, extremely efficient secretary, Claire Martin, who made sure that I had the time required to complete this book. The editors of Polity Press have been exemplary. John Thompson has been most gracious and efficient. Halina

Boniszewska carefully supervized the production of this book. Penny Rendall is one of the best copy-editors with whom I have worked. As always, my wife Carol has been my best and most perceptive critic.

"Philosophy, History, and Critique" was originally published with the title "History, Philosophy, and The Question of Relativism" in *At the Nexus of Philosophy and History*, ed. Bernard P. Dauenhauer (Atlanta: University of Georgia Press, 1987). Earlier versions of "The Rage Against Reason" appeared in *Philosophy and Literature*, 10 (1986), and in *Construction and Criticism*, ed. Ernan McMullin (Notre Dame: University of Notre Dame Press, 1988). "Incommensurability and Otherness Revisited" was prepared for the Sixth East–West Philosophers' Conference held in Hawaii in August, 1989. It will be published in the proceedings of the conference. "Foucault: Critique as a Philosophic *Ēthos*" was published in *Zwischenbetrachtungen*, eds. A. Honneth, T. McCarthy, C. Offe, A. Wellmer (Frankfurt: Suhrkamp, 1989). "Serious Play: The Ethical-Political Horizon of Jacques Derrida," was published in *The Journal of Speculative Philosophy*, 1 (1987). "One Step Forward, Two Steps Backward: Rorty on Liberal Democracy and Philosophy," together with Rorty's reply, "Thugs and Theorists," appeared in *Political Theory*, 15 (1987). "Rorty's Liberal Utopia" was published in *Social Research*, 57 (1990). "Pragmatism, Pluralism, and the Healing of Wounds," is the presidential address delivered before the Eighty-fourth Annual Eastern Division Meeting of the American Philosophical Association in Washington, DC on December 29, 1988. It was published in the *Proceedings and Addresses of the American Philosophical Association*, 63 (1989). All of the above essays have been revised for publication in this volume. I want to acknowledge my gratitude to the editors and publishers for permission to reprint revised versions of these essays.

Introduction

Soon after the publication of *Beyond Objectivism and Relativism* (1983), a sympathetic critic wrote to me about the book. His comments were perceptive and incisive. But he concluded by abruptly asking: "When are you going to 'take on' Heidegger and the 'French'? When are you going to confront the 'postmodern' challenges – and deconstruction – of the philosophic orientation that you develop in the book?" At first I was somewhat bemused by these questions. They were similar to questions I had been asked before. When I had published *Praxis and Action* (1971) and *The Restructuring of Social and Political Theory* (1976), there was always someone who asked why I had not also treated some theme, some problem or thinker that the reader took to be "really" central to my inquiry.

But my critic's questions had a more pointed significance. In *Beyond Objectivism and Relativism* I claimed that

> a new conversation is now emerging among philosophers – a conversation about human rationality – and as a result of this dialogue we are beginning to gain a new understanding of rationality that has important ramifications for both theoretical and practical life.[1]

I also declared that

> the contours of the conversation about human rationality, especially as it pertains to science, hermeneutics and *praxis*, have recently taken on a new and exciting shape. I want not only to reveal the common

themes of this dialogue – the shared assumptions, commitments, and insights – but also to do justice to the different individual voices and emphases within it.[2]

The questions directed to me were a challenge to defend these "shared assumptions, commitments, and insights." According to *one* reading of what has been called "the postmodern moment," a rupture has occurred, a radical break that calls into question all philosophic projects. In an article written as a preparatory study for *Beyond Objectivism and Relativism*, I had even risked naming my critical philosophic orientation "non-foundational pragmatic humanism."[3] This label was deliberately provocative, especially the use of the signifier "humanism." I wrote that

> "humanism" ... has become something of a dirty word in recent times. It has been used by critics to identify everything that they think is wrong in the modern world ... In the new postmodern, poststructuralist Manichean theology, "humanism" seems to function as a name for the kingdom of Darkness .... But it is more than a matter of perversity to hold on to this sign and *not* to abandon it in the face of such varied criticisms.[4]

I was, of course, fully aware of the objections that Heideggerians and "postmodern" writers might raise. For had not Heidegger in his famous "Letter on Humanism" definitively shown us that humanism is nothing but a consequence of the metaphysical tradition that has its "origins" in Plato and reaches its culmination in Nietzsche, "the last metaphysician"? This metaphysical tradition is now "over" and needs to be overcome (*überwinden*). Had not Heidegger shown us that the *essence* of humanism – in all its guises – is *nihilism*, the nihilism that is becoming our destiny in the modern age of technology? Had not Heidegger shown the ontological need to rupture humanism in order to bring us into the clearing for "original thinking" – the thinking (of) Being?[5] Not only Heidegger but virtually every poststructuralist writer has railed against humanism – even though there are the most diverse understandings about what constitutes humanism and what is being damned. Consider, for example, the rhetorical flourish with which Foucault ends *The Order of Things*:

> Rather than the death of God – or rather in the wake of that death and in profound correlation with it – what Nietzsche's thought heralds

is the end of his murderer; it is the explosion of man's face in laughter
.... As the archaeology of our thought easily shows, man is an invention of recent date. And one perhaps nearing its end.[6]

Or again, in "The Ends of Man," where Derrida seeks to root out the
vestiges of humanism in French thought, he declares (speaking of
Zarathustra's laughter) that

> His laughter then will burst out, directed toward a return which no
> longer will have the form of the metaphysical repetition of humanism,
> nor, doubtless, "beyond" metaphysics, the form of a memorial or a
> guarding of the meaning of Being, the form of the house and of the
> truth of Being. He will dance, outside the house, the *aktive
> Vergesslichkeit*, the "active forgetting" and the cruel (*grausam*) feast of
> which the *Genealogy of Morals* speaks.[7]

In short, one might say that once "we" fully experience the rupture that has occurred with the "postmodern" moment, once "we"
grasp the full force and sting of the critiques of humanism that trace
their lineage to Nietzsche, then even the "non-foundational pragmatic humanism" which I had been developing must be discarded –
thrown into the abyss of failed metaphysical and philosophical
projects. Needless to say I do *not* accept this judgment nor am I
impressed by what has now become a cliché among many "postmodern" writers, i.e., that humanism is passé, to be dismissed by
laughter. But I *do* recognize that these critiques and deconstructions
call for a strong response.

There were other reasons why the more I thought about the
questions posed to me, the more I realized they demanded a
response. For even though in several of my books I have critically
examined a wide variety of problems, themes, and thinkers that span
much of twentieth-century Anglo-American and Continental philosophy, I had not focused on Heidegger or the heterogeneous writings
of those who are frequently labeled "postmodern." Nor had I
squarely confronted those Nietzschean motifs that have so deeply
affected these texts. Consequently, despite my claims about a "new
conversation concerning human rationality," I could justifiably be
accused of ignoring and excluding some of the most important
"voices" in this conversation – or more accurately those "voices"
that questioned and challenged this conversation and the "shared
assumptions" I sought to articulate. Furthermore I could justifiably

be accused of violating a fundamental principle that I have always advocated and have sought to put into practice. This is a principle that I originally learned from my reading of the Platonic Dialogues and which was reinforced by my study of Hegel and the American pragmatic thinkers. It is the principle that has most recently been eloquently and subtly expressed by Hans-Georg Gadamer.[8] The basic condition for all understanding requires one to test and risk one's convictions and prejudgments in and through an encounter with what is radically "other" and alien. To do this requires imagination and hermeneutical sensitivity in order to understand the "other" in its strongest possible light. Only by seeking to learn from the "other," only by fully grasping its claims upon one can it be critically encountered. Critical engaged dialogue requires opening of oneself to the full power of what the "other" is saying. Such an opening does not entail agreement but rather the to-and-fro play of dialogue. Otherwise dialogue degenerates into a self-deceptive monologue where one never risks testing one's prejudgments. So the quip about Heidegger, the "French," and "postmodern" challenges was a demand to put into practice what I had been professing – to test and risk my own philosophic convictions by exposing them to the sharpest and most penetrating questioning.

There was still another consideration that was motivating the need to face these challenges. The most persistent and pervasive concern in all my writings is the question(s) of *praxis*. This concern has been in the foreground and background of all my thinking. In *Praxis and Action*, I already affirmed that "the guiding principle of this study is that the investigation of the nature, status, and significance of *praxis* and action has become the dominant concern of the most influential philosophic movements that have emerged since Hegel."[9] But again it might be objected that this is simply not true for Heidegger, the most original and influential Continental philosopher of the twentieth century, the figure who stands behind and who casts his shadow over "postmodern" writers. *Praxis* is associated with the metaphysical humanism that Heidegger so devastatingly attacks. The entire thrust of Heidegger's thinking is to displace the question of *praxis* with a far more "fundamental" question – the question of Being (*Seinsfrage*). Furthermore in much of the French poststructuralist writings there is scarcely even the mention of "*praxis*" – except as an object of suspicion. So what then is the basis for the claim that *praxis* and action have become "the dominant concern of the most influential philosophic movements that have emerged since Hegel"?

Furthermore I felt the need to take account of a phenomenon that could not be denied. In the post-Second World War period through the 1960s, the evocation of *praxis* had powerful and rich resonances for many left intellectuals throughout the world. It called to mind the early Marx, the tradition of Western Marxism and the Critical Theory of the Frankfurt School. Throughout Eastern Europe *"praxis"* became the banner for those left intellectuals who were battling Stalinism, dogmatism, and totalitarianism. Yet by the end of the 1960s there were already many signs of the fading of Western Marxism. There was a turning away from the talk about *praxis* (and such related concepts as alienation). A new generation of thinkers no longer drew their radical inspiration from such "heroes" as Adorno, Horkheimer, Benjamin, Marcuse, Gramsci, Lukács and Korsch. New "names" began to displace these older heroes – Foucault, Derrida, Deleuze, Lacan. There was even the emergence of strange hybrids – "left Heideggerians," "left Nietzscheans." For French intellectuals, the striking and ambiguous events of May 1968, and the revelations about Stalin's Gulag signaled a break with all forms of Marxism. Initially I found this rapid displacement of the "heroes" of Western Marxism extremely perplexing. With the possible exception of Foucault, the writings of the so-called "postmodern" intellectuals rarely dealt with ethical-political issues, or so it seemed. What was it about these "new" currents that spoke to so many younger intellectuals? How was one to account for the growing influence of "French" poststructuralism? What was it about the new interest in otherness, *différance*, the decentering of the subject, in fragments and fissures, in power/knowledge regimes that appeared to be so relevant for coming to grips with modernity and its discontents? What distinguished the "radical" gestures of "postmodernism" from older varieties of reactionary anti-modernism?

In order to answer these questions, I decided to reread and rethink what was happening in these "postmodern" interventions. To use a Hegelian turn of phrase, I wanted to discover the "truth" implicit in these heterogeneous writings. For I had become increasingly dissatisfied with the typical responses to recent developments in Continental philosophy – especially by Anglo-American philosophers. Roughly speaking, these fall into three categories: (1) total ignorance and uninformed silence; (2) polemical attacks;

(3) endless internal commentary and textual analysis. Many – indeed most – Anglo-American analytic philosophers totally ignore twentieth-century Continental philosophy. For them it simply does not count as "serious" philosophy and is not worthy of consideration. It is a quagmire of confusion, obfuscation, and pretentious gesturing – flouting even the most minimal standards of clarity and rational argumentation. The occasional references to Continental philosophy are usually only polemical and disparaging – in order to "expose" its confusion and triviality. But I find no more satisfactory the defensive attitude of those who have become so enamored with Continental philosophy that they never achieve any critical distance. They become "groupies" who seize upon the latest fashionable trends. Frequently they treat these texts as if they were sacred texts calling forth endless commentary. Some of these "commentaries" even read like parodies. With the exception of Richard Rorty (whose contro-versial writings are discussed in the following essays) there is scarcely another significant Anglo-American *philosopher* who has cre-atively appropriated "postmodern" themes. There is a paucity of judicious critiques of this work – the type of critique where one seeks to do justice to what is being said *and* also "steps back" in order to evaluate critically strengths and weaknesses, insights and blind-nesses, "truth" and "falsity." In the highly charged polemical debates there are even those who ridicule the very idea of "judicious critique." They think this is only a devious power play in order to "domesticate" and contain the radical "other." But to abandon inde-pendent critique is to abandon independent thinking. Of course, there is always the risk that any critique will distort or fail to do justice to what is being criticized. But if this happens, it can only be corrected by further critique.

At an early stage of my rereading of Heidegger, the "French," and deconstructive writings, I kept noticing something which had not been adequately thematized. For despite the apparent neglect and displacement of ethical-political questions, there is a strong under-current in these writings that gravitated toward ethical-political issues. Gradually I began to focus on the question of critique itself – the sense in which these writings were critical and the self-under-standing of critique. The question I wanted to probe is "critique in the name of what?" For in Wittgenstein's sense, the very "grammar" of critique requires some standard, some measure, some basis for critique. Otherwise there is – as Habermas claims – the danger of the critical impulse consuming itself. To put the issue in a slightly different way, I fully agree with Derrida when he says "I cannot conceive of a radical critique which would not be ultimately motivated by some sort of affirmation, acknowledged or not."[10] But then one must ask what precisely is being affirmed and *why*? What is it that deconstruction affirms? What is Heidegger affirming when he thinks *against* humanism? What does Foucault affirm in his archaeological and genealogical critiques? The reason why these are such perplexing and crucial questions is because of an *aporia* that seems to lie at the heart of these critiques. On the one hand, the primary rhetorical gesture of the "postmodern" moment is to be critical – of Western rationality, logocentrism, humanism, the Enlightenment legacy, the centered subject, etc. But on the other hand, there is also a questioning, undermining and deconstruction of any and all fixed standards of critique, a relentless questioning of any appeal to *archai* or foundations. Does this mean that "postmodern" writers are ensnared in what Habermas and Apel call "performative contradictions" where critique is at once affirmed and undermined?[11] Or is there a way of reading these texts so that we can interpret them as developing new genres of critique without requiring affirming norms of critique?

With respect to basic ethical-political norms of critique, much of twentieth-century thinking has fluctuated between two extremes. There are those like Max Weber who tell us that we must frankly acknowledge that there is not – and cannot be – any *rational grounding* of the basic ethical-political norms. With cold lucidity we are compelled to commit ourselves to warring gods and demons. This is a matter of decision and commitment without the comfort of rational grounding. Consequently, there is no rational basis for our ultimate affirmations. Despite the consequential differences among Weber, decisionists and emotivists, there is a common agreement that the attempt to ground norms is a futile project. We will see that this is also true for the ironic stance taken by Richard Rorty.

At the other extreme are those who claim that the project of rationally grounding norms is not only a viable one but can be carried out. Furthermore this can be done in a way that avoids the treacherous pitfalls of "bad" foundationalism. Advocates of such a "position" like Apel and Habermas typically employ strong or weak transcendental or quasi-transcendental arguments. For they argue that speech and communication, when properly understood and analyzed, show that there are *necessary* and *unavoidable* rational norms of both theoretical and practical discourse.

We seem then to be drawn into a grand Either/Or: *either* there is a rational grounding of the norms of critique *or* the conviction that there is such a rational grounding is itself a self-deceptive illusion. But again both of these extreme alternatives have themselves been subject to sharp criticism. So the question arises, can we avoid these extremes? Is there some third way of understanding critique that avoids – passes between – the Scylla of "groundless critique" and the Charybdis of rationally grounded critique that "rests" upon illusory foundations? There are many who think that the achievement of the "postmodern" moment is to open up the space for new styles and genres of critique that avoid the extremes and twin dangers of this grand Either/Or. But is this so? Is there a new way of understanding and practicing critique that escapes this grand Either/Or? In several of the following essays I probe this question from a variety of perspectives. This is – if not *the* central question – then at least *a* central question that is at the very heart of "modern/postmodern" debates.

In light of the above reflections I can now explain why I have entitled this volume, *The New Constellation: The Ethical-Political Horizons of Modernity/Postmodernity*. "Constellation" is a metaphor that I have taken from the writings of Theodor Adorno and Walter Benjamin. Martin Jay gives a succinct characterization of what they mean when he writes that a constellation is a "juxtaposed rather than integrated cluster of changing elements that resist reduction to a common denominator, essential core, or generative first principle."[12] The reason why I find this metaphor so fertile is because I want to show that our "modern/postmodern" situation or predicament is one that defies and resists any and all attempts of reduction to "a common denominator, essential core, or generative first principle." "Constellation" is deliberately intended to displace Hegel's master metaphor of *Aufhebung*. For, as I will argue, although we cannot (and should not) give up the *promise* and demand for reconciliation – a reconciliation achieved by what Hegel calls "determinate negation," I do not think we can any longer responsibly claim that there is or can be a final reconciliation – an *Aufhebung* in which all difference, otherness, opposition and contradiction are reconciled. There are always unexpected contingent ruptures that dis-rupt the project of reconciliation. The changing elements of the new constellation resist such reduction. What is "new" about this constellation is the growing awareness of the depth of radical instabilities. We have to learn to think and act in the "in-between" interstices of forced reconciliations and radical dispersion.

Jay also calls attention to another metaphor that is central for Adorno and which I have also appropriated: force-field (*Kraftfeld*). A force-field is a "relational interplay of attractions and aversions that constitute the dynamic transmutational structure of a complex phenomenon."[13] This is also an extremely fertile metaphor for "comprehending" the "modern/postmodern" situation. For I want to show that this situation can be characterized as a dynamic "relational interplay of attractions and aversions." The task of comprehension today requires doing justice to the delicate unstable balance of these attractions and aversions.

Throughout I use the hyphenated expression "ethical-political." I do so in order to invoke and recall the classical (Greek) understanding of the symbiotic relation between ethics and politics. Ethics is concerned with *ēthos*, with those habits, customs and modes of response that shape and define our *praxis*. Politics is concerned with our public lives in the *polis* – with the communal bonds that at once unite and separate us as citizens. The essential link between *ēthos* and *polis* is *nomos*. Although we can distinguish ethics and politics, they are inseparable. For we cannot understand ethics without thinking through our political commitments and responsibilities. And there is no understanding of politics that does not bring us back to ethics. Ethics and politics as disciplines concerned with *praxis* are aspects of a unified practical philosophy. It is because *ethics* and *politics* are so intimately related that both Plato and Aristotle are so concerned with the tensions between them, and with the central question of what is the relation between leading a good life and becoming a good citizen. The scope of what the Greeks took to be the proper ethical-political domain is far broader and richer than modern understandings of morality. Recently, thinkers as different as Alasdair MacIntyre, Charles Taylor, Bernard Williams, Martha Nussbaum and HansGeorg Gadamer (and many others) have developed a multifaceted critique of the narrowing of morality as it has been treated by modern philosophy. Despite their differences they all appeal to the classical Greek understanding of the domain of the ethical-political in order to criticize modern morality and moral philosophy.

My use of ethical-political is also intended to remind us of the Hegelian concept of *Sittlichkeit*. Hegel is the "modern" philosopher par excellence who at once appreciated the achievement and limitations of modern (Kantian) *Moralität*. He sought to integrate and reconcile the "truth" of modern *Moralität* (which emphasizes individual autonomy) and *Sittlichkeit* with its stress on communal "ethical substance." He argued that a new *mediated Sittlichkeit* is in the process of emerging in our (his) time. Even if one rejects (as I do) Hegel's claims about what he thought was occurring in his time, Hegel – perhaps more than any other "modern" philosopher – had a profound grasp of both the strong tensions and mutual dependence of *Moralität* and *Sittlichkeit*. Many of the contemporary battles between those who insist upon the primacy of individual rights and those who emphasize the primacy of communal bonds stand in the shadow of Hegel's analysis of the achievements and discontents of modernity.

"Horizons" is a metaphor that has taken on increasing importance ever since Nietzsche used it in his celebrated "God is dead" passage: "How could we drink up the sea? Who gave us the sponge to wipe away the entire horizon?"[14] Since Nietzsche's time, "horizon" has assumed a life of its own. It became a central philosophic concept in the phenomenological tradition – in Husserl, Merleau-Ponty, Heidegger, and in Gadamer's ontological hermeneutics. Throughout the following essays I play on (with) the multiple polysemic meanings of "horizon." Sometimes I use it to focus attention on what lies in the background of someone's thinking but which is never explicitly thematized. At times I use it to call attention to what always seems to be receding but nevertheless orients one's thinking. I agree with Gadamer when he tells us that "in a conversation, when we have discovered the other person's standpoint and horizon, his ideas become intelligible without our necessarily having to agree with him."[15] "Horizon" also has a normative aura, for example when we speak of a loss of horizon or an enlargement of one's horizon. The use of the plural "horizon*s*" is important because I do not think that there is a single all-encompassing ethical-political horizon of "modernity/postmodernity" but rather an irreducible plurality of horizons. It will become clear why I have skeptical doubts about the way in which Gadamer speaks of the "fusion of horizons." For "fusion" does not do adequate justice to those ruptures that dis-turb our attempts to reconcile different ethical-political horizons.

Throughout I have placed "modernity/postmodernity" in scare quotes to signal that it must be used with extreme caution. Anyone with even the most superficial acquaintance with recent debates can scarcely avoid noticing that the terms "modernity" and "postmodernity" are slippery, vague, and ambiguous. They have wildly different meanings within different cultural disciplines and even within the same discipline. There is no consensus or agreement about the multiple meanings of these treacherous terms. Furthermore there is the paradox that many thinkers who are labeled "postmodern" by others, do not think of themselves as "postmodern" or even use this expression. For example, when asked to name "postmodern" thinkers I suspect many would include Heidegger, Derrida, Foucault, and perhaps Nietzsche. But none of them ever rely on this term. For reasons that I set forth, I think it is best to use the expression "modern/postmodern" to signify what Heidegger calls a *Stimmung*, a mood – one which is amorphous, protean, and shifting but which nevertheless exerts a powerful influence on the ways in which we think, act, and experience. So when I speak of "modernity/postmodernity," it is primarily this *Stimmung* that I want to elicit.

Although the essays in this volume deal with a variety of different problems, themes, and thinkers, they are intended to support a thesis about the *Stimmung* of "modernity/postmodernity." I want to show that there has been a dialectical development at work. Initially it appears that ethical-political questions about *praxis* are excluded and marginalized. In the early writings of Heidegger, Derrida, Foucault and Rorty these questions do not even *seem* to be considered. Yet as we follow the pathways of their thinking and writings something curious begins to happen – for each of these thinkers begins to gravitate more and more to confronting the ethical-political consequences of their own thinking. I do not think this is merely contingent or accidental but rather a dialectical consequence of the questions they themselves raise. Like the "return of the repressed" we will see how and why their thinking necessitates this turn. And this dialectical turn has a much broader and deeper significance. For the "modern/ postmodern" *Stimmung* compels us to confront anew the classic Socratic question, "How one should live."

Understanding the "modern/postmodern" *Stimmung* in this way, where ethical-political questions come into the foreground of our horizons, can help explain why Jean-François Lyotard's *The Post-modern Condition* caused such a stir when it first appeared and has given rise to so much controversy.[16] For whatever one thinks of his characterization of "postmodern" (I think it is both too narrow and contentious) he did touch upon a vital intellectual nerve when he "pushed" ethical-political questions into the foreground. There is an analogy between the appearance of Thomas Kuhn's *The Structure of Scientific Revolutions* (1962) and Lyotard's *The Postmodern Condition* (1979). In retrospect we can see that many of Kuhn's claims about science were – so to speak – in the air. Nevertheless the rhetorical force of his monograph and the controversy it generated were due to Kuhn's gift for articulating and bringing together in a focused manner what many other scholars were saying and exploring. So too, Lyotard's monograph achieved its rhetorical force because he succinctly gave expression to something that was increasingly in the air – the need to confront ethical-political concerns that had been emerging in the "modern/postmodern" *Stimmung*.

This collection of essays is not quite the book that I intended to write when I began working on it. My plan was first to write a number of independent essays, experiments, what Hannah Arendt calls "exercises," in order to approach issues and thinkers from a variety of perspectives. My original plan was to rewrite essays in order to relate a coherent narrative – to fill in gaps and supply transitions. But every time I attempted to unify the essays into an integrated whole, I was frustrated. I felt that I was attempting a "forced reconciliation" – seeking to reduce the elements that resisted reduction. It was only gradually that I came to realize that there was a reason for this – that my claims about the new constellation were self-referential – that I too had to resist the temptation to reduce the changing elements to a "common denominator, essential core, or genernative principle." Nevertheless this is not a miscellaneous collection of independent essays. They are all variations on the same or similar themes. They interweave and even at times repeat motifs. Some passages are repeated in order to emphasize the continuities of these essays. They are all shaped by a horizon from which I seek to understand the ethical-political consequences and deficiencies of the "modern/postmodern" *Stimmung*.

When editing these essays for publication I discovered something of which I had not been fully aware when I originally wrote them. There are two essays explicitly devoted to the work of Richard Rorty, but a discussion of Rorty crops up in many of the other essays. Rorty has been a dialogical partner and friend for more than forty years since we were both undergraduates at the University of Chicago. On several occasions we have engaged in public debates. We share a great deal although we have had our disagreements. Both of us draw our inspiration from the American pragmatic movement. (My first book dealt with John Dewey, and Rorty calls himself a "Deweyean pragmatist.")[17] Nevertheless we each emphasize very different aspects of the pragmatic legacy. So my frequent discussions and allusions to Rorty can be read as an ongoing *Auseinandersetzung* where what is at issue is the ethical-political consequences of this common pragmatic legacy. The sharpness of my critique of Rorty's recent work in these essays must be seen within the context of our common bonds.

NOTES

1 *Beyond Objectivism and Relativism*: *Science, Hermeneutics, and Praxis* (Philadelphia: University of Pennsylvania Press, 1983), p. 2.

2 Ibid.

3 "What is the Difference that Makes a Difference? Gadamer, Habermas, and Rorty," reprinted in *Philosophical Profiles* (Philadelphia: University of Pennsylvania Press, 1986), pp. 86–93.

4 Ibid, p. 92.

5 See my critical discussion of Heidegger, "Heidegger on Humanism," reprinted in *Philosophical Profiles*.

6 Michel Foucault, *The Order of Things* (New York: Vintage Books, 1973), p. 385.

7 Jacques Derrida, "The Ends of Man," *Margins*, trans. Alan Bass (Chicago: University of Chicago Press, 1982), p. 136.

8 See my discussion of Gadamer in *Beyond Objectivism and Relativism*.

9 *Praxis and Action: Contemporary Philosophies of Human Activity* (Philadelphia: University of Pennsylvania Press, 1971), p. xiii.

10 Jacques Derrida, "Dialogue with Jacques Derrida," in Richard Kearney, ed., *Dialogues with Contemporary Continental Thinkers* (Manchester: Manchester University Press, 1984), p. 118.

11 See Jürgen Habermas, *The Philosophical Discourse of Modernity*, trans. F. Lawrence (Cambridge, Mass.: MIT Press, 1987).

12 Martin Jay, *Adorno* (Cambridge, Mass.: Harvard University Press, 1984), pp. 14–15.

13 Ibid.

14 Friedrich Nietzsche, *The Gay Science*, trans. Walter Kaufman (New York: Vintage Books, 1974), p. 181 (paragraph 125). See also *Untimely*

Meditations, trans. R. J. Hollingdale (Cambridge: Cambridge University Press, 1983), especially the second essay.

15 Hans-Georg Gadamer, *Truth and Method*, second revised edn, trans. and revised J. Weinsheimer and D. G. Marshall (New York: Crossroad, 1989), p. 303. See Gadamer's perceptive discussion of "horizon," pp. 300–307.

16 Jean-François Lyotard, *The Postmodern Condition: A Report on Knowledge*, trans. G. Bennington and B. Massumi (Minneapolis: University of Minnesota Press, 1984).

17 See Richard J. Bernstein, *John Dewey* (1966; reprinted Atascadero, Cal.: Ridgeview, 1981).

1

Philosophy, History, and Critique

In her preface to *Between Past and Future*, Hannah Arendt imaginatively interprets a parable by Franz Kafka. Kafka's parable reads as follows:

> He has two antagonists: the first presses him from behind, from the origin. The second blocks the road ahead. He gives battle to both. To be sure, the first supports him in his fight with the second, for he wants to push him forward, and in the same way the second supports him in his fight with the first, since he drives him back. But it is only theoretically so. For it is not only the two antagonists who are there, but he himself as well, and who really knows his intentions? His dream, though, is that some time in an unguarded moment – and this would require a night darker than any night has ever been yet – he will jump out of the fighting line and be promoted, on account of his experience in fighting, to the position of umpire over his antagonists in their fight with each other.[1]

Arendt's interpretation of this parable illuminates the gap in which the activity of thinking takes place – thinking that is situated in "a battleground on which the forces of the past and the future clash with each other." It is in this gap that the experience of thinking occurs – thinking that must be practiced and exercised over and over again but which knows no finality.

Kafka's parable is sufficiently rich so that it can be interpreted as a parable of the relation of philosophy to its past, to its history. For just as the "He" of the parable gains his identity in the battle with the two antagonists, so I want to suggest that this is the situation of philosophy. While it may dream of jumping out of the fighting line and achieving the position of a neutral umpire, it is an illusory dream. And like Kant's analysis of dialectical illusion, and Wittgenstein's Tractarian understanding of the limits of language, even when we are dimly aware that we cannot break out of these limits, that we cannot "jump out of the fighting line," we are still tempted to try. We never escape the battlefield in which there is always uneasy resolution and unresolved tension. It is a battle that is fraught with different types of dangers and illusions. For there is the illusion that philosophy can once and for all cut itself off from its past, jump out of its own history – something it never succeeds in doing. If it could, it would simply disappear and lose its identity. And there is the illusion of imagining that it can completely identify itself with its past, an illusion which, if it could be realized, would also mean a loss of its identity. For its proper place, its *topos* is always in the gap, and in fighting the battle between past and future.

When the danger is perceived as being overwhelmed by its past, philosophy fights back. We see this moment exemplified by Descartes, Kant, Nietzsche, Husserl, and more recently by logical positivists and analytic philosophers. At such moments philosophers are prone to make a sharp distinction between "doing philosophy" and the history of philosophy, with the confidence that once we hit on the right method, discover the way of making philosophy into a rigorous discipline, then we can simply abandon to antiquarians what appears to be the "dead weight" of the past. At such moments the history of philosophy is viewed with extreme suspicion, a repository of confusions and obscurities, an endless battleground of competing opinions with no resolution, a trap that can ensnare us. We need to make a break with the past; we need to forget in order to get on with the serious endeavor of philosophizing. And there are times when there is a backlash against the pretensions of the ahistorical character of philosophy, when we realize that even the boldest attempts to break with history fail, when we see how even those philosophers who thought that they were laying entirely new foundations for philosophy are themselves deeply marked by prejudices and biases which they have inherited from the very past that they have been battling. At such moments there is sometimes the temptation to claim that philosophy itself is nothing but the history of philosophy – a stance which ironically is itself unhistorical insofar as it tends to forget that there would be no history of philosophy unless philosophers themselves (who make this history) thought of themselves as breaking with the past.

I do not think that this unstable, in-between status of philosophy is a cause for despair, but rather that it is the *topos* in which philosophy always dwells. It would only be a cause for despair if we had reason to think that there can be an end to the battle, that philosophy could and should achieve the position of a neutral umpire. The quest for certainty, the search for an Archimedean point which can serve as a foundation for philosophy, the aspiration to see the world aright *sub specie aeternitatis*, the metaphysics of presence where we desire to break out of the endless process of signification and interpretation and face reality with immediacy and directness, are all variations on the dream of "He" to jump out of the fighting line. And even if we judge these attempts to fail in their ultimate objective, we do a serious injustice to philosophy if we fail to realize how much is achieved and illuminated in these failed attempts. Philosophers – especially since the beginnings of modern philosophy – have been plagued by the anxiety that unless we can discover fixed, indubitable foundations, we are confronted with intellectual and moral chaos, radical skepticism, and self-defeating relativism – a situation that is metaphorically described by Descartes when he says it is "as if I had all of a sudden fallen into very deep water [and] I am so disconcerted that I can neither make certain of setting my feet on the bottom, nor can I swim and so support myself on the surface."[2] In another context I have labeled this anxiety "the Cartesian Anxiety" and have argued that it is an anxiety that needs to be exorcized, that can only be cured by a type of philosophic therapy.[3] But here I want to focus on the critical space of this unstable gap between philosophy and its past. For the theme that I want to explore is the way in which an appeal to history (and not just the history of philosophy) serves a *critical* function in the battle of philosophy. It is not simply that we locate the critical function of philosophy in those moments when philosophy fights back and seeks to push back its past, but also in those moments when this process is reversed, when we appeal to history and the history of philosophy in order to uncover, challenge, and criticize current prejudgments and prejudices – prejudices that can run so deep that we are not even aware of them as uncritical biases. I do not want to suggest that this is the only function which the study of history of philosophy can serve, but it is a function which I think has not always been fully appreciated. So let me turn to several attempts and several different ways in which the appeal to history has been used critically in our contemporary situation.

The uses of history for philosophic critique

The two major philosophic movements of the twentieth century have prided themselves on their ahistorical thrust, and both initially helped to foster a deep suspicion of the positive role that the study of history might play for philosophy. In this respect, both analytic philosophy and phenomenology were true heirs of the Cartesian bias. Both in very different ways sought to rid us once and for all from what they took to be the dangers of historicism and to delineate ways in which philosophy might "finally" become a rigorous discipline that would no longer be burdened by past errors and dead ends. This anti-historical animus was no less fundamental for Frege and Husserl than it was for later logical positivists and conceptual analysts. To the extent that either movement showed an interest in the history of philosophy, it was motivated by the desire to show how what was valuable and viable in this tradition could be interpreted as seeing through a glass darkly what now was supposedly seen so perspicaciously – to show how the task of philosophy, properly understood, could correct the mistakes and confusions of the past.

Although I think parallel stories can be told about the breakdown of the anti-historical bias of analytic philosophy and phenomenology, a breakdown which can be seen as a "return of the repressed," I want to focus on the development of analytic philosophy and some of its recent critics. Analytic philosophy as a style of philosophizing has undergone many internal transformations from its early origins in logical positivism and the writings of Russell and Moore. But even when we follow its sometimes tortuous paths and its diverse currents from positivism to ordinary-language analysis to the philosophy of language and formal semantics, the anti-historical bias of this style of philosophizing has persisted. Recently, however, there are many signs of the breakup of the hegemony of analytic philosophy. Even a generation ago there seemed to be an optimistic confidence among many analytic philosophers that philosophy had finally discovered its proper subject matter, its problems and its procedures, so that genuine progress could be made in solving or dissolving philosophic problems. But even among the staunchest defenders of analytic philosophy this confidence is now seriously questioned. Recently there have been a growing number of critiques of the presuppositions, unquestioned assumptions, and metaphors that have characterized so much of contemporary analytic philosophy.

Two of the most forceful and controversial critics of analytic philosophy have been Richard Rorty and Alasdair MacIntyre. Philosophers are frequently insensitive to the criticisms of "outsiders," but what has disturbed (or delighted) so many philosophers is that both Rorty and MacIntyre are "insiders." I do not simply mean that they have established their credentials as professional philosophers, but more specifically that each has contributed to discussions which have been in the foreground of analytic philosophy. But the distinctive feature of their recent critiques is the use that they make of history in carrying out these critiques. Rorty, in *Philosophy and the Mirror of Nature*,[4] not only "goes after" the pretensions of analytic philosophy, he also seeks to deconstruct what he calls the "Cartesian-Lockean-Kantian" tradition, and the obsession with epistemology and foundationalism that he takes to be characteristic of so much of modern philosophy. Rorty typically begins his critiques with a "softening-up" strategy in which he shows his dexterity in picking apart the typical argumentative strategies that have been valorized by analytic philosophers. But the subversive quality of his critique soon becomes evident, for he is calling into question just this adversarial, argumentative style of philosophizing. He wants to dig deeper and come to some understanding of why philosophers engage in the language games that they do. And this requires a historical critique, a type of genealogical unmasking where we become aware of the historical accidents and contingencies that shape what we frequently take to be intuitive and self-evident.

One of the many spinoffs of Rorty's reflections is a distinctive (and controversial) interpretation of how the history of philosophy has developed. He rejects the view that there are perennial problems of philosophy which arise as soon as we reflect. He is equally relentless in his criticism of a variant of this, where we take the more charitable and self-congratulatory attitude that our philosophic ancestors were dealing with basic problems, but the trouble is that they lacked the proper conceptual tools for solving them. His alternative, which can be seen as a novel blending of themes suggested by Heidegger, Derrida, Foucault, Kuhn, and Feyerabend, may be stated as follows.

There are moments in history when, because of all sorts of historical accidents – like what is going on in some part of culture such as science or religion – a new set of metaphors, distinctions, and problems is invented and captures the imagination of followers. For a time, when a particular philosophic language game gets entrenched, it sets the direction for "normal" philosophizing. After a while, because of some other historical accidents – like the appearance of a new genius or just plain boredom and sterility – another cluster of metaphors, distinctions, and problems usurps the place of what is now a dying tradition. At first the abnormal talk of some new genius may be dismissed as idiosyncratic, as not being "genuine" or "serious" philosophy. But sometimes this abnormal talk will set philosophy in new directions. We must resist the Whiggish temptation to rewrite the history of philosophy in our own image – where we see our predecessors as "really" treating what we now take to be fundamental problems. The crucial point for Rorty is to realize that a philosophical paradigm does *not* displace a former one because it can better formulate the legitimate problems of a prior paradigm; rather, because of a set of historical contingencies, it nudges the former paradigm aside. This is what happened in the seventeenth century when within a relatively short period of time the entire tradition of scholasticism collapsed and no longer seemed to have much point. After such a revolution or upheaval occurs, philosophers have a difficult time figuring out the point of the elaborate language game that had evolved. While Rorty refuses to make predictions, he certainly suggests that this is likely to happen again with modern philosophy and its offspring, analytic philosophy. To understand a historical movement such as analytic philosophy, we must uncover the metaphors, distinctions, and problems that characterize its form of normal philosophizing, and this requires historical digging into how a distinctive type of problematic was invented.

I do not want to suggest that I uncritically accept Rorty's understanding of how the history of philosophy develops, or rather moves by fits and starts. There is plenty to criticize in the specific genealogies that he elaborates. But I do want to highlight the seriousness (and playfulness) of Rorty's critique, for if he is right then many analytic philosophers are self-deceived in what they think they are doing – solving and dissolving the "genuine" problems of philosophy. In this context the most important point to emphasize is that Rorty's forays into the history of philosophy and the normal philosophizing of analytic philosophers is primarily critical in its intent. His historical analyses are intended to uncover prejudgments and prejudices, to expose their historical contingencies. At the very least, he forces us to ask new sorts of questions about just what analytic philosophers are doing, and these critical questions could not even be raised without a historical perspective on the present.

MacIntyre, who has been critical of Rorty's historical interpretations and more generally Rorty's conception of the history of philosophy, makes an even more ambitious use of history in his critique of contemporary moral philosophy in *After Virtue*. In the main, Rorty restricts himself to the history of philosophy. But in a quasi-Hegelian manner, MacIntyre thinks that if we want to understand philosophy and its history, we can only properly make sense of it in terms of more pervasive themes in culture and society. This is evidenced in the way in which he examines emotivism. For emotivism is not just a curious minor chapter in the history of moral philosophy. We can argumentatively show why an emotivist theory of meaning is mistaken, but this does not yet touch what MacIntyre takes to be a more fundamental issue. For he claims that,

> to a large degree people now think, talk, and act *as if* emotivism were true, no matter what their avowed theoretical standpoint may be. Emotivism has become embodied in our culture. But of course in saying this I am not merely contending that morality is not what it once was, but also and more importantly that what once was morality has to a large degree disappeared ... and that this marks a degeneration, a grave cultural loss.[5]

MacIntyre seeks to show us that emotivism has become embodied in our culture and sketches a historical account of just how this came to be – a historical account which is not meant to be neutral but rather has the critical intent of showing us why this is a degeneration and a cultural loss. A degeneration from what? From what MacIntyre calls the "tradition of the virtues" – a tradition that began long before Aristotle, but where Aristotle's ethical and political writings are the canonical texts, a tradition which according to MacIntyre continued to develop creatively through the Middle Ages. If MacIntyre is to complete his narrative argument, it is not sufficient simply to describe and evoke the memory of this tradition. He must also defend it. To use his own words, he seeks to make "the rational case" for a tradition in which the Aristotelian ethical and political texts are canonical. The Aristotelian tradition of the virtues must be "rationally vindicated." According to MacIntyre's narrative it was the Enlightenment project of seeking to justify moral principles that bears a great deal of the responsibility for the "catastrophe" of the collapse of the tradition of the virtues. This Enlightenment project, when unmasked – as it was by Nietzsche – ineluctably leads to emotivism. According to MacIntyre we are confronted with a grand Either/Or.

> *Either* one must follow through the aspirations and the collapse of the different versions of the Enlightenment project until there remains only the Nietzschean diagnosis and the Nietzschean problematic *or* one must hold that the Enlightenment project was not only mistaken, but should never have been commenced in the first place. There is no third alternative.[6]

Once again, in citing MacIntyre, my main point is not to endorse what he is claiming, but to highlight another variation of the way in which the appeal to history can serve a critical philosophical function.[7] To anticipate a point that I want to emphasize later in this essay, MacIntyre's own historical critique of contemporary morality and moral philosophy itself demands a close critical examination of his "rational vindication" of the Aristotelian tradition. To return to Kafka's parable, both Rorty and MacIntyre help us to see how "He" uses one antagonist in his fight with the second, how the appeal to history can enable us to think critically in the gap between past and future. But "He" must give battle to both antagonists. Rorty and MacIntyre are not just telling us likely stories that are intended to make sense of our present predicament. They are making claims to validity, claims which have an implicit future reference and which must themselves be subjected to careful scrutiny and evaluation. In carrying out this critical task, an appeal to the past, to the history of philosophy, or to a more general cultural and social history is never sufficient. But before dealing more explicitly with the doubly critical character of the fight of philosophy, I want to extend the horizon of the ways in which the appeal to history has served a critical function in recent philosophy.

One of the most dramatic consequences of the appeal to history in recent philosophy has been the appeal to history in the understanding of the nature of science. Kuhn was certainly prophetic when he opened *The Structure of Scientific Revolutions* with the following claim:

> History, if viewed as a repository for more than anecdote or chronology, could produce a decisive transformation in the image of science by which we are now possessed. That image has been previously drawn, even by scientists themselves, mainly from the study of finished scientific achievements as these are recorded in the classics, and more recently, in the textbooks from which each new scientific generation learns to practice its trade. Inevitably, however, the aim of such books is persuasive and pedagogic; a concept of science drawn from them is no more likely to fit the enterprise that produced them than an image of a national culture drawn from a tourist brochure or a language text. This essay attempts to show that we have been misled by them in fundamental ways. Its aim is to sketch a quite different concept of science that can emerge from the historical record of research activity itself.[8]

If we place Kuhn's remarks in their historical context we can grasp why *The Structure of Scientific Revolutions* had such an impact on our understanding of science and also influenced many other areas of inquiry. For Kuhn gave expression to a new emerging orientation – to emphases and concerns that were being fed by a wide variety of sources. By 1962, the "received" or "orthodox" view of the structure of scientific theory and explanation was coming under increased attack.[9] Not only was there a questioning of the fundamental dogmas of logical empiricism, including a sharp analytic–synthetic distinction, the observational–theoretical distinction, the dichotomy between the context of discovery and the context of justification, and the primacy of the deductive-nomological analysis of scientific explanation, there was a growing sense that there was something artificial and distortive about the very way in which problems in the philosophy of science were formulated. Hanson, Feyerabend, Toulmin, Lakatos, and even Popper emphasized how a sensitivity to science as a historical, ongoing activity transformed our "image of science." The appeal to history was not anecdotal, it was critical. I do not want to underestimate the differences among those who transformed our understanding of scientific inquiry, but this should not blind us to the common themes and affinities that emerged in these debates and controversies.[10] Although Kuhn's slippery and ambiguous term "paradigm" has been seriously challenged for clarifying the character of scientific development, Kuhn helped to initiate a "paradigm shift" in the philosophy and history of science. The new sensitivity to the relevance of the history of scientific inquiry for gaining a philosophical perspective on science was itself fraught with dangers. For there was the danger of displacing the "epistemological myth of the given" with a "historical myth of the given," where we falsely imagine that global interpretations of the nature of science can be resolved by direct appeals to history.[11] But the appeal to history is not sufficient to bear this weight. The history of science has served a powerful critical function in our understanding of science, but the diverse appeals to history themselves demand careful critical scrutiny.

Thus far, in discussing Rorty, MacIntyre, and Kuhn, I have been focusing on diverse uses of history in criticizing some of the anti-historical biases of analytic philosophy, but I have already suggested that we can find affinities with what has happened in Continental philosophy since the early days of phenomenology. To illustrate what I mean, let me briefly consider some of the contributions of Hans-Georg Gadamer and Michel Foucault.

The transition from Rorty, MacIntyre, and Kuhn to Gadamer is an easy and natural one. Rorty himself appropriated the expression "hermeneutics" from Gadamer. (The penultimate chapter of *Philosophy and the Mirror of Nature* is entitled "From Epistemology to Hermeneutics.") Kuhn, too, recognizes the affinity of his approach to understanding scientific inquiry and hermeneutics.[12] There are many family resemblances between MacIntyre's understanding of the role of narrative and tradition – and especially his appeal to Aristotle – and Gadamer's appropriation of Aristotle. (Indeed, I think one of the most exciting aspects of recent philosophy is the increased crisscrossing that is taking place between Anglo-American and Continental philosophy.)

Gadamer not only is constantly making a critical use of the history of philosophy, he is a thinker who has sought to challenge the Enlightenment's prejudice against prejudice. He has defended the centrality of tradition and rightful authority in all human understanding. We are beings thrown into the world who are always shaped by and shaping the traditions that form us. Tradition for Gadamer is a repository of truth, and in the dialogical conversation with tradition our task is to recover this truth. This is not the occasion for a full-scale explication and assessment of Gadamer's claims, but I would like to focus on one dominant theme in Gadamer which exemplifies what he means by hermeneutics, and how it can enable us to gain a critical perspective on our contemporary situation: his interpretation of Aristotle's conception of *praxis* and *phronēsis*.[13] All understanding for Gadamer involves appropriation; and this is what he seeks to do with Aristotle's texts. Appropriation itself for Gadamer requires what Aristotle called *phronēsis*, where knowledge is not detached from our being but is determinative of what we are in the process of becoming. Hermeneutical understanding for Gadamer is itself a form of *phronēsis*, a judgmental mediation between the universal and the particular. And Gadamer himself has sought to delineate the ways in which the practical wisdom of *phronēsis* differs from *epistēmē* and *technē*. But Gadamer's interest in Aristotle's ethical and political writings is not merely philological or antiquarian. He tells us: "When Aristotle, in the sixth book of the *Nicomachean Ethics*, distinguishes the manner of 'practical' knowledge ... from theoretical and technical knowledge, he expresses, in my opinion, one of the greatest truths by which the Greeks throw light upon 'scientific' mystification of the modern society of specialization."[14]

He spells out what he means when he writes:

> In my own eyes, the great merit of Aristotle was that he anticipated the impasse of our scientific culture by his description of the structure of practical reason as distinct from theoretical knowledge and technical skill. By philosophical arguments he refuted the claim of the professional lawmakers whose function at that time corresponded to the role of the expert in the modern scientific society. Of course, I do not mean to equate the modern expert wth the professional sophist. In his own field he is a faithful and reliable investigator, and in general he is well aware of the particularity of his methical assumptions and realizes that the results of his investigation have a limited relevance. Nevertheless, the problem of our society is that the longing of the citizenry for orientation and normative patterns invests the expert with an exaggerated authority. Modern society expects him to provide a substitute for past moral and political orientations. Consequently, the concept of *"praxis"* which was developed in the last two centuries is an awful deformation of what practice really is. In all the debates of the last century practice was understood as application of science to technical tasks .... It degrades practical reason to technical control.[15]

Here, too, we witness still another subtle and powerful critical encounter with the present – an encounter informed by the appropriation of Aristotle's reflections on *praxis* and *phronēsis*. But again there is double movement in this critique. If Gadamer is right about what he takes to be "one of the greatest truths" found in Aristotle, then this needs to be rationally vindicated. It is here that the "He" of Kafka's parable needs to fight back. If we accept Gadamer's analysis of the problem of our scientific civilization, it cannot be simply because when compared with the classical Greek understanding of *praxis* and *phronēsis* we judge our society to be deficient and deformed, but rather because we are *now* prepared to defend and argumentatively justify what we take to be the "truth" in the tradition of practical philosophy. Such an argumentative defense always makes an implicit reference to the future, to the openness of critical examination of validity claims. It is a bad or degenerate form of historicism to think we can justify such validity claims by the appeal to tradition and inherited authority. In this respect, I am in complete agreement with Habermas, who has forcefully argued against Gadamer that in any critical encounter with tradition we never escape the demand to warrant our validity claims, to defend them by the best possible arguments and reasons which are available to us. This is the "truth" in the Enlightenment tradition that still needs to be preserved and defended.[16] This is the "truth" in Kant's call for "the freedom to make public use of one's reason at every point."[17]

Before returning explicitly to the double gesture – the dialectical tension – between philosophy and its history, I want to consider how we can enlarge our appreciation of the critical function of the appeal to history by briefly considering the work of Michel Foucault. At first glance Foucault is problematic in several respects. Whereas Gadamer seeks to show continuities and affinities between the past and the present, to enable us to fuse alien horizons, Foucault's characteristic emphasis is on epistemological ruptures and radical breaks of *epistēmē* and discursive practice. He has an uncanny ability to make the familiar appear strange and alien. His histories, archaeological excavations, and genealogical unmaskings strike us as anti-histories.[18] Moreover, his texts defy any easy genre classification. Are they history, philosophy, sociology, fictions? Transgression is not only a constant theme in Foucault, it is embodied in his rhetorical style – a style that makes us acutely aware of the exclusionary tactics of all forms of discourse, including the discourse of philosophers. Just as he is an anti-historical "historian," he sometimes appears to be an anti-philosophical philosopher. When he asks the question: how is a given form of knowledge possible? – he is not searching for transcendental conditions but for an analysis of these micropractices and "unthought" rules embedded in what seems so marginal – the substructure of our discourses.

Foucault is always throwing us off-center, forcing us to ask new sorts of questions and engaging in new sorts of inquiries to write a "history of the present." Consider his *Discipline and Punish*, which strikingly begins with a description of the brutal public execution of Damiens, a description juxtaposed with the "timetable" – the rules for "the house of young prisoners in Paris" which was drawn up eighty years later by Léon Faucher.[19] What does any of this have to do with philosophy? What concern for philosophers is there in a study which announces itself as "The Birth of the Prison"? And yet, as Foucault's own "narrative" unfolds, we gradually become aware that such themes as "knowledge," "power," "truth," "subjectivity," the nature of "man," "the character of the human sciences" – themes which have been central for philosophy – come obliquely into the foreground. He concludes with a chilling analysis of the "Panopticon society," "the disciplinary society," "the carceral city" – which turns out to be our society. In short, Foucault presents us with nothing less than a radical critique of our present condition, radical not only in the sense of holding up to us a mirror of what we have become, but radical in the sense of getting at its archaeological underpinnings: "the historical background to various studies of the power of normalization and the formation of knowledge in modern society." Foucault frequently leaves us with more questions than he resolves. His analyses force us to raise new questions about freedom, power, knowledge, and emancipation.[20] We witness a penetrating critique that could only be achieved by "historical" digging – a digging not into the history of philosophy but the "history" that makes philosophy itself possible.

The double critical gesture of philosophy

My brief discussions of Rorty, MacIntyre, Kuhn, Gadamer, and Foucault are intended to be a series of reminders – signposts – of some of the diverse ways in which the appeal to history serves the critical function of philosophy. For all their differences, they share the intent to expose prejudgments, prejudices, and illusions. Each manifests a negative moment which calls into question what has been unquestioned. In this respect they share in the *ēthos* that is perhaps the deepest and most persistent theme in the tradition of philosophic reflection. There is a double character, a double gesture in all these "historical" critiques. For the more seriously we take them, the more seriously we must critically evaluate them, exploring their ramifications, testing their validity, pursuing the questions that they raise. We are not only thrust backward, but forward. "He" must always engage in a double battle. Philosophy becomes thin and is in danger of losing its identity when it forgets its past, when it gives up trying to grapple with both the strangeness and familiarity of what is "other" and alien. But it also becomes thin when it is seduced into thinking that the appeal to tradition is sufficient to answer its questions. It should be clear that I reject foundationalism in its multifarious forms. I not only reject the idea that philosophy itself can be grounded on permanent foundations and that philosophy itself is a foundational discipline, an arbitrator for the rest of culture; I also reject the idea that history – in any of its forms – is or can be a foundational discipline, that it can answer the questions we ask in philosophy. I do not believe that there are perennial problems in philosophy or philosophical intuitions which are so deep that they escape historical contingencies. But there is another way of understanding the perennial character of philosophy, for there is a perennial impulse of wonder that can take a variety of forms. There is a deep impulse to understand, to make sense of, to comprehend "that articulated and integrated vision of man-in-the-universe – or shall I say, discourse-about-man-in-all-discourse – which has traditionally been its goal,"[21] even when this discourse seeks to unravel what has been taken to be intelligible. And this impulse and the task it sets for us – although it may be suppressed or repressed – has itself an uncanny way of reasserting itself, even when it appears most moribund.

Let me conclude with a passage from John Dewey. For the interpretation of Kafka's parable that I have sketched above might well be taken as commentary on what Dewey wrote:

> There is current among those who philosophize the conviction that, while past thinkers have reflected in their systems the conditions and

perplexities of their own day, present-day philosophy in general, and one's own philosophy in particular, is emancipated from the influence of that complex of institutions which forms culture. Bacon, Descartes, Kant each thought with fervor that he was founding philosophy anew because he was placing it securely upon an exclusive intellectual basis, exclusive, that is, of everything but intellect. The movement of time has revealed the illusion; it exhibits as the work of philosophy the old and ever new undertaking of adjusting that body of traditions which constitute the actual mind of man to scientific tendencies and political aspirations which are novel and incompatible with received authorities. Philosophers are parts of history, caught in its movement; creators perhaps in some measure of its future, but also assuredly creatures of its past.[22]

NOTES

1 Cited in Hannah Arendt, *Between Past and Future* (New York: Viking Press, 1961), p. 7.
2 René Descartes, *The Philosophical Works of Descartes*, trans. Elizabeth S. Haldane and G. R. T. Ross, 2 vols. (Cambridge: Cambridge University Press, 1969), 1, p. 149.
3 See *Beyond Objectivism and Relativism: Science, Hermeneutics, and Praxis* (Philadelphia: University of Pennsylvania Press, 1983), pp. 16–20.
4 The following paragraph is based upon my critical study of Rorty's *Philosophy and the Mirror of Nature* (Princeton: Princeton University Press, 1979). See "Philosophy in the Conversation of Mankind," in Richard J. Bernstein, *Philosophical Profiles* (Philadelphia: University of Pennsylvania Press, 1986), p. 86.
5 Alasdair MacIntyre, *After Virtue* (Notre Dame: University of Notre Dame Press, 1981), p. 21.
6 Ibid., p. 111.
7 For my critique of MacIntyre, see "Nietzsche or Aristotle? Reflections on Alasdair MacIntyre's *After Virtue*," *Philosophical Profiles*, pp. 115–40.
8 Thomas Kuhn, *The Structure of Scientific Revolutions*, second enl. edn (Chicago: University of Chicago Press, 1970), p. 1.
9 For a detailed elaboration of the "received view" and the criticisms brought against it, see the foreword to Frederick Suppe, ed., *The Structure of Scientific Theories*, second edn (Urbana: University of Illinois Press, 1977).
10 I have analyzed this historical shift in the understanding of science in *Beyond Objectivism and Relativism*, part 2.
11 See my discussion of this danger in *Beyond Objectivism and Relativism*, pp. 71ff.
12 See Kuhn's preface to *The Essential Tension* (Chicago: University of

Chicago Press, 1977). See also my discussion of hermeneutics and the philosophy of science in *Beyond Objectivism and Relativism*.

13   See my discussion and critique of Gadamer in *Beyond Objectivism and Relativism*, part 3.

14   Hans-Georg Gadamer, "The Problem of Historical Consciousness," reprinted in Paul Rabinow and William Sullivan, eds, *Interpretive Social Science: A Reader* (Berkeley and Los Angeles: University of California Press, 1979), p. 107.

15   Hans-Georg Gadamer, "Hermeneutics and Social Science," *Cultural Hermeneutics* 2 (1975), p. 312.

16   I have developed this theme more fully in *Beyond Objectivism and Relativism*. See especially pp. 150ff.

17   Immanuel Kant, "What is Enlightenment?" in *Foundations of the Metaphysics of Morals*, trans. Lewis White Beck (New York: Library of Liberal Arts, 1959), p. 87.

18   See Hayden White, "Foucault Decoded: Notes from Underground," in *Tropics of Discourse* (Baltimore: Johns Hopkins Press, 1978).

19   Michel Foucault, *Discipline and Punish: The Birth of the Prison*, trans. Alan Sheridan (New York: Vintage, 1979), pp. 3–7.

20   For a critique of Foucault, see Charles Taylor, "Foucault on Freedom and Truth," in David Hoy, ed., *Foucault: A Critical Reader* (Oxford: Basil Blackwell, 1986).

21   Wilfrid Sellars, *Science, Perception and Reality* (New York: Humanities Press, 1963), p. 171.

22   John Dewey, *Philosophy and Civilization* (New York: Mouton, Balch and Company, 1931), pp. 3–4.

2

The Rage Against Reason

Recently, a number of philosophers including Alasdair MacIntyre, Richard Rorty, Paul Ricoeur, and Jean-François Lyotard have reminded us about the central (and problematic) role of narratives for philosophic inquiry. I say "reminded us" because narrative discourse has always been important for philosophy. Typically, every significant philosopher situates his or her own work by telling a story about what happened before he or she came along – a story that has its own heroes and villains. This is the way in which philosophers are always creating and recreating their own traditions and canons. And the stories that they tell are systematically interwoven with what they take to be their distinctive contributions. Consider Aristotle's narrative in the first book of the *Metaphysics* about the insights and blindnesses of his predecessors in grasping the multidimensional character of our scientific knowledge of causes. Or – to leap to the contemporary scene – think of the story that logical positivists have told us about the confusions and linguistic blunders of most of their predecessors – with a few bright moments of anticipation of their own radical program for reforming philosophy. Or again, there is the powerful, seductive story that Husserl tells, where the entire history of philosophy is viewed as a teleological anticipation of the new rigorous *Wissenschaft* of transcendental phenomenology. There is a common rhetorical pattern in these narratives. They tell stories of anticipations, setbacks, and trials, but they culminate with the progressive realization of truth and reason, which is normally identified with what the philosopher/storyteller *now* sees clearly – a "truth" which his or her predecessors saw only through a glass darkly.

There is also the genre of philosophic narratives – which have become so fashionable in the nineteenth and twentieth centuries – that dramatically reverse this pattern. They tell of relentless decline, degeneration, catastrophe, and forgetfulness. A "classic" instance of this is Nietzsche's genealogical unmasking of the "history" of reason, truth, and morality, which culminates in the dominance and spread of a pernicious all-encompassing nihilism. But we also find variations of this pattern in MacIntyre's saga of the decline and degeneration of moral philosophy and moral life since the Enlightenment. And – as we shall see – this is the way in which Heidegger reads (in his "strong reading") the destiny of Western philosophy and meta-physics, which is interwoven with the history of the forgetfulness and concealment of Being.

It is not my intention to develop a typology of narrative patterns in philosophy, although I am convinced that such a typology would be extremely illuminating. Rather I want to set a context for what I will attempt to do in this essay. For I want to outline a narrative – or more accurately and modestly – a narrative sketch. Even though I will be schematic, my tale is a complex one for several reasons. First, because it is a narrative about narratives, specifically narratives which themselves relate stories about the development of reason, or what thinkers such as Weber and Habermas call "rationalization" processes.[1] Secondly, because it is a narrative that isolates different story lines, a plot and a counterplot that stand in an uneasy and unresolved tension with each other. Thirdly, because it is not one of those narratives where all the loose threads are neatly tied together at the end – or to switch metaphors, there is no grand *Aufhebung* because it is essentially an unfinished story.

In the spirit of this prologue, let me introduce the four main characters of my *first* story line and tell you what I hope to achieve. The names of the main characters are Condorcet, Weber, Adorno, and Heidegger. My aim is to confront some deeply troubling contem-porary questions. For I want to understand why today there are so many "voices" screeching about Reason. Why is there a rage against Reason? What precisely is being attacked, criticized, and damned? Why is it that when "Reason" and "Rationality" are mentioned, they evoke images of domination, oppression, repression, patriarchy, sterility, violence, totality, totalitarianism, and even terror? These questions are especially poignant and perplexing when we realize that not so long ago the call to "Reason" elicited associations with autonomy, freedom, justice, equality, happiness, and peace. I not only want to understand what is happening but – even more important – what ought to be our response to the disturbing and confusing situation. Without further introduction, let me begin my tale of the battle of lightness and darkness.

The dialectic of Enlightenment

In July 1793, Marie-Jean-Antoine-Nicolas Caritat, Marquis de Condorcet, under the threat of death by the Jacobins who had condemned him and declared him to be *hors la loi*, went into hiding in the house of Madame Vernet, 21 rue Servandoni, where he wrote his now famous *Esquisse d'un tableau historique des progrès de l'esprit humain* (Sketch for a historical picture of the progress of the human mind). Published posthumously in 1795 (Condorcet died the day after he was apprehended and dragged to prison in April 1794), the *Esquisse* was immediately hailed as a testament of the French Enlightenment. It was officially adopted as the philosophical manifesto of the post-Thermidorian reconstruction when the Convention voted funds to distribute copies throughout France.

It is a remarkable document. In less than two hundred pages Condorcet sweeps through the nine stages or epochs of the history of mankind, culminating with a euphoric description of the tenth epoch, "The Future Progress of the Human Mind." "Progress" for Condorcet never simply means growth, development, and differentiation. It has a teleological normative aura – progress *toward* the indefinite perfectibility of the human species. The hero of his narrative is Reason – first manifested in philosophy, then in the natural sciences, and finally in the "moral and political sciences." Furthermore, in the course of human history, Reason gains in strength and power. With the discovery of printing, the good works of publicists and especially through public education, the full illumination of Reason spreads to all of humankind. Reason passes through difficult trials. It must triumph over the devious tactics of priests, tyrants, despots, and cunning hypocrites. But in the course of its journey through history, it gains an overwhelming momentum.

The moral of Condorcet's narrative is announced in the very beginning of the *Esquisse*. He will show us

> in the modifications that the human species has undergone, cease-lessly renewing itself through the immensity of the centuries, the path that it has made towards truth and happiness.
>
> Such observations upon what man has been and what he is today, will instruct us about the means we should employ to make certain and rapid further progress that his nature allows him still to hope for.
>
> Such is the aim of the work I have undertaken, and its result will be to show by appeal to reason and fact that nature has set no term to the perfection of human faculties; that the perfectibility of man is truly indefinite, and that the progress of this perfectibility, from now onwards independent of any power that might wish to halt it, has no other limit than the duration of the globe upon which nature has cast us.[2]

This progress will never again be reversed as the linkage of reason, justice, virtue, equality, freedom, and happiness becomes stronger and stronger. Condorcet's history of mankind is itself teleologically oriented toward the tenth epoch – the future. He begins his "description" of "the future progress of the human *esprit*" by echoing that eighteenth-century rhetoric which was so confident that the future could be predicted on the basis of "the general laws directing the phenomena of the universe."[3] But Condorcet's "predictions" read more like utopian dreams and "hopes for the future condition of the human race."[4] There will be the eventual abolition of all forms of pernicious inequality. There will be cultural, political, and economic equality among nations and within each nation. There will be the indefinite perfection of the human faculties. Private and public happiness will prevail. Condorcet even explicitly speaks of the elimination of sexual inequality and hints (in an ambiguous manner) about stamping out racism. War will be no more, peace will eternally reign. There will even be a transformation of our biological nature. For the duration of human life will be indefinitely extended and our faculties will be strengthened.

> The time will therefore come when the sun will shine only on free men who know no other master but their reason; when tyrants and slaves, priests and their stupid or hypocritical instruments will exist only in the works of history and on the stage; and when we shall think of them only to pity their victims and their dupes; to maintain our-

selves in a state of vigilance by thinking on their excesses; and to learn how to recognize and so to destroy, by force of reason, the first seeds of tyranny and superstition should they ever dare to reappear amongst us.[5]

From the perspective of the final decades of the twentieth century with living memories of barbaric totalitarianism, death camps, and the ever-present danger of nuclear cataclysm, it is difficult to resist the temptation to read the *Esquisse*, Condorcet's testament to the future – our present – with sardonic irony. Even such a sympathetic interpreter of the Enlightenment as Peter Gay says "the *Esquisse*, we must conclude, is as much a caricature of the Enlightenment as its testament; it is rationalism run riot, dominated by a simple-minded faith in science that confuses, over and over again, the improvement of techniques with advances in virtue and happiness."[6] Condorcet's "predictions" and "hopes" have relentlessly turned into surrealistic nightmares. Many would concur with the judgment of Horkheimer and Adorno when they wrote: "the Enlightenment has always aimed at liberating men from fear and establishing their sovereignty. Yet the fully enlightened earth radiates disaster triumphant."[7]

Yet it behooves us to remember how many of Condorcet's hopes – frequently in more modulated tones – have animated and still animate those who come after him. For we still hope and dream of the end of oppressive inequality, the institutionalization of freedom, and a reign of peace. Many of us still share his faith in the potential power of public discussion and education. Let us not forget that throughout the nineteenth and twentieth centuries, when the "social sciences" (a term already used by Condorcet) were being developed, many of their practitioners believed – and still believe – that they provide "the means we should employ to make certain and rapid further progress" toward human improvement and the alleviation of human suffering.

A storyteller always has the license to skip historical time, so let me abruptly jump a century and continue my narrative with Max Weber. I want to juxtapose Weber's chilling prognosis of our future "progress" with Condorcet's "apocalyptic" vision.[8] Weber is at once an heir to the Enlightenment in his passionate commitment to reason and the "calling" (*Beruf*) of science, and at the same time one of its harshest and most devastating critics. Weber begins to expose what Horkheimer and Adorno call the "dialectic of Enlightenment" –

the dark side of the Enlightenment, which fosters its own self-destruction. One reason why Weber is so important for my narrative is because I basically agree with Alasdair MacIntyre when he writes: "the present age in its presentation of itself is dominantly Weberian."[9]

For all of Weber's insistence on tenaciously adhering to the postulate of freedom from value judgments when engaging in empirical sociological research, his own writings (as he well knew) are filled with striking and strong judgments. Perhaps the most famous and drastic judgment – which reads like an epigraph for the twentieth century – is his "conclusion" to *The Protestant Ethic*:

> No one knows who will live in this cage in the future, or whether at the end of this tremendous development entirely new prophets will arise, or there will be a great rebirth of old ideas and ideals, or, if neither, mechanized petrifaction embellished with a sort of convulsive self-importance. For of the last stage of this cultural development, it might well be said: "Specialists without spirit, sensualists without heart; this nullity imagines that it has attained a level of civilization never before achieved."[10]

Weber was a relentless critic of the type of philosophy of history, social evolutionism, and even a "stage model" theory of human development which are presupposed by Condorcet and his successors (even though recent commentators have argued there are vestiges of these in Weber's own narrative of the emergence, development, and fate of "Occidental Rationality").[11] If the Enlightenment was committed to destroying myths, superstitions, illusions, and prejudices, then Weber – in this tradition – seeks to expose and smash the mythic thought patterns of the Enlightenment itself. He scorns the very idea of teleological progress – except if we think of "progress" with bitter irony. Freedom and republican democracy are not the "natural" *telos* of human history – as Condorcet believed. On the contrary, the primary trends that characterize modernity, especially those exhibited in the development of capitalism (and socialism) pose the greatest threat to freedom and democracy. In 1906, Weber wrote:

> It is utterly ridiculous to see any connection between the high capitalism of today – as it is now being imported into Russia and as it exists

in America – with democracy or with freedom in any sense of these words. Yet this capitalism is an unavoidable result of our economic development. The question is: how are freedom and democracy in the long run at all possible under the domination of highly developed capitalism? Freedom and democracy are only possible where the resolute will of a nation not to allow itself to be ruled like sheep is permanently alive. We are individualists and partisans of "democratic" institutions "against the stream" of material constellations. He who wishes to be the weathercock of an evolutionary trend should give up those old-fashioned ideals as soon as possible. The historical origin of modern freedom has had certain unique preconditions which will never repeat themselves.[12]

Not only is "mechanized petrification" an imminent historical possibility, but freedom and democracy are endangered. Weber is just as relentless in deconstructing other key elements of Condorcet's prediction/hopes. In one of his more nationalist pronouncements, he warns us: "It is not peace and happiness that we shall have to hand to our descendants, but rather the principle of eternal struggle for the survival and higher breeding [*Emporzüchtung*] of our national species."[13] Modernity is not characterized by a universal assent to, and institutionalization of, natural rights, but by a new polytheism of warring, incommensurable value commitments, by a new and violent struggle of gods and demons.

But perhaps the most severe threat to Condorcet's hopes is Weber's challenge to the very idea that science – as it has "progressively" developed – can tell us how we should live our lives. Condorcet never seriously questions that the sciences not only provide the *means* for human perfectibility but also reveal the *ends* to be achieved. But this myth is precisely what Weber seeks to explode. Here, too, we can detect another ironic reversal. For in Condorcet's version of Enlightenment aspirations, there is a fusion and confusion of the "is" and the "ought" – of instrumental means and normative ends. But Weber pushes to the extreme that other version of Enlightenment thinking that highlights the logical gap between the "is" and the "ought." For Kant, recognizing and insisting upon the categorical distinction of the "is" and the "ought" is the way, indeed the only way, *rationally* to ground the universal moral imperative. But for Weber, opening this abyss has the consequence of showing that there cannot be any scientific – or, more generally, *rational* – foundation for our ultimate norms.

When Weber poses the question, "What is the meaning of science?" his answer is unequivocal. He tells us:

> Tolstoy has given the simplest answer with the words: "Science is meaningless because it gives no answer to our question, the only question important for us: What shall we do and how shall we live?" That science does not give an answer to this is indisputable. The only question that remains is the sense in which science gives "no answer," and whether or not science might yet be of some use to the one who puts the question correctly.[14]

In the background of these passionate pronouncements is a figure who, like an ominous specter, hovers not only over Weber's thought but over my own narrative: the specter of Nietzsche. There is scarcely a criticism advanced by Weber or any other critic of the Enlightenment that was not anticipated by Nietzsche – frequently in a much sharper, more succinct, and aphoristic form.

If we simply contrast the visionary optimism of Condorcet with the tragic cultural and sociological resignation of Weber, we would leave untouched the primary question that needs to be confronted. Why? How are we to account for this striking and consequential difference?

An adequate answer would itself require a detailed narrative of the economic, political, and cultural developments of the century that separates them.[15] But let me suggest that an essential clue is to be found in what stands as *the* cherished concept of the Enlightenment – Reason. Compared with Weber, Condorcet's understanding of Reason and how it operates as a force in history is naive and simplistic. However, Weber's frequent uses of *Rationalism, Rationalität,* and *Rationalisierung* are so complex, multidimensional and polysemous that one can well understand why someone like Steven Lukes claims that Weber's use of "rational" and its cognates is "irredeemably opaque and shifting."[16] Nevertheless one of the most fruitful and promising developments in recent Weber scholarship has been the attempt to sort out the different meanings of "rationality" and its cognates, the plethora of shifting distinctions that Weber introduces, and to reconstruct the outlines of his comprehensive theory of rationalization. Habermas is right when he suggests that using Weber's theory of rationalization as a guideline,

it is possible to reconstruct his project as a whole.[17] Indeed, it is possible to reveal the deep tensions and paradoxes that lie at the very
heart of his thought.

I cannot enter into the details of contemporary controversies and
reinterpretations of Weber, but I do want to highlight a few commonly accepted key points that are important for my narrative. If we
take account of Weber's entire project for a sociology of religion and
do not exclusively focus on *The Protestant Ethic*, then it becomes clear
that Weber's understanding of modern rationalization processes is
embedded within a much more comprehensive framework. He seeks
to understand the specific and peculiar rationalism of the Occident,
its manifestation in the domains of culture, society, and personality,
as well as the different types and developmental rhythms of
rationalization.[18] Even posing the problem in this way, i.e., asking
what is *distinctive* about Western rationality, indicates that Weber
thinks there are forms of rationality and rationalization which are
characteristic of non-Occidental cultures and societies. Furthermore, the question of Occidental rationalism needs to be further
differentiated in order to comprehend the developmental patterns
of Western rationality, and the distinctive forms of *modern*
rationalization processes. Thus, for example, Weber's thesis about
the disenchantment (*Entzauberung*) of the world (literally "de-
magification") is not unique to modernity, but is a developmental
process involved in the history of world religions and worldviews.
This de-magification, which is itself the result of complex
rationalization processes, is a necessary precondition for the appearance of modern forms of Western rationality.

Later I will return to the significance of Weber's comprehensive
and internally complex scheme, but virtually all commentators
on Weber agree that the type of rationalization processes that
loomed so large for him in understanding the modern age are those
tied to one of the four types of social action that he discrimi-
nated: purposive-rational (*zweckrational*) action.[19] "Action is purposive-
rational when it is oriented to ends, means, and secondary results.
This involves rationally weighing the relations of means to ends, the
relations of ends to secondary consequences, and finally the relative
importance of different ends."[20] This concept of purposive-rational
action is the key to Weber's more complex concept of "practical
rationality" – which itself is a combination of "purposive-rational"

and "value-rational" action.[21] What Weber sought to show in virtually every domain of modern culture and society – including science, morality, law, politics, economics, administration, bureaucracy, even the arts – is the relentless pressure and spread of *Zweckrationalität*, which shapes every aspect of our everyday lives. It is this complex developmental process – from which there is no "turning back" – that reinforces the "iron cage" and leads to "mechanical petrification," which threatens freedom and democracy and even has the potential for undermining the very existence of the autonomous individual. This has been called "the paradox of rationalization." Albrecht Wellmer characterizes this paradox succinctly when he writes:

> through his analysis of the institutional correlates of progressive rationalization – capitalist economy, bureaucracy, and professionalized empirical science – [Weber] shows at the same time that the "rationalization" of society does not carry any utopian perspective, but is rather likely to lead to an increasing imprisonment of modern man in dehumanized systems of a new kind of increasing "reification," as Weber's disciple Lukács later would call it. The paradox, that "rationalization" connotes both emancipation and reification at the same time, remains unresolved in Weber's theory.[22]

It is this unresolved paradox that prompted Herbert Marcuse, in his own stinging critique of Weber, to remark: "It is difficult to see reason at all in the ever more solid 'shell of bondage' which is being constructed. Or is there perhaps already in Max Weber's concept of reason the irony that understands but disavows? Does he by any chance mean to say: And this you call 'reason'?"[23]

We can now understand that *if* Weber is right, *if* this is what rationality and rationalization have become in the modern world, *if* this is the "inevitable" consequence of the very type of emancipation which the Enlightenment fostered and legitimized, then we can well understand why there is a rage against reason – or, more precisely, a revulsion against what rationality has become in the contemporary world. We can see how subsequent twentieth-century critiques of the Enlightenment and its privileged forms of rationality can be understood as variations of Weberian themes. There is not only thematic continuity with Adorno's damning portrait of the "administered world," but also with Heidegger's ontologizing of Weber's paradox in his questioning of the triumph of "the will to will," the self-destructiveness of "metaphysical humanism," and the supreme danger of *Gestell* (enframing). There are also strong affinities with Foucault's microanalyses of the discursive practices of the "disciplinary society," "the carceral archipelago."

Since I still have a long way to go in my narrative, let me be briefer in introducing the two other characters of my first story line: Adorno and Heidegger. I can introduce them by highlighting a motif that runs through virtually all the types of rationality that Weber delineates – the motif of *mastery* and *control*.

Stephen Kahlberg brings out this motif when he writes:

> However much they vary in content, mental processes that consciously strive to *master reality* are common to all the types of rationality. Regardless of whether they are characterized by sheer means-end calculation, the subordination of diffuse realities to values, or abstract thought processes; regardless also of whether they take place in reference to interests, formal rules and laws, values, or purely theoretical problems – all of these processes systematically confront, for Weber, social reality's endless stream of concrete occurrences, unconnected events, and punctuated happenings. In *mastering reality*, their common aim is to banish particularized perceptions by ordering them into comprehensible and "meaningful" regularities (emphasis added).[24]

This is the motif that Adorno seizes upon, deepens, and seeks to explode in his negative dialectics. To capture the flavor of Adorno's paratactic and atonal style of thinking, one has to do justice to the fragile dynamic antithetical tensions which he so tightly holds together and which are manifested by his selective critical appropriation of strands from Hegel, Marx, Schopenhauer, Nietzsche, Lukács, and Benjamin. If one searches for some overall coherent organic perspective to integrate Adorno's conflicting and even contradictory claims, one will easily be defeated. For Adorno, fantasies of "organic wholeness" are always regressive. The style and content of his forays (he rejects any distinction between style and content) always aim at undermining and defeating any final synthesis – any positive *Aufhebung*. This is one of the many reasons why we can find in Adorno anticipations of the deconstructive critiques of logocentrism.[25] Martin Jay suggests that we approach Adorno by applying two of his favorite metaphors to his own style of thinking.

The first of these is the force-field (*Kraftfeld*), by which Adorno meant a relational interplay of attractions and aversions that constituted the dynamic transmutational structure of a complex phenomenon. The second is the constellation, an astronomical term Adorno borrowed from Benjamin to signify a juxtaposed rather than integrated cluster of changing elements that resist reduction to a common denominator, essential core, or generative first principle.[26]

I want to relate these metaphors to two deep antithetical traces which need to be juxtaposed in Adorno's own constellation.

On the one hand, the cultural and sociological pessimism that flows from Weber's formulation of the paradox of rationalization begins to look like innocent child's play compared with Adorno's unrelentingly bleak portrait of the "administered world" and the contemporary "culture industry." While Weber still differentiated conflicting elements in modern forms of rationalization processes, these are fused together in Adorno's nightmarish characterization of "instrumental rationality" gone mad. In Adorno's allegorical representation of the Enlightenment's conception of Reason, which he labels "identity logic" or "the philosophy of identity," repressive Reason did not arise in the eighteenth century, but has its origins in the very beginnings of Western culture. The cunning Odysseus is the first "bourgeois" Enlightenment figure.[27] The hidden structure of the "identity logic," which is expressed in conceptual form in the beginnings of Western philosophy and reaches its culmination in Hegel, who is tempted by the lure of the System, turns out to be the will to mastery and control. This is just the motif that runs through Weber's characterizations of the types of rationality. But for Adorno this identity rationality always seeks to deny, repress, and violate otherness, difference, and singularity. *This* form of reason – when unmasked – is intrinsically domination (*Herrschaft*); the domination and control over nature inexorably turns into the domination of men over men (and indeed men over women) and culminates in sadistic-masochistic self-repression and self-mutilation. The hidden "logic" of Enlightenment reason is violently repressive; it is totalitarian.

On the other hand, however, despite Adorno's scathing exposure of the dark sado-masochistic side of the Enlightenment, whose legacy is epitomized in that single horrible name, *Auschwitz*, he is still an heir – albeit in a different way than Weber – to Enlightenment aspirations. Even in the introduction to the co-authored *Dialectic of*

Enlightenment, which many have read as Horkheimer's and Adorno's most pessimistic work, the authors declare:

> We are wholly convinced – and therein lies our *petitio principii* – that social freedom is inseparable from enlightened thought. Nevertheless, we believe that we have just as clearly recognized that the notion of this very way of thinking, no less than the actual historic forms – the social institutions – with which it is interwoven, already contains the seed of the reversal universally apparent today.[28]

Initially, what seems so paradoxical – indeed aporetic – is the way in which Adorno self-consciously affirms the wildest utopian dreams of the Enlightenment – its *promesse de bonheur* and the end of all human suffering. The utopian hopes of the Enlightenment which Weber scorned as "unrealistic" and "irrational" are hyperbolically affirmed by Adorno. And happiness for Adorno is not a pale public *eudaimonia* or private well-being, but an aestheticized, unrepressed sensuous gratification and ease. Adorno – in his own *mimesis* of redemption – holds up before us the vision of a non-antagonistic, non-hierarchical, non-violent, and non-repressive society.

Adorno presses to radical extremes these two elements into a new constellation – the unlimited *dynamis* of the *promesse de bonheur* and the devastating distorting power of "identity logic" – not to foster the illusion of a grand *Aufhebung* but rather to crack open encrusted repressive social reality.

> The only philosophy which can be responsibly practised in the face of despair is the attempt to contemplate all things as they would present themselves from the standpoint of redemption. Knowledge has no light but that shed on the world by redemption: all else is reconstruction, mere technique. Perspectives must be fashioned that displace and estrange the world, reveal it to be, with its rifts and crevices, as indigent and distorted as it will appear one day in the messianic light.[29]

Adorno bequeaths us a whole cluster of *aporias*. But the fragile and taut thread that still connects Adorno with the deepest strata of the Enlightenment's *promesse de bonheur* is broken by Heidegger. For all of Adorno's explicit scorn for Heidegger and despite his barbed condemnation of the "jargon of authenticity," Adorno provides the bridge – or to use Nietzsche's phrase, "the tightrope" – to

Heidegger's ontological rendering of the history and destiny of *logos* and reason which culminates in metaphysical humanity's blindness and forgetfulness of the silent call of Being. In Heidegger's fateful strong reading of the "history of Being," which is already fore-shadowed in *Being and Time* (1927) but becomes more and more pronounced in his "middle" and "late" writings, we find a thematic affinity with Adorno's own claim that the seeds of "identity logic" with its hidden will to mastery are to be found in the very origins of Western rationality. For Heidegger, there is a direct continuity – a single story to be told of the playing out of "prefigured possibilities" from Plato to Nietzsche, the last metaphysical thinker. "With Nietzsche's metaphysics, philosophy is completed."[30] The very idea of *animal rationale* – metaphysical man – is emblematic of the oblivion of Being. The mood (*Stimmung*) of Heidegger's "history of Reason" and more encompassing "history of Being" is manifest when he writes:

> The decline of the truth of beings occurs necessarily, and indeed as the completion of metaphysics. The decline occurs through the col-lapse of the world characterized by metaphysics, and at the same time through the desolation of the earth stemming from metaphysics. Col-lapse and desolation find their adequate occurrence in the fact that metaphysical man, the *animal rationale*, gets fixed as the laboring ani-mal. This rigidification confirms the most extreme blindness to the oblivion of *Being*. But man wills *himself* as the volunteer of the will to will, for which all truth becomes error which it needs in order to be able to guarantee for itself the illusion that the will to will can will nothing other than empty nothingness, in the face of which it asserts itself without being able to know its own completed nullity.[31]

The specter of Nietzsche which haunts Weber and Adorno now takes on an ominous hyper-reality. It is difficult to resist the con-clusion that we are – as Gadamer says of Heidegger – living in "the 'cosmic night' of the 'forgetfulness of being,' the nihilism that Nietzsche prophesied."[32] Heidegger does tantalize us by suggesting that we may yet overcome (*überwinden*) metaphysics, we may still be "saved" from the supreme danger, the essence of technology, *Gestell*, by a new/old event/appropriation of thinking and poetic building.[33] But we can bring to a closure this story line by recalling Condorcet's posthumously published testament to the tenth epoch of mankind and juxtaposing it with Heidegger's own posthumously published testament:

Philosophy will be unable to effect any immediate change in the current state of the world. This is true not only of philosophy but of all purely human reflection and endeavor. Only a god can save us. The only possibility available to us is that by thinking and poetizing we prepare a readiness for the appearance of a god or for the absence of a god in [our] decline, insofar as in view of the absent god we are in a state of decline.[34]

After Heidegger, it would seem that all talk of humanism – *human* freedom, happiness, and emancipation – has become a mockery. If this were the history and fate of Western rationality, then the rage against Reason would be eminently "reasonable." For it would seem to be impossible to resist the "conclusion" that the working through of the "prefigured possibilities" of *logos* ineluctably results not in illumination and Enlightenment, but the cosmic black night of nihilism.

Dialectical rationality

Thus far I have followed my first story line without hinting at my other story line or counterplot. I want to introduce it *in medias res* by returning to Weber and specifically to Habermas' recent critical response to Weber. The "Habermas" who is a character in this narrative is not the Habermas who has recently given birth to what may strike many as a new form of academic scholasticism or a new culture industry. The mark of an original thinker is to gravitate toward a single thought or intuition which is explored, amplified, and probed over and over again. Indeed, if asked, as Rabbi Hillel once was in another situation, to sum up this single dominant thought in a phrase, I can think of no better phrase than one recently used by Habermas in an interview. He speaks of "the conviction that a humane collective life depends on the vulnerable forms of innovation-bearing, reciprocal and unforcedly egalitarian everyday communication." (Incidently, and the significance of this will soon become evident, Habermas makes this remark in speaking about the "intuition" that he sees as linking him with Richard Rorty – an "intuition" which "Rorty retains from the pragmatist inheritance.")[35]

But let me turn to Habermas' encounter with Weber to show how central this intuition is for him and for my own narrative. In the second chapter of *The Theory of Communicative Action*, Habermas – in what is virtually an independent monograph on Max Weber – seeks to reconstruct Weber's theory of rationalization. The details of this reconstruction are complex, challenging, and controversial – worthy of careful systematic analysis. But, informally, I think it is fair and accurate to say that what motivates Habermas throughout his critical reconstruction is almost a "gut feeling" that something has gone desperately wrong in Weber's analysis of modern rationalization processes, that something is askew and distorted. In part, Habermas seeks to show deep tensions within Weber's own project and that the "conclusions" Weber draws about the "iron cage" of modern forms of rationalization processes do not follow from, and indeed are even inconsistent with, his more comprehensive understanding of different types of rationalization processes. But perhaps even more important, Habermas wants to understand what led Weber astray – what led him to the seductive story of the ineluctable triumph of *Zweckrationalität*, which has so pervasively influenced subsequent critiques of the Enlightenment legacy. To put a very complex story into a nutshell, Habermas argues that despite all of Weber's enduring insights, the primary "conceptual bottleneck"[36] that prejudices Weber's understanding of societal rationalization can be traced back to his limited understanding of social action. By giving such prominence to purposive-rational (*zweckrational*) action, Weber slights the distinctiveness, centrality, and indeed (for Habermas) the primacy of communicative action – the type of action manifested most clearly in speech that is oriented not to success, but to mutual understanding. Whereas the rationalization of purposive-rational action, as Weber well understood, involves "the empirical efficiency of technical means and the consistency of choice between suitable means," the rationalization of communicative action is radically different:[37]

> Rationalization here means extirpating those relations of force that are inconspicuously set in the very structures of communication and that prevent conscious settlement of conflicts, and consensual regulation of conflicts, by means of intrapsychic as well as interpersonal communicative barriers. Rationalization means overcoming such systematically distorted communication in which the action-supporting consensus concerning the reciprocally raised validity claims – especially consensus concerning the truthfulness of intentional expressions and the rightness of underlying norms – can be sustained in appearance only, that is, counterfactually.[38]

This reference to "counterfactuality" is extremely important for several reasons. First, because Habermas argues that there is no historical necessity involved in specific forms and domination of *Zweckrationalität* in the modern world. (Weber, who himself eschewed all appeals to "historical necessity," might even agree.) In this respect Habermas is also strongly opposing those tendencies in Adorno and Heidegger which suggest the ineluctable destiny of the working out of "identity logic" or the pernicious domination of *Gestell*.

Secondly, the conceptual shift that Habermas introduces dissolves the so-called paradox of rationalization. Wellmer points this out clearly when he writes:

> Habermas objects that this paradox of rationalization does *not* express an internal *logic* (or dialectic) of modern rationalization processes; it is strictly speaking not a paradox *of rationalization*.... rather it would be more adequate to speak of a "selective" process of rationalization, where the selective character of this process may be explained by the peculiar restrictions put upon communicative rationalization by the boundary conditions and the dynamics of a capitalist system of production.[39]

But what is most important about Habermas' conceptual re-orientation, his paradigm shift, is that it enables us to grasp more perspicaciously what Weber described without accepting his aporetic prophesies about the "iron cage" which imprisons us. The "paradox of rationalization" is now reinterpreted as the powerful, and indeed the dominant, tendency in the modern world toward the deformation of the life-world (with its distinctive communicative rationality) by the distorting pressures of systems of purposive rationality. This conceptual shift does not mean that Habermas is any more optimistic than Weber was about our future prospects. Rather this conceptual shift alters our *theoretical* understanding of the dynamic and conflicting rationalization processes of modernity and also our *practical* evaluation of new social movements. For we can evaluate them as defensive strategies for protecting and furthering the integrity of an undistorted life-world. This is the perspective from which Habermas himself evaluates the women's movement – a movement which he suggests may potentially be the most radical contemporary social movement.

I cannot go into the exposition and critique of the complex way in which Habermas seeks to explain and defend these striking claims.[40] My primary intention here is to make use of Habermas' insights to expand my narrative by pursuing two lines of affinity. The first goes back to that "intuition" which Habermas says links him with the pragmatic tradition. For Habermas is profoundly right in recognizing that the basic intuition or judgment that stands at the center of his own vision is also central to the pragmatic tradition. Both share an understanding of rationality as intrinsically dialogical and communicative. And both pursue the ethical and political consequences of this form of rationality and rationalization. It was Peirce who first developed the logical backbone of this thought in his idea of the fundamental character of a self-corrective critical community of inquirers without any absolute beginning points or finalities. It was Dewey who argued that the very idea of such a community, when pressed to its logical extreme, entails the moral ideal of a democratic community where "the task of democracy is forever that of creation of a freer and more human experience in which all share and to which all contribute."[41] Dewey, no less than Habermas, knew how vulnerable such "innovation-bearing, reciprocal and unforcedly egalitarian" communities can be in the face of all those tendencies in the contemporary world which seek to undermine, crush, and deform communicative rationality. And it was Mead who saw that the linkage of dialogic communicative rationality and the institutionalization of democratic forms of life require a new understanding of the genesis and development of practical sociality – what one recent perceptive commentator aptly calls Mead's theory of practical intersubjectivity.[42] I vividly recall my own shock of recognition when I first started reading Habermas in the 1960s. For I realized that he, who was primarily intellectually shaped by the German tradition from Kant through Hegel to Marx and by his creative appropriation from the Frankfurt School, was moving closer and closer to the central themes of the American pragmatic tradition.[43]

To amplify my counterplot, it is helpful to pursue another line of affinity which takes us in a very different direction – Habermas' affinity with Gadamer and with the tradition of hermeneutics and practical philosophy that Gadamer has helped to revivify. I am certainly aware of the consequential differences between Habermas and Gadamer in the understanding of the character and preconditions required for dialogic rationality.[44] Habermas' broad sociological concerns are completely alien to Gadamer's ontological hermeneutics and to Gadamer's own self-identification with the tradition of German Romanticism.[45] But in this context, I want to focus on the common ground – what Gadamer would call *die Sache* – that binds them together in the twists and turns of their ongoing debate, which has lasted now for more than twenty years.

By an independent pathway – which owes a great deal to his critical appropriation of themes in Plato, Aristotle, Hegel, and Heidegger – Gadamer in his ontological version of hermeneutics has been arguing that our ontological condition, our very being-in-the-world, is to *be* dialogical *beings*. We find in Gadamer one of the subtlest and most sensitive phenomenological analyses of the internal play and essential openness of dialogue.[46] His very practice of philosophy is constantly showing us what authentic dialogue involves. The main reason, however, why Gadamer is so important for my second story line is that he shows us a way of recognizing that *die Sache* of Habermas' understanding of communicative rationality is *not* a discovery of the twentieth century. Rather it is one of the oldest and most persistent – albeit subterranean – themes in Western philosophy. Although Gadamer's great hero is the Plato of the Socratic/Platonic Dialogues, he finds traces of this theme already in Heraclitus. Even when he integrates Aristotle into his narrative of the history of Western rationality, he highlights the communicative aspects of *phronēsis* by showing us how it presupposes and fosters the civic virtue of friendship. Gadamer is not motivated by a nostalgia for a "golden" past. He wants to redeem those "truths" in the tradition of philosophy that can enable us to understand and critically evaluate the deformations of modern scientific technological culture with its deification of technical expertise. Just as I rashly attempted to sum up Habermas in a sentence, let me try to do the same for Gadamer. For I believe that Gadamer's entire corpus can be read as an invitation to join him in the rediscovery and redemption of the richness and concreteness of our dialogical being-in-the-world.

By now it should be clear that I could have told my narrative as a series of footnotes to Plato. The first plot can be traced back to the "construction" of the metaphysical Plato, with his two-world theory, his denigration of corporeality, and his celebration of eternal immutable forms which are the erotic *telos* of *dianoia* and *noesis*. This Plato (sometimes called "Platonism") is the villain to whom we can trace back everything that has subsequently gone wrong with Western rationality. This is the Plato who is attacked and "deconstructed" by Nietzsche, Heidegger, Derrida, and Rorty.

But there is the "other" Plato – the progenitor of my second story line – who is the great defender of the *spoken* and *written* dialogue – which is always open to novel turns and which knows no finality.[47] Much of what Habermas, the pragmatists, and even Gadamer have explored may well be understood as a commentary on the claim that it is a fiction to think "Socratic dialogue is possible everywhere and at any time."[48] All are concerned, although in very different ways, with probing the conditions required to foster the concrete embodiment of this "ideal fiction." John Dewey, who some might think an unlikely advocate of a back-to-Plato movement, put the point beautifully when he wrote:

> Nothing could be more helpful to present philosophizing than a "Back to Plato" movement; but it would have to be a back to the dramatic, restless, cooperatively inquiring Plato of the Dialogues, trying one mode of attack after another to see what it might yield; back to the Plato whose highest flight of metaphysics always terminated with a social and practical turn, and not to the artificial Plato constructed by unimaginative commentators who treat him as the original university professor.[49]

The new constellation

My narrative is not yet finished because the story I am telling is still unfolding. At the beginning I warned that this is not one of those stories where all the loose threads are neatly tied up at the "end." Let me once again recall Benjamin's and Adorno's metaphor of a "constellation," and suggest that today we find ourselves in a new constellation. In our "post-era" – whether we label it postmodernist, poststructuralist, postmetaphysical (or any of the dozen or so "post" appellations which are being bandied around), there are those who are telling us that the very idea of dialogue and communicative rationality belong to the dustbin of the now discredited history of Western rationality and metaphysics. These ideas and ideals are part of the now exhausted metaphysics of presence, logocentrism, phonocentrism, ethnocentrism, and phallocentrism which comprise the violent history of the West. To the extent that this has now become the fashionable, "sophisticated" skeptical claim of the movement called deconstruction, I think it is radically mistaken. Furthermore – and this may surprise you – I do not for a moment think that this is what Derrida, with whom the name "deconstruction" has become entangled, is really telling and showing us. Since I am coming to the end of my tale, let me state briefly and forcefully what I take to be – to use an old-fashioned term – the *truths* to be appropriated from so-called postmodern debates. Isaiah Berlin once commented that "the history of thought and culture is, as Hegel showed with great brilliance, a changing pattern of great liberating ideas which inevitably turn into suffocating straitjackets, and so stimulate their own destruction by new emancipating, and at the same time, enslaving conceptions."[50]

What such thinkers as Derrida – and in a very different manner, Foucault – have shown us is that such ideas as authentic dialogue, community, communication, and communicative rationality *can* potentially – and indeed *have* in the past – become "suffocating straitjackets," and "enslaving conceptions." This is already anticipated by Benjamin's and Adorno's deep suspicion of what "communication" has become in an administered world: little more than the technological exchange of information to be utilized – input and output of "data."

But there are more subtle, unobtrusive, and even more pernicious dangers that need to be unmasked and revealed. There can be no dialogue, no communication unless beliefs, values, commitments, and even emotions and passions are shared in common. Furthermore, I agree with Gadamer and MacIntyre that dialogic communication presupposes moral virtues – a certain "good will" – at least in the willingness to really listen, to seek to understand what is genuinely other, different, alien, and the courage to risk one's more cherished prejudgments. But too frequently this commonality is not really shared, it is *violently* imposed. A false "we" is projected. As I read Derrida, few contemporary writers equal him in his sensitivity and alertness to the multifarious ways in which the "history of the West" – even in its institutionalization of communicative practices – has always tended to silence differences, to exclude outsiders and exiles, those who live on the margins. The so-called "conversation of mankind" has been just that – a conversation of *mankind*, primarily white mankind. This is one of the many *good* reasons why Derrida "speaks" to those who have felt the pain and suffering of being excluded by the prevailing hierarchies embedded in the text called "the history of the West" – whether they be women, Blacks, or others bludgeoned by exclusionary tactics. Even Derrida's deconstructive inversion and reinscription of speech and writing can be read as a warning against the nostalgic belief that face-to-face spoken language is sufficient to guarantee communication. He teaches us how much can go wrong – even tragically wrong – in the folds of communication.

As for Foucault – at his best – he shows us that if we take a cold, hard look at the discursive practices that underlie so much of modern "humanism" and the human sciences, we discover power/ knowledge complexes that belie what their ideologues profess. In novel ways Foucault shows us the truth of Benjamin's claim, "There is no document of civilization which is not at the same time a document of barbarism."[51] Sometimes what is required to communicate – to establish a reciprocal "we" – is rupture and break – a *refusal* to accept the common ground laid down by the "other." It is extremely easy to pay lip service to recognizing and respecting genuine plurality, difference, otherness, but nothing perhaps is more difficult than to achieve this in practice – and such practice is *never* completely stable or permanent. It is a self-deceptive illusion to think that the "other" can always be heard in a friendly dialogue.

I would go further and argue that Derrida, Foucault, Lyotard, and many others are important not only for their "negative" cautious moral skepticism in warning us of the hidden dangers of "false" consensus, dialogue, community, a "false" we, but that when we think through what they are saying, when we try to make sense of their own moral passion, we are led back to the fragile, but persistent "ideal" of dialogical communicative rationality – an ideal which is more often betrayed than honored.

We must learn again and again to hear what Weber, Adorno, Heidegger, and their successors are telling and showing us. But we must resist the temptation to be seduced by "arguments" of necessity, destiny, and ineluctable decline. We must resist those essentialist stories of the history of Western rationality that see it as *only* ending in hidden forms of violence and despairing nihilism. For then we would surely be enclosed in the darkness of forgetfulness and betrayal. Let us not forget that "communicative reason operates in history as an avenging force,"[52] and that the claim to reason has a "stubbornly transcending power, because it is renewed with each act of unconstrained understanding" and with "each moment of living together in solidarity." But never before has *this* claim to communicative reason been so threatened from so many different directions. A *practical* commitment to the avenging *energeia* of communicative reason is the basis – perhaps the only honest basis – for hope.

NOTES

1 The expression "rationalization" can be misleading because, in an Anglo-American context, it typically connotes a false, misleading, and distortive justification. We speak, for example, of a rationalization of hidden motives. But the expression, as used by Weber, Habermas, and others influenced by the German sociological tradition, does not have a pejorative connotation. It refers to a developmental process by which a type of rationality increases over time. Thus for Weber an increase in the efficiency of bureaucratic administration or the development of empirical science would both be understood as rationalization processes.

2 Antoine-Nicolas de Condorcet, *Sketch for a Historical Picture of the Progress of the Human Mind*, trans. June Barraclough (London: Weidenfeld and Nicolson, 1955), p. 4.

3 Ibid., p. 173.

4 Ibid.

5 Ibid., p. 179.

6 Peter Gay, *The Enlightenment: An Interpretation* (New York: Alfred A. Knopf, 1969), 2, p. 122.

7 Max Horkheimer and Theodor W. Adorno, *Dialectic of Enlightenment*, trans. John Cumming (New York: Continuum, 1972), p. 3.

8 Louis-Gabriel-Ambroise Bonald hailed the *Esquisse* as the "apocalypse of the new gospel." See Keith Michael Baker, *Condorcet: From Natural Philosophy to Social Mathematics* (Chicago: University of Chicago Press, 1975), p. 393.

9 Alasdair MacIntyre, *After Virtue* (Notre Dame: University of Notre Dame Press, 1981), p. 108.

10 Max Weber, *The Protestant Ethic and the Spirit of Capitalism*, trans. Talcott Parsons (New York: Scribner's, 1958), p. 182.

11 See Wolfgang Schluchter, *The Rise of Western Rationalism: Max Weber's Developmental History*, trans. Guenther Roth (Berkeley: University of California Press, 1981), and Jürgen Habermas, *The Theory of Communicative Action*, trans. Thomas McCarthy, 2 vols. (Boston: Beacon, 1981), 1, chap. 2, "Max Weber's Theory of Rationalization."

12 *Archiv für Sozialwissenschaft und Sozialpolitik*, 12, no. 1, pp. 347ff., cited in

H. H. Gerth and C. Wright Mills, eds., *From Max Weber: Essays in Sociology* (New York: Oxford University Press, 1946), p. 71.

13 Cited by Wolfgang J. Mommsen, *The Age of Bureaucracy* (New York: Harper and Row, 1974), p. 30.

14 Max Weber, "Science as a Vocation," in *From Max Weber: Essays in Sociology*, p. 143.

15 See Habermas' account in his analysis of "Max Weber's Theory of Rationalization."

16 Steven Lukes, "Some Problems about Rationality," in Bryan Wilson, ed., *Rationality* (New York: Harper and Row, 1971), p. 207.

17 Habermas, *The Theory of Communicative Action*, 1, p. 143.

18 See the Introduction to *The Protestant Ethic*, which is a translation of the *Vorbemerkung* to his studies in the sociology of religion.

19 The other three types of social action are affectual, traditional, and value-rational action. See Stephen Kahlberg's discussion of the types of social action and the types of rationality in "Max Weber's Types of Rationality: Cornerstones for the Analysis of Rationalization Processes," *American Journal of Sociology* 85 (1980), pp. 1145–79. Kahlberg distinguishes four types of rationality: theoretical, practical, substantive, and formal.

20 Max Weber, *Economy and Society*, trans. Guenther Roth and Claus Wittich, 2 vols. (Berkeley: University of California Press, 1978), 1, p. 26. The translation is slightly modified.

21 See Habermas' "reconstruction" of the concept of practical rationality in *The Theory of Communicative Action* 1, p. 168ff.

22 Albrecht Wellmer, "Reason, Utopia, and the *Dialectic of Enlightenment*," in Richard J. Bernstein, ed., *Habermas and Modernity* (Cambridge, Mass.: MIT Press, 1985), p. 41.

23 Herbert Marcuse, "Industrialization and Capitalism in the Work of Max Weber," in *Negations*, trans. Jeremy J. Shapiro (Boston: Beacon, 1968), pp. 225–6.

24 Kahlberg, "Max Weber's Types of Rationality," pp. 1159–60.

25 See Martin Jay's discussion of Adorno's anticipations of deconstructionism in *Adorno* (Cambridge, Mass.: Harvard University Press, 1984), p. 21.

26 Ibid., pp. 14–15.

27 See Horkheimer and Adorno, *Dialectic of Enlightenment*. I am focusing here on Adorno's thought, leaving aside some of the important differences between Horkheimer and Adorno. In the preface to the new English (1972) edition of *Dialectic of Enlightenment*, the authors write, p. ix: "No outsider will find it easy to discern how far we are both responsible for every sentence. We jointly dictated lengthy sections; and the vital principle of the *Dialectic* is the tension between the two intellectual temperaments conjoined in it."

28 Ibid., p. xiii.

29 Theodor W. Adorno, *Minima Moralia*, trans. E. F. N. Jephcott (London: Verso, 1974), p. 247.

30 Martin Heidegger, "Overcoming Metaphysics," in *The End of Philosophy*, trans. Joan Stambaugh (New York: Harper and Row, 1973), p. 95.

31 Ibid., p. 86.

32 Hans-Georg Gadamer, *Truth and Method*, second revised edn, trans. and revised J. Weinsheimer and D. G. Marshall (New York: Crossroad, 1989), p. xxxvii.

33 See "The Question Concerning Technology," especially Heidegger's interpretation of Hölderlin's lines "But where danger is, grows/The saving power also" in *Martin Heidegger: Basic Writings*, ed. and trans. David F. Krell (New York: Harper and Row, 1977), pp. 283–318. See my critical discussion, "Heidegger on Humanism," in Richard J. Bernstein, *Philosophical Profiles* (Philadelphia: University of Pennsylvania Press, 1986).

34 Martin Heidegger, "Only a God Can Save Us," trans. William J. Richardson, SJ, in Thomas Sheehan, ed., *Heidegger: The Man and the Thinker* (Chicago: Precedent, 1981), p. 57.

35 Jürgen Habermas, "A Philosophico-Political Profile," in *New Left Review* 151 (May/June 1985), p. 12. Habermas makes this remark in response to the question "And could you explain the discrepancy between your condemnation of poststructuralism, and your comparatively friendly reception of the work of Richard Rorty, which provides parallels to, and has in some cases been directly influenced by, poststructuralist themes?" Habermas replies:

> As far as Richard Rorty is concerned, I am no less critical of his contextualist position. But at least he does not climb aboard the 'anti-humanist' bandwagon, whose trail leads back in Germany to figures as politically unambiguous as Heidegger and Gehlen. Rorty retains from the pragmatist inheritance, which in many, though not all, respects he unjustly claims for himself, an intuition which links us together – the conviction that a humane collective life depends on the vulnerable forms of innovation-bearing, reciprocal and unforcedly egalitarian everyday communication.

36 *The Theory of Communicative Action*, 1, pp. 270ff.

37 Jürgen Habermas, *Communication and the Evolution of Society*, trans. Thomas McCarthy (Boston: Beacon, 1979), p. 117.

38 Ibid., pp. 119–20.

39 Wellmer, "Reason, Utopia, and the *Dialectic of Enlightenment*," p. 56.

40 For a critical discussion of some aspects of Habermas, see my discussion of his work in *The Restructuring of Social and Political Theory* (Philadelphia: University of Pennsylvania Press, 1978), and *Beyond Objectivism and Relativism: Science, Hermeneutics, and Praxis* (Philadelphia: University of Pennsylvania Press, 1983).

41 John Dewey, "Creative Democracy – The Task Before Us," reprinted in M. Fisch, ed., *Classic American Philosophers* (New York: Appleton-Century-Crofts, 1951), p. 394. See my discussion of Peirce and Dewey in *Praxis and Action: Contemporary Philosophies of Human Activity* (Philadelphia: University of Pennsylvania Press, 1971).

42 Hans Joas, *G. H. Mead: A Contemporary Re-examination of His Thought* (Cambridge, Mass.: MIT Press, 1985).

43 See Habermas' comments about Peirce, Dewey, and Mead in "A Philosophico-Political Profile," pp. 76–7.

44 See my discussion of Gadamer and Habermas in *Beyond Objectivism and Relativism.*

45 See "A Letter by Professor Hans-Georg Gadamer," included as an Appendix in *Beyond Objectivism and Relativism.*

46 See *Beyond Objectivism and Relativism,* part 3, "From Hermeneutics to Praxis."

47 For an illuminating interpretation of Plato's *Phaedrus* which shows how Plato defends "a philosophic art of writing," see Ronna Burger, *Plato's Phaedrus: A Defense of a Philosophic Art of Writing* (University, Ala.: University of Alabama Press, 1980). Compare this with Jacques Derrida, "Plato's Pharmacy," in *Disseminations,* trans. Barbara Johnson (Chicago: University of Chicago Press, 1981).

48 Jürgen Habermas, *Knowledge and Human Interests,* trans. Jeremy J. Shapiro (Boston: Beacon, 1971), p. 314.

49 John Dewey, "From Absolutism to Experimentalism," in Richard J. Bernstein, ed., *John Dewey: On Experience, Nature, and Freedom* (New York: Library of Liberal Arts, 1960), p. 13.

50 Isaiah Berlin, "Does Political Theory Still Exist?" in *Philosophy, Politics, and Society* (2nd series), in Peter Laslett and W. G. Runciman, eds. (Oxford: Basil Blackwell, 1962), p. 17.

51 Walter Benjamin, "Theses on the Philosophy of History," in Hannah Arendt, ed., *Illuminations* (New York: Schocken, 1969), p. 256.

52 Jürgen Habermas, "A Reply to My Critics," in John B. Thompson and David Held, eds., *Habermas: Critical Debates* (London: Macmillan, 1982), p. 227. See my elaboration of this theme in the Introduction to *Habermas and Modernity.*

3

Incommensurability and Otherness Revisited

"Incommensurability," "otherness," "alterity," "singularity," "*différance*," "plurality." These signifiers reverberate throughout much of twentieth-century philosophy. For all their differences, they are signs of a pervasive amorphous mood – what Heidegger calls a *Stimmung*. It is a mood of deconstruction, destabilization, rupture and fracture – of resistance to all forms of *abstract* totality, universalism, and rationalism. In the most diverse philosophic currents – ranging from Anglo-American post-empiricist philosophy of science to Continental poststructuralism, we can detect family resemblances in this complex reaction against some of the dominant tendencies in the history of Western philosophy. Sometimes the object of attack is what Richard Rorty calls the Cartesian-Lockean-Kantian tradition of modern epistemology. Sometimes the rebellion is against the Enlightenment legacy. Sometimes, as in Nietzsche, Heidegger and Derrida, it is the entire tradition of Western metaphysics that is made to tremble. But whatever is the specific target of destabilization and deconstruction, and regardless of the philosophic "vocabulary" in which these objections are articulated, there is also a profound convergence in the mood that they express.

I want to unravel some of the threads that are interwoven by these signifiers – especially those that cluster around the notions of incommensurability and otherness. What is at issue here? Why have these themes become so central in our time? What can we learn from the intensive debates concerning them? And what is to be rejected as misleading and/or false?

In order to orient my questioning, let me step back to gain some perspective. One of the oldest and most persistent questions in Western philosophy – and as far as I understand it, in Eastern thought too – has been the "problem" of the one and the many and/ or identity and difference. One might even argue that Western philosophy began with this "problem." I speak of *the* "problem" in scare quotes, because – as so often happens in philosophy – we are really dealing with *many* problems under this rubric. Nevertheless, we can say that philosophers have always been concerned with understanding what underlies and pervades the multiplicity, diversity, and sheer contingency that we encounter in our everyday lives. Is there some fundamental essential unity that encompasses this multiplicity? Is there a one, *eidos*, universal, form, genus that is essential to the multiplicity of particulars? What is the character of this essential unity? It can be argued – and indeed has been – that the dominant tendency in Western philosophy and metaphysics has been to privilege and valorize unity, harmony, totality and thereby to denigrate, suppress, or marginalize multiplicity, contingency, particularity, singularity. The problem of the one and the many and/or identity and difference can take on many different ontic forms – it arises not only in metaphysics, but also in epistemology, ethics, politics and religion. Even the recent debates between so-called communitarians and anti-communitarians can be viewed from this perspective. Anti-communitarians are deeply suspicious of any claim that compromises the independence and ontological irreducibility of individuals, while communitarians argue that a theory of the individual or self that does not acknowledge the reality of common bonds that unite individuals leads to a shallow and inadequate understanding of social and political life.

If we read the history of philosophy as an attempt to reconcile identity with difference, then we can understand why Hegel might be seen as the culmination of this tradition. More systematically and thoroughly than any previous philosopher, Hegel sought to think through a "final solution" to this problem. Hegel himself claimed that the entire tradition of Western philosophy achieves its *telos* with the unity of identity with difference. Ironically, almost every philosopher since Hegel has rejected his "solution."

But Hegel already brilliantly noted and indeed anticipated what has been deeply troubling for many post-Hegelian thinkers. We can see this clearly in the section "Absolute Freedom and Terror" in the *Phenomenology of Spirit*. Hegel adumbrates the dialectic of what happens when an abstract universalism, an abstract "universal will" ascends the throne "without any power being able to resist it."[1] The demand for (of) abstract universal freedom inevitably leads to terror. "In this absolute freedom, therefore, all social groups or classes which are the spiritual spheres into which the whole is articulated are abolished."[2] It is doubly ironic that even though Hegel contrasts the terror of abstract universal freedom with the struggle for, and actualization of, concrete freedom as the *telos* of history, post-Hegelian philosophers have not only been skeptical of Hegel's relentless drive toward a grand *Aufhebung*, they have accused him of furthering a new more subtle and pernicious form of terror in his demand for *totality*. Indeed this charge has become a cliché for those who think of themselves as "postmodern." But I am getting ahead of my story. Let me turn to the question of incommensurability.

Incommensurability: from Kuhn to MacIntyre

"Incommensurability" was thrust into the center of Anglo-American philosophic debates because of Thomas Kuhn's provocative book, *The Structure of Scientific Revolutions*. Kuhn tells us that "In applying the term 'incommensurability' to theories, I had intended only to insist that there was no common language within which both could be fully expressed and which could there be used in a *point-by-point* comparison between them" (emphasis added).[3]

Now it is important to remember the context in which Kuhn introduced incommensurability – just as it is essential to distinguish carefully commensurability, compatibility, and comparability.[4] Kuhn never intended to deny that paradigm-theories can be compared – indeed *rationally* compared and evaluated. In insisting on incommensurability, his main point was to indicate the ways in which paradigm-theories *can* and *cannot* be compared. Furthermore incompatibility is not to be confused with, or assimilated to, incommensurability. For incompatibility is a logical concept that presupposes – as Kuhn himself notes – a common language in which we can specify incompatible logical relations. What then is the meaning and significance of the incommensurability of paradigm-theories?

Kuhn's main (although very brief) explicit discussion of incommensurability occurs in the context of his analysis of the resolution of scientific revolutions. Kuhn seeks to explain why proponents of competing paradigms "may [each] hope to convert the other to his way of seeing his science and its problems [but] neither may hope to prove his case."[5] He specifies three reasons why "the proponents of competing paradigms must fail to make *complete* contact with each other's viewpoints" (emphasis added).[6] These are the reasons for claiming there is "incommensurability of the pre- and post-revolutionary normal scientific traditions."[7] "In the first place, the proponents of competing paradigms will often disagree about the list of problems that any candidate for a paradigm must resolve. Their standards or their definitions of science are not the same."[8] "More is involved, however, than the incommensurability of standards."[9] Secondly, then, "within the new paradigm, old terms, concepts, and experiments fall into new relationships one with the other."[10] But there is a third – and for Kuhn, this is the "most fundamental aspect of the incommensurability of competing paradigms."[11] In a provocative and ambiguous passage he writes:

> In a sense that I am unable to explicate further, the proponents of competing paradigms practice their trades in different worlds. One contains constrained bodies that fall slowly, the other pendulums that repeat their motions again and again. In one, solutions are compounds, in the other mixtures. One is embedded in a flat, the other in a curved, matrix of space. Practicing in different worlds, the two groups of scientists see different things when they look from the same point in the same direction. Again that is not to say that they can see anything they please. Both are looking at the world, and what they look at has not changed. But in some areas they see different things, and they see them in different relations to the other. That is why a law that cannot even be demonstrated to one group of scientists may occasionally seem intuitively obvious to another. Equally, it is why, before they can hope to communicate fully, one group or the other must experience the conversion that we have been calling a paradigm shift. Just because it is a transition between incommensurables, the transition between competing paradigms cannot be made a step at a time, forced by logic and neutral experience. Like the gestalt switch, it must occur all at once (though not necessarily in an instant) or not at all.[12]

It is passages like this one that provoked strong reactions among philosophers. Such expressions as "different worlds," "conversion," "gestalt switches" led (or rather, misled) many sympathetic and unsympathetic readers to think that his conception of a paradigm is like a total self-enclosed windowless monad – and that a paradigm shift necessitates an "irrational conversion." Even Karl Popper interpreted Kuhn as being guilty of "the myth of the framework" – the myth that "we are prisoners caught in the framework of our theories; our expectations; our past experiences; our language."[13] Presumably we are so imprisoned in these frameworks or paradigms that we cannot even communicate with those imprisoned in "radically" incommensurable paradigms. In another context I have argued that this is an inaccurate and distortive reading of Kuhn – although, unfortunately, a very common one.[14] Despite Kuhn's repeated protests that he never intended to suggest that paradigm switches involve an irrational mystical conversion, the rhetoric of extreme relativism has continued to haunt the appeal to incommensurability.

Although there are many ambiguities in Kuhn's discussion of incommensurability, one point is clear. Kuhn is primarily concerned with the incommensurability of *scientific* paradigms. But the very idea of incommensurability became so fertile and suggestive that it was soon generalized and extended to problems and contexts far beyond Kuhn's original concern to analyze scientific inquiry.

We can witness this in Richard Rorty's use of incommensurability in *Philosophy and the Mirror of Nature*. Rorty stretches the idea of commensuration and incommensurability to call into question the main tradition of modern epistemology – the "Cartesian-Lockean-Kantian tradition."[15] He characterizes "commensurable" as follows:

> By "commensurable" I mean able to be brought under a set of rules which will tell us how rational agreement can be reached on what would settle the issue on every point where statements seem to conflict. These rules tell how to construct an ideal situation, in which all residual disagreements will be seen to be "noncognitive" or merely verbal, or else merely temporary – capable of being resolved by doing something further. What matters is that there should be agreement about what would have to be done if a resolution *were* to be achieved. In the meantime, the interlocuters can agree to differ – being satisfied of each other's rationality the while.[16]

According to Rorty, "epistemology proceeds on the assumption that all contributions to a given discourse are commensurable."[17] "The dominating assumption of epistemology is that to be rational, to be fully human, to do what we ought, we need to be able to find agreement with other human beings."[18] Hermeneutics, according to Rorty, is a struggle against the assumption of commensuration; hermeneutics indicates the desire to keep open the cultural space opened up after the demise of epistemology. Rorty is calling for the ever new "invention" of incommensurable vocabularies – ever new forms of dissensus, not epistemological consensus. By generalizing and pressing the incommensurability thesis to this extreme, Rorty not only raised the specter of an extreme relativism but has provoked strong and hostile reactions. We can see this backlash in the reassertion of the varieties of metaphysical and scientific realism that has dominated so much of recent analytic philosophy.[19]

Instead of attempting to sort out the tangled issues involved in the crossfire of realist and anti-realist arguments, I want to discuss briefly the significance of Donald Davidson's contribution to the debate about incommensurability in what has become a "classic" paper, "On the Very Idea of a Conceptual Scheme." Davidson questions the intelligibility of the idea of a conceptual scheme, a framework, a paradigm that is presupposed – but rarely critically examined – in the debates about incommensurability. The main force of his argument is to show that the very idea of a conceptual scheme (in which we use sentences with truth values) that is presumably "radically" incommensurable with alternative conceptual schemes is – when we think it through – incoherent.

Summing up his conclusion, Davidson writes:

> It would be wrong to summarize by saying we have shown how communication is possible between people who have different schemes, a way that works without need of what there cannot be, namely a neutral ground, or a common coordinate system. For we have found no intelligible basis on which it can be said that schemes are different. It would be equally wrong to announce the glorious news that all mankind – all speakers of language, at least – share a common scheme and ontology. For if we cannot intelligibly say that schemes are different, neither can we intelligibly say that they are one.[20]

Davidson is not denying that there may be a sense in which different languages or vocabularies are incommensurable. Rather he is rejecting the "dogma of scheme and reality" whereby we assume different conceptual schemes are partial representations of a common uninterpreted reality. He is challenging the idea that we can intelligibly conceive of different conceptual schemes so that it makes sense to say that the truth values of sentences in "one" conceptual scheme may not share any of the truth values of sentences in different alternative conceptual schemes.[21]

Before drawing out the lessons of what can be learned from the use and abuse of appeals to incommensurability, I want to consider briefly one further appropriation of this controversial concept. Alasdair MacIntyre applies the concept of incommensurability to what he calls "tradition-constituted and tradition-constitutive" inquiries. In this respect, MacIntyre wants to show how rival traditions themselves may be incommensurable – especially traditions where the concepts of justice and practical rationality are central. The position developed by MacIntyre in *Whose Justice? Which Rationality?* is complex and nuanced – and, I would argue, not completely persuasive.[22] Let me outline some of his main theses. MacIntyre presents a "rational reconstruction" of three primary traditions – the Aristotelian, the Augustinian and the Scottish "common sense" tradition in order to show how each of these traditions can be viewed as *rationally* resolving conflicts (or failing to resolve conflicts) generated *within* each of these traditions. Although each of these traditions is formed by historically contingent beliefs, nevertheless *within* each of these traditions universal claims are made about what is justice and what is practical rationality – claims which are, in important ways, incompatible and incommensurable with those made in rival traditions. Each of these traditions develops its own standards of rationality. But despite this incommensurability we are not forced into an epistemological situation of relativism or perspectivism.[23] The rational superiority of a tradition can be vindicated without (falsely) presupposing that there are universally neutral, ahistorical standards of rationality. There is no "rationality as such." However it is possible to show that a specific tradition – say the Aristotelian tradition – can be rationally vindicated and shown to be rationally progressive by its own "standards of rationality." Furthermore, we can show – and MacIntyre thinks he has shown this – that rival incompatible and incommensurable traditions fail, not only according to Aristotelian standards of rationality, but according to their own standards of rationality. This is precisely what MacIntyre claims to have demonstrated about the "tradition" of liberalism that has its roots in the Enlightenment. We cannot ever hope to provide a *final* rational vindication for any "tradition-constituted and tradition-constitutive inquiry" because there cannot be an epistemological guarantee that a living tradition will be able to continue to solve the problems and conflicts it inevitably generates. Traditions undergo what MacIntyre calls "epistemological crises." We cannot know in advance whether or not a specific tradition will be able to resolve these "epistemological crises." But this claim does not mean we should be agnostic about the traditions in which we participate. Rather it means recognizing our historical finitude and fallibilism. Fallibilism itself presupposes that there is a truth which can be known. We can support our allegiance to a tradition by showing how it is rationally progressing according to its own historically developing "standards of rationality" and how it can successfully meet the challenges of rival traditions. There is no way to jump "out" or "over" history.

Now despite MacIntyre's apparently tolerant claims in acknowledging the "legitimacy" of radically incommensurable traditions of justice and practical rationality, there is an *implicit* cultural imperialism in his view. For it is a necessary consequence of his claims that a given tradition *may* contingently turn out to be rationally superior to all its rivals. And indeed MacIntyre does believe he has shown that:

> an Aristotelian tradition with resources for its own enlargement, correction, and defense, resources which suggest that *prima facie* at least a case has been made for concluding ... that those who have thought their way through the topics of justice and practical rationality, from the standpoint constructed by and in the direction pointed out first by Aristotle and then by Aquinas, have every reason so far to hold that *the rationality of their tradition has been confirmed* in its encounters with other traditions (emphasis added).[24]

I have indicated that I do not find MacIntyre's complex argument fully persuasive. Specifically, I do not think he has justified the claim that the Aristotelian-Thomistic tradition of justice and practical rationality *is* rationally *superior* to its rivals – even the few rival traditions he has analyzed. But this is not the place to develop fully the reasons why I think he fails to justify *this* claim.[25] However I do think MacIntyre deepens our understanding of incommensurability by applying this concept to a "thick description" of traditions. Furthermore I agree with MacIntyre that acknowledging such incommensurability does not mean giving up the universality of truth claims made within a given tradition. The incommensurability of traditions does not entail relativism or perspectivism.

But the time has come to sum up what I think are the proper conclusions to be drawn from the debates about incommensurability. Although I cannot develop a full-scale justification for these claims here, I do believe they can be adequately justified. I want to sum up these "conclusions" in a series of theses.

1   The controversies concerning incommensurability have challenged and raised serious doubts about the belief that there is – or must be – a determinate, universal, neutral, ahistorical framework in which all languages or "vocabularies" can be *adequately* translated and which can enable us to evaluate rationally the validity claims made within these disparate languages. In this respect one of the most fundamental foundational claims of Western philosophy and epistemology has been called into question.

2   The incommensurability of languages and traditions does not entail a self-defeating or self-referentially inconsistent form of relativism or perspectivism.

3   The concept of incommensurability is not to be confused with, or reduced to logical incompatibility or incomparability. Incommensurable languages can be compared and rationally evaluated in *multiple* ways. Practically, such comparison and evaluation requires the cultivation of hermeneutical sensitivity and imagination.

4   Incommensurable languages and traditions are not to be thought of as self-contained windowless monads that share nothing in common. In Wittgenstein's phrase, this is a (false) picture that holds us captive. There are always points of overlap and criss-crossing, even if there is not perfect commensuration. We must not succumb to "the myth of the framework." Our linguistic horizons are always open. This is what enables comparison, and even sometimes a "fusion of horizons."

5   We can never escape the real practical possibility that we may fail to understand "alien" traditions and the ways in which they are incommensurable with the traditions to which we belong.

6   But the response to the threat of this practical failure – which can sometimes be tragic – should be an ethical one, i.e., to assume the responsibility to listen carefully, to use our linguistic, emotional, and cognitive imagination to grasp what is being expressed and said

in "alien" traditions. We must do this in a way where we resist the dual temptations of *either* facilely assimilating what others are saying to our own categories and language without doing justice to what is genuinely different and may be incommensurable *or* simply dismissing what the "other" is saying as incoherent nonsense. We must also resist the double danger of imperialistic colonization and inauthentic exoticism – what is sometimes called "going native."[26]

7   Within a given language or tradition which may be incommensurable with its rivals, participants are always already making validity claims that "transcend" their local contexts.

8   Above all, we must always strive to avoid a false essentialism when we are trying to understand the traditions to which we belong or those alien traditions that are incommensurable with "our" traditions. For frequently discussions of East–West lapse into such a false essentialism where we are seduced into thinking there are essential determinate characteristics that distinguish the Western and Eastern "mind." This false essentialism violently distorts the sheer complexity of overlapping traditions that cut across these artificial, simplistic global notions.

9   Learning to live with (among) rival pluralistic incommensurable traditions – which is one of the most pressing problems of contemporary life – is always precarious and fragile. There are no algorithms for grasping what is held in common and what is genuinely different. Indeed, commonality and difference are themselves historically conditioned and shifting. The search for commonalities and differences among incommensurable traditions is always a task and an obligation – an *Aufgabe*. It is a primary responsibility for reflective participants in any vital substantive tradition. In this sense the plurality of rival incommensurable traditions imposes a *universal* responsibility upon reflective participants in any tradition – a responsibility that should not be confused with an indifferent superficial tolerance where no effort is made to understand and engage with the incommensurable otherness of "the Other."

I agree with a theme which has been just as central for Gadamer as it has been for Derrida – that it is only through an engaged encounter with the Other, with the otherness of the Other, that one comes to a more informed, textured understanding of the traditions to which "we" belong. It is in our genuine encounters with what is other and alien (even in ourselves) that we can further our own self-understanding.

Otherness: Levinas/Derrida

Let me abruptly switch contexts and take up the themes of otherness and alterity. But I hope to show – as my last remarks suggest – that this is not really an abrupt change at all. Although the thematization of "otherness" has not been in the foreground of twentieth-century Anglo-American philosophy, it has been at the very center of twentieth-century Continental philosophy – especially German and French philosophy. Michael Theunissen begins his impressive book, *The Other*, with the following claim – a claim with which I fully agree:

> Few issues have expressed as powerful a hold over the thought of this century as that of "The Other." It is difficult to think of a second theme, even one that might be of more substantial significance, that has provoked as widespread an interest as this one; it is difficult to think of a second theme that so sharply marks off the present – admittedly a present growing out of the nineteenth century and reaching back to it – from its historical roots in the tradition. To be sure the problem of the other has at times been accorded a prominent place in ethics and anthropology, in legal and political philosophy. But the problem of the other has certainly never penetrated as deeply as today into the foundations of philosophical thought – the question of the other cannot be separated from the most primordial questions raised by modern thought.[27]

But what precisely is the "problem" of the Other? Here too we must be careful to avoid a false essentialism. When we "look and see," we discover that it "names" a cluster of problems related by family resemblances rather than a single well-defined problem. Theunissen tells us: "Generally speaking, 'the Other' comprehends all those concepts by means of which contemporary philosophy has sought to set out the structure of being-with, or its original transcendental form. Thus, among other things, it comprehends the difference between 'Thou' on the one side and the 'alien I' – the 'alter ego' or being-with-the-other – on the other side."[28] But even this broad formulation does not encompass all the issues raised by the question of "the Other." Indeed it does not explicitly mention those analyses where "the Other" is taken to be a generic term for what is excluded, repressed, suppressed or concealed. Thus for example, one can speak of "the Other" of Reason – regardless of how this "Other" is characterized. Theunissen primarily intends to call attention to the "problem of the other" where the Other is understood as a *personal* Other – whether a first person "alien I" or a second person "thou" – (although what is meant by "personal" is itself problematic and contested). In French, for example, this systematic ambiguity in the neutral English term "Other" is reflected in the distinction between *"autre"* and *"l'autrui."*[29]

To pursue the vicissitudes of reflections on "the Other" would require nothing less than a comprehensive narrative of twentieth-century Continental philosophy. The theme of "the Other" – and specifically what constitutes the otherness of "the Other" – has been at the very heart of the work of every major twentieth-century Continental philosopher. But in order to leap into the center of controversies concerning "the Other," I want to begin by considering one of the most extreme and radical formulations of the problem of "the Other" – the one developed by the French Jewish thinker, Emmanuel Levinas.

Levinas, perhaps more than any other French thinker, is responsible for the original French encounter with, and appropriation of Husserl and Heidegger. It was from Levinas' early writings on Husserl that even Sartre first learned of the importance of phenomenology. But for my purposes, I want to focus on the way in which "the Other" – specifically *l'autrui* – becomes increasingly predominant in Levinas' thinking. This notion becomes a lever for a questioning and challenging of the entire project of philosophy, including the phenomenology of Husserl and the fundamental ontology of Heidegger. According to Levinas, both Husserl and Heidegger still think in the shadow of Greek philosophy – which has set the terms for the entire tradition of Western philosophy. Simplifying to the extreme, we can say that Levinas reads the entire project of the history of Western philosophy, whose destiny has been shaped by the classical Greek problematic, as functioning within what he calls "the Same and the Other." Furthermore, the primary thrust of this Western tradition has always been to reduce, absorb, or appropriate what is taken to be "the Other" to "the Same." This is manifested not only in ontology but also in epistemology and in the main traditions of Western politics and ethics. This drive to reduce or assimilate "the Other" to "the Same" is already reflected in the Parmenidian identification of thought and being – where difference and otherness disappears. This imperialistic gesture – this gesture to conquer, master and colonize "the Other" – reveals the violence that is implicit in the reduction of "the Other" to "the Same." For Levinas, this violence reaches its apogee in Hegel. Commenting on Hegel, Levinas tells us:

> The I is not a being that always remains the same, but is the being whose existing consists in identifying itself, in recovering its identity throughout all that happens to it. It is the primal identity, the primordial work of the identification .... Hegelian phenomenology, where self-consciousness is the distinguishing of what is not distinct, expresses the universality of the same identifying itself in the alterity of objects thought and despite the opposition of self to self.[30]

To illustrate what he means, Levinas cites a famous passage from the *Phenomenology of Spirit* where Hegel declares:

> I distinguish myself from myself; and therein I am immediately aware that this factor distinguished from me is not distinguished. I, the selfsame being thrust myself away from myself; but this which is distinguished, which is set up as unlike me, is immediately on its being distinguished no distinction for me.[31]

Levinas reads this as affirming that "the difference is not a difference; the I, as other, is not an 'other'."[32] In short, even though "alterity" drives the Hegelian dialectic, this "alterity" is ultimately *aufgehoben*, swallowed up in the Absolute Subject. Consequently "alterity" has no singular *metaphysical* status outside what is *ontologically* the same – it is only a "moment" within "the Same."[33] Of course, Levinas is not the first to raise this type of objection against Hegel. We find variations upon it in thinkers as diverse as Kierkegaard, Nietzsche, Sartre, Heidegger, Foucault and Derrida. What is distinctive about Levinas, what makes him so "radical" is his claim that even Husserlian phenomenology and Heidegger's fundamental ontology – despite protests to the contrary – do not escape this reduction of "the Other" to "the Same." (Adorno too makes this critique of Husserl and Heidegger.)

Levinas boldly seeks to escape this philosophical imperialism of "the Same" and "the Other" by opening the space for the absolute exteriority of the metaphysical Other (*l'autrui*) which he sharply distinguishes from the ontological Other (*autre*). The metaphysical Other is an "other with an alterity that is not formal, is not the simple reverse of identity, and is not formed out of resistance to the same, but is prior to every initiative, to all imperialism of the same. It is other with an alterity constitutive of the very content of the other."[34] To acknowledge the otherness of the Other (*l'autrui*), to keep it from falling back into the other of the same requires Levinas to speak of it as the "absolute other." It is the Stranger (*L'Etranger*) who genuinely dis-turbs or ruptures the being at home with oneself (*le chez soi*).[35] It is this radically asymmetrical relation between the I and the Other (a "relation" that defies reduction to reciprocal equality) that characterizes what Levinas calls *the ethical relation*. As he boldly pursues this pathway of thinking, he categorically asserts the metaphysical priority and primacy of the ethical (which is not to be confused with the Kantian primacy of practical reason) – a primacy that reigns over all ontology. We can see just how radical Levinas' thinking is when he distances himself from Heidegger.

> Even though it opposes the technological passion issued forth from the forgetting of Being hidden by existants, Heideggerian ontology, which subordinates the relationship with the Other to the relation with Being in general, remains under obedience to the anonymous, and leads inevitably to another power, to imperialist domination, to tyranny.[36]

Initially, Levinas' idiom may strike us as idiosyncratic (which it is) and abstract (which it is not). We can begin to relate these reflections on "the Other" (*l'autrui*) with our discussion on incommensurability. For by argumentation and phenomenological description, Levinas seeks to elicit the incommensurability of "the Other" with the I. This incommensurability and asymmetry of "the Other" (*l'autrui*) is manifested in what he calls the "face-to-face," the primary ethical relation that can never be reduced to the "totality" of "the Same" and "the Other." Against the tendency so deeply ingrained in Western discourse that highlights and valorizes reciprocity, likeness, and symmetry in "personal" relationships, e.g., in Western discourses of friendship (*philia*), Levinas emphasizes the lack of reciprocity, unlikeness, asymmetry – and indeed incommensurability – in the ethical relation of the "face-to-face." This even has consequences for understanding the asymmetry of responsibility where I, in responding to "the Other" (*l'autrui*), am always responsible for (to) "the Other" (*l'autrui*), regardless of "the Other's" response to me.

We can appreciate the thought-provoking quality of Levinas' thinking when we realize that he is at once reiterating and radicalizing a theme that has been sounded over and over again in the aftermath of Hegel and which has become so dominant in what is loosely and vaguely called "postmodern" thought. This is the theme that *resists* the unrelenting tendency of the will to knowledge and truth where Reason – when unmasked – is understood as always seeking to appropriate, comprehend, control, master, contain, domi- nate, suppress, or repress what presents itself as "the Other" that it confronts. It is the theme of the violence of Reason's imperialistic welcoming embrace.

The metaphors of "imperialism," "colonization," "domination," "mastery," "control" are not to be taken as "dead" metaphors. For the "logic" at work here *is* the "logic" at work in cultural, political, social, and economic imperialism and colonization – even the "logic" of ethical imperialism where the language of reciprocal recognition and reconciliation masks the violent reduction of the alterity of "the Other" (*l'autrui*) to "more of the same." What is at issue here is acknowledging the radical incommensurable *singularity* of the Other (*l'autrui*), to recover a sense of radical plurality that defies any facile total reconciliation.

In "using" Levinas as exemplar of a radical thinker who seeks to take us beyond the limits of the "logic" of "the Same" and "the Other" – which *he* takes to be the logic of Western philosophy shaped by the Greek problematic – I do *not* want to suggest that I agree with him. Derrida's own brilliant deconstruction of Levinas' texts exposes the double-bind logic that ensnares Levinas. For Derrida's close reading brings out the aporetic quality and instability of Levinas' "position." Derrida's reading has consequences that reach far beyond the interpretation of Levinas. For Levinas comes precipit- ously close to reinstituting a new set of rigid dichotomies, e.g., ontology/metaphysics; philosophy/ethics; Greek/Jew.

Derrida questions the intelligibility of Levinas' notion of *the* Absol- ute Other and absolute exteriority. He even shows how "Levinas is very close to Hegel, much closer than he admits, and at the very moment when he is apparently opposed to Hegel in the most radical fashion. This is a situation he must share with all anti-Hegelian thinkers."[37]

Derrida agrees with Levinas that "the other is the other only if his alterity is absolutely irreducible, that is, infinitely irreducible."[38] But, contrary to Levinas, who claims that "to make the other an alter ego ... is to neutralize its absolute alterity," Derrida argues that "if the other was not recognized as ego, its entire alterity would collapse."[39] Against Levinas' reading of Husserl, Derrida (rightly) claims that according to Husserl "the other as alter ego signifies the other as other, irreducible to *my* ego, precisely because it is an ego, because it has the form of the ego .... This is why, if you will, he is a face, can speak to me, understand me, and eventually command me."[40]

Derrida presses this point even further when he declares "the other, then would not be what he is (my fellowman as foreigner) if he were not alter ego .... the other is absolutely other only if he is an ego, that is, in a certain way, if he is the same as I."[41] This last claim sounds *as if* Derrida is siding with Hegel against Levinas. But to draw this inference would miss the subtlety (and instability) of Derrida's point. His "logic" here is a "both/and" rather than "either/or" – but it is not the "logic" of *Aufhebung* in which all differences and oppositions are ultimately reconciled. In short, there is both sameness and radical alterity, symmetry and asymmetry, identity and difference in my relation with "the Other," and above all in the ethical relation.

Just as Derrida plays off Hegel and Husserl against Levinas (indeed with Levinas' *own* reading of Hegel and Husserl), Derrida also turns Heidegger against Levinas. When he does this, the ethical (or rather the meta-ethical) implications of Derrida's deconstruction and destabilization become vivid. For Derrida writes:

> Not only is the thought of Being not ethical violence [as Levinas claims], but it seems no ethics – in Levinas' sense – can be opened without it ... [The thought of Being] conditions the *respect* for the other *as what it is*. Without this acknowledgement, which is not a knowledge, or let us say, without this "letting-be" of an existent (other) as something existing outside me in the essence of what it is (first in its alterity), no ethics would be possible .... to let the other be

in its existence and essence as other means that what gains access to thought, or (and) what thought gains access to, is that which is essence and that which is existence; and that which is the Being which they presuppose. Without this, no letting-be would be possible, and first of all, the letting be of respect and of the ethical commandment addressing itself to freedom. Violence would reign to such a degree that it would no longer even be able to appear and be named.[42]

Derrida, who begins his essay on Levinas with a citation from Matthew Arnold:

Hebraism and Hellenism, – between these two points of influence moves our world. At one time it feels more powerfully the attraction of one of them, at another time of the other; and it ought to be, though it never is, evenly and happily balanced between them.[43]

concludes his essay with a much more ambiguous – and what he would call "undecidable" – question:

And what is the legitimacy, what is the meaning of the *copula* in this proposition from perhaps the most Hegelian of modern novelists: "JewGreek is greekjew. Extremes meet"?[44]

Derrida's citation from James Joyce can be read as allegorical – and is just as applicable to EastWest. For playing with Derrida's citation of Joyce, we can ask: "And what is the legitimacy, what is the meaning of the *copula* in the proposition: 'Eastwest is westeast. Extremes meet'?"

Now despite the allusions to my earlier discussion of incommensurability in exploring the alterity of the Other, one may wonder what does this strange Continental talk about "the Other" have to do with the original problematic of incommensurability? If there are "family resemblances" aren't they only extremely superficial? I do not think so. So – in a manner that roughly parallels the theses I advanced in the discussion of incommensurability – let me conclude with a number of theses concerning the alterity and singularity of the otherness of the Other that interweave with the discussion of incommensurability.

1   The controversies concerning the otherness or alterity of "the Other" do highlight a deep tendency in Western philosophy to

reduce (violently) "the Other" to "the Same." And they deeply question and challenge this tendency – showing us the consequences of this reduction. They show us what is silenced or obliterated when we fail to acknowledge the alterity (the incommensurability) of the Other.

2   This irreducible alterity does not mean that there is nothing in common between the I and its genuine "Other." If there were nothing in common, we would once again find ourselves in the *aporias* of self-defeating relativism and/or perspectivism.

3   Acknowledging the radical alterity of "the Other" does not mean that there is *no* way of understanding the Other, or comparing the I with its Other. Even an asymmetrical relation is still a *relation*. Alternatively we can say that to think of "the Other" as an "absolute Other," where this is taken to mean that there is *no* way whatsoever for relating the I to "the Other," is unintelligible and incoherent. We must cultivate the type of imagination where we are at once sensitive to the sameness of "the Other" with ourselves *and* the radical alterity that defies and resists reduction of "the Other" to "the Same."

4   Acknowledging radical alterity does not mean that we should think of the "terms" of this relation of the "I" or "we" to its "Other" as windowless monads completely impenetrable to each Other.

5   We can never escape the real practical possibility that we will fail to do justice to the alterity of "the Other."

6   But the response to the threat to this practical failure should be an ethical one – to assume the responsibility to acknowledge, appreciate and not to violate the alterity of "the Other." Without such acknowledgment and recognition no ethics is possible. We must resist the dual temptation of *either* facilely assimilating the alterity of "the Other" to what is "the Same" (this is what Levinas so acutely emphasizes) *or* simply dismissing (or repressing) the alterity of "the Other" as being of no significance – "merely" contingent. We must also resist the double danger of imperialistic colonization and inauthentic exoticism when encountering "the Other."

7   Contrary to Levinas there *is* a reciprocity between the I and "the Other" (*l'autrui*) which is compatible with their radical alterity. For *both* stand under the reciprocal obligation to seek to transcend their narcissistic egoism in understanding the alterity of the Other.

8   Above all, we must always strive to avoid a false essentialism

that sees *only* more of the Same in the Other – that fails authentically to confront "the terror of Otherness."[45]

9   Learning to live with the instability of alterity; learning to accept and to encounter radical plurality which fully acknowledges *singularity* – is always fragile and precarious. It makes no sense to even speak of a "final solution" to this problem – *the* problem of human living. No one can ever fully anticipate the ruptures and new sites of the upsurgence of alterity. This is a lesson that we must learn again and again. And it has been painfully experienced in our time whenever those individuals or groups who have been colonized, repressed, or silenced rise up and assert the legitimacy and demand for full recognition of their own non-reducible alterity. The search for commonalities and precise points of difference is always a task and an obligation – an *Aufgabe*. Without a *mutual* recognition of this *Aufgabe*, without a self-conscious sensitivity of the need always to do justice to "the Other's" *singularity*, without a heightened awareness of the inescapable risks that can never be completely mastered, we are in danger of obliterating the radical plurality of the human condition.[46] It is an *Aufgabe* not only when we seek to understand our own traditions (whether "West" or "East") but when we authentically try to encounter and understand Eastwest and Westeast.

NOTES

1   G. W. F. Hegel, *The Phenomenology of Spirit*, trans. A. V. Miller (New York: Oxford University Press, 1977), p. 357.

2   Ibid.

3   Thomas Kuhn, "Theory-Change as Structure-Change: Comments on the Sneed Formalism," *Erkenntnis* 10 (1976), pp. 190–91. In this passage Kuhn speaks of the incommensurability of *theories*. Kuhn has not always carefully distinguished between theories and paradigms. Not all theories are to be construed as paradigms. But in this context it is clear that Kuhn is referring to paradigm-theories. See my discussion of Kuhn's "ambiguous concept of a paradigm" in *The Restructuring of Social and Political Theory* (Philadelphia: University of Pennsylvania Press, 1978), pp. 84–93.

4   See my discussion of incommensurability in *Beyond Objectivism and Relativism: Science, Hermeneutics, and Praxis* (Philadelphia: University of Pennsylvania Press, 1983), part 2, "Science, Rationality, and Incommensurability."

5   Thomas Kuhn, *The Structure of Scientific Revolutions*, second enl. edn (Chicago: University of Chicago Press, 1970), p. 148.
6   Ibid.
7   Ibid.
8   Ibid.
9   Ibid., p. 149.
10 Ibid.
11 Ibid.
12 Ibid., p. 150.
13 Karl Popper, "Normal Science and Its Dangers," in Imre Lakatos and Alan Musgrave, eds., *Criticism and the Growth of Knowledge* (Cambridge: Cambridge University Press, 1970), p. 56.
14 See *Beyond Objectivism and Relativism*, pp. 79–93.
15 Richard Rorty, *Philosophy and the Mirror of Nature* (Princeton: Princeton University Press, 1979). See especially "From Epistemology to Hermeneutics," pp. 315–56.
16 Ibid., p. 316.
17 Ibid.
18 Ibid.
19 See Rorty's discussion of the "backlash" of realism in his Introduction to *Consequences of Pragmatism* (Minneapolis: University of Minnesota Press, 1982).
20 Donald Davidson, "On the Very Idea of a Conceptual Scheme," *Proceedings and Addresses of the American Philosophical Association* 47 (1973–4), p. 20.
21 Giving up the dualism of "scheme and world" does not entail relinquishing the notion of objective truth.

> In giving up dependence on the concept of an uninterpreted reality, something outside all schemes and science, we do not relinquish the notion of objective truth – quite the contrary. Given the dogma of a dualism of scheme and reality, we get conceptual relativity, and truth relative to a scheme. Without the dogma, this kind of relativity goes by the board. Of course, truth of sentences remains relative to language, but that is as objective as can be. In giving up the dualism of scheme and world, we do not give up the world, but reestablish unmediated touch with the familiar objects whose antics make our sentences and opinions true or false. (Ibid., p. 20)

22 Alasdair MacIntyre, *Whose Justice? Which Rationality?* (Notre Dame: University of Notre Dame Press, 1988). See especially the last three chapters: "The Rationality of Traditions"; "Tradition and Translation"; and "Contested Justices, Contested Rationalities."
23 MacIntyre distinguishes between the "relativist" challenge and the "perspectivist" challenge.

> The relativist challenge rests upon a denial that rational debate and rational choice among rival traditions is possible; the perspectivist challenge puts in question the possibility of making truth-claims from within any one tradition. (Ibid., p. 352)

MacIntyre develops and seeks to answer these challenges in his chapter, "The Rationality of Traditions," pp. 349–69.

24 Ibid., pp. 402–403.

25 My main reasons for arguing that MacIntyre fails to justify *this* central claim concern some of the aporetic consequences of his analysis of "truth," and how truth claims about justice and practical rationality are justified. Furthermore I do not think that MacIntyre squarely faces the issue of how much disagreement there can be about what *are* the standards of rationality even *within* a "tradition-constituted and tradition-constitutive inquiry." For he fails adequately to indicate how disputes about "standards of rationality" (whether *within* a tradition or among rival traditions) are to be *rationally* resolved. But to justify my objections requires a more detailed analysis and critique of MacIntyre's understanding of "truth" and "rationality" (including both practical and theoretical rationality).

26 See Clifford Geertz's sensitive and subtle discussion of this double danger in "From the Native's Point of View: On the Nature of Anthropological Understanding" in Paul Rabinow and William Sullivan, eds., *Interpretive Social Science: A Reader* (Berkeley: University of California Press, 1979). See also my discussion of Geertz in *Beyond Objectivism and Relativism*, pp. 93–108.

27 Michael Theunissen, *The Other*, trans. Christopher Macann (Cambridge, Mass.: MIT Press, 1984), p. 1.

28 Ibid.

29 In distinguishing the neutral generic sense of "the Other" from the personal senses of "the Other" – as it is investigated, for example, in what is sometimes called "the problem of intersubjectivity" or "sociality" – I do *not* want to suggest that these are unrelated. On the contrary, what characterizes most treatments of "the Other" is the interweaving of the multiple senses of "the Other."

30 Emmanuel Levinas, *Totality and Infinity*, trans. Alphonso Lingis (Pittsburgh: Duquesne University Press, 1969), p. 36.

31 Ibid.

32 Ibid.

33 Levinas sharply distinguishes *metaphysics* from *ontology*. "The metaphysical desire tends toward *something else entirely*, toward the absolutely other" (ibid., p. 33). "Thus the metaphysician and the other cannot be *totalized*" (p. 35). But ontology involves "a reduction of the other to the same by interposition of a middle and neutral term that ensures the

comprehension of being" (p. 43). According to Levinas, "Western philosophy has most often been an ontology ..." (p. 43). See *Totality and Infinity*, "Metaphysics and Transcendence," pp. 33–52.

34   Ibid., p. 38.

35   Ibid., p. 39.

36   Ibid., pp. 46–7.

37   Jacques Derrida, "Violence and Metaphysics: An Essay on the Thought of Emmanuel Levinas," in *Writing and Difference*, trans. Alan Bass (Chicago: University of Chicago Press, 1978), p. 99.

38   Ibid., p. 104.

39   Ibid., p. 125.

40   Ibid.

41   Ibid., p. 127.

42   Ibid., p. 138.

43   Ibid., p. 79.

44   Ibid., p. 153.

45   This is David Tracy's phrase. See David Tracy, *Plurality and Ambiguity: Hermeneutics, Religion, Hope* (New York: Harper and Row, 1987).

46   This allusion to Hannah Arendt is deliberate. Although I have discussed the "problem" of "the Other" primarily with reference to Levinas and Derrida, I might have concentrated on Arendt's own analysis of plurality as a fundamental characteristic of the human condition. Indeed Arendt – with a specific emphasis on action, speech, public space and politics – develops one of the most perceptive analyses of plurality that does justice to both singularity (alterity) *and* togetherness (commonality). See Hannah Arendt, *The Human Condition* (Chicago: University of Chicago Press, 1958). See also my discussion of Arendt's understanding of plurality in "Judging – the Actor and the Spectator" and "Rethinking the Social and the Political" included in Richard J. Bernstein, *Philosophical Profiles* (Philadelphia: University of Pennsylvania Press, 1986).

4

Heidegger's Silence?
Ēthos and Technology*

No short circuit can be set up between work and person. Heidegger's philosophical work owes its autonomy, as does every other such work, to the strength of its arguments. But then a productive relation to his thinking can be gained only when one engages these *arguments* – and takes them out of their ideological context. The farther the argumentative substance sinks into the unchallengeable morass of ideology, the greater is the demand of the critical force of an alert and perceptive appropriation.

Jürgen Habermas, "Work and Weltanschauung"

Thomas Sheehan begins his critical review of recent revelations about Heidegger and the Nazis with the stark claim: "Two facts about Martin Heidegger ... are as incontestable as they are complicated: first that he remains one of the century's most influential philosophers, and second, that he was a Nazi."[1] It is the second "complicated" fact that has recently stirred up (once again) so much controversy. How could a thinker of Heidegger's stature and originality – who is judged by his critics and admirers to be one of the greatest philosophers of the twentieth century – give his enthusiastic support to Hitler and "the movement" of National Socialism? No one writing about Heidegger can ignore these two "complicated" facts and question what precisely is the relation (or non-relation) between them. This is what makes writing about Heidegger so difficult, challenging, and disturbing.

* Throughout his writings, Heidegger typically uses masculine forms of speech. To avoid artificiality, I have followed his usage.

Many of the facts about Heidegger's brief but active support of Hitler and the Nazis during the ten-month period when he served as Rector of the University of Freiburg between April 1933 and February 1934 have been known for a long time. But with the publication of Victor Farias' controversial book, *Heidegger et le nazisme*, the careful archival scholarship of the German historian Hugo Ott, the detailed analyses of Heidegger's student and commentator, Otto Pöggler, and the publication of the memoirs and recollections of Karl Löwith and Karl Jaspers we are gaining a much more detailed and accurate account of what Heidegger said and did, as well as an increased awareness of his evasions, misleading statements, and crucial silences. The accumulation of these details reveals a horrendous portrait of Heidegger's fantastic illusions about the possibility of a "spiritual" renewal of the German *Volk* led by Hitler, Heidegger's delusion that he might serve as the *Führer* of the *Führer*, his attempt to "reform" the German University in order to destroy its liberal constitution, his scorn for so-called "academic freedom," his complicity with the ugly process of *Gleichschultung* – the "streamlining" of the university so that it would submit to the Party and state power – and his betrayal of academic colleagues.[2] What is still most scandalous and incomprehensible is not what he did and said in 1933–4, but his refusal after 1945 to confront *directly* and *unambiguously* the full horror of the *Shoah* and the barbaric crimes of the Nazis. How can we explain why Heidegger – who claimed that what is most thought-provoking about our epoch is the refusal to think – failed himself to think through the most shocking events of the twentieth century that "call forth" thinking?

One of the consequences of the recent intense scrutinizing of Heidegger's pronouncements and deeds has been a deconstruction, a dismantling of the "Heidegger myth" – a myth cultivated by Heidegger himself, many of his admirers, and even some of his critics. According to this myth, it was only during the relatively brief period of his rectorship that Heidegger "erred" so greatly. But after he resigned, Heidegger retreated into "internal exile" – to his native dwelling place of thinking. There are even those who argue that almost immediately after his resignation – in his lectures and seminars – Heidegger began to develop a sharp critique of Nazi ideology, especialy its ultra-nationalism, racism, and biologism. The myth of Heidegger's brief descent into a world of human affairs and his rapid retreat into his "proper residence" of thinking was eloquently expressed by Hannah Arendt on the occasion of his eightieth birthday in 1969 when she compared Heidegger with Plato:

> Now we all know that Heidegger too, once succumbed to the temptation to change his "residence" and to get involved in the world of human affairs. As to the world, he was served somewhat worse than Plato, because the tyrant and his victims were not located beyond the sea, but in his own country. As to Heidegger himself, I believe the matter stands differently. He was still young enough to learn from the shock of the collapse, which after ten short hectic months thirty-seven years ago drove him back to his residence, and to settle in his thinking what he experienced.[3]

But this myth of Heidegger as the pure thinker who was briefly tempted "to get involved in the world of human affairs" and then retreated to his proper "residence" is belied by the stubborn facts of what he said and did before and after those "ten short hectic months." We can even interpret the twists and turns in his thinking – from at least 1929 on – as, *in part* a response to his understanding of the political events he was witnessing.[4]

Still the most difficult and thorny questions concern the complex relation between Heidegger's philosophic texts (and which texts?) to his more overt political pronouncements and deeds. Almost every shade of opinion has been expressed – ranging from those like Richard Rorty who claim that there is no correlation between Heidegger's philosophy and his "moral character" to those like Adorno who wrote that Heidegger's "philosophy is fascist right down to its innermost components" (*dessen Philosophie bis in ihre innersten Zellen faschistisch ist*).[5]

Rorty tells us that, as a human being, Heidegger "was a rather nasty piece of work – a coward and a liar, pretty much from first to last." But "there is no way to correlate moral virtue with philosophical importance or philosophical doctrine. Being an original philosopher (and Heidegger was as an original philosopher as we have had in this century) is like being an original mathematician or an original microbiologist or a consummate chess master, it is the result of some neural kink that occurs independently of other kinks."[6] Rorty draws an analogy between Frege and Heidegger. We do not condemn Frege's contributions to formal logic even though he was "a vicious anti-semite and a proto-Nazi."[7] So we should also sharply distinguish Heidegger's philosophic importance from the deficiencies of his "moral character." Although Rorty thinks that "Heidegger and Hitler had a lot in common: blood-and-soil rhetoric, anti-semitism, self-deception, a conviction that philosophy must be taken seriously, and a desire to found a cult" we should not consider "Heidegger as Hitler's equivalent."[8] Rather, we should read Heidegger's "books as he would have not wished them to be read: in a cool hour, with curiosity, and an open tolerant mind."[9]

Insofar as Rorty is endorsing the claim that no "short circuit can be set up between [Heidegger's] work and person," one can be sympathetic with his plea for a tolerant reading of his works even if we are appalled by his "moral character." Nevertheless Rorty's sharp dichotomy between "philosophic originality" and "moral character" is misleading for several reasons. First, because it obscures and displaces the question of whether there is anything about Heidegger's "philosophy" that lends support to, justifies, or would enable us to account for why he "erred" so greatly. Secondly, it ignores the question of whether – and in what ways – Heidegger's "philosophic" writings were influenced by ideological biases, especially the mandarin "reactionary modernism" so prevalent in Germany between the two World Wars.[10] Thirdly, Rorty's exclusive focus on the lack of correlation between philosophic originality and moral character diverts attention from exploring the political and ethical consequences of Heidegger's philosophic writings. Fourthly, the analogy Rorty draws between philosophy and mathematics or microbiology is itself misleading. Heidegger was concerned – directly or indirectly – with *Dasein* – the questioning being. Heidegger is the thinker who even harshly condemns "metaphysical humanism" because it does "not realize the proper dignity of man" (Humanism, 210; 21).[11] It would be a gross distortion of Heidegger's "philosophic" writings to think that they have nothing to say about our being-in-the-world – including the ethical and political aspects of our existence. The relation between Heidegger's philosophic concerns and his politics becomes even more complex because the textual evidence (as well as reports of his own personal testimony) is overwhelming that he drew upon, appropriated and reinterpreted his central philosophic concepts in such texts as his infamous "Rectoral Address."[12] Karl Löwith, one of Heidegger's closest associates, reports that when he met Heidegger in Rome in 1936 and suggested that Heidegger's support of the Nazis came from the very essence of his philosophy, "Heidegger agreed with me without reservations and spelled out for me that his concept of historicity was the basic for his political engagement."[13]

One cannot begin with the apriori (and unjustified) assumption that there is no relation between Heidegger's philosophy and his politics. One must "look and see," one must carefully examine Heidegger's texts *before* making any such judgment.

In contrast to Rorty's rigid and misleading demarcation, there are those who have argued that Heidegger's fundamental philosophic concerns are not only compatible with his political engagement, but were appropriated by Heidegger when he supported the "movement" of National Socialism. Karsten Harries, who develops a subtle argument along these lines, claims that "Authenticity as Heidegger himself understands it, rules out a separation of the political stance of the author and his philosophy."[14] Harries argues that an analysis of such key Heideggerian concepts as "authenticity," "conscience," "guilt," and especially the treacherously ambiguous concept of "resolve" (*Entschlossenheit*) in *Sein und Zeit* reveal crucial links between Heidegger's philosophy and his Rectoral Address.[15] According to Harries we cannot ignore Heidegger's changing political stances if we want to understand his philosophy. Heidegger's turn "towards National Socialism was genuine and cannot be erased from the development of his thought."[16] Furthermore the intimate relation between Heidegger's philosophy and politics is crucial for understanding his development. For Heidegger's "disastrously misplaced enthusiasm for National Socialism" and his "unfounded hope for a new beginning which would rescue Germany from disintegration and madness" is the key for understanding what Harries calls the "apolitical" turn of his subsequent rethinking of his own "philosophy and its relationship to the age."[17]

Unlike Rorty who focuses almost exclusively on the single question of the relation of Heidegger's philosophy to his nasty moral character, Harries opens up the questions of the ways in which Heidegger's philosophy – and the changes in his development – are related to his interpretations of the political events that he was witnessing. The current Heidegger debate set off by the publication of Farias' book has aroused so much passion and polemic – pro and con – that issues which need to be carefully distinguished are confused and jumbled together. Indeed there is a danger that the recent outpouring of secondary literature on *l'affaire Heidegger* can obscure these issues rather than clarify them.

Without denying that these are interrelated, we can nevertheless discriminate the following issues: (1) there is a need to specify accurately the historical facts about what Heidegger said and did – when, where, and to whom; (2) there are questions concerning the apparent disparities between what happened and Heidegger's subsequent accounts, evasions and rationalizations. One must examine carefully the ways in which Heidegger was reinterpreting and perhaps falsifying his own past;[18] (3) there is need to ask whether and in what ways Heidegger's philosophy and thinking was influenced by his interpretation of historical and political events. Is his thinking "contaminated" by ideological biases? (4) There is also the question of how his changing philosophic concerns shaped his reading of these events. Careful textual analysis is required to determine what philosophic concepts Heidegger himself drew upon in his overt political pronouncements; (5) we must also ask whether Heidegger was betraying his own deepest thinking. For one may want to argue that even though Heidegger did "err greatly" his "failure" was one of misjudgment and that we can find the resources in his own philosophy for critically evaluating his own errors and misjudgments; (6) finally, we must ask what precisely are the political and ethical implications of Heidegger's texts (and which texts) – what are the consequences of the "pathways" of his thinking for understanding the political and ethical dimensions of our being-in-the-world?

It is this last question that I want to explore with reference to Heidegger's questioning concerning technology. For *l'affaire Heidegger* compels us to ask again – for our time – a classic question, Socrates' question. Bernard Williams reminds us of this question in his *Ethics and the Limits of Philosophy*:

> It is not a trivial question, Socrates said: what we are talking about is how one should live. Or so Plato reports him, in one of the first books written about the subject. Plato thought that philosophy could answer the question. Like Socrates, he hoped that one could direct one's life, if necessary redirect it, through an understanding that was distinctively philosophical – that is to say, general and abstract, rationally reflective, and concerned with what can be known through different kinds of inquiry.
>
> The aims of moral philosophy, and any hopes it may have of being worth serious attention, are bound up with the fate of Socrates' question, even if it is not true that philosophy itself can reasonably hope to answer it.[19]

Despite the vicissitudes of Socrates' question through the history of philosophy, we are still haunted by it. We not only continue to ask Socrates' question, we want to know whether philosophy can or cannot "answer the question" – or more minimally whether philosophy can or cannot help to clarify Socrates' question. One of the primary reasons why Heidegger's Nazi involvement is so thought-provoking is because it compels us to *question* Socrates' question – it forces us to ask what is the relation of philosophy to the question, "how one should live."

Heidegger, despite his scorn and skepticism about the traditional philosophic discipline of "ethics" and his apocalyptic declaration that "philosophy is over" was obsessed with Socrates' question – or more accurately – with questioning this question. For Socrates' question is central to all of Heidegger's thinking. My focus here will be quite specific. I intend to concentrate on some of Heidegger's late thinking concerning technology and the essence of technology – what he names *Gestell* (enframing) – the "supreme danger," and the sense in which he claims that this danger harbors the "growth of the saving power." There are several reasons for this concentrated focus. It is this late period – from 1945 on – that has most troubled and scandalized commentators on Heidegger. For this is the time when there were no longer any serious doubts about the full horror of the Nazi regime. This is the time of Heidegger's apparent "silence." George Steiner speaks for many when he wrote (before the recent Heidegger controversy): "But nauseating as they are, Heidegger's gestures and pronouncements during 1933–34 are tractable. It is the complete silence on Hitlerism and the holocaust after 1945 which is very nearly intolerable."[20] (Later we will see that it isn't completely accurate to speak of Heidegger's "complete silence.") So the question arises whether we can discern in his late thinking anything that enables us to account for his virtual silence.[21] My primary concern is to show in detail the seductive power of Heidegger's thinking, and to reveal his insights and blindnesses, especially as they pertain to Socrates' question: "how one should live."

But the following objection will be raised. Heidegger was not primarily concerned with Socrates' question. Rather the fundamental question for Heidegger is the *Seinsfrage* – the question of Being. He never wrote an "ethics" and resisted all attempts to draw ethical implications from his writings – what he called "moral-existentiell" or "anthropological" conclusions (Humanism, 212; 23). He explicitly criticized those who interpreted his concept of authenticity (*Eigentlichheit*) as a "moral-existentiell" concept. He tells us that "if man is to find his way once again into the nearness of being ... he must recognize the seductions of the public realm as well as the impotence of the private. Before he speaks man must first let himself be claimed by Being" (Humanism, 199; 10). Consequently the very attempt to draw out ethical-political implications from his texts is fundamentally misguided. The classic text used to support this objection is the "Letter on Humanism" where Heidegger speaks directly about ethics. But this objection is itself based on a misreading of the "Letter on Humanism." So before turning directly to Heidegger's questioning concerning technology, I want to probe what Heidegger says about ethics and *ēthos*.

Ēthos and "The Original Ethics"

In the "Letter on Humanism", Heidegger tells us:

> Soon after *Being and Time* appeared, a young friend asked me, "when are you going to write an ethics?" Where the essence of man is thought so essentially i.e., solely from the question concerning the truth of Being, but still without elevating man to the center of beings, a longing necessarily awakens for a preemptory directive and for rules that say how man, experienced from existence toward Being, ought to live in a fitting manner. The desire for an ethics presses ever more ardently for fulfillment as the obvious no less than the hidden perplexity of man soars to immeasurable heights. The greatest care must be fostered upon the ethical bond at a time when technological man, delivered over to mass society, can be kept reliably on call only by gathering and ordering all his plans and activities in a way that corresponds to technology. (Humanism, 231; 43)

Heidegger never wrote an "ethics" that deals with "rules that say how man ... ought to live in a fitting manner." He expressed his skepticism about the period when ethics emerged as a distinctive philosophic discipline. "Even such names as 'logic', 'ethics', and 'physics', began to flourish only when original thinking comes to an end. During the time of their greatness the Greeks thought without such headings" (Humanism, 195; 7). One might draw further support for Heidegger's skepticism about "ethics" (or any form of "value" theory) in his disparaging remarks about the very concept of "value." For all the modern chatter about "values," the concept itself is a consequence of "modern subjectivism" – "the age of the world picture."[22] "It is important finally to realize that precisely through the characterization of something as 'a value', what is so valued is robbed of its worth. That is to say, by the assessment of something as a value what is valued is admitted only as an object for man's estimation .... Every valuing, even where it values positively, is subjectivizing. It does not let beings: be" (Humanism, 228; 39). Heidegger is never more explicit than when he declares: "the thinking that inquires into the truth of Being and so defines man's essential abode from Being and toward Being is neither ethics nor ontology" (Humanism, 236; 48).

But to leave the matter here, to think that Heidegger is simply dismissing "ethics" is to fail to follow the pathway of his thinking. Paraphrasing a distinction that becomes all important for Heidegger, we can say that although this is "correct," it is not yet "true." We gain an essential clue to what Heidegger means when he speaks of "man's essential abode." For this essential abode is what Heidegger calls *"ēthos."* Let us follow this closely.

> Along with "logic" and "physics," "ethics" appeared for the first time in the school of Plato. These disciplines arose at a time when thinking was becoming "philosophy," philosophy, *epistēmē* (science), and science itself a matter of schools and academic pursuits. In the course of a philosophy so understood, science waxed and thinking waned. Thinkers prior to this period knew neither a "logic" nor an "ethics" nor "physics." Yet their thinking was neither illogical nor immoral. But they did think *physics* in a depth and breadth that no subsequent "physics" was ever again able to attain. The tragedies of Sophocles – provided such a comparison is at all permissible – preserve the *ēthos* in their sagas more primordially than Aristotle's lectures on "ethics." A saying of Heraclitus which consists of only three words says something so simply that from it the essence of the *ēthos* immediately comes to light. (Humanism, 232; 44)

What then is "the essence of the *ēthos*," and how is it related to the thinking that waned when "ethics" first appeared as a discipline?

> The saying of Heraclitus (Frag. 119) goes: *ēthos anthrōpōi daimōn.* This is usually translated, "A man's character is his daimon." This translation thinks in a modern way, not in a Greek one. *Ēthos* means abode,

dwelling place. The word names the open region in which man dwells. The open region of his abode allows what pertains to man's essence, and what in thus arriving resides in nearness to him, to appear. The abode of man contains and preserves the advent to what belongs to man in his essence. According to Heraclitus' phrase this is *daimōn*, the god. The fragment says: Man dwells, insofar as he is man, in the nearness of god. (Humanism, 233; 45)

But still, we want to know what this understanding of *ēthos* as abode or dwelling place has to do with "ethics." Heidegger is quite explicit. "If the name of 'ethics' in keeping with the basic meaning of the word *ēthos*, should now say that 'ethics' ponders the abode of man, then that thinking which thinks the truth of Being as the primordial element of man, as one who eksists, is in itself the original ethics" (*die ursprüngliche Ethik*) (Humanism, 235; 47).

In what sense is *ēthos* as abode *the original* ethics? It is a mistake to think that Heidegger is simply engaging in a "nostalgia" for a time of the "greatness" of the Greeks, for a time when there was a "thinking more rigorous than the conceptual." For Being is always far and near. There is always the possibility of a "thinking which thinks the truth of Being." This motif of original ethics – abode, dwelling, *ēthos* – is intimately related to what Heidegger understands to be the "homelessness of contemporary man from the essence of Being's history" (Humanism, 217; 28). It is this homelessness that is coming to be the destiny of the world – a homelessness that consists in the abandonment of Being by beings. We might say that the pathways of Heidegger's late thinking keep returning to a reflection upon this homelessness and what it would mean to exist in one's "proper" abode. In this sense, Heidegger's thinking can be characterized as gravitating toward "the original ethics." This primordial concern with *ēthos* is the basis for Heidegger's critique of metaphysical humanism which distorts, and is forgetful of, man's proper dwelling in nearness to Being. It is the key for understanding what he means by the essence of technology, the supreme danger that it harbors, and what Heidegger calls "the growth of the saving power." (For " 'to save' is to fetch something home into its essence, in order to bring the essence for the first time into its genuine appearing" [Technology, 310; 32].)[23] "This thinking is a deed, but a deed that surpasses *theoria* and all *praxis*" (Humanism, 239; 51). This "original ethics" is more essential than the discipline called "ethics." "More essential than instituting rules is that man find the way to his abode in the truth of Being" (Humanism, 239; 51).

It should be clear how superficial the objection is that Heidegger is not concerned with "ethics." On the contrary, given his under-standing of *ēthos* and "the original ethics" as pondering "the abode of man," then this is Heidegger's primordial (obsessive) concern. But if we are to probe and open up more fully Heidegger's pondering of the proper abode of man we must turn to his questioning concerning technology. For let us recall his claim that "the greatest care must be fostered upon the ethical bond at a time when technological man, delivered over to mass society, can be kept reliably on call only by gathering and ordering all his plans and activities in a way that corresponds to technology" (Humanism, 231–2; 43). What does Heidegger mean by "technological man"? Heidegger's brief but poignant remarks about technology in the "Letter on Humanism" anticipate his much more detailed questioning in "The Question Concerning Technology." This essay, published in 1953, is itself based upon a lecture first delivered in 1949. By closely examining and commenting on this essay/lecture we will not only come to understand why Heidegger is such a provocative thinker but also be able to examine in detail Heidegger's insights and blindness con-cerning "the original ethics."

"Technology is not equivalent to the essence of technology"

As always with Heidegger, it is essential to pay close attention to the openings of his finely crafted and densely textured essays. When we read his opening remarks carefully, they announce the central themes, establish the tone, anticipate what is to come, and orient the readers by sending us along the pathway that we are to follow. At crucial stages in "The Question Concerning Technology" Heidegger returns again and again to his opening paragraph.

> In what folows we shall be *questioning* concerning technology. Ques-tioning builds a way. We would be advised, therefore, above all to pay heed to the way, and not to fix our attention on isolated sentences and topics. The way is one of thinking. All ways of thinking, more or less perceptibly, lead through language in a manner that is

extraordinary. We shall be questioning concerning *technology*, and in so doing we should like to prepare a free relationship to it. The relationship will be free if it opens our human existence to the essence of technology. When we can respond to this essence, we shall be able to experience the technological with its own bounds. (Technology, 247; 9)

The two words that are so prominent in this opening paragraph (and are italicized) are "questioning" (*fragen*) and technology (*Technik*). Emphasizing "questioning" is not an innocent gesture when we realize that Heidegger already began *Being and Time* with questioning questioning – with exploring the conditions for the possibility of questioning and focusing his attention on the questioning being – *Dasein*. Furthermore, the final sentence of this essay – which returns us to the beginning – is: "For questioning is the piety of thought" (*Denn das Fragen ist die Frömmigheit des Denkens*) (Technology, 317; 40). The linkage of questioning with thinking is clearly indicated when Heidegger says "questioning builds a way" and the "way is one of thinking." Furthermore questioning and thinking are linked with language – to what Heidegger calls "the house of Being" (Humanism, 193; 5). Our questioning/thinking concerns (*nach*) technology. The polysemia of the title of the essay is indicated by the multiple meanings of "*nach*" – concerning, about, after, belated.

In this first paragraph, Heidegger – almost inadvertently – introduces a distinction that will be crucial for everything that follows – the distinction between technology and "the essence of technology" (*Wesen der Technik*). He begins his second paragraph by emphatically declaring: "Technology is not equivalent to the essence of technology" (*Die Technik is nicht des gleiche wie das Wesen der Technik*) (Technology, 287; 9). At this preliminary stage of Heidegger's questioning he relies upon our common understanding of "essence" as quiddity or whatness. "When we are seeking the essence of 'tree', we have to become aware that what pervades every tree, as tree, is not itself a tree that can be encountered among all other trees" (Technology, 287; 9). Distinguishing something from its essence seems almost obvious and trivial. But we will discover how consequential is the distinction between technology and the essence of technology. (Only later does Heidegger return to questioning the meaning of "essence" when we speak of the "essence of technology.")

But focusing on questioning, thinking, language, technology and the essence of technology does not yet capture what is most important and distinctive about Heidegger's opening paragraph. He indicates that his primary concern is "to prepare a free relationship" (*eine freie Beziehung*) to technology. "The relationship will be free if it opens our human existence to the essence of technology." So as we follow the way that Heidegger is building, we must keep in mind what precisely is this "free relationship" – this response to the essence of technology.

Initially we may think that a "free relationship" is one where we are not enslaved to technology, where we do not allow it to control us, but where we master it in order to achieve our freely chosen ends. But Heidegger abruptly and startlingly declares that thinking about technology in this manner blinds us to, and conceals, the essence of technology.

> But we are delivered over to [technology] in the worst possible way when we regard it as something neutral; for this conception of it, to which today we particularly like to do homage, makes us blind to the essence of technology. (Technology, 287–8; 9)

This is startling because it seems to go against our common deeply entrenched ways of thinking about technology. We tend to think of technology as being itself intrinsically neutral. Everything depends on how we *use* technology. There are beneficial technologies such as the many new medical technologies that enable us to alleviate human suffering and save human lives. There are also lethal technologies that can be used to annihilate human existence. Everything depends on how we freely use the technologies available to us. This common way of thinking about technology is what Heidegger calls "the instrumental and anthropological definition of technology" (Technology, 288; 10). Technology is understood to be a neutral instrument or means for achieving human purposes (whatever they may be).

Such a definition is not wrong. Indeed it is correct (*rechtig*). It is uncannily correct (*unheimlich rechtig*) (Technology, 288; 10). From the perspective of this correct definition, Heidegger states what is commonly thought to be *the* question concerning technology (but which, as we shall see, conceals the essence of technology).

Everything depends on our manipulating technology in the proper manner as means. We will, as we say, "get" technology "spiritually in hand." We will master it. The will to mastery becomes all the more urgent the more technology threatens to slip from human control. (Technology, 289; 11)

It is against the background of this common instrumental and anthropological conception of technology that Heidegger begins his questioning. He anticipates the way he is building by raising a tentative doubt. "But suppose now that technology were no mere means, how would it stand with the will to master it?" (Technology, 289; 11). It is here that Heidegger emphasizes the all-important distinction between the correct (*das Richtige*) and the true (*das Wahre*) – and tells us that "only the true brings us into a free relationship with that which concerns us from its essence" (Technology, 289; 11).

The correct always fixes upon something pertinent in whatever is under consideration. However, in order to be correct, this fixing by no means needs to uncover the thing in question in its essence. Only at the point where such an uncovering happens does the true come to pass. Only the true brings us into a free relationship with that which concerns us from its essence. Accordingly, the correct instrumental definition of technology still does not show us technology's essence. In order that we may arrive at this, or at least come close to it, we must seek the true by way of the correct. (Technology, 289; 11)

This last sentence makes clear the way (*methodos*) in which Heidegger will proceed. We are seeking to prepare a "free relationship" to technology. A "free relationship" requires that we open "our human existence to the essence of technology." What then is the essence of technology? To answer this we must begin with the correct instrumental and anthropological definition of technology. But we must not remain fixated on this correct definition. We must seek the true by way of the correct. When we reflect on the correct definition of technology as a means to an end and as a human activity then what is most manifest is that technology is "a contrivance – in Latin, an *instrumentum*" (Technology, 288; 10).

What is the instrumental itself? Within what do such things as means and end belong? A means is that whereby something is effected and thus attained. Whatever has an effect as its consequence is called a cause. But not only that by means of which something else is effected is a cause. The end in keeping with which the kind of means to be used is determined is also considered a cause. Wherever ends are pursued and means are employed, wherever instrumentality reigns, there reigns causality. (Technology, 289; 11)

So our initial probing of the correct instrumental and anthropological definition of technology leads us to investigate what lies at the heart of this definition – causality.

At this point, Heidegger pursues what initially seems to be an esoteric and irrelevant digression – a byway. For rather than directly examining the concept of causality involved in technology as an instrumental means to an end, he gives a novel interpretation of the Aristotelian doctrine of the four causes. We will discover just how important this "digression" is for everything that follows – that it is really not a "digression" at all.

For centuries philosophy has taught that there are four causes: (1) the *causa materialis*, the material, the matter out of which, for example, a silver chalice is made; (2) the *causa formalis*, the form, the shape into which the material enters; (3) the *causa finalis*, the end, for example, the sacrificial rite in relation to which the chalice required is determined as to its form and matter; (4) the *causa efficiens*, which brings about the effect that is the finished, actual chalice, in this instance, the silversmith. What technology is, when represented as a means, discloses itself when we trace instrumentality back to fourfold causality. (Technology, 289–90; 11–12)[24]

Heidegger's "digression," his reflections on the traditional notion of a fourfold causality may seem perverse. They *are* perverse insofar as they direct us away from what is correct. But this is characteristic of Heidegger's way of thinking. For to think through what is correct requires us to "step back" in order to provoke new ways of thinking. Our common ways of "thinking" have become so familiar and entrenched that they conceal what needs to be unconcealed. It is only by showing how the familiar and the correct appear strange and uncanny (*unheimlich*) that thinking can be called forth. This is even related to the peculiarities of Heidegger's style(s) of writing. His strange use of familiar words, his seemingly perverse etymologies, his deceptively simple gnomic sentences, his repetitions and staccato rhythms are rhetorical devices to dis-rupt and dis-turb "normal" argumentative philosophic discourse. They have the uncanny effect of compelling us to think, to question what we "normally" do not question.

In order not to stray too far from the way Heidegger is building, let me highlight some of the key claims that he makes in his reflections upon the traditional doctrine of a fourfold causality. His most provocative claim is that our modern conception of causality (which lies at the heart of the correct definition of technology) has "nothing at all to do" with the Greek way of understanding causality. For we think of causality as "that which brings something about ... to bring about means to obtain results, effects" (Technology, 290; 12). But the fourfold causality, thought in a Greek way (not a modern way) "are the ways, all belonging at once to each other, of being responsible for something else" (Technology, 290; 12). To illustrate what he means, Heidegger gives an example of the four interrelated, co-responsible ways occasioned in the bringing-forth of a sacrificial silver chalice:

> Silver is that out of which the silver chalice is made. As the matter (*hyle*), it is co-responsible for the chalice. The chalice is indebted to i.e., owes thanks to the silver for that of which it consists. But the sacrificial vessel is indebted not only to the silver. As a chalice, that which is indebted to the silver appears in the aspect of a chalice, and not in that of a broach or a ring. Thus the sacred vessel is at the same time indebted to the aspect (*eidos*) of chaliceness. Both the silver into which the aspect is admitted as chalice and the aspect in which the silver appears are in their respective ways co-responsible for the sacrificial vessel.
>
> But there remains yet a third that is above all responsible for the sacrificial vessel. It is that which in advance confines the chalice within the realm of consecration and bestowal. Through this the chalice is circumscribed as sacrificial vessel. Circumscribing gives bounds to the thing. With the bounds the thing does not stop; rather, from within them it begins to be what after production it will be. That which gives bounds, that which completes, in this sense is called in Greek *telos*, which is all too often translated as "aim" and "purpose," and so misinterpreted. The *telos* is responsible for what as matter and as aspect are together co-responsible for the sacrificial vessel.
>
> Finally, there is a fourth participant in the responsibility for the finished sacrificial vessel's lying before us ready for use, i.e., the silversmith – but not at all because he, in working, brings about the finished sacrificial chalice as if it were the effect of a making: the silversmith is not a *causa efficiens*. (Technology, 290–91; 12–13)

We may be utterly baffled by this "poetic" description of the fourfold causality "thought as the Greeks thought it." Furthermore we may think that Heidegger, with his references to "co-responsibility," "indebtedness," "owing thanks," is lapsing into a moralistic and anthropocentric way of thinking of causality. But Heidegger warns us against this misreading.

> Today we are too easily inclined either to understand being responsible and being indebted moralistically as a lapse, or else to construe them in terms of effecting. In either case we bar to ourselves the way to the primal meaning of that which is later called causality. So long as the way is not opened up to us we shall also fail to see what instrumentality, which is based on causality, actually is. (Technology, 292; 14)

This may only increase our perplexity and unease. For it is not *yet* clear how this excursus enables us "to see what instrumentality ... actually is."

What is most important for Heidegger is that when we think this fourfold co-responsible bringing-forth "in the sense in which the Greeks thought it" we understand this bringing-forth as *poiēsis*, as presencing (*Anwesen*), as "starting something on its way into arrival." Furthermore "*physis* also, the arising of something from out of itself, is a bringing-forth, *poiēsis*. *Physis* is indeed *poiēsis* in the highest sense" (Technology, 293; 15). This bringing-forth which "comes to pass only insofar as something concealed comes into unconcealment" is what Heidegger calls revealing (*das Entbergen*) (Technology, 293–4; 15).

Heidegger concludes his "digression" with what seems to be a casual remark. (But nothing in Heidegger's text is quite what it initially seems to be!) He tells us:

> The Greeks have the word *alētheia* for revealing. The Romans translate this with *veritas*. We say "truth" and usually understand it as correctness of representation. (Technology, 294; 15–16)

This "casual remark" takes on a much deeper and richer significance when we realize that a major theme of Heidegger's thinking is to stress the difference between *alētheia* as revealing or unconcealing and our modern conception of truth as "correctness of representation."[25] The history of metaphysics that "begins" with Plato and culminates with Nietzsche, "the last metaphysician," can itself be read as a forgetfulness and concealment of this consequential distinction.

We are likely to have an ambivalent reaction to Heidegger's "digression," his probing the Greek way of thinking causality. For what he says is so cryptic and oracular that we may wonder what precisely he is saying and why. Presumably he took up the question of the meaning of causality in order to understand the instrumentality of technology. But we seem to be getting farther and farther away from any such understanding. Instead of tracing "instrumentality back to fourfold causality," we are discovering that the modern instrumental conception of causality as "bringing about and effecting" has nothing to do with the bringing-forth of *poiēsis.* Yet we may begin to sense that this "digression" provides some sort of transition (or more accurately, a rupture) for coming closer to understanding the essence of technology. But how? Heidegger anticipates our perplexity:

> But where have we strayed to? We are questioning concerning technology, and we have arrived now at *alētheia*, at revealing. What has the essence of technology to do with revealing? The answer: everything. For every bringing-forth is grounded in revealing. Bringing-forth, indeed, gathers within itself the four modes of occasioning – causality – and rules them throughout. Within its domain belong end and means as well as instrumentality. Instrumentality is considered to be the fundamental characteristic of technology. If we inquire step by step into what technology, represented as means, actually is, then we shall arrive at revealing. The possibility of all productive manufacturing lies in revealing.
>
> Technology is therefore no mere means. Technology is a way of revealing. If we give heed to this, then another whole realm for the essence of technology will open itself up to us. It is the realm of revealing i.e., of truth. (Technology, 294; 16)

We are now led to new questions. What does Heidegger mean by "revealing"? In what sense is the essence of technology a way of revealing? What is the relation between the essence of technology as a way of revealing and the way of revealing (*alētheia*) of *poiēsis*, bringing-forth?

There is always a danger in reading Heidegger's late essays that we become so mesmerized by his strange idiom that we lose any critical distance in understanding what he is saying and doing.

(There is the opposite danger that we are so "put off" by his apparently "oracular" pronouncements that we are tempted to dismiss them as pretentious and vacuous.) Before proceeding, let me give a brief prosaic summary of what Heidegger has shown us thus far.

We are questioning concerning technology. Our first task is to start with how we commonly represent or define technology. What initially appears most manifest about technology is that it is a neutral means or instrument for achieving human ends and purposes. Given this instrumental and anthropological characterization of technology, the main problem concerning technology – if we are to achieve a "free relationship" to it – *seems* to be how to master technology. But we must understand what it means to characterize technology as an instrument. Perhaps thinking about technology in this way – a way that seems so obvious and correct – conceals more than it reveals. But we cannot simply turn away from the instrumental and anthropological definition of technology. For it is correct. When we question it further we realize that the very concept of instrumentality involves and presupposes causality. Probing causality we are led back to its Greek origins and we discover that causality (thought of in a Greek way) is a fourfold co-responsible occasioning, a mode of revealing (*alētheia*), a bringing-forth. Furthermore, this way of thinking causality has nothing to do with the modern conception of causality as "bringing about or effecting" – the notion of causality that is presupposed in conceiving of technology as an instrument. So it would seem that this excursus in the doctrine of the four causes is a blind alley – for it does not reveal what is the essence of our modern instrumental conception of causality. But perhaps we can gain a truer understanding of the essence of modern technology if we think of it also as a mode of revealing rather than as a means to an end. But then we need to ask what it means to speak of modern technology as a way of revealing. What is distinctive about this way of revealing, and how it is related to the *technē* that "belongs to bringing-forth"? This is the turn that Heidegger's questioning now takes.

> What then is modern technology? It too is a revealing. Only when we allow our attention to rest on this fundamental characteristic does that which is modern technology show itself to us.
> And yet the revealing that holds sway throughout modern technology does not unfold into a bringing-forth in the sense of *poiēsis*.

The revealing that rules in modern technology is a challenging [*Herausforderung*], which puts to nature the unreasonable demand that it supply energy which can be extracted and stored as such. (Technology, 296; 18)

Heidegger gives a series of examples to illustrate what he means by the "challenging" or "challenging-forth" that rules modern technology, especially the way in which it contrasts with *poiēsis* and *technē* of "bringing-forth." He tells us: "Agriculture is now the [motorized] food industry" (*Ackerbau ist jetzt motorisierte Ernährungsindustrie*) (Technology, 296; 18). Here there is a "setting-in-order, which *sets upon nature.*" But this can be contrasted with the work of the peasant who does not *challenge* the soil of the field. "In sowing grain it places seed in the keeping of the forces of growth and watches over its increase" (Technology, 296; 18). Or again, he contrasts the "old windmill" whose "sails do indeed turn in the wind" with the modern "hydroelectric plant set into the current of the Rhine" (Technology, 296; 18–19). Modern technology as a challenging or challenging-forth orders, manipulates, controls, sets upon nature.

The revealing that rules throughout modern technology has the character of a setting-upon, in the sense of a challenging-forth. Such challenging happens in that energy concealed in nature is unlocked, what is unlocked transformed, what is transformed is stored-up, what is stored-up in turn distributed, what is distributed is switched about ever anew. Unlocking, transforming, storing, distributing and switching about are ways of revealing. But the revealing never simply comes to an end. (Technology, 297–8; 20)

It may be objected that Heidegger is indulging in a sentimental, pastoral nostalgia by invoking images of a simpler time when human beings were more attuned to nature, when human rhythms corresponded to the rhythms of nature – *physis*. (Heidegger's prose is filled with pastoral and sacred images when he seeks to elicit the bringing-forth of *poiēsis*.) But his main point is to highlight the difference between the mode of revealing of *bringing-forth* and mode of revealing of modern technology – *challenging-forth*.

He explicitly disclaims the "absurd wish to revive what is past."

Therefore, in the realm of thinking, a painstaking effort to think through still more primally what was primally thought is not the absurd wish to revive what is past, but rather the sober readiness to be astounded before the coming of the dawn. (Technology, 303; 26)

If modern technology, like the bringing-forth of *poiēsis*, is a way of revealing (*alētheia*), then we must deepen our understanding of what is distinctive about the way in which it *both* reveals and conceals.

What kind of unconcealment is it, then, that is peculiar to that which results from this setting-upon that challenges? Everywhere everything is ordered to stand by, to be immediately on hand, indeed to stand there just so that it may be on call for a further ordering. Whatever is ordered about in this way has its own standing. We call it the standing-reserve [*Bestand*]. (Technology, 298; 20)

As we follow Heidegger's questioning/thinking we experience a series of disturbing shocks, ruptures, inversions. I suggested that this is related to the stylistic devices by which Heidegger seeks to disrupt and dis-turb our common patterns of understanding in order to call forth a thinking and questioning of what we "normally" do not question. At this point in his essay we are on the verge of a major and consequential rupture. Recall that according to the "correct" instrumental and anthropological definition of modern technology, the primary question concerning technology seemed to be how to master it, how to get it "spiritually in hand." But now we discover that when modern technology is understood as the mode of revealing of "challenging-forth" then we realize "man does not have control over unconcealment itself, in which at any given time the real shows itself or withdraws" (Technology, 299; 21). We can appreciate now the significance of the doubt that Heidegger artfully interposed earlier when he asked, "But suppose now that technology were no mere means, how would it stand with the will to master it?" (Technology, 289; 11).

Although it is "correct" to speak of man controlling technology as a means, he does not control the unconcealment itself that is the *essence* (the presencing or revealing) of technology. On the contrary:

Yet precisely because man is challenged more originally than are the energies of nature, i.e., into the process of ordering, he never is transformed into mere standing-reserve. Since man drives technology forward, he takes part in ordering as a way of revealing. But the unconcealment itself, within which ordering unfolds, is never a human handiwork, any more than is the realm man traverses every time he as a subject relates to an object. (Technology, 299–300; 22)

The "correct" definition of technology is being deconstructed. For the "correct" definition focuses our attention on how man uses, masters, controls technology in order to achieve human purposes. But it obscures and conceals the way in which human beings themselves are responding to, and are *claimed by*, the unconcealment – the revealing of challenging-forth in which human beings become "human resources." This unconcealment is not the result of human handiwork or doing. On the contrary, this unconcealment determines what human activity has become in the modern epoch.

Heidegger does not make any explicit reference to Marx, Weber or Lukács. But his analysis of the "economy" of the essence (presencing) of modern technology as a way of revealing bears strong family resemblances with their social analyses. For it recalls Marx's analysis of alienation, Weber's analysis of the growth and spread of *Zweckrationalität*, and Lukács' analysis of reification. In particular there is a parallel insofar as they also seek to show that human beings do not freely control the products of their labor but become alienated, rationalized and reified. Human beings become standing-reserve, human resources, commodities, congealed labor-power. Human beings become functioning cogs in the interlocking ordering of "challenging-forth." This claim upon human beings shapes every aspect of our lives – the ways in which we experience the world, act, and think.

Thus when man, investigating, observing, pursues nature as an area of his own conceiving, he has already been claimed by a way of revealing that challenges him to approach nature as an object of research, until even the object disappears into the objectlessness of standing-reserve. Modern technology, as a revealing which orders, is thus no mere human doing [*menschliches Tun*]. (Technology, 300; 22)

But the differences between Heidegger and Marx, Weber and Lukács are as consequential as any affinities that they share. For the latter three were primarily concerned with describing and analyzing the social, economic, and political factors in modernization processes that can account for this alienation, rationalization, and reification. Furthermore, thinkers in the Marxist tradition have been concerned with the type of human acting – *praxis* – that can overcome and break with the ways in which modern technology in capitalist societies "claims" and distorts human *praxis*. But Heidegger is deeply skeptical about whether *any* form of human doing or *praxis* can escape from the ordering of challenging-forth that is the way of revealing of modern technology. Why? Because what human activity, *praxis*, has become in the modern technological epoch is itself a challenging-forth. To think that there is some form of human doing that can master the unconcealment that "has already come to pass" and which "calls man forth into the modes of revealing allotted to him" (Technology, 300; 22) is to be ensnared in the delusions of metaphysical humanism.[26]

It is becoming increasingly apparent that Heidegger's questioning/thinking concerning technology is no mere "supplement" to his late thinking. Or rather, it is a "supplement" in that Derridean sense that reveals the core of his thinking. For the essence (presencing) of technology is itself the culmination of the metaphysical tradition, specifically the metaphysical humanism that can be traced back to the "origins" of philosophy. The correct definition of technology is itself an expression of what is so deeply entrenched in metaphysical humanism where man is taken to be a *subject* that *represents* and stands over against an *objective* world. By representing this objective world, man presumably exercises his free will in controlling, manipulating and mastering it in order to achieve human purposes. This metaphysical humanism – when its "logic" is exposed – reveals man as the "lord of beings." But Heidegger seeks to undermine and deconstruct this metaphysical humanism.

Let us return to the way that Heidegger is building in his questioning/thinking. We have reached a stage where Heidegger is now ready to "name" the essence of modern technology – the way of revealing he has characterized as "challenging-forth."

> We now name that challenging claim which gathers man thither to order the self-revealing as standing-reserve: "*Ge-stell*" [enframing].
> We dare to use this word in a sense that has been thoroughly unfamiliar up to now. (Technology, 301; 23)

Linguistically, Heidegger has anticipated this "eerie" (*schaurig*) use of the word *Gestell* in his play of the family of German words that have "*stell*" as their root, e.g., *her-stellen* (to produce); *dar-stell-en* (to represent); *be-stell-en* (to order). (Recall that in his opening paragraph Heidegger said: "All ways of thinking, more or less perceptively, lead through language in a manner that is extraordinary" [Technology, 287; 9].)

> Enframing means the gathering together of that setting-upon that sets upon man i.e., challenges him forth, to reveal the real, in the mode of ordering, as standing-reserve. Enframing means that way of revealing that holds sway in the essence of modern technology and that is itself nothing technological.

> Ge-stell heisst das Versammelnde jenes Stellens, das den Menschen stellt, d.h. herausfordert, das Wirkliche in der Weise des Bestellens als Bestand zu entbergen. Ge-stell heisst die Weise des Entbergens, die im Wesen der modernen Technik waltelt und selber nichts Technisches ist. (Technology, 302; 24)

Here again, we can see how artfully and compactly Heidegger has organized this lecture/essay. We can now understand the full significance of the distinction that Heidegger makes between technology and the essence of technology which he introduced in his opening paragraph. We can now also appreciate the importance of the apparently innocuous claim "Technology is not equivalent to the essence of technology." Once we understand that *Gestell* – enframing – is the essence of modern technology then we realize that the "correct" or "merely instrumental, merely anthropological definition of technology is therefore in principle untenable" (Technology, 302; 25) for it conceals the essence of technology as a way of revealing. Furthermore, we can better understand why Heidegger's earlier apparent "digression" where he explores the fourfold causality of the Greeks was not really a digression. For it enabled us to understand *poiēsis* and *technē* as bringing-forth – a distinctive way of revealing (*alētheia*). We can now grasp that while *Gestell* is also a way of revealing, it is "fundamentally different" from *poiēsis* – "and yet they remain related in their essence" (Technology, 302; 24).

> This producing that brings forth, e.g. erecting a statue in the temple precinct, and the ordering that challenges now under consideration are indeed fundamentally different, and yet they remain related in their essence. *Both are ways of revealing, of alētheia.* In enframing that unconcealment comes to pass in conformity with which the work of

modern technology reveals the real as standing-reserve. (Technology, 302; 24; emphasis added)

There is another strange, seemingly "perverse" claim that Heidegger makes about *Gestell*; but when we comprehend what he is saying, it deepens our understanding of *Gestell* as the essence of modern technology. Heidegger tells us that the essence of technology "historically" precedes the "chronological" development of modern technology. We normally think that modern technology is based upon the achievements of the modern physical experimental sciences. Technology is an application of the physical sciences. So it seems perverse to claim that the essence of technology "historically" precedes the "chronological" development of modern technology. To heighten the paradox, Heidegger says:

> But after all, mathematical science arose two centuries before technology. How, then, could it have already been set upon by modern technology and placed in its service? The facts testify to the contrary. Surely technology got underway only when it could be supported by the exact physical science. Reckoned chronologically, this is correct. Thought historically, it does not hit upon the truth. (Technology, 303; 25)

Why doesn't it "hit upon the truth"? Heidegger's point – and it is essential to his analysis of *Gestell* – is that already with the rise of the exact physical sciences, there is a *mentalité* that prepares the way and "heralds" the development of modern technology. The ordering that is required and presupposed for the development of modern technology is itself embodied in the practices that define the exact physical sciences. So "the modern physical theory of nature prepares the way not simply for technology but for the essence of modern technology" (Technology, 303; 25).

Heidegger's meaning can be clarified with reference to the way in which Kant characterizes the revolution that occurred with the rise of exact physical science.

> When Galileo caused balls, the weights of which he had himself previously determined, to roll down an inclined plane; when Torricelli made the air carry a weight which he had calculated beforehand to be equal to that of a definite column of water; or in more recent times, when Stahl changed metals into oxides, and oxides back into metal, by

withdrawing and then restoring it, a light broke upon all students of nature. They learned that reason has insight only into that which it produces after a plan of its own, and that it must not allow itself to be kept, as it were, in nature's leading-strings, but must itself show the way with principles of judgment based upon fixed laws, constraining nature to give answers to questions of reason's own determining.[27]

In Heidegger's terminology, we can say that Kant's portrayal of what happened in the revolutionary formation of the exact physical sciences portends the coming to pass of *Gestell*. "Modern physics is the herald of enframing, a herald whose origin is still unknown" (Technology, 303; 25). So although it is correct to say that modern technology chronologically comes after the exact physical experimental sciences, this development itself historically presupposes the *mentalité* of *Gestell* which is already heralded in the development of the modern physical sciences. This *mentalité* is itself a precipitate of metaphysical humanism where primacy is assigned to a subject who represents an objective world and seeks to know and master it by experimentation and manipulation; setting upon and "constraining nature to give answers to questions of reason's own determining." In this happening the very concept of causality is radically transformed.

> Causality now displays neither the character of occasioning that brings forth nor the nature of the *causa efficiens*, let alone that of *causa formalis*. It seems as though causality is shrinking into a reporting – a reporting challenged forth – of standing-reserves that must be guaranteed either simultaneously or in sequence. (Technology, 304; 26–7)

We must not lose our bearings on the way that Heidegger's questioning/thinking is building. Heidegger is not simply concerned with elucidating and contrasting two ways of revealing – the bringing-forth of *poiēsis* and the challenging-forth of modern technology. His primary concern – as indicated in his opening paragraph – is "to prepare a free relationship" to technology by opening "our human existence to the essence of technology," in order to enable us to "respond to this essence." Although we have begun to understand the essence of technology as *Gestell*, we still do not yet understand what is a free relationship to this essence. At best we have achieved the negative knowledge that freedom is *not* to be thought of as the will to master technology. So Heidegger now reminds us:

We are questioning concerning technology in order to bring to light our relationship to its essence. The essence of modern technology shows itself in what we call enframing. But simply to point to this is still no way to answer the question concerning technology, if to answer means to respond, in the sense of correspond, to the essence of what is being asked about. (Technology, 305; 27)

Our focus now shifts to the question of a *response* to *Gestell*. We must properly understand what is involved in this response. We have already learned that it is not as if man "stands apart" from the essence of technology; it is not "external" to him. *Gestell* itself claims man – it challenges forth man himself.

As the one who is challenged forth in this way, man stands within the essential realm of enframing. He can never take up this relationship to it subsequently. Thus the question as to how we arrive at a relationship to the essence of technology, asked in this way, always comes too late. But never too late comes the question as to whether we actually experience ourselves as the ones whose activities everywhere, public and private, are challenged forth by enframing. *Above all, never too late comes the question as to whether and how we actually admit ourselves into that wherein enframing itself comes to presence.* (Technology, 305; 27; emphasis added)

How are we to answer *this* question? (And what does it even mean?) Everything Heidegger says from this point on can be related to this strange question – even though we must pass through what seems to be a series of devious byways.

To understand how Heidegger proceeds let us pause and reflect upon what appears to be an *aporia* in Heidegger's questioning/thinking. We have been told that man does not control the way of revealing of *Gestell*, the essence of technology and that this way of revealing historically precedes modern technology. If this is so then we may wonder what it can even mean to speak of a "free relationship" to the essence of technology? Heidegger himself asks: "Does such revealing happen somewhere beyond all human doing?" We might think the answer is affirmative. But Heidegger emphatically answers: "No. But neither does it happen exclusively *in* man, or definitively *through* man" (Technology, 305; 27). If *Gestell* were somehow *fated*, it would make no sense to even speak of a "free relationship" to *Gestell*.

Heidegger now introduces a crucial distinction between fate (*Schicksal*) and destining (*Geschick*). Fate compels. Fate means "inevitableness of an unalterable course" (*das Unausweichliche eines unabänderlichen Verlaufs*) (Technology, 307; 29). But technology is *not* the "fate of our age." This is all important for Heidegger. He is *not* claiming that there is a predetermined logic of history that is working itself out behind our backs and which entraps men in the iron cage of *Gestell*.

Rather *Gestell* is a *destining*, a sending, a starting upon a way. (Heidegger here, as he does throughout his essay, desubstantializes language in order to emphasize the *happening* of *alētheia*.)

> Enframing, as challenging-forth into ordering, sends into a way of revealing. Enframing is an ordering of destining, as is every way of revealing. Bringing-forth, *poiēsis*, is also a destining in this sense. (Technology, 306; 28)

Destining is never a fate that compels. Indeed the all-important distinction between fate and destining enables us to begin to comprehend what Heidegger means by freedom. "For man becomes truly free only insofar as he belongs to the realm of destining and so becomes one who listens, though not one who simply obeys" (Technology, 306; 28).

In a manner analogous to his deconstruction of the "correct" definition of technology, Heidegger deconstructs what might be called the "correct" definition of freedom.

> The essence of freedom is *originally* not connected with the will or even the causality of human willing.
>
> Freedom governs the open in the sense of the cleared and lighted up, i.e., the revealed. To the occurrence of revealing, i.e., of truth, freedom stands in the closest and most intimate kinship. All revealing belongs within a harboring and a concealing. But that which frees – the mystery – is concealed and always concealing itself. All revealing comes out of the open, goes into the open, and brings into the open. The freedom of the open consists neither in unfettered arbitrariness nor in the constraint of mere laws. Freedom is that which conceals in a way that opens to light, in whose lighting shimmers that veil that hides the essential occurrence of all truth and lets the veil appear as what veils. Freedom is the realm of the destining that at any given time starts a revealing on its way. (Technology, 306; 28)

Heidegger's remarks linking revealing, destining and freedom are so enigmatic and cryptic – despite their evocative power – that we may experience a sense of vertigo – an utter confusion about what he is even saying and why. But we are coming very close to the dramatic climax and denouement of this essay/lecture. He hints at this when he tells us that we are not confined "to a stultified compulsion to push on blindly with technology or, what comes to the same, to rebel helplessly against it and curse it as the work of the devil. Quite to the contrary, when we once open ourselves expressly to the *essence* of technology we find ourselves unexpectedly taken into a freeing claim" (Technology, 307; 29). If we can understand what this means – what it means to "open ourselves expressly to the *essence* of technology" then we may be able to understand Heidegger's cryptic remarks about freedom.[28]

Throughout this essay Heidegger uses the rhetorical device of repetition. He repeats with ever so slight variations and nuances. It is a stylistic device that moves us step by step along the way he is building. So Heidegger repeats what he has already said in order to move us one step further.

> The essence of technology lies in enframing. Its holding sway belongs within destining. Since destining at any given time starts man on a way of revealing, man, thus underway, is continually approaching the brink of the possibility of pursuing and pushing forward nothing but what is revealed in ordering, and of deriving all his standards on this basis. Through this the other possibility is blocked, that man might be admitted more and sooner and ever more primordially to the essence of what is unconcealed and to its unconcealment, in order that he might experience as his essence the requisite belonging to revealing.
>
> Placed between these possibilities, man is endangered by destining. The destining of revealing is as such, in every one of its modes, and therefore necessarily, *danger* [*Gefahr*]. (Technology, 307; 29)

Note that Heidegger says that the destining of revealing is *necessarily* – and *in every one of its modes* – *danger*. Destining at once opens and closes possibilities. The danger that a destining harbors is "that man may misconstrue the unconcealed and misinterpret it" (Technology, 307; 29). For he may fail to realize that a way of revealing that claims him is *a* mode of revealing that at once opens possibilities and necessarily closes off other possibilities. "The destining of revealing is in itself not just any danger, but *the* danger." And the danger that primarily concerns Heidegger is the supreme danger (*die höchste Gefahr*). *Gestell* harbors this supreme danger.

> Yet when destining reigns in the mode of enframing, it is the supreme danger. This danger attests itself to us in two ways. As soon as what is unconcealed no longer concerns man even as object, but exclusively as standing-reserve, and man in the midst of objectlessness is nothing but the order of the standing-reserve, then he comes to the very brink of a precipitous fall, that is, he comes to the point where he himself will have to be taken as standing-reserve. Meanwhile, man, precisely as the one so threatened, exalts himself to the posture of lord of the earth. In this way the illusion comes to prevail that everything man encounters exists only insofar as it is his construct. This illusion gives rise in turn to one final delusion: it seems as though man everywhere and always encounters only himself.... *In truth, however, precisely nowhere does man today any longer encounter himself* i.e., *his essence.* Man stands so decisively in attendance on the challenging-forth of enframing that he does not grasp enframing as a claim, that he fails to see himself as the one spoken to, and hence also fails in every way to hear in what respect he ek-sists, from out of his essence in the realm of an exhortation or address, so that he *can never* encounter only himself. (Technology, 308; 30–31)

Technology then is not what is dangerous. "Technology is not demonic; but its essence is mysterious." Rather "the essence of technology, as a destining of revealing, is the danger" (Technology, 309; 32). "Where enframing reigns, there is *danger* in the highest sense" (Technology, 309; 32). Why? Because man not only comes to the "very brink of a precipitous fall" where he himself is claimed as standing-reserve, but even more important because he fails to realize that *Gestell* is a destining of revealing. He fails to grasp *Gestell* as a claim – one which at once opens a range of possibilities of how we think, act and feel and closes off –"drives out every other possibility." We are on the brink of accepting *Gestell* as *fated* rather than as *destining* – a sending. The sign of this "precipitous fall" is that we are deluded into thinking that man is the "lord of the earth." Metaphysical humanism conceals from us the supreme danger of *Gestell*. Once again – and in a new light – we see the significance of Heidegger's "digression" in elucidating the way of revealing of *poiēsis*. For as destining, enframing "banishes man into that kind of revealing that is an ordering" – a challenging-forth.

Where this ordering holds sway, it drives out every other possibility of revealing. Above all, enframing conceals that revealing which, in the sense of *poiēsis*, lets what presences come forth into appearance. As compared with that other revealing, the setting-upon that challenges forth thrusts man into a relation to whatever is that is at once anti-thetical and rigorously ordered. Where enframing holds sway, regulating and securing of the standing-reserve mark all revealing. They no longer even let their own fundamental characteristic appear, namely this revealing as such. (Technology, 309; 31)

The supreme danger of *Gestell* is that it conceals revealing itself. "Thus the challenging-enframing not only conceals a former way of revealing, bringing-forth, but it conceals revealing itself and with it that wherein unconcealment i.e., truth, comes to pass" (Technology, 309; 31). To emphasize this point, Heidegger declares "the rule of enframing threatens man with the possibility that it could be denied to him to enter into a more original revealing and hence to experi-ence the call of a more primal truth" (Technology, 209; 31). The supreme danger of *Gestell* is that it threatens and blocks a "free relationship" to the essence of technology.

If Heidegger's questioning/thinking stopped here, we would be confronted with only the bleakest possibility. The very distinction between a fate that compels and a destining that sends man on a way of revealing would be in danger of collapsing. For it would seem that *Gestell* as the essence of technology over which we have no con-trol claims and threatens us, ordering everything as standing-reserve, driving out every other possibility of revealing, and concealing revealing itself. This would mean, as Heidegger says in "Overcoming Metaphysics,"

> The still hidden truth of Being is withheld from metaphysical humanity. The laboring animal [technological man, RJB] is left to the giddy whirl of its products so that it may tear itself to pieces and annihilate itself in empty nothingness.[29]

Thus far, nothing Heidegger has said is intended to rule out this possibility. On the contrary, only by facing this possibility do we con-front "that where enframing reigns, there is danger in the highest sense" (Technology, 309; 32).

It is at this point that we encounter the most striking turn (rupture) in Heidegger's questioning concerning technology. But everything Heidegger has said thus far prepares us for this turn. The denouement comes so rapidly that we can fail to appreciate its significance. For we are on the verge of finally understanding what it means to prepare a "free relationship" to technology – to opening our human existence to the essence of technology. At this juncture, Heidegger cites the famous lines from Hölderlin's *Patmos*:

> But where danger is, grows
> The saving power also
>
> Wo aber Gefahr ist, wacht
> Das Rettende auch (Technology, 310; 32).

What is "the saving power," and what does it mean "to save"?

> Let us think carefully about these words of Hölderlin. What does it mean to "save"? Usually we think that it means only to seize hold of a thing threatened by ruin in order to secure it in its former continuance. But the verb "to save" says more. "To save" is to fetch something home into its essence, in order to bring the essence for the first time into its genuine appearing. If the essence of technology, enframing, is the extreme danger, if there is truth in Hölderlin's words, then the rule of enframing cannot exhaust itself solely in blocking all lighting-up of every revealing, all appearing of truth. Rather, precisely the essence of technology must harbor in itself the growth of the saving power. But in that case, might not an adequate look into what enframing is, as a destining of revealing, bring the upsurgence of the saving power into appearance? (Technology, 310; 32)

Heidegger's remarks about the meaning of "to save" bring us back to the primordial theme of *ēthos*, dwelling, abode – to the "original ethics" where we reflect upon how man in his homelessness can find his way back to his *ēthos*, his abode. Enframing as the essence of technology is the way of revealing of challenging-forth. But enframing itself blocks *all* revealing; it conceals its essence as a destining. Insofar as it blocks this, it is the supreme danger. But the supreme danger *also* harbors in itself the growth of the saving power. If we open ourselves to this danger then we prepare ourselves for the "upsurgence of the saving power"; we prepare ourselves for a "free relationship" to the essence of technology.

This linkage of the supreme danger and the growth of the saving power is mysterious. In what respect does the saving power "most profoundly take root and thence thrive even where the extreme danger lies – in the holding sway of enframing"? We need to take "a last step upon our way, to look with yet clearer eyes into the danger" (Technology, 310; 32).

This "last step" requires us to examine the word which has been fundamental throughout Heidegger's questioning but which he has not yet fully explained – "essence." Heidegger tells us that

> Thus far we have understood "essence" in its current meaning. In the academic language of philosophy "essence" means *what* something is; in Latin, *quid*. *Quidditas*, whatness, provides the answer to the question concerning essence. (Technology, 311; 33)

But the *essence* of technology is *not* to be understood as *quidditas*, whatness, genus, universal, kind. We must break with – rupture – this metaphysical way of conceiving of the essence of technology. And indeed, Heidegger's way of speaking of essence as the revealing that has the character of destining has been preparing us for a different way of thinking essence – or more accurately, *essencing*.

So once again Heidegger repeats the steps we have taken in order to prepare us for "the last step upon our way."

> Enframing is a way of revealing which is a destining, namely the way that challenges forth. The revealing that brings forth (*poiēsis*) is also a way that has the character of destining. But these ways are not kinds that, arrayed beside one another, fall under the concept of revealing. Revealing is that destining which, ever suddenly and inexplicably to all thinking, apportions itself into the revealing that brings forth and the revealing that challenges, and which allots itself to man. The revealing that challenges has its origin as a destining in bringing-forth. But at the same time enframing, in a way characteristic of a destining, blocks *poiēsis*.
>
> Thus enframing, as a destining of revealing, is indeed the essence of technology, but never in the sense of genus and *essentia*. If we pay heed to this, something astounding strikes us: it is technology itself that makes the demand on us to think in another way what is usually understood by "essence." But in what way? (Technology, 311; 34)

It is almost as if Heidegger keeps deferring this "last step" where we can grasp the sense in which the supreme danger harbors "the upsurgence of the saving power" – where we can prepare ourselves to experience a free relationship to the essence of technology. For first he comments on the meaning of "to save," and then on the meaning of "essence." This *seems* to be taking us farther away from the question we are trying to answer.

Rather than thinking of essence as a genus, kind or universal we need to think "of the essence of something as what essences, what comes into presence, in the sense of what endures" (Technology, 312; 34). By now Heidegger's strategy of seeking the "true" by way of the "correct" – the true which breaks with and shows how the correct is untenable – should be familiar to us. Thus, we can also say that although it is correct to think of essence as *quidditas* it is not yet "the true." "All essencing endures." But this doesn't mean that this enduring is only a permanent enduring "based solely on what Plato thinks as *idea* and Aristotle as *ti en einai* (that which any particular thing has always been), or what metaphysics in its most varied interpretations thinks as *essentia*" (Technology, 321; 34). We need to break with the compulsion to think of essence as a metaphysical *quidditas*.

Heidegger moves us a bit further by playing upon the linguistic associations of *wahr* (true), *währen* (to endure), and *ge-währen* (to grant). He tells us:

> And if we now ponder more carefully than we did before what it is that actually endures and perhaps alone endures, we may venture to say: Only what is granted endures. What endures primally out of the earliest beginning is what grants [*Nur das Gewährte währt. Das anfanglich aus der Frühe Währende ist das Gewährende*]. (Technology, 313; 35)

Saving – essencing – enduring – granting. Is this simply punning – word play? How does this enable us to understand how the supreme danger harbors the saving power? What does "granting" mean and how is it related to enframing?

> Does enframing hold sway at all in the sense of granting? No doubt the question seems a horrendous blunder. For according to everything that has been said, enframing is rather, a destining that gathers together into the revealing that challenges forth. Challenging is any-

thing but a granting. So it seems, so long as we do not notice that the challenging-forth into the ordering of the real as standing-reserve still remains a destining that starts man upon a way of revealing. (Technology, 313; 35)

What is going on here? What is Heidegger seeking to show us at the crucial juncture in the way he is building? He wants to reveal what seems extraordinarily paradoxical and mysterious – what we might call the *double* character, the radically ambiguous character, of the essence of technology. For it is at once the extreme danger that threatens us, that claims and can consume us as standing-reserve *and* – at the same time – opens us to a free relationship to the essence of technology. We need to confront the double character of the essencing of technology as *destining* – a destining that "starts man upon a way of revealing."

To emphasize this paradox, this mystery, this sense in which the supreme danger harbors the growth of the saving power, Heidegger tells us:

> But if this destining, enframing, is the extreme danger, not only for man's coming to presence but for all revealing as such, should this destining still be called a granting? Yes, most emphatically, if in this destining the saving power is said to grow. Every destining of revealing comes to pass from a granting and as such a granting. For it is granting that first conveys to man that share in revealing that the coming-to-pass of revealing needs. So needed and used, man is given to belong to the coming-to-pass of truth. The granting that sends one way or another into revealing is as such the saving power. For the saving power lets man see and enter into the highest dignity of his essence. This dignity lies in keeping watch over the unconcealment – and with it, from the first, the concealment – of all coming to presence on this earth. (Technology, 313; 36)

To heighten the mystery of the radical ambiguous character of enframing, Heidegger continues:

> It is precisely in enframing which threatens to sweep man away into ordering as the supposed single way of revealing and so thrusts man into danger of the surrender of his free essence – it is precisely in this extreme danger that the innermost indestructible belongingness of man within granting may come to light, provided that we, for our part, begin to pay heed to the essence of technology.

Thus the coming to presence of technology harbors in itself what we least suspect, the possible upsurgence of the saving power. (Technology, 313–14; 36)

"The ambiguous essence of technology" (*das zweideutige Wesen der Technik*) is revealed when we fully realize and experience that we may succumb to the threat of the supreme danger of *Gestell or* we may become witnesses of "the possible upsurgence of the saving power."

Everything, then, depends upon this: that we ponder this arising and that we, recollecting, watch over it. (Technology, 314; 36)

What we hear here – once again – is the call to what Heidegger says is the "original ethics" – to ponder and reflect upon (*bedenken und andenken*) our *ēthos*, dwelling, abode. We "re-turn" to this abode when we ponder the upsurgence of the saving power and watch over it. For, as we have been told, "'to save' is to fetch something home into its essence, in order to bring the essence for the first time into its genuine appearing" (Technology, 310; 32). It is only when we realize that the essence of technology is at once the supreme danger and harbors the upsurgence of the saving power that we have prepared ourselves to experience a free relationship to *Gestell*. Our freedom and our dignity consists in "keeping watch over the unconcealment."

We can now grasp the full force of Heidegger's critique of the correct instrumental and anthropological definition of technology. If we allow ourselves "to represent technology as an instrument, we remain transfixed in the will to master it." To the extent that we remain transfixed "we press on past the essence of technology"; we allow ourselves to be caught up in "the frenziedness of ordering that blocks every view into the coming-to-pass of revealing" (Technology, 314; 36).

We are "not yet saved" when "we look into the danger and see the growth of the saving power." "But we are thereupon summoned to hope in the growing light of the saving power. How can this happen? Here and now in little things, that we may foster the saving power in its increase. This includes holding always before our eyes the extreme danger" (Technology, 315; 37).

But what are we to *do*? In one sense, Heidegger is telling us this is the *wrong* question to ask. For this question still tempts us to think that human activity can counter or master this danger. Rather the answer to the question, "What are we to do?" is to ponder, to recollect, to reflect, to question, to think, to prepare, to wait.

> The coming to presence of technology threatens revealing, threatens it with the possibility that all revealing will be consumed in ordering and that everything will present itself only in the unconcealedness of standing-reserve. Human activity [*menschliches Tun*] can never directly counter this danger. Human achievement [*menschliche Leistung*] alone can never banish it. But human reflection [*menschliche Besinnung*] can ponder the fact that all saving power must be of a higher essence than what is endangered, though at the same time hindered to it. (Technology, 315; 38)

Still we want to know how this pondering, how this *menschliche Besinnung* furthers the growth of the saving power. Heidegger (typically) responds with another question.

> But might there not perhaps be a more primally granted revealing that could bring the saving power into its first shining-forth in the midst of the danger that in the technological age rather conceals than shows itself? (Technology, 315; 38)

What then is this "more primally granted revealing"? It is no longer surprising that Heidegger "re-turns" to what originally seemed to be an unnecessary "digression" but which is actually the key to "The Question Concerning Technology" – his elucidation of *poiēsis*, bringing-forth, *technē*.

> There was a time when it was not technology alone that bore the name *technē*. Once that revealing which brings forth truth into the splendor of radiant appearance was also called *technē*. (Technology, 315; 38)

As we approach the end of Heidegger's essay, his style becomes even more cryptic, aphoristic, and apocalyptic.

> Once there was a time when the bringing-forth of the true into the beautiful was called *technē*. *The poiēsis* of the fine arts was also called *technē*. (Technology, 315; 38)

But Heidegger has already warned us that we cannot simply turn away from modern technology and "re-turn" to the revealing of bringing-forth of *poiēsis* and *technē*. So why does Heidegger invoke "the more primally granted revealing" of *poiēsis* and *technē*?

It is important to realize that Heidegger's narrative of the epochal history of Being which has culminated in the holding sway of *Gestell* is not simply the story of decline – even though there is a powerful strand in his thinking that tempts us to read him in this way. To give in to this temptation is to misread him. It is to slip into thinking that *Gestell* is fated rather than a destining. It is to forget what Heidegger keeps telling us, that Being is always near and far. It conceals that *Gestell* is not only the danger in "the highest sense," but that this danger harbors the saving power. Furthermore, Heidegger is not saying that what we today call the artistic and the aesthetic – art as a "sector of cultural activity" – can save and redeem us. For in the age of technology artworks themselves are deprived of their power of revealing the "truth." They have become artworks to be "enjoyed aesthetically." But this is not what art, *poiēsis*, *technē* were "at the outset of the destining of the West, in Greece" when "the arts soared to the supreme height of the revealing granted them" (Technology, 315; 38).

> What was art – perhaps only for the brief but magnificent age? Why did art bear the modest name *technē*? Because it was revealing that brought forth and made present, and therefore belonged within *poiēsis*. It was finally that revealing which holds complete sway in all the fine arts, in poetry, and in everything poetical that obtained *poiēsis* as its proper name. (Technology, 316; 38)

Heidegger now cites Hölderlin once again in order to bring together what he has been struggling to bring forth – the mysterious relation between the growth of the saving power harbored in the supreme danger of *Gestell* and poetic revealing.

The same poet from whom we heard the words

> But where danger is, grows
> the saving power also ...

says to us

> ... poetically dwells man upon this earth (Technology, 316; 39).

Like a leitmotif we "re-turn" to dwelling, *ēthos*, to the "original eth-ics." For the growth of the saving power is a fetching home where poetically dwells man upon the earth.

As Heidegger comes to the end of the way his questioning/think-ing has been building, he is extremely tentative – provoking us with more questions. But this tentativeness is itself grounded in the rad-ical ontological ambiguity of *Gestell.*

> Could it be that the fine arts are called to poetic revealing? Could it be that revealing lays claim to the arts most primally, so that they for their part may expressly foster the growth of the saving power, may awaken and found a new vision of that which grants and our trust in it? (Technology, 316; 39)

Heidegger emphasizes the precariousness and openness of this possibility.

> Whether art may be granted this highest possibility of its essence in the midst of the extreme danger, no one can tell. Yet we can be astounded. Before what? Before this other possibility: that the frenziedness of technology may entrench itself everywhere to such an extent that someday, throughout everything technological, the essence of technology may come to presence in the coming-to-pass of truth. (Technology, 316–17; 39)

Heidegger's essay/lecture culminates in opening up – in bring-ing into a clearing – this other possibility before which we may be astounded, viz., that what *may* yet happen, through the very frenziedness of technology, is the growth of the saving power – a "re-turn" to poetic dwelling. He knows how paradoxical, mysterious, and astounding this may sound. But the "free relationship" to tech-nology that is being opened is one where we open ourselves to this "highest possibility."

He "re-turns" to the beginning of his essay, to the opening para-graph of the way he has been building, to the relation of technology, the essence of technology and questioning/thinking. But now he relates this to the essence of art and poetic revealing.

> Because the essence of technology is nothing technological, essential reflection upon technology and decisive confrontation with it must happen in a realm that is, on the one hand, akin to the essence of technology and, on the other, fundamentally different from it.

Thus questioning, we bear witness to the crisis that in our sheer preoccupation with technology we do not yet experience the coming to presence of technology, that in our sheer aesthetic-mindedness we no longer guard and preserve the coming to presence of art. Yet the more questioningly we ponder the essence of technology, the more mysterious the essence of art becomes.

The closer we come to the danger, the more brightly do the ways into the saving power begin to shine and the more questioning we become. For questioning is the piety of thought. (Technology, 317; 39–40)

Heidegger's silence?

Thus far, I have presented a close reading and commentary on "The Question Concerning Technology" in order to show its power, density and thought-provoking quality. Since the time of its publication in 1953 volumes have been written on the question(s) concerning technology. There is now a "culture industry" dealing with every aspect of technology. But it would be difficult to name another short text that is so provocative and calls into question many of the ways in which we commonly think about technology. As we tenaciously follow the way Heidegger is building, he scandalizes us and compels us to raise the most fundamental questions about technology. Heidegger exposes what is rarely questioned, viz., the very "framework" for asking questions about technology. We can understand the rationale for his gnomic, oracular, apocalyptic style, his strange and seemingly forced etymologies, his syntactical and grammatical violence. These are rhetorical devices used to rupture our normal "correct" modes of thinking (i.e., non-thinking) in order to provoke questioning/ thinking. Heidegger is forging a new idiom – what Richard Rorty calls a new "vocabulary" which dis-turbs. This is what is required if we are not to fall back into simply repeating "more of the same." The difficulties, frustrations and obscurities that a reader experiences are not merely the result of Heidegger's self-indulgent idiosyncracies. They are all intended to awaken reflection. Heidegger repeatedly tells us that what is most thought-provoking about the modern age of technology is that we do not think.[30] "The Question Concerning Technology" is an exemplar of what Heidegger means by thinking. It shows what he means when he says: "What is needed in the present world crisis is less philosophy, but more attentiveness to thinking" (Humanism, 242; 54).

I have suggested that the themes and threads in this essay/lecture are interwoven with every aspect of his late thinking and that it can deepen our understanding of his thinking. We can even gain a new perspective on Heidegger's posthumously published interview in *Der Spiegel* when we juxtapose it with "The Question Concerning Technology." We can give a more subtle reading of the striking claim that "only a god can save us." Consider the context of this claim:

> Philosophy will be unable to effect any immediate change in the cur-
> rent state of the world. This is true not only of philosophy but of all
> purely human reflection and endeavor. Only a god can save us. The
> only possibility available to us is that by thinking and poetizing we
> prepare a readiness for the appearance of a god, or for the absence of
> a god in [our] decline, insofar as in view of the absent god we are in a
> state of decline.[31]

The language Heidegger uses here echoes the language of "The Question Concerning Technology." For the upshot of the essay – what Heidegger calls a "free relationship" to the essence of technology is to help "prepare a readiness" – a readiness that can only be achieved by thinking and *poiēsis*. To say that "only a god can *save* us" is to say that we can only prepare ourselves for "the *possible* upsurgence of the saving power." The radical ambiguity of the appearance *or* absence of a god parallels the radical ambiguity of the essence of technology which at once threatens us and harbors the growth of the saving power. Furthermore, in this passage we find echoes of Heidegger's emphatic claim: "Human activity can never directly counter this danger. Human achievement alone can never banish it. But human reflection can ponder the fact that all saving power must be of a higher essence than what is endangered, though at the same time kindred to it" (Technology, 315; 38).

We can also see how "The Question Concerning Technology" is a response to Socrates' question, "How one should live." It does not, of course, provide us with rules for living our lives, nor does it provide any guidance for how we are to "safeguard and secure the existing bonds ... that hold human beings together ever so tenuously" (Humanism, 232; 43). But it does direct us toward the task of preparing ourselves to "enter into the highest dignity of [our] essence" – the dignity that "lies in keeping watch over the unconcealment" (Technology, 313; 36). It directs us to reflecting on man's dwelling, abode, *ēthos* – to the "original ethics" – where we ponder the abode of man, to "that thinking which thinks the truth of Being as the primordial element of man" (Humanism, 235; 47).

But Heidegger's essay/lecture not only reveals, it also conceals. I want to – using Heidegger's own expression – "step back" and question what it conceals, especially as it pertains to the ethical-political consequences of Heidegger's late thinking. I will begin by staying close to what Heidegger says (and does not say) in order to highlight gaps and fissures in the way he is building, and to note his silences. Stepping back further, I want to expose the more momentous and horrendous ethical-political consequences of Heidegger's questioning concerning technology. For once we understand these, we can better understand what has disturbed so many of Heidegger's readers – his virtual silence about the Holocaust and the atrocities of the Nazis.

What then precisely is concealed – and passed over in silence – in this essay? Let me return to an early stage of his questioning, to the place where Heidegger first introduces "the Greek way" of thinking *poiēsis* and *technē* as "bringing-forth." This is the place where Heidegger explicitly introduces revealing (*das Entbergen*) and tells us "the Greeks have the word *alētheia* for revealing." To explain what he means, Heidegger refers to a discussion of Aristotle that has "special importance."

> Aristotle, in a discussion of special importance (*Nicomachean Ethics*, BK. VI, Chaps. 3 and 4) distinguishes *epistēmē* and *technē* and indeed with respect to what and how they reveal. *Technē* is a mode of *alētheuein*. It reveals whatever does not bring itself forth and does not yet lie here before us, whatever can look and turn out now one way and now another. Whoever builds a house or a ship or forges a sacrificial chalice reveals what is to be brought forth, according to the terms of the four modes of occasioning. (Technology, 295; 17)

If we turn to these chapters of the *Nicomachean Ethics*, we are immediately struck by a curious omission, a striking silence by Heidegger. Aristotle does indeed distinguish between *epistēmē* and *technē* and relates them to *alētheia*. But Aristotle does not stop there. Indeed, Aristotle's main point is to distinguish *phronēsis* from the other "intellectual virtues." *Phronēsis* is the intellectual virtue or "state of the soul" that pertains to *praxis*, just as *technē* relates to *poiēsis*. This is one of the classic texts in which Aristotle carefully distinguishes *praxis* (the subject matter of the *Ethics*) from *poiēsis*. In Heidegger's idiom *phronēsis* is also a "mode of *alētheuein*."

Aristotle begins Book VI, chapter 3 by telling us:

> Then let us begin over again, and discuss these states of the soul. Let us say, then, that there are five states in which the soul grasps the truth [*alētheia*] in its affirmations or denials. These are craft [*technē*], scientific knowledge [*epistēmē*], [practical] intelligence [*phronēsis*], wisdom [*sophia*], and understanding [*nous*] ...[32]

Much of Book VI is dedicated to examining *phronēsis* and distinguishing it from the other "intellectual virtues." After surveying these "states of the soul" Aristotle tells us that "the remaining possibility, then is that [practical] intelligence [*phronēsis*] is a state grasping the truth [*alētheia*], involving reason, concerned with action [*praxis*] about what is good or bad for a human being."[33]

But neither here nor at any other place in "The Question Concerning Technology" does Heidegger even mention "*phronēsis*" and "*praxis*." Why is this omission so striking and important? It might be objected that Heidegger's concern in this essay is with *technē* and technology, and that the point of referring to Aristotle is to emphasize that *technē* is a mode of *alētheuein*. But such a rejoinder is a bit too facile. Throughout his essay Heidegger speaks as if there are a *plurality* of modes of revealing, but he only explicitly considers two modes: *poiēsis* (bringing-forth) and *Gestell* (challenging-forth). Again it might be objected that these are the only modes of revealing that are relevant to questioning technology. But is this so? Recall the decisive step in the denouement of the essay – the point where Heidegger asks:

> But might there not perhaps be a more primally granted revealing that could bring the saving power into its first shining-forth in the midst of the danger that in the technological age rather conceals than shows itself?

And Heidegger immediately comments:

> There was a time when it was not technology alone that bore the name *technē*. Once that revealing which brings forth truth into the splendor of radiant appearance was also called *technē*. (Technology, 315; 38)

But there is a significant gap here in the way in which Heidegger has shown us to think about revealing (*alētheia*). For why should we think that the response that modern technology calls forth is to be found by "re-turning" to *technē* and *poiēsis*, rather than *phronēsis* and *praxis*? At the very least – because *phronēsis* is also a mode of *alētheuein* – we might expect Heidegger to consider, to reflect upon, *this* possibility. But he doesn't. The entire rhetorical construction of "The Question Concerning Technology" seduces us into thinking that the only alternative to the threatening danger of *Gestell* is *poiēsis*. It excludes and conceals the possible response of *phronēsis* and *praxis*.

I do not think that this is simply a philological omission. On the contrary, if Heidegger had been rigorous in his own questioning/thinking then this requires pondering *phronēsis* itself as a mode of revealing. This omission begins to show a much more significant concealment which affects everything he says in his late writings. This is indicated by the ways in which Heidegger typically speaks about "human activity" (*menschliches Tun*). Why does Heidegger think that human activity can never directly counter the danger of *Gestell*? Why does he tell us in the *Spiegel* interview that all purely human endeavor "will be unable to effect any immediate change in the current state of the world"? Because he thinks that what human activity has become in the age of technology is *only* a variation of *Gestell* – the will to will, to mastery and control. This is already evident in the "Letter on Humanism" where Heidegger announces in his opening lines: "We are still far from pondering the essence of action decisively enough. We view action as causing an effect." This is the same formulaic pattern by which action is conceived as the causality of the "correct" instrumental and anthropological definition of technology.

The "Letter on Humanism" displays the same pattern we have discovered in "The Question Concerning Technology" where Heidegger passes over *phronēsis* and *praxis* – or rather *displaces* them with the "highest action" of thinking, thinking that ponders man's *ēthos*.

> We are still far from pondering the essence of action decisively enough. We view action as causing an effect. The actuality of the effect is valued according to its utility. But the essence of action is accomplishment. To accomplish means to unfold something into the fullness of its essence, to lead forth into this fullness – *producere*. Therefore only what already is can really be accomplished. But what

"is" above all is Being. Thinking acomplishes the relation of Being to the essence of man. It does not make or cause the relation. Thinking brings this relation to Being solely as something handed over to it from Being. Such offering consists in the fact that in thinking Being comes to language. Language is the house of Being. In its home man dwells. Those who think and those who create with words are the guardians of this home. Their guardianship accomplishes the manifestation of language and maintains it in language through their speech. Thinking does not become action only because some effect issues from it or because it is applied. Thinking acts insofar as it thinks. Such action is presumably the simplest and at the same time the highest, because it concerns the relation of Being to man. (Humanism, 193; 5)[34]

Note how here too Heidegger speaks only of the two modes of action – action as causing an effect, and the highest mode of action, thinking. How are we to explain why Heidegger – for all his subtlety in drawing distinctions – leads us over and over again to a stark dichotomy that conceals the other ways of pondering human activity? One might reply that this is Heidegger's emphatic way of compelling us to confront what action has become in the age of technology, action as *Gestell* which is itself the consequence of metaphysical humanism. But even if we were to say that to conceive of action as only causing an effect is "correct," we might think with Heidegger *against* Heidegger. We might ask whether this correct definition of action reveals "the true." And furthermore we may question whether revealing what is true leads us only to thinking as the highest action. Heidegger himself is closing, concealing other possibilities.

We might account for Heidegger's passing over *phronēsis* as a mode of *alētheuein* and his denigration of *praxis* in another way. After all, for Aristotle *phronēsis* and *praxis* are essential for understanding not only ethics but also politics – the distinctive form of human activity in the *polis*. But Heidegger – certainly by 1947 when the "Letter on Humanism" was published – was completely disillusioned about any and all forms of political public activity. His remarks about public life are disparaging, for example when he speaks of "the peculiar dictatorship of the public realm" (Humanism, 197; 9) in the modern technological age. This is what several commentators have called the "apolitical" turn in Heidegger's late thinking. But it is misleading to call this an "apolitical turn." For to condemn the "political realm," to characterize it as only a manifestation of *Gestell* is an *extreme* political gesture – one that contributes to Heidegger's exclusive focus on art and poetic revealing as the saving power.

I do not think that we can underestimate the extent to which the twists and turns of Heidegger's thinking were responses to his understanding of the political events he was witnessing. But Heidegger's blindness goes much deeper. Despite Heidegger's own appreciation of Aristotle's *Ethics*, he never does justice to what distinguishes *praxis* from *poiēsis*, or *phronēsis* from *technē* – to what Hannah Arendt calls the human condition of plurality – the basic condition of both action and speech. Typically Heidegger speaks of man – not *men* or *human beings* in their plurality – beings who are at once alike and different in their otherness and who in their speech and deeds reveal their uniqueness.[35]

Jacques Taminiaux characterizes this imperviousness to human plurality, to human affairs in the *polis* – where the clash of *doxa* prevails as Heidegger's "Platonic bias." He argues that we can already detect this bias in the way in which Heidegger transforms Aristotle's distinctions in *Being and Time*.[36] For despite Heidegger's subtle discussion of care (*Sorge*), solicitude (*Forsorge*), co-being (*Mitsein*), and *Dasein*'s being-with (*Mitdasein*) in his fundamental ontology, there is a powerful monological bias at work in his analyses. Heidegger rarely shows a sensitivity to the ambiguity and contingency in our everyday public engagements, our everyday involvement with other human beings in their otherness. Commenting on the "Letter on Humanism," Taminiaux writes:

> Here the Platonic bias reappears again: the utmost, the innermost, the highest possibility of action is nothing else but thinking, which is something that Heidegger repeats in 1950 in the lecture on *Kehre*: "Thinking is acting at the innermost." To be sure this thinking is no longer aiming at the science of Being .... But should we not consider it a sign of Platonism that Heidegger's notion of "action," involvement or "engagement" ... never gives the slightest consideration to the insertion with a human plurality which the word connotes?[37]

And Taminiaux, following Hannah Arendt's analysis of plurality and *praxis*, says:

> The entire issue of *praxis* for the Greeks of the isonomic city was the aiming at a form of excellence strictly conditioned by the free manifestation of the individuals, by their sharing in words and deeds

of a common world whose reality could not be separated from the pluralistic perspectives invested in it. It is this pluralistic and ambiguous manifestation which Aristotle in his *Ethics* was attempting to preserve, over against Plato, in his refusal to absorb *phronēsis* into *sophia*. *Phronēsis* in this sense had to be recognized as the general aptitude of each and every one – something that was not limited to the professionals of thought – to pass judgment in public matters as in the private ones.[38]

Now whether one agrees or disagrees with Taminiaux's characterization of Heidegger's affirmation that thinking is the highest possibility of action as a "Platonic bias," he is certainly right in calling attention to Heidegger's neglect of the pluralistic character of *praxis* and *phronēsis* – and the need to preserve *phronēsis* from being absorbed into (or displaced by) *sophia* or *Denken*.

There is a profound historical irony in Heidegger's neglect and denigration of these dimensions of *phronēsis* and *praxis*. For two of Heidegger's most distinguished students were at once inspired by and strongly resisted Heidegger's reading of Aristotle's *Nicomachean Ethics:* Hans-Georg Gadamer and Hannah Arendt. Both Gadamer and Arendt attended the famous seminar that Heidegger gave in 1924 that focused on Book VI of the *Nicomachean Ethics*. Central to their intellectual projects is a probing of aspects of *praxis* and *phronēsis* that Heidegger conceals.[39] What is especially important is that they – in different ways – draw upon and interpret *praxis* and *phronēsis* in order to confront the very question that so concerns Heidegger – how are we to respond to what is happening in the age of technology?

Gadamer argues that Aristotle's understanding of *praxis* and *phronēsis* provides a *critical* basis for responding to what Heidegger calls *"Gestell."*

When Aristotle, in the sixth book of the *Nicomachean Ethics* distinguishes the manner of "practical" knowledge ... from theoretical and technical knowledge, he expresses in my opinion, one of the greatest truths by which the Greeks throw light upon "scientific" mystification of modern society of specialization.[40]

And in a passage that at once echoes Heidegger's questioning concerning technology – and radically departs from Heidegger – Gadamer writes:

In a scientific culture such as ours the fields of *technē* and art are much more expanded. Thus the fields of mastering means to pre-given ends have been rendered even more monological and controllable. The crucial change is that practical wisdom [*phronēsis*] can no longer be promoted by personal contact and the mutual exchange of views among citizens. Not only has craftsmanship been replaced by industrial work; many forms of our daily life are technologically organized so that they no longer require personal decision. In modern technological society public opinion itself has in a new and radically divisive way become the object of very complicated techniques – and this, I think, is the main problem facing our civilization.[41]

But for Gadamer – as for Taminiaux – our destiny does not rest solely with "the thinkers and the poets" who are guardians of the abode in which man dwells. There is an urgent need to nurture *phronēsis* in our everyday lives as citizens. Gadamer is fully aware of his strong divergence from Heidegger. With explicit reference to Heidegger he writes,

Don't we all then run the risk of a terrible intellectual hubris if we equate Nietzsche's anticipations and the ideological confusions of the present with life as it is actually lived with its own forms of solidarity? Here, in fact, my divergence from Heidegger is fundamental.[42]

What Gadamer means by "solidarity" is closely related to what Arendt and Taminiaux mean by "plurality." Each of them is aware of the ordering power – the challenging-forth of *Gestell*. But each of them strongly resists the Heideggerian bias to denigrate public life – to collapse *praxis* into *Gestell*, or to displace *praxis* by thinking.

Arendt too is sensitive to what Heidegger calls *Gestell*. Her own description of *homo faber* echoes Heidegger:

Among the outstanding characteristics of the modern age from its beginning to our time we find the typical attitudes of *homo faber*: his instrumentalization of the world, his confidence in tools and in the productivity of the maker of artificial objects, his trust in the all comprehensive range of the means–end category, his conviction that every issue can be solved and every human motivation, which regards everything given as material and thinks of the whole of nature as of "an immense fabric from which we can cut out whatever we want to renew it however we like"; his equation of intelligence with ingenuity, that is, his contempt for all thought which cannot be considered to be "the first step ... for the fabrication of artificial objects, particularly tools to make tools, and to vary fabrication indefinitely"; *finally his matter-of-course identification of fabrication with action* (emphasis added).[43]

This last clause indicates Arendt's sharp departure from Heidegger's analysis of *Gestell*. She would certainly agree that in the age of technology there is a strong overwhelming tendency to identify fabrication with action. Indeed this is just what Heidegger himself has done. She also claims that the "activity of thinking is the highest and perhaps purest activity of which men are capable" and she would endorse Heidegger's claim that "we are still far from pondering the essence of action decisively enough." But for Arendt this means that we must carefully distinguish what Heidegger merges and fuses together: the distinctive non-reducible modes of the *vita activa* – labor, work, and action (*praxis*). It is action which is exhibited in the public space of political debate, action that presupposes the human condition of plurality and natality that is the highest form of the *vita activa*. Arendt also thinks that *praxis* has been deformed in the modern technological age. There has been a consequential inversion of the classical hierarchy of action, work and labor. We have become blind and forgetful of what is distinctive about action, and are on the verge of becoming a "laboring society." But her analysis of action is intended as an act of retrieval, to reveal a possibility that can never be completely obliterated, and to show how this possibility is rooted in human plurality and natality – the capacity to initiate, to begin to act in concert with others.[44] We can relate Arendt's retrieval and opening of the possibility of action – action that is not reducible to fabrication and *Gestell* – directly to Heidegger's text. For I have been arguing that Heidegger seduces us into thinking that the *only* possible response (the highest possibility) to the supreme danger of *Gestell* is poetic revealing. This is evident when he asks:

Could it be that the fine arts are called to poetic revealing? Could it be that revealing lays claim to the arts most primally, so that they for their part may expressly foster the growth of the saving power, may awaken and found anew our vision of that which grants and our trust in it? (Technology, 316; 39)

But why is this the "highest possibility," indeed the only possibility? Arendt can be read as showing that Heidegger himself conceals what needs to be unconcealed – "the possible upsurgence of the saving power" may be revealed in action (*praxis*) and not only in "poetic dwelling."

The primary issue is not simply one of retrieving dimensions of Aristotle's understanding of *praxis* and *phronēsis* that Heidegger distorts and conceals. Rather the primary issue is answering the very question that Heidegger takes to be fundamental – how does one respond to *Gestell*, the essence of technology? Even Habermas, who is one of Heidegger's sharpest critics, and who is also skeptical of recent neo-Aristotelianism, makes a point that parallels what Taminiaux, Gadamer and Arendt emphasize when he declares:

> The real difficulty in the relation of theory and *praxis* does not arise from this new function of science as a technological force, but rather from the fact that we are no longer able to distinguish between practical and technical power. Yet even a civilization that has been rendered scientific is not granted dispensation from practical questions; therefore a peculiar danger arises when the process of scientification transgresses the limit of technical questions, without, however, departing from the level of reflection of a rationality confined to the technological horizon. For then no attempt is made to attain a rational consensus on the part of citizens concerning the practical control of their destiny. Its place is taken by the attempt to attain technical control over history by perfecting the administration of society, an attempt that is just as impractical as it is unhistorical.[45]

Why is Heidegger blind to those aspects of *praxis* and *phronēsis* highlighted by Taminiaux, Gadamer, Arendt, and Habermas? Why is he so silent about the possibility of *praxis* in "The Question Concerning Technology"? Why does he lead us to think that we are confronted with only two ways of revealing: the bringing-forth of *poiēsis* and the challenging-forth of *Gestell*? Why does he focus exclusively on poetic dwelling when he considers the growth of the saving power that is harbored in the supreme danger of *Gestell*? Is Heidegger guilty – as Gadamer suggests – of "a terrible intellectual hubris" when he leads us to think that the only proper (authentic) response to the supreme danger is to prepare ourselves to watch over unconcealment? I think that he is, and that this is itself revealed in the very way that he characterizes thinking, destining, essencing. To explain what I mean we need to recall the historical context in which this essay/lecture was written.

"The Question Concerning Technology" is an expanded version of one of the four lectures that Heidegger delivered in Bremen in December 1949. The general title of the four lectures – "The Thing," "Enframing," "The Danger," and "The Turning" – is "Insight into What Is." We know that the period immediately following the end of World War II was one of the most troubling and traumatic periods in Heidegger's life. There was no longer any possibility of deceiving oneself about the extent and horrors of Nazi atrocities. Heidegger himself was experiencing the "humiliation" of de-Nazification proceedings. In September 1945, the de-Nazification committee set up to investigate Heidegger's conduct during the Third Reich issued its report and charged Heidegger with four things: "having an important position in the Nazi regime; changing the structure of the university by introducing the *Führer*-principle; engaging in Nazi propaganda; and inciting students against allegedly reactionary professors."[46] Heidegger was required to submit a statement explaining his conduct. Debate over the report extended through 1946. In March 1946 Heidegger suffered a nervous breakdown and spent three weeks in a sanatorium. The de-Nazification proceedings continued through March 1949 when Heidegger was officially prohibited from teaching at Freiburg University. (The university and the Freiburg philosophy department came to Heidegger's defense. In 1951 he was granted emeritus status and allowed to teach and lecture again at the university.) We know that during this period Heidegger was being pressed by former students and colleagues to speak directly about the Nazi atrocities and specifically about the extermination of the Jews. But Heidegger answered only with evasive replies. When Herbert Marcuse wrote Heidegger in 1948 asking him to make a public statement about the Holocaust, Heidegger answered by comparing the extermination of the Jews to the Soviet Union's treatment of Germans in Eastern Europe:

> I can only add that instead of the word "Jews" [in your letter] there should be the word "East Germans," and then exactly the same [terror] holds true of one of the Allies, with the difference that everything that has happened since 1945 is public knowledge world-wide, whereas the bloody terror of the Nazis was in fact kept a secret from the German people.[47]

In reading such texts as the "Letter on Humanism" and "The Question Concerning Technology" we cannot neglect the historical context in which they were written. There is a subtext in both of these documents. For they can both be read as an *apologia* – a defense in which Heidegger's condemnation of metaphysical human- ism and his analysis of *Gestell* are intended to account for, to "justify" his silence about the Holocaust.

As indicated earlier, to speak of Heidegger's silence is not completely accurate. I previously cited a passage from "The Ques- tion Concerning Technology" where Heidegger first contrasts the essence of technology as challenging-forth with the revealing of bringing-forth. To illustrate what he means he writes: "But mean- while even the cultivation of the field has come under the grip of another kind of setting-in-order, which *sets upon* nature. It sets upon it in the sense of challenging it. Agriculture is now [motorized] food industry" (Technology, 296; 18).

But in the unpublished manuscript of the 1949 lecture there is a passage which has been deleted from the published text of "The Question Concerning Technology." The manuscript reads:

> Agriculture is now motorized food industry – in essence the same as the manufacturing of corpses in gas chambers and extermination camps, the same as blockading and starving of nations [it was the year of the Berlin blockade], the same as the manufacture of hydrogen bombs.[48]

This is one of the passages that Thomas Sheehan says is "characterized by a rhetoric, a cadence, a point of view that is damning beyond commentary."[49] But, strictly speaking, it is not "beyond commentary." On the contrary, in the context of Heideg- ger's questioning concerning technology, we can understand precisely why Heidegger would make this horrendous comparison between motorized agriculture and "manufacturing corpses in gas chambers." From the "heights" of thinking, the key phrase here is "in essence the same" (*im Wesen das Selbe*). Heidegger is question- ing the essence of technology – *Gestell*, the challenging-forth and setting-upon that claims man and where everything becomes "standing-reserve," including human beings who become "human resources." We are scandalized by Heidegger's comparison because – he might say – we are still wedded to the "correct" definition of tech- nology where we think of technology as a neutral instrument which can be used for benign ends of increasing food production or the malignant end of extermination of human beings. But if we focus on the *essence* of technology then these differences are "non-essential." The manufacturing of corpses in gas chambers more fully reveals the essence of technology.[50] Heidegger doesn't flinch from the scandal of thinking that is an affront and an offence to our normal "correct" ways of thinking (or rather, non-thinking). Unless we fully acknowledge and confront the essence of technology, even in "manufacturing of corpses in gas chambers," unless we realize that *all* its manifestations are "in essence the same," we will never confront the supreme danger and the possible upsurgence of the saving power.

So Heidegger's "cool" comparison of motorized agriculture, mass extermination and manufacturing of hydrogen bombs is not – from the heights of thinking, "the highest form of activity," some grotesque lapse or incidental "insensitive remark"; it is a *necessary* consequence of the very way in which Heidegger characterizes *Gestell* – the unconcealment that claims man and over which he has no control. When we realize that this is a necessary consequence – that there is a hidden "logic" in these comparisons, our sense of scandal is not diminished, it is intensified. It compels us to question the essence of Heidegger's thinking that sees no essential differences between modern agriculture, the murder of millions of human beings, and the genocide of Jews. What calls forth thinking *is* Heidegger's *thinking*, i.e., his *failure* of thinking.[51] When we examine Heidegger's post-Second World War texts, we discover that the formulaic pattern involved here is typical, not atypical.

In an extremely perceptive article dealing with this passage, Jack Caputo notes:

> One might suppose that this is an offhand comment, strange and atypical, which Heidegger prudently chose to omit from the published text. Actually, the opposite is the case. Heidegger says things of this sort with disturbing regularity. The passage obeys the deepest laws of Heideggerian discourse. It is heavily coded, almost formulaic, a profoundly typical gesture on his part.[52]

From the "Letter on Humanism" to the end of his life, Heidegger is obsessed with poetic dwelling and pondering one's true abode, one's *ēthos*. From the "heights" of his thinking all other distinctions fall by the wayside. The formulaic pattern we discover is one that is always distinguishing the "correct" from "the true," always focusing on extreme (and simplistic) contrasts, leading us away from everyday human suffering, plights and dangers to our "real plight" and danger.

In "Building Dwelling Thinking," a lecture delivered to the Darmstadt Symposium on *Man and Space* (August 5, 1951), we discern the same formulaic pattern; we can "hear" the same rhythms.

> On all sides we hear talk about the housing shortage, and with good reason. Nor is there just talk; there is action too. We try to fill the need by providing houses, by promoting the building of houses, planning the whole architectural enterprise. However hard and bitter, however hampering and threatening the lack of housing remains, the *real* plight [*eigentliche Not*] *of dwelling* does not lie merely in a lack of houses. The real plight of dwelling is indeed older than the world wars with their destruction, older also than the increase of the earth's population and the condition of the industrial workers. The real dwelling plight lies in this, that mortals ever search anew for the essence of dwelling, that he *must ever learn to dwell*. What if man's homelessness consisted in this, that man still does not even think of the *real* plight of dwelling as *the* plight? Yet as soon as man *gives thought* to his homelessness, it is a misery no longer. Rightly considered and kept well in mind, it is the sole summons that *calls* mortals into their dwelling.[53]

The motif of homelessness which "is coming to be the destiny of the world" that was articulated in "The Letter on Humanism" is reiterated here. But this homelessness is not to be confused with mundane pain and misery. For the "real" homelessness is that we do not *think* of the *real* (true) plight – the failure to ponder the abode of man. Presumably when we respond to the "call of Being" our misery is "no longer." This corresponds to the claim that the real danger is not technology itself – even if it is used to manufacture corpses – but *Gestell*, the essence of technology.

Or again, in *Gelassenheit*, we see the same formulaic pattern at work – a pattern that turns us away from such "mundane" issues as mass extermination, human misery, life and death, to the "real" plight, the "real" danger – the failure to keep meditative thinking alive.

> But for the time being – we do not know for how long – man finds himself in a perilous situation. Why? Just because a Third World War might break out unexpectedly and bring about the complete annihil-

ation of humanity and the destruction of the earth? No. In this dawning atomic age a far greater danger threatens – precisely when the danger of a third world war has been removed. A strange assertion! Strange indeed, but only as long as we do not meditate ...

What great danger then might move upon us? Then there might go hand in hand with the greatest ingenuity in calculative planning and inventing indifference toward meditative thinking, total thoughtlessness. And then? Then man would have denied and thrown away his own special nature – that he is a meditative being. Therefore, the issue is the saving of man's essential nature. Therefore, the issue is keeping meditative thinking alive.[54]

The formulaic pattern is clear. We may, from our "correct" understanding think there is an incommensurability between agriculture and manufacturing corpses in gas chambers. We may think the misery of concrete homelessness is the "real plight." We may think that the real danger is the "complete annihilation of humanity and the destruction of the earth." All of this is correct (*richtig*). But none of it is "the true," *alētheia*. From the heights of true, genuine, authentic thinking *the* real danger (danger in the highest sense) is the threat to saving man's essential nature, restoring our true "dignity," keeping alive meditative thinking that ponders our dwelling, our *ēthos*. This rhetorical call to true, meditative thinking is an operation that Habermas calls "abstraction via essentialization" where "the history of being is thus disconnected from political and historical events" whether they be extermination of Jews or the threat of nuclear annihilation. None of this is *essential*. "Under the leveling gaze of the philosopher of Being even the extermination of Jews seems merely an event equivalent to many others. Annihilation of Jews, expulsion of Germans – they amount to the same."[55]

What calls forth thinking here is Heidegger's own understanding of a type of meditative thinking that *anesthetizes* us to the frightful contingencies of human life and death, that is so obsessed with the "real" danger, the "real" plight that it can dismiss the difference between motorized agriculture and mass murder as "nonessential."[56] When we question Heidegger's questioning, when we think about his thinking, then the entire uplifting rhetoric of the growth of the saving power begins to crumble and sound hollow.

This is much more – and much worse – than a "Platonic bias" or even a blindness to the human condition of plurality. It is as if in Heidegger's obsession with man's estrangement from Being, nothing

else counts as essential or true except pondering one's *ēthos*. Furthermore, we can begin to question the Heideggerian discourse of
response and responsibility. When Heidegger explicitly discusses
responsibility in "The Question Concerning Technology" it is exclusively in regard to the co-responsibility in the occasioning of the
four causes in bringing forth, *poiēsis*. He tells us that this sense of
responsibility has nothing to do with our normal "correct" understanding of moral responsibility. It becomes clear that the only
response that is really important and appropriate is the response to
the silent call of Being, not to the silent screams of our fellow human
beings. If *Gestell* is the destining of modern technology, if it "claims
man," then "mere" human responsibility for Auschwitz is absolved.
For this too is part of the destining of *Gestell*. We can well understand
why Heidegger never expressed any remorse for *his* responsibility for
supporting the Nazi regime. Gadamer, who has consistently
defended Heidegger's philosophic originality and profundity, speaks
directly to this issue when he writes:

> People may wonder: did Heidegger feel no responsibility at all for the
> terrible consequences of Hitler's accession to power – the new barbar-
> ism, the Nuremberg laws, the terror, the blood sacrifice for all
> humanity of two world wars – and finally, the inextinguishable shame
> of the extermination camps. The answer is unequivocal: no. All that
> was merely a ruined revolution and not the great renewal based in the
> spiritual and moral strength of the people, which Heidegger dreamed
> of and yearned for as the preparation for a new human religion.[57]

There is no place in Heidegger's *thinking* for a response and responsibility for the mundane pain and suffering of other human beings. As
Caputo says:

> It is a world in which a wholly *other* kind of responsiveness and
> responsibility has been silenced, a responsibility to those who live and
> die, to those who are embodied, who suffer or are in pain, who grow
> old and infirm, above all, to innocent victims. The thinker leaves no
> room at all for the victim in the history of Being's self-showing.[58]

When we think through the "pathways" of Heidegger's thinking
we realize – to turn his own phrase against him – it is "correct" to
say he is silent about the Nazi atrocities, but this is not "the truth."
For once we grasp the hidden logic of *his* thinking, once we expose

what Caputo calls "the deepest laws of Heideggerian discourse" then it becomes strikingly clear that he is *not* silent.[59] For "the manufacturing of corpses in gas chambers and extermination camps" is itself only a manifestation of the destining of *Gestell* – a destining which man furthers by his actions but over which he has no control. It is all part of the epochal history of Being.

I want to conclude by returning to the "Letter on Humanism" where Heidegger tells us that "thinking which thinks the truth of Being as the primordial element of man, as one who eksists, is in itself the original ethics" (Humanism, 235; 47). I have already indicated that the "Letter on Humanism" can be read as an *apologia*. Heidegger defends himself against what he condemns as superficial objections – that his thinking against metaphysical humanism is itself an "irresponsible and destructive nihilism." He sums up those objections when he declares:

> Because in all the respects mentioned we everywhere speak against all that humanity deems high and holy our philosophy teaches an irresponsible and destructive "nihilism". (Humanism, 226; 37)

Heidegger's defense is that it is not *his* questioning that is nihilistic but rather metaphysical humanism and *Gestell* that is essentially nihilistic. Both here and in "The Question Concerning Technology" he presents himself as the one who speaks for, and defends human dignity. "The highest determinations of the essence of man in humanism still do not realize the proper dignity of man" (*die eigentliche Würde des Menschen*) (Humanism, 210; 21). This "concern" for human dignity is reiterated in "the Question Concerning Technology" when he tells us that "the saving power lets man see and enter into the highest dignity [*in die höchste Würde*] of his essence. This dignity lies in keeping watch over the unconcealment – and with it, from the first, the concealment – of all coming to presence on this earth" (Technology, 313; 36).

We need not denigrate Heidegger's thought-provoking questioning/thinking. We can read and think about his texts "as he would not have wished them to be read: in a cool hour, with curiosity, and an open tolerant mind." We can acknowledge Heidegger's originality in leading us to think about technology and the essence of technology in new ways. Nevertheless we can question his *apologia* and his response to Socrates' question, how one should live – pondering our *ēthos.* For "the proper dignity of man" that he wants to defend and guard is a strange type of dignity. For this "dignity" is blind and impervious to mundane suffering and misery, victimization and mass extermination. None of this is our "real plight" or real danger. It is "correct" to say that Heidegger was virtually silent about Nazi atrocities, and *his* responsibility in supporting the "movement" of National Socialism. But this is not the *truth.* On the contrary, when we listen carefully to what he is saying, when we pay attention to the "deepest laws of Heideggerian discourse" then Heidegger's "silence" is resounding, deafening and damning.

NOTES

1 Thomas Sheehan, "Heidegger and the Nazis," *New York Review of Books* (June 16, 1988), p. 38. In his text and notes, Sheehan cites many of the documents that are relevant to the recent controversy concerning Heidegger's politics. See also Michael E. Zimmerman, *Heidegger's Confrontation with Modernity: Technology, Politics, Art* (Bloomington: Indiana University Press, 1990) and Richard Wolin, *The Politics of Being: The Political Thought of Martin Heidegger, 1927–1966* (New York: Columbia University Press, 1990).

2 Victor Farias' book, *Heidegger et le nazisme,* has been translated into English, *Heidegger and the Nazis* (Philadelphia: Temple University Press, 1989). See also Hugo Ott, *Martin Heidegger: Unterwegs zu seiner Biographie* (Frankfurt: Campus, 1988); Otto Pöggler, "Den Führer führen? Heidegger und kein Ende," *Philosophische Rundschau* 32 (1985); Annette Gethmann-Siefert and Otto Pöggler, eds., *Heidegger und die praktische Philosophie* (Frankfurt: Suhrkamp, 1988); Karl Löwith, *Mein Leben in Deutchland vor und nach 1933* (Stuttgart: J. B. Metzler, 1986). Zimmerman discusses the three waves of controversy about Heidegger's politics. See especially chap. 3, "Heidegger, National Socialism, and Modern Technology," in *Heidegger's Confrontation With Modernity.*

3 Hannah Arendt, "Martin Heidegger at Eighty," reprinted in Michael Murray, ed., *Heidegger and Modern Philosophy* (New Haven: Yale University Press, 1978), pp. 301–302.

4 Jürgen Habermas, "Work and Weltanschauung: The Heidegger Controversy from a German Perspective," *Critical Inquiry* 15 (Winter 1989). This article is an English translation of Habermas' introduction to the German edition of Farias, *Heidegger et le nazisme.* See also the afterword to the second edtion of Otto Pöggler, *Der Denkweg Martin Heideggers* (Pfullingen: Neske, 1983).

5   Theodor Adorno, *Diskus* (January 1963). See Philippe Lacoue-Labarthe's discussion of the context of Adorno's remark, *Heidegger, Art and Politics* (Oxford: Basil Blackwell, 1990), p. 105 and note 1, pp. 117–18. See also Habermas, "Work and Weltanschauung," note 8, p. 433.

6   Richard Rorty, "Taking Philosophy Seriously," *The New Republic* (April 11, 1988), pp. 32–3.

7   Ibid., p. 33.

8   Ibid., p. 34.

9   Ibid.

10 See Jeffrey Herf, *Reactionary Modernism: Technology, Culture, and Politics in Weimar and the Third Reich* (New York: Cambridge University Press, 1984). See also Zimmerman, *Heidegger's Confrontation with Modernity*, especially his discussion of the influence of Ernst Jünger on Heidegger.

11 Martin Heidegger, "Letter on Humanism," reprinted in *Martin Heidegger: Basic Writings*, ed. and trans. David F. Krell (New York: Harper and Row, 1977), *Über den Humanismus* (Frankfurt: Vittorio Klostermann, 1981). Page references to the "Letter on Humanism" are indicated by Humanism, followed by the English and German page numbers.

12 Martin Heidegger, *Die Selbstbehauptung der deutschen Universität. Rede, gehalten bei feierlichen Übernahme des Rektorats der Universität Freiburg l. Br. am 27.5.1933*, trans. Karsten Harries, "The Self-Assertion of the German University: Address, Delivered on the Solemn Assumption of the Rectorate of the University of Freiburg," *The Review of Metaphysics* 38 (March 1985). Harries' translation also includes "The Rectorate 1933/34: Facts and Thoughts."

13 Löwith, *Mein Leben in Deutschland vor und nach 1933*, p. 57.

14 Karsten Harries, "Heidegger as a Political Thinker," reprinted in Murray, ed., *Heidegger and Modern Philosophy*, p. 305.

15 See also Wolin, *The Politics of Being*.

16 Harries, "Heidegger as a Political Thinker," p. 306.

17 Ibid., pp. 319, 326.

18 The primary texts where Heidegger addresses the question about his Nazi involvement are: "The Rectorate 1933/34: Facts and Thoughts"; the posthumously published interview in *Der Spiegel* (1976), trans. William J. Richardson, SJ, "Only a God Can Save Us" in Thomas Sheehan, ed., *Heidegger: The Man and the Thinker* (Chicago: Precedent, 1981). See Heidegger's letter to the Chairman of the De-Nazification Committee at Freiburg University (1945); and Heidegger's request for reinstatement addressed to the Rector of Freiburg University. The German texts of these letters are reprinted in Karl A. Moehling, "Martin Heidegger and the Nazi Party," unpublished Ph.D. dissertation, Northern Illinois University, 1972. Heidegger also made misleading claims about the following controversial sentence included in the 1953 republication of his *Introduction to Metaphysics*:

> The stuff which is now being bandied about as the philosophy of National
> Socialism – but which has not the least to do with the inner truth and
> greatness of this movement (namely, the encounter between global tech-
> nology and modern man) – is casting its net in these troubled waters of
> "values" and "totalities."

Thomas Sheehan discusses Heidegger's comment on this passage in
"Heidegger and the Nazis," pp. 42–3. See Habermas' discussion in
"Work and Weltanschauung," pp. 451–2.

19   Bernard Williams, *Ethics and the Limits of Philosophy* (Cambridge, Mass.:
Harvard University Press, 1985), p. 1.

20   George Steiner, *Martin Heidegger* (Harmondsworth and New York:
Penguin, 1978), p. 123. See also Maurice Blanchot, "Thinking the
Apocalypse: A Letter from Maurice Blanchot to Catherine David,"
and Emmanuel Levinas, "As if Consenting to Horror." These texts are
translated and reprinted in *Critical Inquiry* 15 (1989), pp. 475–80;
485–8.

21   The periodization of Heidegger's thinking is a matter of controversy,
especially in regard to the so-called *Kehre*. In this context, when I speak
of Heidegger's late thinking I am referring to his post-World War II
writings.

22   Martin Heidegger, "The Age of the World-Picture," in *The Question Concerning Technology and Other Essays*, trans. William Lovitt (New York:
Harper and Row, 1977).

23   Martin Heidegger, "The Question Concerning Technology," reprinted
in Krell, ed., *Martin Heidegger: Basic Writings*, "Die Frage nach der
Technik" in *Vorträge und Aufsätze* (Pfullingen: Neske, 1985). Page
references to "The Question Concerning Technology," are indicated by
Technology, followed by the English and German page numbers.

24   It is not accidental that Heidegger introduces his discussion of the four
causes by using the Latin terms for these causes rather than the original Greek. This is also "correct." But Heidegger wants to show how
this Latin "translation" obscures and conceals the meaning of this fourfold causality thought "in a Greek way."

25   See "On the Essence of Truth" reprinted in *Martin Heidegger: Basic
Writings*.

26   See my essay, "Heidegger on Humanism," in Richard J. Bernstein,
Philosophical Profiles (Philadelphia: University of Pennsylvania, 1986).

27   Immanuel Kant, *Critique of Pure Reason*, trans. Norman Kemp Smith
(New York: MacMillan, 1964), p. 20.

28   See Fred Dallmayr's perceptive analysis of freedom in "Heidegger, The
Ontology of Freedom," *Political Theory* 12 (1984), pp. 205–34.

29   Martin Heidegger, "Overcoming Metaphysics," in *The End of Philosophy*,
trans. Joan Stambaugh (New York: Harper and Row, 1973), p. 87.

30   See *What is Called Thinking?*, trans. J. Glenn Gray (New York: Harper

and Row, 1968). See also *Discourse on Thinking*, trans. John M. Anderson and E. Hans Freund (New York: Harper and Row, 1966).

31 "Only a God Can Save Us," p. 57.

32 Aristotle, *Nicomachean Ethics*, trans. Terence Irwin (Indianapolis: Hackett, 1985), p. 151.

33 Ibid., p. 154.

34 I analyze this passage in detail in my essay, "Heidegger on Humanism." For a radically different and extremely thought-provoking interpretation of the consequences of Heidegger's texts for understanding politics and action, see Reiner Schürmann, *Heidegger on Being and Acting: From Principles to Anarchy* (Bloomington: Indiana University Press, 1987).

35 See Hannah Arendt, *The Human Condition* (Chicago: University of Chicago Press, 1958).

36 Jacques Taminiaux, "The Connection Between Heidegger's Fundamental Ontology and the Nazi Liability of 1933," unpublished paper presented as part of the conference "Heidegger and Practical Life" sponsored by the Greater Philadelphia Philosophy Consortium, March 18, 1989. Taminiaux's extremely perceptive paper is based in part on a reading of the still unpublished analysis of the *Nicomachean Ethics* developed by Heidegger in his 1924 course on Plato's *Sophist*.

37 Ibid., p. 22.

38 Ibid., p. 23.

39 See my discussion of Arendt and Gadamer on *phronēsis* and *praxis* in *Beyond Objectivism and Relativism: Science, Hermeneutics, and Praxis* (Philadelphia: University of Pennsylvania Press, 1983).

40 Hans-Georg Gadamer, "The Problem of Historical Consciousness," reprinted in Paul Rabinow and William Sullivan, eds., *Interpretive Social Science: A Reader* (Berkeley: University of California Press, 1979), p. 107.

41 Hans-Georg Gadamer, "Hermeneutics and Social Science," *Cultural Hermeneutics* 2 (1975), pp. 313–14.

42 "A Letter by Professor Hans-Georg Gadamer," in Bernstein, *Beyond Objectivism and Relativism*, p. 264.

43 Arendt, *The Human Condition*, p. 305.

44 For an analysis of what Arendt means by natality, see Patricia Bowen-Moore, *Hannah Arendt's Philosophy of Natality* (New York: St Martin's Press, 1989).

45 Jürgen Habermas, "Dogmatism, Reason, and Decision: On Theory and *Praxis* in our Scientific Civilization," in *Theory and Practice*, trans. John Viertel (Boston: Beacon, 1973), p. 255.

46 Sheehan, "Heidegger and the Nazis," p. 42.

47 This passage is cited by Sheehan, ibid. In his response to Heidegger's letter, Marcuse replied:

> You write that everything I say about the extermination of the Jews holds equally for the Allies, if instead of "Jew" we write "Eastern German."

With this sentence, do you not place yourself outside the realm in which a conversation among humans is possible at all – outside the logos? For only from fully beyond the "logical" dimension is it possible to explain, adjust, "comprehend" a crime by saying that others did the same thing too. More: how is it possible to place the torture, mutilation, and annihilation of millions of people on the same level as the forcible resettlement of groups in which none of these misdeeds has occurred (save perhaps in a few exceptional cases)?

Marcuse's letter is reprinted in *Pflasterstrand* (Frankfurt, Jan. 1988), p. 48–9.

48   "Ackerbau ist jetzt motorisierte Ernährungsindustrie, im Wesen das Selbe wie die Fabrikation von Leichen in Gaskammern und Vernichtungslagern, das Selbe wie die Blockade und Aushungerung von Ländern, das Selbe wie die Fabrikation von Wasserstoffbomben." Cited in Wolfgang Schirmacher, *Technik und Gelassenheit* (Freiburg: Alber, 1983), p. 25. This citation is from p. 25 of Heidegger's original typescript.

49   "Heidegger and the Nazis," p. 41.

50   See Lacoue-Labarthe's analysis of the passage from Heidegger's original lecture, *Heidegger, Art and Politics*, pp. 34ff. Although Lacoue-Labarthe claims that Heidegger's sentence is "scandalously inadequate" his reasoning is extremely involuted. Ironically, Lacoue-Labarthe fails to appreciate how close he is to Heidegger when he claims "In the Auschwitz apocalypse, it was nothing less than the West, in its essence, that revealed itself." Even though Heidegger does not say this, nevertheless this is entailed by his analysis of the destining of *Gestell*. For *Gestell* itself is a consequence of the metaphysical humanism that has been the *essence* of the West. When we focus our attention on the *essence* of technology then Heidegger would agree that "in the Auschwitz apocalypse, it was nothing less than the West, *in its essence*, that revealed itself."

51   See David F. Krell's discussion of *Ein Versagen des Denkens* (a failure of thinking) in "Heidegger's Rectification of the German University," unpublished manuscript.

52   Jack Caputo, "Heidegger's Scandal: Thinking and the Essence of the Victim," unpublished manuscript, p. 3. My own reading of "the deepest laws of Heideggerian discourse" is indebted to Caputo's analysis.

53   "Building Dwelling Thinking" in *Martin Heidegger: Basic Writings*, p. 339.

54   *Gelassenheit, Discourse on Thinking*, pp. 55–6.

55   Habermas, "Work and Weltanschauung," pp. 55–6. In 1953 when Habermas was still a student, he addressed the following questions to Heidegger – questions that Heidegger never answered:

Can even the planned mass murder of millions of people, about which all of us know today, be made understandable in terms of the history of

Being, as a fateful error? Is it not a factual crime of those who were responsible for carrying it out – and the bad conscience of an entire people? ("Zur Vernöffentlichung von Vorlesungen aus dem Jahre 1935," Frankfurt *Allgemeine Zeitung*, 25 July 1953.)

56 See Jean-François Lyotard, *Heidegger and "the jews,"* trans. Andreas Michel and Mark Roberts (Minneapolis: University of Minnesota Press, 1990). Lyotard is also critical of Lacoue-Labarthe's analysis of Heidegger and the Jews. Caputo puts the issue sharply when he asks, "is there not something deeply unsettling in a thinking which is anesthetized before unspeakable suffering, deaf to the cries of the victim?" ("Heidegger's Scandal," p. 19). Caputo's critique of Heidegger in this article shows the influence of Levinas and Lyotard. Caputo, like them, argues that "the victim is invisible in the history of Being, is not a matter of concern, is not what is at issue ... the victim has no voice in the call of Being, cannot speak, cannot be heard," p. 24.

57 Hans-Georg Gadamer, "Back from Syracuse?", *Critical Inquiry* 15 (1989), p. 429.

58 I fully agree with Caputo when he writes:

> the ethical has been "naturalized," not in the sense of naturalism or materialism, but rethought in terms of *physis*, of emerging into presence. The only *ēthos* which is permitted is a more essential, originary *ēthos*, an early Greek poetic *ēthos*, which dictates a more poetic mode of dwelling on the earth. There is no call of conscience, no response which says guilty, and so there are no victims. ("Heidegger's Scandal," p. 23)

59 Ibid.

5

Foucault
Critique as a Philosophic *Ēthos*

> Our age is, in especial degree, the age of criticism, and to criticism everything must submit.
>
> Kant, Preface to *The Critique of Pure Reason*

One of the last essays that Foucault wrote before his untimely death is a short text, "What is Enlightenment?"[1] It is a remarkable text – for many reasons. When we recall Foucault's sharp critique of Kant and the Kantian problematic in *The Order of Things*, it may seem surprising that he turns to a reading of Kant's famous essay, published in November 1784, in order to show the thread that connects his own work with the "type of philosophical interrogation" (p. 42) that Foucault claims Kant initiated. But as any close reader of Foucault knows, his writings are filled with surprises and novel twists. It is almost as if Foucault started each new project afresh, bracketing what he had written previously, constantly experimenting with new lines of inquiry. This is one reason why reading Foucault is so provocative, disconcerting, and frustrating. For just when we think we have grasped what Foucault is saying and showing, he seems to dart off in new directions (and even seems to delight in frustrating attempts to classify and fix what he is doing). But Foucault's essay is much more than a reflection on the question "What is Enlightenment?" and its relation to the "attitude of modernity." It is – in the classical sense – an *apologia*, a succinct statement and defense of his own critical project. It is also an *apologia* in the sense that Foucault seeks to answer (at least obliquely) the objections of many of his critics. During the last decade of his life Foucault was being pressed about the normative status of his own critical stance. It becomes clear that he is defending himself against what he calls the "blackmail" of the Enlightenment. Although he emphasizes the importance of Kant's text for defining a certain manner of philosophizing that is concerned with the present, one which also reflects on the *relation* of philosophizing to the present, this

> does not mean that one has to be "for" or "against" the Enlightenment. It even means precisely that one has to refuse everything that might present itself in the form of a simplistic and authoritarian alternative: you either accept the Enlightenment and remain within the tradition of its rationalism (this is considered a positive term by some and used by others, on the contrary, as a reproach); or else you criticize the Enlightenment and then try to escape from its principles of rationality (which may be seen once again as good or bad). And we do not break free of this blackmail by introducing "dialectical" nuances while seeking to determine what good and bad elements there may have been in the Enlightenment. (p. 43)

The last sentence is an allusion to the German tradition of critical theory, and specifically to Habermas. For perhaps the most formidable critic of Foucault is Habermas, for whom the question of critique and its normative foundations has been one of the central issues of his corpus.[2] Habermas, who acknowledges the insight and force of Foucault's brilliant critical analyses of modernity, nevertheless argues that Foucault "contrasts his critique of power with the 'analysis of truth' in such a fashion that the former becomes deprived of the normative yardsticks that it would have to borrow from the latter."[3] In short, Habermas thinks that Foucault's critical project – for all its insight – is nevertheless enmeshed in serious "performative contradictions." But from Foucault's perspective, Habermas – like others who develop similar lines of argument – is engaged in Enlightenment blackmail.

The question that I want to probe here is: what does Foucault mean by critique, especially when he speaks of an attitude – "a philosophical ethos that could be described as a permanent critique of our historical era" (p. 42). I want to focus on what precisely is *critical* in this "permanent critique." This question is not only crucial for understanding Foucault but has a much more general significance. For the question of critique – especially a critique of the present historical era – has become one of the most important issues of our time. To use a Wittgensteinian expression, the very "grammar" of critique seems to presuppose some measure or standard, some basis for critique. And yet there has been so much skepticism about any and all appeals to standards and "foundations" that one is compelled to reflect on the very intelligibility of the concept of critique. The issue is especially poignant in regard to Foucault because he has been read as calling into question and undermining any privileged discourse or "position" from which we can engage in critique. For Foucault, talk about "normative foundations" elicits "normalization," which he takes to be one of the primary dangers of the "disciplinary society." To phrase it in a slightly different way, we want to know whether it makes sense to speak of critique without implicitly or explicitly presupposing some "basis" for the critique – a "basis" which in *some* sense is defended, warranted or affirmed. Foucault's critics argue that his concept of critique is confused and/ or incoherent. Yet Foucault and many of his defenders appear to claim that Foucault has developed a new type of critical stance that does *not* implicitly or explicitly appeal to any basis, ground, or normative foundations.

The question of the status, character, and meaning of critique has already received a great deal of attention both by critics and defenders of Foucault. Much of the recent prolific literature on his thought has gravitated toward "an effort to think through the practical or political consequences of Foucault's genre of critical thinking."[4] But what precisely is this "genre of critical thinking"? To answer this question I will proceed in three stages. First, I want to highlight some of Foucault's key claims in "What is Enlightenment?" as they pertain to the question of critique. Secondly, I want to consider the strong case that has been made against Foucault, one that seeks to expose his confusions, contradictions, and incoherence. Thirdly, I will consider the ways in which Foucault and his defenders have sought to defuse and answer these objections. Proceeding in this manner will enable me to return to the question: what is this "philosophical ethos that could be described as a permanent critique of our historical era"?

What is Enlightenment?

Foucault begins his essay with a thought-experiment. "Let us imagine that the *Berlinische Monatschrift* still exists and that it is asking its readers the question: what is modern philosophy? Perhaps we could respond with an echo: modern philosophy is the philosophy that is attempting to answer the question raised so imprudently two centuries ago: *Was ist Aufklärung?*" (p. 32). According to Foucault, this is the question that philosophers have been confronting ever since Kant, "a question which modern philosophy has not been capable of answering and yet which it has never managed to get rid of, either" (p. 32). Foucault claims that Kant confronted this question in a novel way, that he initiated a new way of thinking about philosophy and its relation to its historical present. For Kant, the *Aufklärung*

> is neither a world era to which one belongs, nor an event whose signs are perceived, nor the dawning of an accomplishment. Kant defines *Aufklärung* in an almost entirely negative way, as an *Ausgang*, an "exit," a "way out." He is not seeking to understand the present on the basis of a totality or a future achievement. He is looking for a difference: what difference does today introduce with respect to yesterday? (p. 34)

Foucault is already anticipating the thread that connects him with Kant. For Foucault's experiments with writing a "history of the present" are directed to highlighting what is different in the present without any appeal to a "totality or a future achievement." He ruthlessly excludes any appeal to teleology or the progressive development of history. Foucault tells us that Kant thinks of *Aufklärung* as a "way out," but this doesn't mean we have any basis for hope or looking forward to a future achievement that will redeem us. *Aufklärung* is a process, a task, an obligation that releases us from immaturity — an immature status for which man himself is responsible. Enlightenment means achieving *Mündigkeit*. Enlightenment is "the moment when humanity is going to put its own reason to use, without subjecting itself to any authority .... And it is precisely at this moment that the critique is necessary, since its role is that of defining the conditions under which the use of reason is legitimate in order to determine what can be known, what must be done, and what may be hoped" (p. 38).[5]

But if we are to understand how Kant's text is located "at the crossroads of critical reflection and reflection on history" (p. 38), then we need to examine the other key term that Foucault introduces in his thought-experiment – "modernity." Foucault disclaims any attempt to give a full-scale analysis of modernity or Enlightenment. Nevertheless, drawing upon Baudelaire, Foucault tells us that "modernity" is not primarily a term for denoting a period or epoch of history. Rather he wants to speak of modernity as an attitude, "a mode of relating to contemporary reality," an *ēthos*. It is "a mode of relating to contemporary historical reality where there is an ironic heroization of the present" (p. 40). "For the attitude of modernity, the high value of the present is indissociable from a desperate eagerness to imagine it, to imagine it otherwise than it is, and to transform it not by destroying it but by grasping it in what it is" (p. 41). Summing up, Foucault tells us: "Modern man, for Baudelaire, is not man who goes off to discover himself, his secrets and his hidden truth; he is the man who tries to invent himself. This modernity does not 'liberate man in his own being'; it compels him to face the task of producing himself" (p. 42).

Here too Foucault is at once anticipating and defending his own attitude to the present, his own *ēthos*. For Foucault relentlessly and scathingly attacks the very idea that human beings have some hidden essence which we can presumably discover and which, once revealed, enables us to achieve freedom and autonomy. There is *no* hidden essence to be discovered, there is no hidden *depth* revealing what we truly are, there is only the task of producing or inventing ourselves. This is what Foucault calls "ethics" in his late writings.

It is these converging reflections on Enlightenment and modernity that provide the background for Foucault's central claim that Kant initiated a new type of philosophical interrogation, "one that simultaneously problematizes man's relation to the present, man's historical mode of being, and the constitution of the self as an autonomous subject" (p. 42). The legacy of Kant that Foucault stresses "is not faithfulness to doctrinal elements, but rather the permanent reactivation of an attitude – that is, of a philosophical ethos that could be described as a permanent critique of our historical era" (p. 42).

In order to characterize this *ēthos*, Foucault first gives a negative characterization stressing two points. The first, I have already anticipated. For this permanent reactivation means a refusal of Enlightenment blackmail, a refusal of getting trapped in declaring oneself to be "for" or "against" the Enlightenment. The second point is to distinguish sharply between Enlightenment and humanism. Throughout his writings Foucault has always set himself against humanism (although the meaning of "humanism" and the precise target of Foucault's attack changes in the course of his writing).[6] In this context however, by "humanism" Foucault means a set of themes that reappear in the most diverse contexts ranging from Christian humanism to Nazi humanism where there is an unexamined reliance on dubious conceptions of man "borrowed from religion, science, or politics" (p. 44). Enlightenment must not be confused with humanism. Indeed, Foucault's point is even stronger: Enlightenment as a principle of critique and a permanent creation of ourselves is *opposed* to humanism.

But still, even if we are careful about avoiding Enlightenment blackmail and sharply distinguishing Enlightenment from humanism, we need a "positive" characterization of this philosophic *ēthos* of critique of the historical present. It is at this point in Foucault's own "little text" that we can most clearly discern the sense in which it can be read as an *apologia*. Foucault begins his positive characterization by telling us that this philosophic *ēthos* is a "limit-attitude." This, of course, has Kantian resonances. But here Foucault sharply distinguishes his understanding of a "limit-attitude" from Kant's view. In a succinct but dense passage, Foucault gives one of the most complete statements of what he means by critique.

criticism is no longer going to be practiced in the search for formal structures with universal value, but rather as a historical investigation into events that have led us to constitute ourselves and to recognize ourselves as subjects of what we are doing, thinking, saying. In that sense criticism is not transcendental, and its goal is not that of making metaphysics possible: it is genealogical in its design and archaeological in its method. Archaeological – and not transcendental – in the sense that it will not seek to identify the universal structures of all knowledge or of all possible moral action, but will seek to treat the instances of discourse that articulate what we think, say, and do as so many historical events. And this critique will be genealogical in the sense that it will not deduce from the form of what we are what is impossible for us to do and to know; but it will separate out, from the contingency that has made us what we are, the possibility of no longer being, doing, thinking what we are, do, or think. It is not seeking to make possible a metaphysics that has finally become a science; it is seeking to give new impetus, as far and wide as possible, to the undefined work of freedom. (p. 46)[7]

Such a "historical-critical attitude must also be an experimental one" and it must be local and specific – always pressing specific limits in order to grasp "the points where change is possible and desirable, and to determine the precise form this change should take" (p. 46). Anticipating the objection that he is caught within a self-referential inconsistency, Foucault tells us we have "to give up hope of our ever acceding to any complete and definitive knowledge of what may constitute our historical limits" (p. 47). The possibility of moving beyond these limits is always itself limited. This is why we are always in the position of beginning again. This is why a critique of the present requires *permanent reactivation*.

Foucault reiterates his main points and indicates his affinity with Kant's interrogation when he declares:

The critical ontology of ourselves has to be considered not, certainly, as a theory, a doctrine, nor even as a permanent body of knowledge that is accumulating; it has to be conceived as an attitude, an ethos, a philosophic life in which the critique of what we are is at one and the same time the historical analysis of the limits that are imposed on us and an experiment with the possibility of going beyond them. (p. 50)[8]

The case against Foucault

Now the problem or rather the cluster of problems that has drawn the fire of some of Foucault's sharpest critics is already suggested in this last passage. For Foucault tells us that "the critique of what we are is at one and the same time the historical analysis of the limits that are imposed on us and an experiment with the possibility of going beyond them." But precisely how are these "moments" inter-related? In what ways are Foucault's "interpretive analytics"[9] critical? To sharpen the relevant issues, I want to consider how three critics have pressed their objections to show that Foucault's understanding of critique is confused, incoherent or contradictory. All three acknowledge the incisiveness of Foucault's historical analyses for interpreting modernity, but each seeks to locate what they take to be serious confusions/contradictions.

The title of Nancy Fraser's paper, "Foucault on Modern Power: Empirical Insights and Normative Confusions," indicates the problem she is concerned with.[10] Fraser gives a sympathetic account of Foucault's genealogical method, showing how he seeks to bracket questions concerning legitimacy or normative validity, and how his novel analysis of power, especially modern bio-power, problematizes modernity and even has important political implications.[11] But the problem she locates is: how can we reconcile Foucault's attempt to suspend *all* questions of "normative foundations" with his engaged critique of bio-power? Her conclusion, after working through several unsuccessful possibilities for reconciling these tensions, is that Foucault vacillates between two equally inadequate stances.

> On the one hand, he adopts a concept of power which permits him no condemnation of any objectionable features of modernity. But at the same time, and on the other hand, his rhetoric betrays the conviction that modernity is utterly without redeeming features. Clearly what Foucault needs and needs desperately are normative criteria for distinguishing acceptable from unacceptable forms of power. As it stands now, the unquestionably original and valuable dimensions of his work stand in danger of being misunderstood for lack of an adequate normative perspective.[12]

Fraser never defines what she means by "normative" or even what an "adequate normative perspective" might look like. Care is needed here because "normative" is a term of art that suggests to many some sort of permanent ahistorical universal standards of evaluation. And it is clear that Foucault rejects any such standards. But we can drop the explicit reference to normative standards or foundations and still see the force of Fraser's critique. For she notes that "Foucault calls in no uncertain terms for resistance to domination. But why? Why is struggle preferable to submission? Why ought domination to be resisted?"[13]

It is clear from the way in which Charles Taylor begins his article on Foucault that he is concerned with a problem similar to the one posed by Fraser. For he says certain of Foucault's most interesting historical analyses, while they are highly original, seem to lie along already familiar lines of critical thought. That is, they seem to offer an insight into what has happened, and into what we have become, which at the same time offers a critique, and hence some notion of a good unrealized or repressed in history, which we therefore understand better how to rescue.[14]

Taylor suggests that one might think there are two goods which need rescuing: freedom and truth. These two goods are deeply linked because "the negation of one (domination) makes essential use of the negation of the other (disguise)."[15] But as Taylor notes, "Foucault himself repudiates this suggestion. He dashes the hope, if we had one, that there is some good we can affirm, as a result of the understanding these analyses give us."[16]

In short, what Taylor is claiming is that the force – and indeed the intelligibility of Foucault's "genre" of critique – seems at once to affirm some good and repudiates any appeal to such a good. Unlike Fraser, who takes a more agnostic stance on the question of whether it is possible to supply an "adequate normative perspective" that is compatible with Foucault's "empirical insights," Taylor claims that Foucault's unstable position is "ultimately incoherent."[17]

Taylor seeks to justify this charge by sketching three successive analyses of Foucault, each of which is progressively more radical in the sense that, while each may initially lead us to think that Foucault is affirming some good, the final consequence to be drawn is that there is no such good to be affirmed. The first analysis (taken from *Discipline and Punish*) opposes the classical liturgical idea of punishment to the modern "humanitarian one," but refuses to value the second over the first because "humanitarianism" is seen as a growing system of discipline and control. The second anlysis seems to give "an *evaluational* reason for refusing the evaluation which issues from the first analysis."[18] Foucault calls into question the very idea that we have a hidden nature which is being controlled and repressed. The ideology of "expressive liberation" turns out to be just a strategy of disciplinary power. This might lead us to think that we need to be liberated from *this* illusion; a liberation which is "helped by our unmasking falsehood; a liberation aided by the truth."[19] This is the third analysis. But according to Taylor, Foucault refuses this value position as well. He refuses to affirm the goods of freedom and truth. This is what Taylor calls Foucault's Nietzschean stance – and it is incoherent. Why? Because, Taylor claims, " 'power' belongs in a semantic field from which 'truth' and 'freedom' cannot be excluded."[20] The very concept of power, even in Foucault's refor-mulation, does not make sense unless there is at least an implicit appeal to liberation from dominating forms of power. Furthermore it requires an appeal to "truth" because the imposition of control "proceeds by foisting illusion upon us; it proceeds by disguises and masks." Consequently Foucault's critical stance is incoherent because

> The Foucauldian notion of power not only requires for its sense the correlative notions of truth and liberation, but even the standard link between them, which makes truth the condition of liberation. And yet Foucault not only refuses to acknowledge this, but appears to under-mine anything except an ironical appeal to "freedom" and "truth."[21]

Fraser and Taylor limit themselves primarily to what they take to be the "confusions/contradictions" in Foucault's critique of modern forms of bio-power. But Habermas in his *Philosophical Discourse of Modernity* is much more ambitious. He seeks to give a recon-struction of Foucault's intellectual development from *Madness and Civilization* to the first volume of *The History of Sexuality*. It is a rich and broad canvas on which Habermas wants to show that, despite the twists and turns of Foucault's development, he is trapped within the *aporias* of the "philosophy of the subject" that is now reaching exhaustion. But for my purposes I want to highlight only those aspects of Habermas' analysis that bear on the question of critique. I have already indicated the central theme – one which is a variation of the theme developed by Fraser and Taylor. It is the claim that Foucault contrasts his critique of power with the "analysis of truth in such a manner that the former becomes deprived of the normative yardsticks that it would have to borrow from the latter." Fleshing out what Habermas means, we can say that Habermas accuses Foucault of sliding down the slippery slope of "totalizing critique." Critique – even genealogical critique – must preserve at least one standard by which we engage in the critique of the present. Yet when critique is *totalized*, when critique turns against itself so that all rational standards are called into question, then one is caught in a perfor-mative contradiction.[22]

"Genealogy" according to Habermas "is overtaken by a fate simi-lar to that which Foucault had seen in the human sciences."

To the extent that it retreats into the reflectionless objectivity of a nonparticipatory, ascetic description of kaleidoscopically changing practices of power, genealogical historiography emerges from its cocoon as precisely the *presentistic, relativistic, cryptonormative* illusory science that it does not want to be.[23]

Let me explain what Habermas means. By "presentistic" Habermas is referring to the "felicitous positivistic" stance that Foucault claimed for himself in describing the contingent power/knowledge regimes. This is the "cool façade of a radical historicism."[24] But this stance requires withholding or bracketing any evaluative judgment of the kaleidoscopically changing practices. Such pure "ascetic description" leads to relativism in the sense that there is no basis or position from which one can evaluate or judge this passing array of power/knowledge regimes. It is like adopting the panoptical gaze. But Foucault does not consistently assume such a "position," nor is it even possible. He exhibits "the passions of aesthetic modernism."[25] He assumes a position of "arbitrary *partisanship* of a criticism that cannot account for its normative foundations."[26] Foucault, Habermas claims, is "incorruptible enough to admit these incoherences," but this doesn't mean that he escapes from them.[27]

Although Fraser, Taylor, and Habermas differ in their lines of attack, the cumulative force of their criticisms is to show that Foucault's understanding of a philosophic *ēthos* as "a permanent critique of our historical era" is confused, incoherent and enmeshed in performative contradictions.

Enlightenment blackmail?

Now the question arises: is this Enlightenment blackmail? Are Foucault's critics forcing him into a grid that distorts his critical project? Are they wedded to a set of distinctions and binary oppositions, e.g., normative/empirical, liberation/domination, universal/relative, rational/irrational, that Foucault subverts? Foucault himself suggests that this is so, and this is precisely what many of Foucault's defenders have claimed. Indeed if we juxtapose the "portrait" of Foucault sketched by his critics with what Foucault says in "What is Enlightenment?" we are struck by glaring disparities. Foucault doesn't defend a stance of "felicitous positivism," he defends the permanent reactivation of critique of our historical era. He shows his awareness that a "limit-attitude" is itself always limited. He doesn't bracket the question of freedom and liberation. He even speaks of the need "to grasp the points where change is possible and desirable, and to determine the precise form this change should take" (p. 46). Now, of course, many responses are possible to these discrepancies between what Foucault says and the charges his critics bring against him: he is changing his mind once again, he is adopting a more conciliatory tone, he is rewriting his own history, he is making claims that contradict what he says in other places, etc. But we might also entertain the possibility that something has gone wrong here. Perhaps we can give a different, more sympathetic reading of what Foucault is doing that makes sense of his genre of critique and escapes from the harsh criticisms of those who claim his position is incoherent. This is the possibility that I want to explore by probing a number of interrelated themes in his work. In each case I want to show how they enable us to get a better grasp of his critical intent – and yet still leave us with difficult unresolved problems.

The Rhetoric of Disruption   Throughout his writings Foucault not only returns again and again to the multiple uses of language, he is himself an extraordinary and skillful rhetorician. The question arises, to what end or purpose does he use rhetoric and how does it work? The answer is complex. But the main point is nicely brought out by William Connolly when he says, "The rhetorical figures, to use a phrase of Nietzsche's, incite us to 'listen to a different claim' rather than to accept the findings of an argument."[28] In part, Foucault seeks to break and disrupt the discourse that has preoccupied so much of modern philosophy, a discourse in which we have become obsessed with epistemological issues and questions of normative foundations. And he does this because he wants to show us that such a preoccupation distracts us and even blinds us from asking new kinds of questions about the genesis of social practices that are always shaping us and historically limiting what we are. Foucault deploys "rhetorical devices to incite the experience of discord or discrepancy between the social construction of self, truth, and rationality and that which does not fit neatly within their folds."[29] He seeks "to *excite* in the reader the experience of discord between the social construction of normality and that which does not fit neatly within the frame of these constructs."[30] In this respect we can draw parallels with Nietzsche's multiple style, and also with that other great skeptical gadfly, Socrates, who also sought to disrupt the conventional and comforting convictions of his interlocutors. Viewed in this way, we can make sense of Foucault's attraction to metaphors of strategy and tactics. It is this rhetoric of disruption that is the source of Foucault's critical sting. There are even those, like Dreyfus and Rabinow, who claim that "Foucault uses language to articulate an understanding of our situation which moves us to action."[31] (Later I want to return to this claim.) But how does Foucault *do* this? How do his rhetorical strategies work?

A full-scale answer would have to examine his own micro- and macropractices, i.e. his *specific* use of rhetorical devices and figures as well as the way in which he carefully crafts his works.

> The Foucauldian rhetorical strategy works, for instance, through displacement of ... unifying or mellow metaphors by more disturbing ones; and by conversion of noun forms giving solidity to modern conceptions of truth, subject, and normality into verbs that present them as constructions; and by the posing of questions left unanswered in the text; and by the introduction of sentence fragments that communicate even though they do not fit into the conventional form that gives primacy to the subject.[32]

We can even grasp Foucault's use of that favored rhetorical device of Nietzsche – hyperbole. One might think, for example, that Foucault is heralding the death of the subject, that he is claiming that the subject itself is *only* the result of the effects of power/knowledge regimes, that he completely undermines and ridicules any and all talk of human agency. There is plenty of textual evidence to support such claims. But it is also clear, especially in his late writings when he deals with the question of the self's relation to itself and the possibility of "the man who tries to invent himself," that he is not abandoning the idea that "we constitute ourselves as subjects acting on others."[33]

Or again, especially in his essays in *Power/Knowledge*, it looks as if Foucault is abandoning any appeal to "truth" or reducing truth to a mere effect of power/knowledge regimes. But Foucault also sharply criticizes the polemicist who "proceeds encased in privileges that he possesses in advance" and refuses to recognize his adversary as "a subject having the right to speak." The polemicist objective "will be, not to come as close as possible to a difficult *truth*, but to bring about the triumph of the just cause he has been manifestly upholding from the beginning" (emphasis added).[34]

Or still again, for all of Foucault's skepticism about expressive notions of freedom and liberty, we have seen that in "What is Enlightenment?" he claims his type of critique "is seeking to give new impetus, as far and wide as possible, to the undefined work of freedom."

Now instead of claiming that Foucault is flatly contradicting himself on the question of the subject, truth, and freedom, we can read him in a different way – as deliberately using hyperbolic rhetorical constructions in order to compel us to disrupt and question our traditional *understandings* of these key concepts. And he effectively does this by showing us the dark ambiguities in the construction of these concepts and the role they have played in social practices.[35]

Now I think it is correct to read Foucault in this way. It enables us to understand the critical sting of his writings – a critical sting that results from disrupting cherished convictions and raising new sorts of questions about the historical contingencies that shape our practices. But there are problems that arise when we seek to think through how the Foucauldian rhetoric of disruption works. Let me illustrate this by considering an example of the macro-rhetorical level of his works. Here we can review the analyses that Taylor gave in order to expose Foucault's incoherence.

When Foucault begins *Discipline and Punish* with the detailed, graphic execution of Damiens (which he immediately juxtaposes with the timetable drawn up eighty years later in the rules "for the House of young prisoners in Paris"), it is a stunning rhetorical device for eliciting conflicting disruptive reactions in the reader.[36] For Foucault knows the reader will react with a sense of horror to what initially *appears* to be the barbaric spectacle of gratuitous torture. We are seduced in taking comfort in the realization that "our" methods of punishment – whatever their defects – are much more humane – even though a doubt may be planted by the perplexing juxtaposition of the timetable. It is only gradually that our confidence begins to be undermined as we see what the process of "humanization" involves. For we come to see how "the birth of the prison" is virtually an allegory for the birth of the disciplinary society – the panoptic society of surveillance that makes such effective use of the disciplines that control our bodies. So we might say that the rhetorical power of his analysis depends upon skillfully eliciting and at the same time undermining the evaluative reactions of the reader. And as we react in horror against what strikes us as so constraining and repressive about the disciplinary society, we are tempted to think there is some good here that is being repressed and needs to be liberated, expressed, and affirmed. But again this elicits in us the expectation of some positive theory of liberation from domination and repression.

Foucault has set us up for the critical analysis of *The History of Sexuality* – an analysis which is not simply restricted to the historical genesis of contemporary discourses of sexuality, but seeks to show us that standard understandings of the dynamics of liberation and repression are distortive and misleading. He also seeks to show us that the will to know the "truth" about ourselves turns out to be a "specific form of extortion of truth," the invention of specific types of discourse that do not liberate us from repression but rather subject us to a new, more subtle control of our bodies. And this analysis leaves us again in an ambiguous situation. For to the extent that we accept Foucault's unmasking of the "repressive hypothesis," we are compelled to question traditional narratives of liberation and domination. We are compelled to rethink what these concepts mean. Foucault – as he so frequently does at the end of his books – ironically tantalizes us with new possibilities.

> Moreover, we need to consider the possibility that one day, perhaps, in a different economy of bodies and pleasures, people will no longer quite understand how the ruses of sexuality, and the power that sustains its organization, were able to subject us to that austere monarchy of sex, so that we became dedicated to the endless task of forcing its secret, or exacting the truest of confessions from a shadow.[37]

Now the point that I want to emphasize is that Foucault's rhetoric of disruption "works" because it at once presupposes and challenges an ethical-political horizon. He deliberately seeks to elicit conflicting responses in us, exposing fractures in "our" most cherished convictions and comforting beliefs. I speak of an "ethical-political *horizon*," because this horizon keeps receding. Foucault never quite thematizes this ethical-political perspective and yet it is always presupposed. Without it the rhetoric of disruption would not work. One may well be skeptical of any talk of ahistorical normative standards. But this does not make the question of what one is "for" or "against" disappear. The rhetoric of disruption and genealogical critique does not escape from the implicit affirmation of some "good," some ethical-political valorization. Even the rhetorical sting of the analyses in *The History of Sexuality* depends upon our revulsion against the idea that the will to knowledge exhibited in contemporary discourses of sexuality does not liberate us from repression but rather furthers the normalization of our docile bodies; these discourses are new techniques of control. Even if one thinks that *philosophic* attempts to face this issue have led us into dead-ends, one can't escape the question, what is it that we are *affirming* – and why do "we" affirm it? One can only go so far in clarifying what is distinctive about this new genre of critique by employing the devices of negative theology – stating what it is *not*. Foucault is a master in using these devices.[38] But the more effective he is in employing them, the greater becomes the urgency to give a positive characterization of the ethical-political perspective that informs his critique and enables his rhetoric of disruption to work. This is the issue that Foucault never squarely and unambiguously confronts.

Dangers   In 1983, Foucault was interviewed about his work in progress on the genealogy of ethics. He was asked, "do you think that the Greeks offer an attractive and plausible alternative?" Foucault answered emphatically:

> No! I am not looking for an alternative; you can't find the solution of a problem in the solution of another problem raised at another moment by other people. You see, what I want to do is not the history of solutions, and that's the reason why I don't accept the word *alternative*. I would like to do the genealogy of problems, of *problématiques*. My point is not that everything is bad, but that everything is dangerous, which is not exactly the same as bad. If everything is dangerous, then we always have something to do.[39]

This claim is not only applicable to Foucault's late work in progress concerning the genealogy of ethics, but is relevant to all his genealogical studies – and it is a theme running through all his work. His archaeological-genealogical analyses of *problématiques* are intended to specify the changing constellation of *dangers*. This is what critique as a philosophic *ēthos* is intended to expose. And this theme has been highlighted by many of Foucault's defenders. Thus Dreyfus and

Rabinow assert: "His aim has never been to denounce power *per se* nor to propound truth but to use his analysis to shed light on the specific dangers that each specific type of power/knowledge produces."[40] Or again, they tell us: "Nor did he consider it his main task to offer alternative possibilities for acting. He was simply trying to diagnose *the* contemporary danger" (emphasis added).[41] David Hiley also stresses the danger theme when he says: "Yet while everything may be thought to be dangerous, he nevertheless believed that there was something uniquely dangerous about modernity."[42] What is uniquely dangerous is "the fact that everything becomes a target for normalization."[43]

Now initially this does seem to be an attractive and illuminating way of understanding Foucault. And again it does accord with the stance he takes in his genealogical critical analyses. If one wants to speak of alternatives, the first task is to grasp the dangers we confront. But when we think out this concept of danger we also face some hard problems. For we might say that the very notion of danger is itself *value-laden* – dangers for whom? Dangers from whose perspective? Why are these dangers "dangerous"? There is something comparable to an interpretative or hermeneutical circle here. For the very specification of what are taken to be dangers or the unique dangers of modernity itself only makes sense from an interpretative perspective – one which involves an *evaluation* of our situation, not just a "neutral" description but an evaluative description. After all there are conflicting and perhaps even incommensurable claims about what are the specific dangers of modernity. Think, for example, of Heidegger's very different interpretation of the "supreme danger" we confront – the danger that arises from *Gestell*, enframing: "thus where enframing reigns, there is *danger* in the highest sense."[44] So the talk of "dangers" or being responsive to what is intolerable only shifts the question to the adequacy or perspicuity of the evaluative-interpretative perspective from which one specifies dangers. This is why it is simply evasive or begging the question to say, as Dreyfus and Rabinow do, "What makes one interpretative theory better than another on this view has yet to be worked out, but it has to do with articulating common concerns and finding a language which becomes accepted as a way of talking about social situations, while leaving open the possibility of 'dialogue', or better, a conflict of interpretations, with other shared discursive practices used to articulate different concerns."[45] What are these "common concerns"? Do they include common *evaluations* of dangers? Who shares these common concerns? Here too I think there is danger of failing to see that what gets pushed out the front door is smuggled in through the back door. One might say that "quite consistent with his interpretative stance, Foucault ... has abandoned the attempt to legitimate social organization by means of philosophical grounding" and that he refuses "to articulate normative principles."[46] But we still want to understand what makes something dangerous – or if everything is dangerous, what it is that makes some dangers more intolerable than others. Here too there is an evaluative ethical-political bias that is operative and indeed is the basis for the very intelligibility of the talk of dangers that never becomes fully explicit or thematized.

Specificity and subjugated knowledges   It may be objected that to speak of an "ethical-political" perspective that is at once presupposed and secreted by Foucault's interpretative analyses is itself misleading. For it invites us to think in the very global terms that Foucault wants to avoid. Indeed it may be argued that we can grasp the point of Foucault's genre of critique only when we fully appreciate his extreme nominalism and his insistence on specificity.[47] Despite what at times has the ring of global claims about discourses, social practices, power/knowledge regimes, Foucault is always directing our attention to what is local, specific, and historically contingent. He emphasizes this over and over again when seeking to explicate what he means by a philosophical *ēthos* as "a permanent critique of our historical era." Insofar as such a critique is directed to opening new possibilities for thinking, acting, and grasping the points where change is possible and desirable, then it must be appropriated by those who have been marginalized and subjected. In short, all effective criticism must be *local*. This theme dovetails with Foucault's claim about the changing role of the intellectual and with Foucault's deep aversion to the "inhibiting effect of global, *totalitarian theories*."[48] He tells us "in contrast to the various projects which aim to inscribe knowledges in the hierarchical order of power associated with science, genealogy should be seen as a kind of attempt to emancipate historical knowledge from that subjection, to render them, that is, capable of opposition and of struggle against the coercion of a theoretical, unitary, formal and scientific discourse."[49] Once again I think there is something important about this emphasis in Foucault, although it also raises some hard problems.

One of the many good reasons why Foucault's rhetoric of disruption is so effective and has been so fertile for novel researches is because he at once captures and shapes a pervasive mood (*Stimmung*) of our time. He is not only a master of revealing the dark constraining side of the "humane" practices that shape our lives and our bodies, he is always showing us how discursive practices exclude, marginalize, and limit us.[50] He develops devastating critiques of global solutions to specific problems and exposes the treacherous ambiguities of loose talk about total revolution. We live in a time when it appears that only specific types of resistance, opposition, and revolt seem to make any sense. Contrary to that reading of Foucault which exaggerates the strain in Foucault that shows how what we are, do and think is *only* the precipitate or result of anonymous historically contingent practices, Foucault can be read as always seeking to expose instabilities, points of resistances, places where counter-discourses can arise and effect transgressions and change. It is the nexus of specific limits and transgressions that is his primary concern. Nevertheless, even if we stick to the specific and local – to the *insurrection of subjected knowledges* – there is an implicit valorization here that never quite becomes fully explicit, and yet is crucial for Foucault's genre of critique.[51] For there are the subjected knowledges of women, Blacks, prisoners, gays, who have experienced the pain and suffering of exclusion. But throughout the world there are also the subjected knowledges of all sorts of fundamentalists, fanatics, terrorists, who have their own sense of what are the unique or most important dangers to be confronted. What is never quite clear in Foucault is why anyone should favor certain local forms of resistance rather than others. Nor is it clear why one would "choose" one side or the other in a localized resistance or revolt.

Foucault insists: "where there is power, there is resistance."[52] The existence of power relationships "depends on a multiplicity of points of resistance; these play the role of adversary, target, support, or handle in power relations."[53] But "adversary" and "target" are reversible and symmetrical – in the sense that A is B's adversary or target, B may be A's adversary or target. But when we transfer this way of speaking and place it within the context of the type of power relations that Foucault analyzes, we are compelled to face the evaluative question: which point of resistance is to be favored? By whom? And why? This is why the claim that Foucault's rhetoric is intended to incite us to action is so unsatisfactory. For it is never clear – even in a specific local situation – how one is to act and why. So the appeal to specificity and locality doesn't help us to elucidate the ethical-political question of how one is to act. It only relocates this issue on a specific and local level.[54]

Freedom and Skepticism   "Foucault is the great skeptic of our times. He is skeptical about dogmatic unities and philosophical anthropologies. He is the philosopher of dispersion and singularity." "To question the self-evidence of a form of experience, knowledge, or power, is to free it for our purposes, to open new possibilities for thought or action. Such freedom is the ethical principle of Foucault's skepticism."[55] This line of interpretation, this reading of Foucault, is extremely appealing and it has been developed in different ways by commentators on Foucault who seek to defend him against "Enlightenment blackmail." Foucault does seem to be working in a tradition that has analogies and parallels with Sextus Empiricus and the Pyrrhonian skeptics. This is even another reason why Foucault is at once so provocative and disconcerting. For his distinctive strength is in a radical questioning and a withholding and suspending of judgment. Nothing is to be taken for granted – not even our predisposition to demand that a thinker must "take a position." David Hiley is right when he argues that we misunderstand the tradition of skepticism and Foucault's own skeptical stance if we fail to realize that it is an ethical stance.[56] For it is only by viewing it in this manner that we can appreciate the relationship between skepticism and freedom. Freedom then is not to be understood as the liberation of some human essence that is repressed, or the affirmation and actualization of some good that is locked up in what we "essentially" are. Freedom is a type of detachment or suspension of judgment that opens new possibilities for thought and action. This does accord with the theme in "What is Enlightenment?" that *Aufklärung* is an *Ausgang*, an exit, or way out, and with Foucault's claim that the critique of what we are is at one and the same time the historical analysis of the limits imposed on us and an experiment with the possibility of going beyond them. But skeptical freedom, as Hegel so brilliantly showed in the *Phenomenology of Spirit*, is radically unstable. It is always in danger of becoming merely abstract, i.e., it "ends up with the bare abstraction of nothingness or emptiness and cannot get any further from there, but must wait to see whether something new comes along and what it is, in order to throw it too into the empty abyss."[57] We can see how the radical instability of skepticism shows up in Foucault. For Foucault is not simply adopting a position of detachment and skeptical suspension of judgment. He is constantly tempting us with his references to new possibilities of thinking and acting, of giving new impetus to the undefined work of freedom, of the need to grasp the points where change is possible and desirable, and of determining the precise form this change should take. But the problem is that these references to new possibilities and changes that are desirable are in danger of becoming empty and vacuous unless we have some sense of which possibilities and changes are *desirable* – and why. We can accept Foucault's claim that a permanent reactivation of the philosophical *ēthos* of critique does not require the critic to lay out blueprints for the future, or "alternatives." Foucault himself is in that tradition which stresses that the primary function of the critic is to analyze the present and to reveal its fractures and instabilities, the ways in which it at once limits us and points to the transgression of these limits. But we must be extremely wary of sliding from references to new possibilities of thinking, acting, and being to a *positive* evaluation of such possibilities.

No one has revealed the dark possibilities that can erupt in history better than Foucault. So the same type of problem that we encountered before arises again here. Foucault's rhetoric, even the attraction of the distinctive type of skeptical freedom he adumbrates, the appeal of "the possibility of no longer being, doing, or thinking what we are, do, think" is itself dependent or parasitic upon an ethical-political valorization. What does it even mean to say that some possibilities are desirable? Without thematizing this question it is difficult to discern what precisely is critical about his genre of critique. It is *not* Foucault's critics that have imposed this problem on him – it emerges from Foucault's own insistence that there are changes that are desirable, and that critique enables us "to determine the precise form this change should take." A skeptical freedom that limits itself to talk of new possibilities for thinking and acting but heroically or ironically refuses to provide any evaluative orientation as to which possibilities and changes are desirable is in danger of becoming merely empty – or even worse, it withholds judgment from those catastrophic possibilities which *have* erupted or *can* erupt.

Ethics   Foucault, in his last works, turned to the question of ethics – athough typically he uses the term "ethics" in a novel and apparently idiosyncratic manner: "the kind of relationship you ought to have with yourself, *rapport à soi* ... and which determines how the individual is supposed to constitute himself as a moral subject of his own actions."[58] And if we again turn to the essay "What is Enlightenment?", we can see how important this motif is for Foucault. It is evident in his analysis of Baudelaire's conception of modern man as the "man who tries to invent himself" – who seeks to make his own life a work of art. This is a kind of ethics which is an aesthetics of existence.

As Dreyfus and Rabinow clearly stress, Foucault's critical ontology has two separate but related components: "work on oneself and responding to one's time."[59] In his interview concerning his work in progress on the genealogy of ethics Foucault asks, "But couldn't every one's life become a work of art?"[60] Does Foucault's turn to such an aestheticized understanding of ethics help us to understand his critical stance? One might be inclined to respond affirmatively – at least insofar as Foucault is giving some content to the type of changes he thinks would be desirable. But for a variety of reasons, I think we need to be extremely cautious in assessing this turn to ethics. Foucault himself is extremely tentative and resists the idea that his experimental studies of the genealogy of ethics yield any alternatives to our present situation. Even sympathetic commentators have noted the many problems that he leaves unresolved.[61] Not the least of these is that the very way in which Foucault talks about ethics in terms of the self's relationship to itself *seems* to presuppose a way of speaking about the self that he had previously so effectively criticized. What precisely is a "self"? How is the "self" related to what Foucault calls a "subject"? Who is the "I" that constitutes "itself" as a moral agent? It is difficult to see how Foucault himself escapes the radical instabilities that he exposed in "Man and his Doubles." And there are other problems. For this way of speaking of ethics which is now sharply distinguished from politics *seems* to be radically individualistic and voluntaristic with no consideration of anything or any "other" beyond one's relationship to oneself.[62]

What is perhaps most ironical about Foucault's talk of ethics and freedom – as it pertains to our historical situation – is that its intelligibility presupposes the notion of an ethical or moral agent that *can* be free and that can "master" itself. But Foucault not only fails to explicate *this* sense of agency, his genealogical analyses seem effectively to undermine any talk of agency which is not a precipitate of power/knowledge regimes. Who or what is left to transgress historical limits?

The most generous comment to make about Foucault's tentative probings of ethics is that they are "suggestive" – opening new lines of inquiry. But they do not significantly further our grasp of his genre of critique. Even if one were to grant that Foucault is tentatively exploring possibilities and changes that would be desirable, he never clarifies why an ascetic-aesthetic mode of ethical life *is* desirable.

I can now return to the question of critique as a philosophical *ēthos* that is a permanent critique of our historical era, critique that is practiced as "a historical investigation into the events that have led us to constitute ourselves and to recognize ourselves as subjects of what we are doing, thinking, saying" (p. 4). I do think – as I have tried to show – that it is possible to give a more sympathetic reading of Foucault that at least blunts the criticism of those who argue that he is confused, contradictory, and incoherent. I think we can see that he is inciting us to "*listen* to a different claim." He does disconcert and disrupt. He forces us to ask hard questions about our most cherished beliefs and comforting convictions. He shows us novel ways in which our bodies are controlled and made docile. He consistently refuses to allow us the illusion of easy solutions and alternatives. He has a remarkable ability to compel us to ask new sorts of questions and open new lines of inquiry. He unmasks illusions. To read him as *only* revealing the way in which global power/knowledge regimes supplant each other and completely determine what we are is to misread him. For it is to screen out the many ways in which Foucault is always focusing on instabilities, points of resistance, specific points where revolt and counter-discourse is possible. We can evaluate his hyper-oscillations "positively," i.e., we can see them as showing us how difficult "the undefined work of freedom" is and how much patient labor is required "to give form to our impatience for liberty."

But nevertheless, as I have also tried to show, when we think through what Foucault is saying and showing we are left with hard issues that are not resolved. These all cluster about the question of the ethical-political perspective that informs his critique. And these problems do not arise from imposing an alien grid or set of demands upon Foucault. On the contrary, they arise from his *own* practice of critique. Foucault never thematizes these problems, he never treats them with the rigor that they demand – a type of rigor he exemplified in his genealogical analyses. At best we have only hints and suggestions – not all of which seem compatible. And at times Foucault seeks to deny us the conceptual resources for dealing with the very issues his analyses force us to confront. This is one reason why his critics find him confused, contradictory, and incoherent. Foucault's own inciting rhetoric of disruption forces us to raise questions and, at the same time, appears to deny us any means for effectively dealing with these questions.

Ironically the current polemic about Enlightenment blackmail tends to boomerang; it is a diversionary tactic that obscures more than it illuminates. It tends to close off issues rather than open them up. It seduces us into thinking that we are confronted with only two possibilities: either there are universal ahistorical normative foundations for critique or critique is groundless. This specious "either/or" closes off the *topos* that needs to be opened for discussion – the *topos* toward which so much of the polemic of modernity/postmodernity gravitates. How can we still today – in our historical present – find ways of significantly clarifying and warranting the ethical-political perspectives that inform a critique of the present? This is *the* question that Foucault's genre of critique requires us to raise – a question he never quite answered.

Let me conclude with a statement that Foucault made in an interview conducted in May 1984, just before his death – where Foucault sounds like some of those he accused of Enlightenment blackmail.

I insist on this difference [between discussion and polemics] as something essential: a whole morality is at stake, the morality that concerns the search for the truth and the relation to the other.
In the serious play of questions and answers, in the work of reciprocal elucidation, the rights of each person are in some sense immanent

in the discussion. They depend only on the dialogue situation. The person asking the questions is merely exercising the right that has been given him: to remain unconvinced, to perceive a contradiction, to require more information .... As for the person answering the questions, he too exercises a right that does not go beyond the discussion itself; by the logic of his own discourse he is tied to the questioning of the other.[63]

I can think of no better description of the type of discussion and dialogue that is now required to probe the ethical-political perspective which informs Foucault's genre of critique.

NOTES

1   Michel Foucault, "What is Enlightenment?," in Paul Rabinow, ed., *The Foucault Reader* (New York: Pantheon, 1984). Page numbers in this chapter refer to this text.

2   Habermas did not publish his full-scale critique of Foucault until after Foucault's death. This appears in *The Philosophical Discourse of Modernity*, trans. F. Lawrence (Cambridge, Mass.: MIT Press, 1987). The German text was published in 1985. In two earlier articles, Habermas referred to Foucault and made some critical remarks about him. These remarks and Habermas' discussion of Foucault in *The Philosophical Discourse of Modernity* have set off a storm of controversy. See Habermas' "Modernity versus Postmodernity," in *New German Critique* 22 (1981), pp. 3–14; and "The Entwinement of Myth and Enlightenment: Re-Reading *Dialectic of Enlightenment*," in *New German Critique* 26 (1982) pp. 13–30. After Foucault's death, Habermas wrote an obituary, "Taking Aim at the Heart of the Present," which is reprinted in David Hoy, ed., *Foucault: A Critical Reader* (Oxford: Basil Blackwell, 1986).

3   Habermas, "Taking Aim at the Heart of the Present," p. 108. In this obituary, Habermas relates what most impressed him when he first met Foucault in 1983: "the tension, which resists easy categorization, between the almost serene scientific reserve of the scholar striving for objectivity on the one hand, and, on the other, the political vitality of the vulnerable, subjectively excitable, morally sensitive intellectual" (p. 103).

4   Michael S. Roth, "Review Essay" of recent literature on Foucault, p. 71, in *History and Theory* (1987) pp. 70–80. This is an excellent review of recent discussions of Foucault.

5   Foucault also tells us "it is necessary to stress the connection that exists between this brief article and the three *Critiques*" (p. 37).

6   For a discussion of what Foucault means by humanism and the distinc-

tion between humanism and Enlightenment, see David R. Hiley, *Philosophy in Question: Essays on a Pyrrhonian Theme* (Chicago: University of Chicago Press, 1988), pp. 101–104. The chapter in Hiley's book "Knowledge and Power" presents a lucid but different reading of the issues raised by Foucault's essay "What is Enlightenment?" Hiley defends Foucault against the blackmail of Enlightenment. Nevertheless he concludes his chapter by showing how Foucault's account "that identifies normalization and unfreedom, and that connects liberation with transgression and connects maturity with self-creation – remains deeply problematic for other reasons" (p. 110). These reasons are related to Foucault's ambivalent attitude toward the relation of an "aesthetics of existence" and its relation to a "notion of community."

7   Several commentators have debated the precise relationship between Foucault's understanding of archaeology and genealogy, and whether the "move" to genealogy represents a break or change in his intellectual development. For different interpretations of Foucault's development, see Hubert L. Dreyfus and Paul Rabinow, *Michel Foucault: Beyond Structuralism and Hermeneutics*, second edn (Chicago: University of Chicago Press, 1983); Habermas, *The Philosophical Discourse of Modernity*, lectures IX and X. See also Arnold I. Davidson's essay "Archaeology, Genealogy, Ethics," in Hoy, ed., *Foucault: A Critical Reader*.

8   Foucault takes up a number of other themes in his essay which I have not discussed, e.g., Kant's distinction of the private and public use of reason. He also briefly explores how the "work" on our historical limits has "its generality, its systematicity, its homogeneity, and its stakes" (p. 47).

9   This is the term used by Dreyfus and Rabinow to characterize Foucault's distinctive orientation that is beyond structuralism and hermeneutics. See *Michel Foucault: Beyond Structuralism and Hermeneutics*.

10   Nancy Fraser, "Foucault on Modern Power: Empirical Insights and Normative Confusions," in *Praxis International* 3 (1981), pp. 272–87. One should also see her two subsequent articles on Foucault: "Foucault's Body Language: A Post-Humanist Political Rhetoric?", in *Salmagundi* 61 (1983), pp. 55–70; and "Michel Foucault: A Young Conservative?", in *Ethics* 96 (1985), pp. 165–84.

11   Fred Dallmayr has argued that Fraser and others have given too simplified and undifferentiated an analysis of Foucault's understanding of power. He shows the complexity and the changing nuances of Foucault's understanding of power in "Pluralism Old and New: Foucault on Power," in *Polis and Praxis: Exercises in Contemporary Political Theory* (Cambridge, Mass.: MIT Press, 1984).

12   Fraser, "Foucault on Modern Power," p. 286.

13   Ibid., p. 283.

14   Charles Taylor, "Foucault on Freedom and Truth," reprinted in Hoy, ed., *Foucault: A Critical Reader*, p. 69.

15   Ibid., p. 70.
16   Ibid., p. 69.
17   Ibid., p. 83.
18   Ibid., p. 80.
19   Ibid.
20   Ibid., p. 91.
21   Ibid., p. 93. Taylor also develops a number of other criticisms, which I have not discussed, including the claim that Foucault's conception of "power without a subject" is also incoherent.
22   This is the line of criticism that Habermas first indicated in his brief reference to Foucault in "The Entwinement of Myth and Enlightenment."
23   Habermas, *The Philosophical Discourse of Modernity*, pp. 275–6.
24   Ibid., p. 275.
25   Ibid.
26   Ibid., p. 276.
27   Ibid. Habermas argues that Foucault's

> putative objectivity of knowledge is itself put in question (1) by the involuntary *presentism* of a historiography that remains hermeneutically stuck in its starting situation; (2) by the unavoidable *relativism* of an analysis related to the present that can understand itself only as a context-dependent practical enterprise; (3) by the arbitrary *partisanship* of a criticism that cannot account for its normative foundations. (p. 276)

He then seeks to reveal the unresolved *aporias* and contradictory impulses involved in each of these three areas. See ibid., pp. 276–86.

28   William E. Connolly, "Taylor, Foucault, and Otherness," in *Political Theory* 13 (August 1985), p. 368. Connolly's article is a response to Charles Taylor, "Foucault on Freedom and Truth," which also originally appeared in *Political Theory* 12 (May 1984), pp. 152–83. For Taylor's reply to Connolly, see "Connolly, Foucault, and Truth," in *Political Theory* 13 (August 1985), pp. 377–85. Connolly is one of Foucault's most sympathetic commentators, but he also presses a number of important criticisms. See his *Politics and Ambiguity* (Madison: University of Wisconsin Press, 1987).
29   Connolly, "Taylor, Foucault, and Otherness," p. 368.
30   Ibid.
31   Hubert L. Dreyfus and Paul Rabinow, "What is Maturity? Habermas and Foucault on 'What is Enlightenment?'," in Hoy, ed., *Foucault: A Critical Reader*, p. 114.
32   Connolly, "Taylor, Foucault, and Otherness," p. 368.
33   Michel Foucault, "On the Genealogy of Ethics: An Overview of Work in Progress," in Rabinow, ed., *The Foucault Reader*, p. 351. See also Ian Hacking's discussion of this interview, "Self-Improvement," in Hoy, ed., *Foucault: A Critical Reader*.

34 Michel Foucault, "Polemics, Politics, and Problemization: An Interview," in Rabinow, ed., *The Foucault Reader*, p. 382. Throughout this interview, Foucault speaks of "the search for the truth" and gaining "access to the truth."

35 Maurice Blanchot makes a similar point about Foucault in his subtle appreciative essay, "Michel Foucault as I Imagine Him," in *Foucault/Blanchot* (New York: Zone, 1987). He writes:

> And were not his own principles more complex than his official discourse, with its striking formulations, led one to think? For example, it is accepted as a certainty that Foucault, adhering in this to a certain conception of literary production, got rid of purely and simply, the notion of the subject: no more oeuvre, no more author, no more creative unity. But things are not that simple. The subject does not disappear; rather its excessively determined unity is put in question. (p. 78)

> Similarly, when one ascribes to Foucault a quasi-nihilistic distrust of what he calls the will to truth (or the will to serious knowledge), or, additionally, a suspicious rejection of the idea of reason (possessing universal value), I think one is underestimating the complexity of his concerns. The will to truth, to be sure, but at what cost? What are its guises? What political imperatives are concealed beneath that highly honorable quest? (p. 79)

There is another aspect of Foucault's rhetoric that should be noted. In several of Foucault's interviews given for English-speaking audiences, he adopts a more moderate reasonable "democratic" tone as compared to some of his more extreme "Nietzschean" pronouncements in French. Many of Foucault's American champions tend to portray him as a "radical democrat" – a domesticated Nietzschean without Nietzsche's anti-democratic biases.

36 Michel Foucault, *Discipline and Punish: The Birth of the Prison*, trans. Alan Sheridan (New York: Vintage, 1979).

37 Michel Foucault, *The History of Sexuality, Volume I: An Introduction*, trans. Robert Hurley (New York: Vintage, 1980), p. 159. See also Fraser, "Foucault's Body Language."

38 Blanchot notes how the formulae of negative theology are already effectively employed in *The Archaeology of Knowledge* trans. Alan Sheridan (New York: Harper Colophon, 1972).

> Read and reread *The Archaeology of Knowledge* ... and you will be surprised to rediscover in it many a formula from negative theology. Foucault invests all his talent in describing with sublime phrases what it is he rejects: "It's not ..., nor is it ..., nor is it for that matter ...," so that there remained almost nothing for him to say in order to valorize what is precisely a refusal of the notion of "value". ("Michel Foucault as I Imagine Him", p. 74)

Foucault continued to work and overwork these formulae throughout his writings. Unfortunately, many of Foucault's sympathetic commentators also tend to overwork these devices – informing us what he does *not* say, believe, or intend.

39 Foucault, "On the Genealogy of Ethics," p. 343.

40 Dreyfus and Rabinow, "What is Maturity?", p. 116.

41 Ibid., p. 118.

42 Hiley, *Philosophy in Question*, p. 94.

43 Ibid., p. 103.

44 Martin Heidegger, "The Question concerning Technology," in *Martin Heidegger: Basic Writings*, ed. and trans. David F. Krell (New York: Harper and Row, 1977), p. 309. One may argue that the concept of danger is not necessarily "value-laden." It is being used merely as a non-evaluative *functional* expression. But this line of defense loses plausibility when one speaks of the dangers of modernity or the dangers of the disciplinary society.

45 Dreyfus and Rabinow, "What is Maturity?", p. 115.

46 Ibid. Even Dreyfus and Rabinow say that Foucault "owes us a criterion of what makes one kind of danger more dangerous than another." See the 1983 Afterword to *Michel Foucault: Beyond Structuralism and Hermeneutics*, p. 264.

47 John Rajchman emphasizes Foucault's historical nominalism in his book *Michel Foucault: The Freedom of Philosophy* (New York: Columbia University Press, 1985).

48 Michel Foucault, *Power/Knowledge: Selected Interviews and Other Writings*, ed. Colin Gordon (New York: Pantheon, 1980), p. 80.

49 Ibid., p. 85.

50 Blanchot acutely perceives that even in *Madness and Civilization: A History of Insanity in the Age of Reason* trans. Richard Howard (New York: Vintage, 1973), the primary theme is "the power of exclusion." See "Michel Foucault as I Imagine Him," p. 65.

51 Habermas notes an interesting parallel between Foucault's appeal to specific *insurrections of subjugated knowledges* and Lukács' more global argument about the "privileged" possibilities of knowledge by the proletariat. See *The Philosophical Discourse of Modernity*, p. 280.

52 Foucault, *The History of Sexuality, Volume I*, p. 95.

53 Ibid.

54 Rajchman characterizes Foucault's politics as a post-revolutionary, "politics of revolt." But he never answers the question, why revolt?, or in the name of what? See chap. 2, "The Politics of Revolt," in *Michel Foucault: The Freedom of Philosophy*.

55 Ibid., pp. 2, 4.

56 Like Rajchman, Hiley approaches Foucault by situating him in the tradition of skepticism. See "Knowledge and Power," in *Philosophy in Question*. This is not a new theme in Foucault. In an interview with J. K. Simon, in *Partisan Review*, 38, 1971, he said:

What I am trying to do is grasp the implicit systems which determine our most familar behavior without our knowing it. I am trying to find their origin, to show their formation, the constraint they impose upon us. I am therefore trying to place myself at a distance from them and to show how one could escape.

57 G. W. F. Hegel, *The Phenomenology of Spirit*, trans. A. V. Miller (New York: Oxford University Press, 1977), p. 51.
58 Foucault, "On the Genealogy of Ethics," p. 352.
59 Dreyfus and Rabinow, "What is Maturity?", p. 112.
60 Foucault, "On the Genealogy of Ethics," p. 350.
61 See, for example, Mark Poster, "Foucault and the Tyranny of Greece"; Arnold I. Davidson, "Archaeology, Genealogy, Ethics"; and Ian Hacking, "Self-Improvement." These essays are in Hoy, ed., *Foucault: A Critical Reader*. See also Reiner Schürmann, "On Constituting Oneself as an Anarchistic Subject," in *Praxis International* 6 (1986), pp. 294–310.
62 See Hiley's discussion of this problem in "Knowledge and Power," pp. 110–14.
63 Foucault, "Polemics, Politics, and Problemizations," p. 381.

6

Serious Play
The Ethical-Political Horizon of Derrida

If you want to honor a philosopher, you must catch him where he has not yet gone forth to the consequences, in his fundamental thought; (in the thought) from which he takes his point of departure.

F. W. Schelling

Jacques Derrida is perhaps the most controversial writer of our time. There are those who think that he is a clever intellectual fraud, a "prophet" of nihilism, a whimsical destroyer of any "canons" of rationality, a self-indulgent scribbler who delights in irresponsible word play, punning, parody, and even self-parody. But there are those who hail him as the most significant "philosopher" (or anti-philosopher) to emerge in France since the Second World War, and who see him as a David battling against Goliath. With wit, barbs, and deft swift movements, he is the slayer of the tradition of Western metaphysics and logocentrism. In some circles – primarily literary circles in America – he has become an intellectual guru whose texts are treated as if they were "sacred," calling forth endless commentary, interpretation, and reinterpretation. At the very least Derrida (or his texts) is a gadfly who annoys, stings, and provokes. With the phenomenon of Derrida, a whole new jargon has come into being – one which keeps changing and shifting: "deconstruction," "trace," "*écriture*," "writing under erasure," "*différance*." "*Pharmakon*," "hymen," "supplementarity" have become code terms. There is something of a Proteus quality about his prolific writings, not only because they display a variety of styles and *shapes*, but because every time one tries to pin down what he is or is not saying, his texts appear to change. He sets all sorts of traps and obstacles for any commentator or interpreter. He even tells us:

> Perhaps the desire to write is the desire to launch things that come back to you as much as possible in as many forms as possible. That is, it is the desire to perfect a program or a matrix having the greatest potential, variability, undecidability, plurivocality, et cetera, so that each time something returns it will be as different as possible. This is also what one does when one has children – talking beings who can always outtalk you. You have the illusion that it comes back to you – that these unpredicable words come out of you somewhat. This is what goes on with texts.[1]

So to write about the ethical-political horizon of Derrida is a risky endeavor. Not only because of the "variability, undecidability, plurivocality, et cetera" of his (?) texts, but for other reasons. For if we judge "ethical-political discourse" by what philosophers have taken to be its "proper domain," then this always seems to be peripheral or marginal in Derrida's writings. There is scarcely anything resembling a straightforward analysis of such concepts as right, good, obligation, justice, and virtue – or anything stable enough to label Derrida's ethical-political "position." At times he even mocks and/or deconstructs the very idea of "taking a position." Yet certain motifs such as "responsibility" keep surfacing in his texts. And, at times, one also detects what – in an old-fashioned way – might be called his eloquent moral passion. I want to show not simply that Derrida does have an ethical-political "position," but something which is much more important, that there is a way of reading Derrida's texts so that we can see his ethical-political horizon pervading and influencing virtually everything he has written, everything that bears his signature. In this sense, I want to locate – if not *the* point of a departure – at least *a* point of departure in his "fundamental thought," and to "catch him where he has not yet gone forth to the consequences."

Suppose we take as a clue what Heidegger (the thinker who Derrida almost obsessively interprets and reinterprets) says about the "original" meaning of *ēthos*. In his "Letter on Humanism," when commenting on a fragment from Heraclitus, *ēthos anthrōpōi daimōn*, Heidegger writes: "*Ēthos* means abode, dwelling place. The word names the open region in which man dwells. The open region of this abode allows what pertains to man's essence, and what is thus arriving resides in nearness to him, to appear."[2] The type of thinking (*Andenken*) which reflects on this dwelling – "the essence of being-in-the-world" – can be said to be "the original ethics." Whether or not we are sympathetic with what Heidegger says, we can nevertheless recognize that any reflection on *ēthos* does – directly or indirectly – bear on the question of our dwelling, our being-in-the-world. Furthermore the explicit linkage of dwelling and *ēthos* raises the theme of the *heimlich* and the *unheimlich* – a theme subtly interwoven into the texts of Nietzsche, Heidegger, Freud, and Derrida.

Let me say boldly, as a first approximation for understanding Derrida's ethical-political horizon, that one reason why his writings are at times so powerful and disconcerting is that he has an uncanny (*unheimlich*) ability to *show* us that at the heart of what we take to be familiar, native, at home – where we think we can find our center – lurks (is concealed and repressed) what is unfamiliar, strange, and uncanny.[3] Indeed, for all of Derrida's indebtedness to Heidegger, he seeks to expose what he calls "the dominance of the entire metaphorics of proximity, of simple and immediate presence, a metaphorics associating the proximity of Being with the values of neighboring, shelter, house, service, guard, voice, and listening."[4] And Derrida asks,

> Is not this security of the near what is trembling today, that is, the co-belonging and co-propriety of the name of man and the name of Being, such as this co-propriety inhabits, and is inhabited by, the language of the West, such as it is buried in its *oikonomia*, such as it is inscribed and forgotten according to the history of metaphysics, and such as it is awakened also by the destruction of ontotheology?[5]

Derrida not only writes about decentering, this is what he is always *doing*. In one of his early and more straightforward essays, "Structure, Sign, and Play in the Discourse of the Human Sciences," he writes:

> The concept of centered structure is in fact the concept of a play based on a fundamental ground, a play constituted on the basis of a fundamental immobility and a reassuring certitude, which itself is beyond the reach of play. And on the basis of the certitude anxiety can be mastered.[6]

But there is no "centered structure," no "fundamental ground." Consequently, anxiety can never be *finally* mastered by a "reassuring certitude" – and *this* is what Derrida seeks to show us. Initially, it might seem that Derrida was seeking to deconstruct (and indeed show the common root of) structuralism and transcendental phenomenology. But it is already clear – even in this essay – that Derrida's target is something that he takes to be "central" to the entire "history of metaphysics," and indeed the "history of the West":

> the entire history of the concept of structure ... must be thought of as a series of substitutions of center for center, as a linked chain of determinations of the center. Successively, and in a regulated fashion, the center receives different forms or names. The history of metaphysics like the history of the West is the history of these metaphors and metonymies. Its matrix ... is the determination of Being as *presence* in all senses of this word. It could be shown that all names related to fundamentals, to principles, or to the center have always designated an invariable presence – *eidos, archē, telos, energeia, ousia* (essence, existence, substance, subject) *alētheia*, transcendentality, consciousness, God, man, and so forth.[7]

It is as if Derrida is telling us that the deepest *desire* in the Western philosophic tradition, the metaphysical tradition, has been to locate some fixed permanent center, some Archimedean point, some ground – whether we think of this as "the transcendental signified," or a presence or self-presence in its full transparency and plenitude. This is true not only of the Western metaphysical tradition but also of the theological tradition that construes the narrative of history as a "development" from original innocence through the "fall of man" to a final redemption. And clearly, ethical discourse, *insofar* as it partakes in the search for an *archē*, a first principle to "ground" moral action is part of this same metaphysical, ontotheological history.

Derrida seems to find evidence of the metaphysics of presence almost everywhere, not only in the "canonical" philosophic texts of Plato, Aristotle, Descartes, Rousseau, Hegel, Husserl and Heidegger but also in the writings of Saussure, Levi-Strauss, and even in Austin and Searle. One of the clearest statements of what Derrida means by metaphysics (and what is wrong with it) occurs in what might seem to be an "odd" context – his dispute with Searle about the interpretation of Austin. Suppose we bracket the question of Derrida's fairness to Austin and concentrate on his characterization of metaphysics. He writes:

> Metaphysics in its most traditional form reigns over the Austinian heritage .... Two indications bear witness to this: 1. The hierarchical axiology, the ethical-ontological distinctions which do not merely set up value-oppositions clustered around an ideal and unfindable limit, but moreover *subordinate* these values to each other (normal/abnormal, standard/parasite, fulfilled/void, serious/non-serious, literal/non-literal, briefly: positive/negative and ideal/non-ideal) .... 2. The enterprise of returning "strategically," ideally, to an origin or to a "priority" held to be simple, intact, normal, pure, standard, self-identical, in order *then* to think in terms of derivation, complication, deterioration, accident, etc. All metaphysicians, from Plato to Rousseau, Descartes to Husserl, have proceeded in this way, conceiving good to be before evil, the positive before the negative, the pure before the impure, the simple before the complex, the essential before the accidental, the imitated before the imitation, etc. And this is not just *one* metaphysical gesture among others, it is *the* metaphysical exigency, that which has been the most constant, most profound and most potent.[8]

So metaphysics is not only the history of the search for a series of substitutions of center for center by which we seek a "reassuring certitude," a "metaphysical comfort," it also (always) establishes ethical-ontological hierarchies in which there is subordination and violence. We should pay close attention to Derrida's own "metaphorics" in the above passage. For his critique, his protest against metaphysics is primarily ethical-political. It is the invidious and pernicious tendency toward hierarchy, subordination, and repression that informs his rhetoric and tropes.

Despite Derrida's differences with what he calls those "two Greeks named Husserl and Heidegger,"[9] he shares with them that "strong" reading of the history of philosophy which claims that "the founding concepts of philosophy are primarily Greek, and it would not be possible to philosophize, or to speak philosophically outside this medium."[10] The "event" (which is not quite an event) that Derrida calls a "rupture" is the realization that

> There was no center, that the center could not be thought in the form of present-being, that the center had no natural site, that it was not a

fixed locus but a function, a sort of nonlocus in which an infinite number of sign substitutions came into play. This was the moment when language invaded the universal problematic, the moment when, in the absence of a center or origin, everything became discourse ... that is to say, a system in which the central signified, the original or transcendental signified, is never absolutely present outside a system of differences. The absence of the transcendental signified extends the domain and the play of signification infinitely.[11]

And here is another reason why Derrida's texts are so disconcerting. For, as he well knows, a "point" (*spur*) so effectively made by Descartes, that if there is no center, no foundation, or stable presence, the "alternative" seems to be chaos, formlessness, even madness.[12] (Later I want to show that Derrida himself deconstructs [takes apart] this stark contrast: fixed center or chaos and formlessness.)

But even the above remarks about the "metaphysical exigency" and decentering do not quite get at what Derrida repeatedly *shows* us. For what I have said thus far can too easily be assimilated to a *thesis*, viz., that although the history of metaphysics "must be thought of as a series of substitutions of center for center" *now* we know that there was (is) no center. But Derrida also claims that the "epoch of the thesis" is also passing.[13] If we attempted to encapsulate what he is saying in such a "thesis," we would be left in the situation that Hegel characterizes in the Introduction to the *Phenomenology* when he writes "One bare assurance is worth just as much as another."[14]

We can come closer to what Derrida is doing by considering Freud's discussion of the *heimlich* and the *unheimlich*. Freud begins his famous essay, "The 'Uncanny'" (*Das Unheimliche*) with what can be read as an exemplar of deconstruction *avant la lettre*. He tells us:

The German word "*unheimlich*" is obviously the opposite of "*heimlich*" ..., "*heimisch*" ... the opposite of what is familiar; and we are tempted to conclude that what is "uncanny" is frightening precisely because it is *not* known and familiar.[15]

But as Freud points out, this opposition is a bit too simple and facile. "Something has to be added to what is novel and unfamiliar in order to make it uncanny."[16] Freud meticulously examines the linguistic usage of *"heimlich"* and *"unheimlich"* (and its equivalents in several languages). He reports a "surprising" discovery:

> among its different shades of meaning the word *"heimlich"* exhibits one which is identical with its opposite *"unheimlich."* What is *heimlich* thus comes to be *unheimlich* .... In general we are reminded that the word *"heimlich"* is not unambiguous, but belongs to two sets of ideas, which without being contradictory, are yet very different, on the one hand what is familiar and agreeable, and on the other, what is concealed and kept out of sight.[17]

Later in his essay Freud reveals "that the uncanny [*unheimlich*] is something which is secretly familiar [*heimlich/heimisch*] which has undergone repression and then returned from it, and that everything that is uncanny fulfills this condition: ... the prefix *'un'* ['un-'] is the token of repression."[18] Summing up his "discovery" based on his review of the linguistic usage of *"heimlich"/"unheimlich,"* Freud declares:

> Thus *heimlich* is a word the meaning of which develops in the direction of ambivalence, until it finally coincides with its opposite, *unheimlich*.[19]

Freud's "discovery," and even his initial way of showing it by a close examination of the linguistic usage of *"heimlich"* and *"unheimlich"* may itself be taken as an exemplar of what Derrida *repeatedly* shows us in a variety of different contexts.[20] One of his typical strategies is to start with what seems so familiar, native, at home – and then to show by a meticulous and tenacious (what the French call "rigorous") analysis how it "develops in the direction of ambivalence, until it finally [but not quite, RJB] coincides with its opposite." He performs this type of deconstruction not only with familiar texts of Husserl, Heidegger, Nietzsche, Freud, Kant, Aristotle, Plato, etc., but also with such apparently familiar concepts as speech, sign, structure, center, context. This is a strategy that bears a close resemblance (as Derrida himself notes) with Hegel's "logic of inversion." But Derrida is not only close to Hegel, he is also radically anti-Hegelian. Whereas for Hegel, inversion is a moment in the progressive dialectical unfolding of *Geist*, a moment in the process of *Aufhebung* where there is negating, preserving, and overcoming, Derrida radically questions the teleological thrust of *Aufhebung*. In a parenthetical aside, he tells us "(*Aufhebung* is, more or less implicitly, the dominant concept of nearly all histories of writing, even today. It is *the* concept of history and of teleology)."[21] But for Derrida, we never quite achieve a genuine *Aufhebung*, a reconciliation of oppositions and differences – it is *always* deferred.[22]

Relating this discussion of the *heimlich/unheimlich* to the question of our *ēthos* or dwelling in the world, Derrida seeks to show us that we never quite are or can be at home in the world. We are always threatened by the uncanniness of what is canny; we are always in exile – even from ourselves. We may long and dream of being at home in our world, to find a "proper" center, but we never achieve this form of presence or self-presence.

The mention of "exile" provides another metaphor for approaching Derrida's ethical-political horizon. For throughout his writings he plays on and with this metaphor. In "Structure, Sign, and Play" he already introduces this motif of exile:

> The event I called a rupture, the disruption I alluded to at the beginning of this paper, presumably would have come about when the structurality of structure had begun to be thought, that is to say repeated, and this is why I said that this disruption was repetition in every sense of the word. Henceforth, it became necessary to think both the law which somehow governed the desire for a center in the constitution of structure, and the process of signification which orders the displacements and substitutions from this law of central presence – but a central presence which has never been itself, has always been exiled from itself into its own substitute.[23]

It is tempting (a temptation that Derrida invites when he weaves bits of his autobiography into his texts) to relate the motif of exile to Derrida's own experience as an Algerian Sephardic Jew who has always worked on the margins of ("Greek") philosophy and metaphysics. This sense of the exile who at times is taken to be a parasite, a pariah, a supplement is not only evident in his sensitive writings on such "Jewish" thinkers and poets as Levinas and Jabès, but pervades all his writings. Indeed, it is a dominant motif in his critique of logocentrism and phonocentrism. When, for example, he scrutinizes Saussure's "condemnation" of writing, Derrida says "Saussure sees writing as perversion, debauchery, dress of corruption and disguise, a festival mask that must be exorcised, i.e., warded off by the good word" – in short as that which is to be exiled.

Susan Handelman, who interprets Derrida's work as "the latest in the line of Jewish heretic hermeneutics" is particularly insightful in stressing the exile motif. She writes:

> Derrida is a vigorous polemicist adept at contorting the arguments of others to fit his own needs, but his particular ironic use of passages and adjectives to characterize negative attitudes towards writing is curious: "The perverse cult of the letter-image," "the sin of idolatry," "perversion that engenders monsters," "deviation from nature," "principle of death," "deformation, sacrilege, crime," "the wandering outcast of linguistics," "expatiated, condemned to wandering and blindness, to mourning," "expelled other." The descriptions are overtly theological and the logos described as the "historical violence of a speech dreaming its full self-presence, living itself as its own resumption ... auto-production of a speech declared alive ... a logos which believes itself to be its own father, being lifted above written discourse," is obviously the Christian logos, the son dreaming himself to be his own father born into flesh and elevated above all texts and written discourses. *And that exiled, wandering, mourning, condemned outcast, accused of unredeemed, original sin is the Jew, the carrier of the letter, the cultist of Writing* (emphasis added).[24]

We can read Derrida as showing us, over and over again, that the devious tactics and strategies designed to exclude, outcast, silence, and exile the contaminating "Other" have never been quite successful. This drive toward exclusion and exile is evidenced not only in logocentrism and phonocentrism, but in the "history of the West." Some of Derrida's most moving and passionate prose shines forth in his perceptive descriptions of the dynamics of exclusion and his *apologia* for what is exiled.

Consider how this motif is played out in his essay "Racism's Last Word" which was written for the catalog of an exhibition of art *contre*/against apartheid when it opened in Paris in 1983.[25]

> By isolating being apart in some sort of essence or hypostasis, the word [apartheid] corrupts it into a quasi-ontological segregation. At every point, like all racisms, it tends to pass segregation off as natural – and as the very law of origin. Such is the monstrosity of this political idiom. Surely, an idiom should never incline toward racism. It often does, however, and this is not altogether fortuitous: there is no racism without a language. The point is not that acts of racial violence are only words but rather that they have to have a word. Even though it offers the excuse of blood, color, birth – or rather, because it uses naturalist and sometimes creationist discourse – racism always

betrays the perversion of a man, the "talking animal." It institutes, declares, writes, inscribes, prescribes. A system of marks, it outlines in order to assign forced residence or to close off borders. It does not discern, it discriminates.[26]

Many of the motifs which are played out in Derrida's critique of logocentrism and the metaphysics of presence are given a forceful ethical-political expression here – the motifs of exclusion, violence, the condemnation and abomination of what is taken as other, the power of the "word" (which is never merely the word), the establishment of fixed "natural" hierarchies and borders. Derrida also shows, in this overtly political essay, another theme that surfaces in his critique of the history of metaphysics, viz., the complicity of the West – the sense in which racism itself is a "Western thing." He emphasizes the duplicity, the "double-bind" logic – the hypocrisy of a Europe which at once denounces apartheid and yet preserves it.[27]

Not only does Derrida vividly describe and condemn the violent logic of exclusion and exile, he also plays on the sense of the exile as bearing witness. (And here too *we witness* a motif that weaves through all his writings.) He writes of the exhibition as remaining "in exile in the sight of its proper residence, its place of destination to come – and to create. For such is here the *creation* and the work of which it is fitting to speak: South Africa beyond *apartheid*, South Africa in memory of apartheid."

> While this might be the cape to be rounded, everything will have begun with exile. Born in exile, the exhibition already bears witness against the forced assignment to "natural" territory, the geography of birth. And if it never reaches its destination, having been condemned to an endless flight or immobilized far from an unshakeable South Africa, it will not only keep the archival record of a failure or a despair but continue to *say* something, something that can be heard today, in the present.
>
> This new satellite of humanity, then, will move from place to place, it, too, like a mobile and stabile habitat "mobile" and "stabile," a place of observation, information, and witness. A satellite is a guard, it keeps watch and gives warning: Do not forget *apartheid*, save humanity from this evil, an evil that cannot be summed up in the principal and abstract iniquity of a system. It is also daily suffering, oppression, poverty, violence inflicted by an arrogant white minority ... on the mass of the black population.[28]

Derrida's essay is a forceful, passionate, unequivocal condemnation of apartheid – "Racism's Last Word." But no text of Derrida is simply univocal. Not only can one discern in this text a subtext which is applicable to the Holocaust – especially when he echoes the Jewish lament in the phrase "Do not forget *apartheid*," but the theme of the exile who bears witness is self-referential. For the "position" that Derrida himself most frequently "takes" is that of the exile bearing witness. A further reason why Derrida's texts "speak" to those who have been excluded and exiled – whether Jews, Blacks, women[29] (for all their differences) – is because he writes with enormous sensitivity and discernment about the violence done to those who have been exiled and condemned to the margins.

In his interpretation of the Tower of Babel, which can be read as a parable of the "history of the West," he writes:

> In seeking to "make a name for themselves," to found at the same time a universal tongue and a unique genealogy, the Semites want to bring the world to reason, and this reason can signify simultaneously a colonial violence (since they would universalize their idiom) and a peaceful transparency of the human community. Inversely, when God imposes and opposes his name, he ruptures the rational transparency but interrupts also the colonial violence or the linguistic imperialism.[30]

Here, too, as in his critique of the metaphysics of presence, Derrida's metaphorics reveal his ethical-political orientation; "colonial violence" and "linguistic imperialism" inform his reading of the Tower of Babel.

There is still another important play of the motif of the exile. For we can ask, what is the *relation* of the exile to that from which it is exiled? Whenever Derrida gives a microanalysis of a binary opposition, he seeks to show how the "opposing" terms – despite the attempt to secure "rigid" boundaries – nevertheless mutually implicate each other. So not only is the "position" of the exile dependent on that from which it is exiled, but the exile as a "parasite" lives on and in its "host." Nowhere is this "reciprocal" bonding more evident than in Derrida's critique of metaphysics and logocentrism. At times, Derrida's rhetoric would lead us to believe that we can once and for all make a total break or rupture with the metaphysical tradition. This is the way in which many of his followers and critics have interpreted him. (With this reading there is a curious parallel with the claim made by logical positivists when they announced that we are "now" in the enlightened position of being able to completely dispense with metaphysics.) But Derrida repeatedly tells us that such a total break does not make any sense.

> There is no sense in doing without the concepts of metaphysics in order to shake metaphysics. We have no language – no syntax and no lexicon – which is foreign to this history; we can pronounce not a single destructive proposition which has not already had to slip into the form, the logic, and the implicit postulations of precisely what it seeks to contest.[31]

But even this strong claim is itself open to divergent readings. For it may be interpreted as a statement of what is only our present and perhaps temporary condition – that the tradition of metaphysics has been so powerful and pervasive that we do not yet know how to speak or write in order to escape the snares of metaphysics. But to read Derrida in this manner would only be to replicate what he is constantly exposing – as if "metaphysics" itself is now the negative term in a binary opposition which is to be condemned, excluded, exiled.

It is important to distinguish *at least* two senses of "metaphysics." There is that sense of metaphysics where we think we can finally reach some luminous transcendental signified, some fixed *archē*, center, or absolutely stable ground that does not tremble and which serves as a basis for permanent hierarchies and rigid boundaries. But there is another sense of metaphysics or the metaphysical impulse in which all thinking, speaking and writing necessitates (as Spinoza and Hegel tell us) making distinctions with their inclusions and exclusions – and even endorsing hierarchies. Of course, the danger – one which Derrida is always exposing – is how easily and inadvertently we slide from the second sense of metaphysics to the first. We must always be on our guard against this slippage. The reason why I think this distinction is so important is because there are readers of Derrida (critics and champions) who think he is telling us that there is something futile or contaminating about making *any* distinctions or endorsing *any* hierarchical claims. But this (as, for example, "Racism's Last Word" so effectively shows) is belied by what he constantly does. It is more appropriate to say that Derrida is always encouraging us to *question* the status of what we take to be our center, our native home, our *archē*. Whether it is the "principle of reason" itself or some other authority, Derrida is not advocating that we abandon all authority, but rather that we never cease questioning it.[32] In this respect, Derrida would agree with Heidegger that "questioning is the piety of thought" even when this means questioning Heidegger's own thought.[33] (Let us remember that in the *Euthyphro*, Socrates also shows us that *questioning is the piety of thought*.) In the Socratic sense, Derrida *is* a subversive thinker/questioner. Those who read him as celebrating formlessness and chaos are missing the bite of his deconstructive exercises. Earlier I suggested that Derrida deconstructs the Either/Or which has haunted so much of the history of philosophy, especially modern philosophy: *Either* an absolutely stable foundation and fixed Archimedean point *or* intellectual and moral chaos – madness. I agree with Henry Staten when he writes:

> Derrida does not want to deny the self-identity of concepts or of entities-as-given-to-knowledge: he only denies what we could call the impermeability of the as-such, the transcendentality or logical superhardness of the barrier that marks off the conceptual purity of X from everything that is not-X. It is not that identity is drowned in otherness, but that it is *necessarily* open to it, contaminated by it. Yet the necessity or essential character of this contamination cannot be named unless we first grasp the concept of essence or form as purity, as pure positive self-identity.[34]

Or as Staten puts it succinctly, "Deconstruction is not a defense of formlessness, but a regulated overflowing of established boundaries."[35] The point is *not* that we can get along without demarcating boundaries, but rather there is no "boundary-fixing" that cannot itself be questioned.[36]

Violence and ethics

Let me be forthright, even blunt. Few contemporary thinkers have been so alert and perceptive about the temptations and dangers of violently crushing or silencing differences, otherness, alterity – in "others" or even the "other" in ourselves. Few writers have written with such nuanced understanding about the suffering, mourning "other." In one of his most beautiful and loving essays, his homage to Levinas (from whom he appropriates so much), Derrida writes of – this time playing off Heidegger against Levinas – "the *respect* for the other *as what it is*: other. Without this acknowledgement, which is not a knowledge, or let us say without this 'letting be' of an existent

(Other) as something existing outside me in the essence of what is (first in its alterity), no ethics would be possible."[37]

It is in passages like this one where, despite Derrida's relentless deconstructive critiques – or perhaps it is more accurate to say, *because* of this style of critique – that we can even detect Derrida's affinities with the deepest impulses of transcendental philosophy. For as Kant taught us, what characterizes the transcendental impulse is not its "dogmatism" or even its search for firm foundations, but its persistent questioning of the conditions and possibility of experience – including ethical-political experience. In "Metaphysics and Violence" Derrida risks delineating the "transcendental" conditions for, and the "ideal" of, an ethical community:

> To let the other be in its existence and essence as other means that what gains access to thought, or (*and*) what thought gains access to, is that which is essence and that which is existence; and that which is the Being which they both presuppose. Without this, no letting-be would be possible, and first of all, the letting-be of respect and of the ethical commandment addressing itself to freedom. Violence would reign to such a degree that it would no longer even be able to appear and be named.[38]

And in a sentence that might almost serve as a "justification" of Derrida's "fundamental thought" he writes: "The best liberation from violence is a certain putting into question, which makes the search for an *archē* tremble."[39] To use a Hegelian turn of phrase, the "truth" that Derrida appropriates from Levinas is "permitting to *let* be others in their truth, freeing dialogue and the face to face."[40] But Derrida, who is always alert to ambiguities, ambivalences, and "double binds," also knows how the very idea of an ethical community, a *Gemeinschaft*, can turn into its opposite and become oppressive and repressive. He brings this out in his deconstructive reading of Rousseau when he shows how Rousseau at once is committed to the "image of community immediately present to itself, without difference, a community of speech where all the members are within earshot,"[41] and also how Rousseau's texts raise disturbing questions about the very possibility of such a self-present community that excludes or presumably "mediates" all difference. Once again, Henry Staten nicely brings out the moral "thrust" of Derrida's unstable and ambivalent "position" when – in summing up his perceptive analysis of the Searle–Derrida debate – he writes:

Perhaps what we have in this debate is a conflict between modern Anglo-American clean-mindedness or sincerity and archaic moral rigor that insists on reminding us of the residue of darkness in man's intention. If there is any skepticism in Derrida, it is moral not an epistemological skepticism – not a doubt about the possibility of morality but about an idealized picture of sincerity that takes insufficient account of the windings and twistings of fear and desire, weakness and lust, sadism and masochism and the will to power, in the mind of the most sincere man.[42]

New responsibilities

In a number of recent texts, dealing with the founding, structure, and complicities of the institution of the modern university, Derrida responds to the charges that have been brought against him over and over again – nihilism, obscurantism, irrationalism. He writes about a "new community of thought" which attempts "to define new responsibilities in the face of the university's total subjection to the technologies of 'informatization'. Not so as to refuse them; not so as to counter with some obscurantist irrationalism (and irrationalism, like nihilism, is a picture that is completely symmetrical to, thus dependent upon, the principle of reason)."[43]

Derrida rightfully lashes out at some of his more hysterical critics when he goes on to say:

> We can easily see on which side obscurantism and nihilism are lurking when on occasion great professors or representatives of prestigious institutions lose all sense of proportion and control; on such occasions they forget the principles that they claim to defend in their work and suddenly begin to heap insults, to say whatever comes into their heads on the subject of texts that they obviously have never opened or that they have encountered through mediocre journalism that in other cirumstances they would pretend to scorn.[44]

And in a clear forthright statement about the political consequences of deconstruction – which certainly distances him from many of his Anglo-American literary "appropriators," he writes:

> what is somewhat hastily called deconstruction is not, if it is of any consequence, a specialized set of discursive procedures, even less the rules of a new hermeneutic method, working on texts or utterances in

the shelter of a given and stable institution. It is also, at the very least, a way of taking a position, in its work of analysis, concerning the political and institutional structures that make possible and govern our practice, our competencies, our performances. Precisely because it is never concerned only with signified content, deconstruction should not be separable from this politico-institutional problematic and should seek a new investigation of responsibility, an investigation which questions the codes inherited from ethics and politics. This means that too political for some, it will seem paralyzing to those who only recognize politics by the most familiar road signs.[45]

Taking positions?

By now, I hope, I have conveyed a sense of the committed, questioning, and potentially subversive character of Derrida's ethical-political horizon. And I hope it is also clear that I am not merely saying that in addition to his reflections on speech, writing, metaphysics, logocentrism, etc., he *also* "has" an ethics and politics. My claim is a much stronger one. Derrida's ethical-political horizon *is* "a point of departure" for virtually everything he has written. It is subtly and integrally interwoven in his critique of metaphysics, logocentrism, phonocentrism, phallogocentrism, and ethnocentrism.

But I have not quite come to the end of "honoring" Derrida. I have not yet "gone forth to the consequences" of his thinking. Critique itself is a form of honoring. I want to return to the text where Derrida claims "deconstruction is also, at the very least, a way of taking a position." Derrida has written a good deal about "positions" and "taking a position," especially in his interviews published under the title *Positions*. Here, too, he tells us "Deconstruction, I have insisted, is not *neutral*. It *intervenes*."[46] But *how*? And from *where*? His answer is certainly not, as one might have expected, straightforward. Consider Derrida's "final" P.S. which concludes his letter to Jean-Louis Houdebine, and "ends" his short book:

> P.S. And, if we gave to this exchange, for its (germinal) title, the word *positions*, whose polysemia is marked, moreover, in the letter *s*, the "disseminating" letter *par excellence*, as Mallarmé said? I will add, concerning *positions*: scenes, sets, figures of dissemination.[47]

Here we touch upon what might be called Derrida's "double bind." When Derrida (or the texts that bear the signature Jacques Derrida,

J. D., or Reb Derissa) tells us "Deconstruction, *I have insisted* [emphasis added, RJB] is not *neutral*. It *intervenes*" or that deconstruction *is* taking a position which may be too political for some, he is – to use a "traditional" term – certainly declaring and clarifying his *intentions*. But few writers have raised so many questions about "intentions" and discerning an "author's intentions" from texts that bear his signature. One is reminded of the type of inversion and displacement that Hegel highlights in the disparity between what is *said* (*sagt*) and what is only meant (*nur gemeint*). But we do not need Hegel to make the point. Derrida's texts do it for us.

Derrida is painfully aware of what one commentator says about deconstruction when he notes that "Insofar as one can treat the movement to dismantle the whole as a whole, it has had and continues to have conservative, even quietistic, implications and this in spite of its radical critique of hierarchy and system."[48] Indeed, there is something grotesque and even perverse about the "reception" of Derrida and deconstruction, especially by *some* members of the Anglo-American literary "community" where this "movement" has been most influential. For it is marked by an intellectual elitist arrogance, and frequently degenerates into little more than a sophisticated word play by coteries of academics who delight in their own "precious" verbal wit and cleverness. Despite the claim that deconstruction may be "too political for some," the "reception" of deconstruction has been almost totally apolitical – except, of course, for that domestic parlour game called "academic politics." Indeed, I think Edward W. Said is right when he notes that recent literary criticism (and in particular, deconstruction) bears its own form of complicity with recent "neo-conservatism," with what Said labels, "The Age of Ronald Reagan."[49] For despite all the talk or writing about "radical gestures," critiques of "hierarchy" and "dogmatic authorities," deconstructive discourse at times seems to be completely disengaged or uncoupled from present-day ethical-political conflicts and struggles. And despite Derrida's own insistence and attempts to demonstrate the relevance of deconstructive questioning to the critique of political and social institutions (such as the modern university), the gestures in this direction have, thus far, been rather feeble.

But is it really "fair" to blame Derrida for the "reception" of his texts? Doesn't this situation tell us more about the times we are living through than it does about what he has written? Isn't holding Derrida "responsible" for the perverse reception of his writings analogous to holding Marx responsible for what has happened in his name in the so-called "really existing socialism" of the Soviet orbit or condemning Nietzsche for the Nazi misappropriation and distortion of his writings? Fortunately we do not have to second guess what Derrida would say about this; he has been explicit. As I report what Derrida says about the texts signed "F. N." I ask you to think about how – with appropriate modifications – we might say the "same" about Derrida's texts. When Derrida takes up the question of how Nietzsche was "heard" by his contemporaries and by Nazi ideologues – when he stresses the size and the anatomy of the "ears" that hear – he tells us "the effects or structure of a text are not reducible to its 'truth,' to the intended meaning of its presumed author, or even its supposedly unique and identifiable signatory."[50] After raising the question of whether there is something about Nietzsche's texts – "a powerful utterance-producing machine that programs the movements of the two opposing forces at once"[51] – Derrida writes "Even if the intention of one of the signatures or shareholders in the huge 'Nietzsche Corporation' [substitute 'Derrida Corporation', RJB] had nothing to do with it, *it cannot be entirely fortuitous that the discourse bearing his name in society, in accordance with civil laws and editorial norms, has served as a legitimating reference for idealogues*" (emphasis added). [52]

Again I (RJB) ask you to make the appropriate "translation" when one reads the following:

I do not aim to "clear" its "author" and neutralize or defuse either what might be troublesome in it for democratic pedagogy or "leftist" politics, or what served as "language" for the most sinister rallying cries of National Socialism. On the contrary, the greatest indecency is *de rigueur* in this place. One may even wonder why it is not enough to say: "Nietzsche did not think that," "he did not want that," or "he would have surely vomited this," that there is falsification of the legacy and interpretive mystification going on here. One may wonder how and why what is so naively called a falsification was possible (one can't falsify just anything), how and why the "same" words and the "same" statements – if they are indeed the same – might several times be made to serve certain meanings and certain contexts that are said to be different, even incompatible.[53]

I hope my moral is clear. But if it isn't, let me spell it out. I am certainly *not* suggesting that Derrida's texts are the occasion for "the most sinister rallying cries." It is difficult to imagine texts which are more anti-authoritarian and subversive for any (and all) "true believers." But I am *asking* whether the signatory of these texts bears some responsibility for their reception. If the desire to write "is the desire to perfect a program or a matrix having the greatest potential, variability, undecidability, plurivocality, et cetera, so that each time something returns it will be as different as possible," then doesn't the signatory bear some "responsibility" for the divergent and incompatible ways in which the texts are read and heard? One may wonder "how and why" the texts signed by J. D. can be read (or heard) as being nihilistic, obscurantist, self-indulgent logorrhoea *and* (as I have argued) passionate, political, subversive, committed to opening the spaces for *différance* and *respecting* what is irreducibly other. What is it about the texts of Derrida that allow for, indeed, invite this double reading? After all "one can't falsify just anything." What is it about these texts that allows us to hear them with such different ears and sign them with such different (and incompatible) signatures? Can we absolve the writer – who constantly emphasizes "new responsibilities" – of the responsibility for his texts? It is too glib – as Derrida himself knows – to say that *every* text involves "a program or a matrix having the greatest potential, variability, undecidability, plurivocality, et cetera," for this does not answer the question why *specific* texts are interpreted in the determinate ways in which they have been read. (After all we can well understand the ambiguities that allowed the Nazis to brutalize Nietzsche's texts. But can we even imagine that they might have done the same to the texts of – say – John Dewey?)

My *questions* need to be carefully circumscribed. For I certainly do not think it even makes sense to hold an "author" completely responsible for the reception, interpretation, and appropriation of his/her texts. To do so would violate a fundamental insight that has emerged from hermeneutics, the theory of communicative action, *and* deconstruction, viz., there is no communication, understanding, interpretation, or reading that is not also open to miscommunication, misunderstanding, misinterpretation, and misreading. As Derrida himself reminds us, we must rigorously scrutinize not only the texts that bear the signature of an "author" but also the texts signed by those who appropriate what is said and written. But still "one may wonder how and why what is so naively called a falsification was possible."

In conclusion, let me suggest a hypothesis to account for Derrida's own "double bind" – the double bind where he tells us explicitly what he *intends*, what deconstruction *is* "if it is of any consequence" *and* at the "same" moment undermines or erases the "naïveté" of assessing texts by what we take to be the "author's intentions." Derrida knows all too well that there is no ethics or politics – or even meta-ethics or meta-politics without "taking a position." But few have written more persuasively and imaginatively than he has about all the snares and traps that await us in "taking a position" – how easily we can fall back into the metaphysics of presence and the dream of a fixed center that he has sought so valiantly to question; how a self-deceptive violent dogmatism awaits those for whom *archai* do not tremble. But even if we learn this lesson over and over again, we are still left with the unanswered question: *how can we "warrant" (in any sense of the term) the ethical-political "positions" we do take?* This is *the* question that Derrida never satisfactorily answers. What is worse, despite the overwhelming evidence of his own moral passion and his willingness and courage in "taking positions," he seems to call into question the very possibility of "warranting" ethical-political positions. Or rather, it is not clear how Derrida understands the *practice* of warranting our ethical-political positions. What are we to do after we realize that all *archai* tremble? It is almost as if Derrida wants to bring us out of the wilderness, wants to *überwinden* the violent "history of the West" without providing us with an orientation for avoiding the abyss of nihilism that he so desperately wants to avoid. We lack what he himself calls a *mochlos* – a lever – for displacing the history of violence. He presumably points us toward the promised land of a *postmetaphysical* ethics and politics without adumbrating its geography. Or perhaps, we might say "the promised land" that we may "dream" about is obscured by a hazy and foggy horizon.

But to "end" with a gesture of reconciliation, I do not say this with malicious smugness from some "suspended position" which may itself stand over an abyss, but rather to highlight a problematic which is – if we are intellectually forthright – not only Derrida's, but *our* collective problematic.

NOTES

1 Jacques Derrida, *The Ear of the Other*, trans. Christie V. McDonald (New York: Schocken Books, 1985), p. 158.
2 Martin Heidegger, "Letter on Humanism," in *Martin Heidegger: Basic Writings*, ed. and trans. David F. Krell (New York: Harper and Row, 1977), p. 233.
3 See Sarah Kofman, "Un Philosophie '*Unheimlich*'," in *Ecarts: Quatre Essais à propos de Jacques Derrida* (Paris: Fayard, 1973).
4 Jacques Derrida, "The Ends of Man," in *Margins*, trans. Alan Bass (Chicago: University of Chicago Press, 1982), p. 130.
5 Ibid., p. 133.

> Ce qui s'ébranle peut-être aujourd'hui, n'est-ce pas cette sécurité du proche, cette co-appartenance et cette co-propriété du nom de l'homme et du nom de l'être, telle qu'elle habite et s'habite elle-même dans la langue de l'Occident, dans son *oikonomia*, telle qu'elle s'y est enfoncée, telle qu'elle s'est incrite et oubliée selon l'histoire de la métaphysique, telle qu'elle se réveille aussi par la destruction de l'onto-théologie?

6 Jacques Derrida, "Structure, Sign, and Play in the Discourse of the Human Sciences," in *Writing and Difference*, trans. Alan Bass (Chicago: University of Chicago Press, 1978), p. 277.
7 Ibid., pp. 277–8.
8 Jacques Derrida, *Limited Inc.*, ed. Gerald Graff (Evanston: Northwestern University Press, 1988), p. 93.
9 Jacques Derrida, "Violence and Metaphysics: An Essay on the Thought of Emmanuel Levinas," in *Writing and Difference*, p. 83.
10 Ibid., p. 81.
11 Derrida, "Structure, Sign, and Play," p. 180. Derrida characterizes this event/rupture of decentering as follows:

> Where and how does this decentering, this thinking the structurality of structure, occur? It would be somewhat naïve to refer to an event, a doctrine, or an author in order to designate this occurrence. It is no doubt part of the totality of an era, our own, but still it has always already begun to proclaim itself and begun to *work*. Nevertheless, if we wished to choose several "names," as indications only, and to recall these authors in whose discourse this occurrence has kept most closely to its most radical formulation, we doubtless would have to cite the Nietzschean critique of metaphysics, the critique of the concepts of Being and Truth, for which were substituted the concepts of play, interpretation, and sign (sign without present Truth): the Freudian critique of self-presence, that is, the critique of consciousness, of the subject, of self-identity and of self-proximity or self-possession; and more radically the Heideggerean destruction of metaphysics, of onto-theology, of the determination of Being as presence. (Ibid., p. 280)

12 See my discussion of "The Cartesian Anxiety" in *Beyond Objectivism and Relativism: Science, Hermeneutics, and Praxis* (Philadelphia: University of Pennsylvania Press, 1983), pp. 16ff.

13 Jacques Derrida, "The Time of a Thesis: punctuations," in Alan Montefiore, ed., *Philosophy in France Today* (Cambridge: Cambridge University Press, 1983).

14 G. W. F. Hegel, *The Phenomenology of Spirit*, trans. A.V. Miller (New York: Oxford University Press, 1977), p. 49.

15 Sigmund Freud, "The 'Uncanny'," in *The Standard Edition of the Complete Psychological Works of Sigmund Freud* (London: Hogarth, 1955), XVII (1917–19), p. 220.

16 Ibid., p. 221.

17 Ibid., p. 224.

18 Ibid., p. 245.

19 Ibid., p. 226.

20 Freud himself stresses the "compulsion to repeat" in his analysis of the uncanny:

> For it is possible to recognize the dominance in the unconscious mind of a "compulsion to repeat" proceeding from the instinctual impulse and probably inherent in the very nature of the instincts – a compulsion powerful enough to overrule the pleasure principle, lending to certain aspects of the mind their daemonic character, and still very clearly expressed in the impulses of small children; a compulsion, too, which is responsible for a part of the course taken by the analyses of neurotic patients. All these considerations prepare us for the discovery that whatever reminds us of this inner "compulsion to repeat" is perceived as uncanny. (Ibid., p. 238)

21 Jacques Derrida, *Of Grammatology*, trans. Gayatri Chakravorty Spivak (Baltimore: Johns Hopkins Press, 1974), p. 25.

22 Derrida also writes: "Hegel is *also* the thinker of irreducible difference." Ibid., p. 26.

23 Derrida, "Structure, Sign, and Play," p. 280.

24 Susan A. Handelman, *The Slayers of Moses* (Albany: State University of New York Press, 1982), pp. 168–9. Although Handelman is extremely perceptive in showing the affinities between Derrida and Jewish hermeneutical practices, at times she comes close to falling into a trap characteristic of many commentators on Derrida, i.e., introducing a new set of rigid "binary" oppositions, e.g., Christian *and* Jewish hermeneutics. But Derrida himself is always wary of displacing "old" dichotomies with "new" dichotomies. This is illustrated when in "Violence and Metaphysics" he asks "Are we Jews? Are we Greeks?" and "concludes" by citing "perhaps the most Hegelian of modern novelists [James Joyce]: 'Jewgreek is greekjew. Extremes meet'" (p. 153). See also the discussion of Jewish mystical themes in Derrida by Jürgen

Habermas, *The Philosophical Discourse of Modernity*, trans. F. Lawrence (Cambridge, Mass.: MIT Press, 1987), pp. 182ff.

25   In the preface to the catalog introducing the itinerant exhibition, the organizers write:

> The collection offered here will form the basis of a future museum against apartheid. But first, these works will be presented in a traveling exhibition to be received by museums and other cultural facilities throughout the world. The day will come – and our efforts are joined to those of the international community aiming to hasten that day's arrival – when the museum thus constituted will be presented as a gift to the free and democratic government of South Africa to be elected by universal suffrage.

See Jacques Derrida, "Racism's Last Word," trans. Peggy Kamuf, *Critical Inquiry* 12 (Autumn 1985), p. 290.

For a critical discussion of "Racism's Last Word" and Derrida's response, see Anne McClintock and Rob Nixon, "No Names Apart: The Separation of Word and History in Derrida's '*Le Dernier Mot du Racisme*'"; and Jacques Derrida, "But beyond ... (Open Letter to Anne McClintock and Rob Nixon)," *Critical Inquiry* 13 (Autumn 1986), pp. 140–70.

26   Derrida, "Racism's Last Word," p. 292.

27   Ibid., p. 298:

> If we could forget about the suffering, the humiliation, the torture and the deaths, we might be tempted to look at this region of the world as a giant tableau or painting, the screen for some geopolitical computer. Europe, in the enigmatic process of its globalization and of its parodoxical disappearance, seems to project onto this screen, point by point, the silhouette of its internal war, the bottom line of its profits and losses, the double-bind logic of its national and multinational interests. Their dialectical evaluation provides only a provisional stasis in a precarious equilibrium, one whose price today is *apartheid*. All states and all societies are still willing to pay this price, first of all by making someone else pay .... without minimizing the alleged "reasons of state," we must nevertheless say very loudly and in a single breath. If that's the way it is, then the declarations of the Western states denouncing *apartheid* from the height of international platforms and elsewhere are dialectics of denegation.

28   Ibid., p. 293. In Derrida's open letter "But beyond ..." he emphasizes that his "appeal is indeed an appeal because it calls for something which is not yet .... It is a call to struggle but also to memory. I never separate promising from memory" (p. 160).

29   In addition to Derrida's texts relating to Jews and Blacks, there is also a series of texts dealing with the "position" of women (and men).

Surely one of Derrida's most lyrical passages which "dreams" of a "position" beyond binary opposition – a different relationship to the other – is the following:

> This double dissymmetry perhaps goes beyond known or coded marks, beyond the grammar and spelling, shall we say (metaphorically), of sexuality. This indeed revives the following question: what if we were to reach, what if we were to approach here (for one does not arrive at this as one would at a determined location) the area of a relationship to the other where the code of sexual marks would no longer be discriminating? The relationship would not be a-sexual, far from it, but would be sexual otherwise: beyond the binary difference that governs the decorum of all codes, beyond the distinction masculine/feminine .... As I dream of saying the chance that this question offers I would like to believe in the multiplicity of sexually marked voices. I would like to believe in the masses, this indeterminable number of blended voices, this mobile of non-identified sexual marks whose choreography can carry, divide, multiply the body of each "individual," whether he be classified as "man" or as "woman" according to the criteria of usage. ("Choreographics," *Diacritics* 12 [Summer, 1982], pp. 66–7)

See also "Voice ii: Jacques Derrida et Verena Andermott Conley," *Boundary 2* 12 (Winter 1984); and *Spurs: Nietzsche's Styles*, trans. Barbara Harlow (Chicago: University of Chicago Press, 1979). For an "appropriation" of Derrida to the question of feminism, see Drucilla Cornell and Adam Thurschwell, "Feminism, Negativity, Intersubjectivity," *Praxis International* 5 (January 1986).

30 Jacques Derrida, "Des Tours de Babel," in Joseph F. Graham, ed., *Difference in Translation* (Ithaca: Cornell University Press, 1985), p. 174.
31 Derrida, "Structure, Sign, and Play," p. 280.
32 See Jacques Derrida "The Principle of Reason: The University in the Eyes of its Pupils," *Diacritics* 13 (Fall 1983).
33 Martin Heidegger, "The Question Concerning Technology," in *Martin Heidegger: Basic Writings*, p. 317.
34 Henry Staten, *Wittgenstein and Derrida* (Lincoln: University of Nebraska Press, 1984), p. 18. Several commentators have noted the affinities between Wittgenstein and Derrida, but Staten shows this with great finesse and subtlety. One of Derrida's most explicit and polemical critiques of boundary-fixing (with a direct reference to the ethical-political context of deconstruction) is his response to McClintock's and Nixon's attack on "Racism's Last Word." He concludes his response, "But beyond ..." (pp. 169–70):

> In short, you are for the division of labor and the disciplined respect of disciplines. Each must stick to his role and stay within the field of his competence, none may transgress the limits of his territory. Oh, you wouldn't go so far as to wish that some sort of *apartheid* remain or become

the law of the land in the academy. Besides, you obviously don't like this word. You are among those who don't like this word and do not want it to remain the "unique appellation." No, in the homelands of academic culture or of "political action," you would favor instead reserved domains, the separate development of each community in the zone assigned to it.
　　Not me.

35　Staten, *Wittgenstein and Derrida*, p. 34.
36　Here it is enlightening to pursue the affinities (as well as the differences) between Derrida and Adorno who also stressed the necessity and the dangers of boundary-fixing concepts (*Begriffe*). It is becoming increasingly apparent how Adorno anticipated many deconstructive themes in his negative dialectics. Terry Eagleton writes:

> The parallels between deconstruction and Adorno are particularly striking. Long before the current fashion, Adorno was insisting on the power of those heterogeneous fragments that slip through the conceptual net, rejecting all philosophy of identity, refusing class consciousness as objectively "positive," and denying the intentionality of signification. Indeed, there is hardly a theme in contemporary deconstruction that is not richly elaborated in his work. (*Walter Benjamin or Towards a Revolutionary Criticism* [London: New Left Books, 1981], p. 141)

　　See also Martin Jay, *Adorno* (Cambridge, Mass.: Harvard University Press, 1984), p. 20; and Michael Ryan, *Marxism and Deconstruction* (Baltimore: Johns Hopkins University Press, 1982), pp. 73–80. See also Habermas' discussion of Adorno and Derrida in *The Philosophical Discourse of Modernity*, pp. 185ff.
37　Derrida, "Violence and Metaphysics," p. 138. See also Fred Dallmayr's perceptive discussion of Derrida and Levinas in *Twilight of Subjectivity* (Amherst: University of Massachusetts Press, 1981), pp. 107–15.
38　Derrida, "Violence and Metaphysics," p. 138.
39　Ibid., p. 141.
40　Ibid., p. 146.
41　Derrida, *Of Grammatology*, p. 136.
42　Staten, *Wittgenstein and Derrida*, pp. 126–7.
43　Derrida, "The Principle of Reason," pp. 14–15. Concerning the (Leibnizian) principle of reason and its relation to the university, Derrida asks:

> Are we obeying the principle of reason when we ask what grounds this principle which is itself a principle of grounding? We are not – which does not mean that we are disobeying it, either. Are we dealing here with a circle or with an abyss? The circle would consist in seeking to account for reason by reason, to render reason to the principle of reason, in appealing to the principle in order to make it speak of itself at the very point

where, according to Heidegger, the principle of reason says nothing about reason itself. The abyss, the hole, the *Abgrund*, the empty "gorge" would be the impossibility for a principle of grounding to ground itself. This very grounding, then, like the university, would have to hold itself suspended above a most peculiar void. Are we to use reason to account for the principle of reason? Is the reason of reason rational? Is it rational to worry about reason and its principle? Not *simply*; but it would be over-hasty to seek to disqualify this concern and to refer those who experience it back to their own irrationalism, their obscurantism, their nihilism. Who is more faithful to reason's call, who hears it with a keener ear, who better sees the difference, the one who offers questions in return and tries to think through the possibility of that summons, or the one who does not want to hear any question about the reason of reason? (Ibid., p. 9)

44 Ibid., p. 15.
45 Jacques Derrida, "The Conflict of Faculties: A *Mochlos*" (forthcoming), p. 56. Derrida has become more explicit and insistent on stressing the political consequences of "deconstruction" especially in light of what he calls the "misreading" of deconstruction which is "widespread." In "But beyond ...," he writes:

It is precisely for strategic reasons (set forth at length elsewhere) that I found it necessary to recast the concept of text by generalizing it almost without limit, without any limit that is. That's why there is nothing *"beyond* the text." That's why South Africa and *apartheid* are, like you and me, part of this general text, which is not to say that it can be read the way one reads a book. That's why the text is always a field of forces: heterogeneous, differential, open, and so on. That's why deconstructive readings and writings are concerned not only with library books, with discourses, with conceptual and semantic contents. They are not simply analyses of discourse, such as, for example, the one you propose. They are also effective or active (as one says) interventions, in particular political and institutional interventions that transform contexts without limiting themselves to theoretical or constative utterances even though they must also produce such utterances. (pp. 167–8)

Terry Eagleton, who is at once sympathetic with, and critical of, Derrida's political "intention" writes the following:

If the American deconstructionists considered their textual enterprise was faithful to the spirit of Jacques Derrida, one of those who did not was Jacques Derrida. Certain American uses of deconstruction, Derrida has observed, work to ensure "an institutional closure" which serves the domi-nant political and economic interests of American society. Derrida is clearly out to do more than develop new techniques of reading: deconstruction is for him an ultimately *political* practice, an attempt to dismantle the logic by which a particular system of thought, and behind that a whole system of political structures and social institutions, maintains its force. He is not seeking, absurdly, to deny the existence of relatively determinate truths, meanings, identities, intentions, historical continuities; he is seeking rather to see such things as the effects of a wider and deeper history – of language, of the unconscious, of social institutions and practices. (*Literary Theory: An Introduction* [Minneapolis: University of Minnesota Press, 1983], p. 148)

46 Jacques Derrida, *Positions*, trans. Alan Bass (Chicago: University of Chicago Press, 1981), p. 93.
47 Ibid., p. 96.
48 Steven Cresap, "Review of Martin Jay: *Marxism and Totality*," *New German Critique* 33 (Fall 1984), pp. 262–3.
49 Edward W. Said, "Opponents, Audiences, Constituencies, and Community," *Critical Inquiry* 9 (September 1982).
50 Derrida, *The Ear of the Other*, p. 29.
51 Ibid.
52 Ibid., p. 30.
53 Ibid., pp. 23–4.

7

An Allegory of Modernity/Postmodernity
Habermas and Derrida

During the past decade – in virtually every area of cultural life – there has been an explosion of discourses about "modernity" and "postmodernity." These discourses and the endless symposia dealing with this problematic have been at once heady and confusing. Heady, because they are signs of a prevailing mood – what Heidegger calls a *Stimmung* – one which is amorphous, elusive, protean. It is difficult to pin down and to characterize. Nevertheless it exerts a powerful influence. For there is a prevailing sense that something is happening that radically calls into question entrenched ways of thinking, acting and feeling. Consider the following description of the postmodern movement as a movement of "unmaking" by the literary critic, Iban Hassan.

> It is an antinomian moment that assumes a vast unmaking of the Western mind – what Michel Foucault might call postmodern *epistēmē*. I say "unmaking" though other terms are now *de rigueur*: for instance, deconstruction, decentering, disappearance, demystification, discontinuity, *différance*, dispersion, etc. Such terms express an ontological rejection of the traditional full subject, the *cogito* of Western philosophy. They express, too, an epistemological obsession with fragments, and a corresponding ideological commitment to minorities in politics, sex and language. To think well, to feel well, to act well, to read well according to this *epistēmē* of unmaking, is to refuse the tyranny of wholes: totalization in human endeavour is potentially totalitarian.[1]

Consider also the way in which Jean-François Lyotard defined "modern" and "postmodern" in his polemical monograph, *The Postmodern Condition: A Report on Knowledge* – a tract that draws upon many "postmodern" themes and which has provoked extensive discussion:

> I will use the term modern to designate any science that legitimates itself with reference to a metadiscourse of this kind making explicit appeal to some grand narrative, such as the dialectics of Spirit, the hermeneutics of meaning, the emancipation of the rational or working subject, or the creation of wealth.

> Simplifying to the extreme I define postmodern as incredulity toward metanarratives. This incredulity is undoubtedly a product of progress in the sciences; but that progress in turn presupposes it. To the obsolescence of the metanarrative apparatus of legitimation corresponds most notably, the crisis of metaphysical philosophy and of the university institution which in part relied on it. The narrative function is losing its functors, its great hero, its great voyages, its great goal.[2]

Although these passages give some indication of the "postmodern" mood, it is becoming increasingly evident that the terms "modern" and "postmodern" are not only vague, ambiguous and slippery, they have been used in conflicting and even contradictory ways. Even when this confusion is acknowledged there has been a strong temptation to go on using them, to slide into a quasi-essentialism where we talk as if there are a set of determinate features that mark off the "modern" from the "postmodern." The trouble is that nobody seems to agree about what these distinguishing characteristics are. My own conviction is that we have reached a stage of discussion where these labels (and their cognates) obscure more than they clarify – that it is better to drop these terms from our "vocabularies," and to try to sort out the relevant issues without reifying these labels.

So I want to do something different, but something that is relevant to these debates. I want to play off against each other two thinkers whose names are frequently invoked in the so-called quarrel of "moderns" and "postmoderns," a quarrel that seems to have displaced the venerable quarrel of the "ancients" and the "moderns." Habermas, for whom the concept of modernity is central, is frequently taken to be the boldest defender of the unfinished project of modernity, a forceful champion of the Enlightenment legacy. Derrida, who rarely even mentions "modernity" or "postmodernity," is nevertheless taken to be the "postmodern" thinker par excellence.[3] Initially, the differences between them – differences in focus, style, tone, and the legacies upon which they draw, *seem* so striking that one wonders if they share any common ground. When one turns to the ways in which they write about each other, one may despair of bridging what appears unbridgeable.[4] It is all too easy to think that an abyss separates them, that if ever there were vocabularies that are incommensurable then the vocabularies of Habermas and Derrida qualify as paradigmatic examples. I do *not* think that there is some theoretical perspective in which their crucial differences can be reconciled, *aufgehoben*. They cannot. But I want to show some of the ways in which they supplement each other, how we can view them as reflecting two intertwined strands of the "modern/postmodern" *Stimmung*. The "logic" of my argument is Both/And rather than Either/Or. This Both/And exhibits unresolved, perhaps unresolvable tensions and instabilities.

Drawing upon two metaphors used by Adorno – the metaphors of a force-field and constellation – I intend to show how Habermas/Derrida enable us to gain a deeper grasp of our present cultural and philosophical situation. By a "force-field" Adorno means "a relational interplay of attractions and aversions that constitute the dynamic, transmutational structure of a complex phenomenon."[5] By "constellation" – a metaphor that Adorno borrowed from Benjamin – he means "a juxtaposed rather than integrated cluster of changing elements that resist reduction to a common denominator, essential core, or generative first principle."[6] To refer to Benjamin once again, the force-field and constellation that I will be sketching may be read as an *allegory* of the "modern/postmodern" condition.

My approach to Habermas and Derrida may appear slightly unorthodox. I want to show what they are "up to." I share William James' conviction when he shrewdly remarked:

> If we take the whole history of philosophy, the systems reduce themselves to a few main types which under all technical verbiage in which the ingenious intellect of man envelops them, are just so many visions, modes of feeling the whole push, and seeing the whole drift of life, forced on one by one's total character and experience and on the whole *preferred* – there is no other truthful word – as one's best working attitude.[7]

I reject the approach to Habermas and Derrida that reads them as if they consisted only in a collection of disembodied texts with little regard to their flesh and blood experiences. We cannot gain a nuanced understanding of what they are "up to," to their "modes of feeling the whole push" unless we pay some attention to the vital formative personal experiences that have shaped even their most theoretical writings. Specifically, I am concerned with the ways in which they have experienced the threats, dangers and challenges of the horrendous – almost incomprehensible – events of the twentieth century.

The unfinished project of the Enlightenment

For Habermas, one of these central formative experiences was his shock as a young adolescent when he discovered the full horrors of Nazism. It is in the background of almost everything he has written. Habermas, who was born in 1929, tells us:

> At the age of 15 or 16, I sat before the radio and experienced what was being discussed before the Nuremberg tribunal, when others, instead of being struck by the ghastliness, began to dispute the justice of the trial, procedural questions, and questions of jurisdiction, there was that first rupture, which still gapes. Certainly, it is only because I was still sensitive and easily offended that I did not close myself to the fact of a collectively realized inhumanity in the same measure as the majority of my elders.[8]

The painful awareness of "the ghastliness," of "a collectively realized inhumanity," a sharp sense of "rupture" were the traumatic experiences of the young Habermas. A question began to take shape – a question that has haunted Habermas ever since: how could one account for the "pathologies of modernity"? How could one explain that rupture in the cultural tradition of Kant, Hegel and Marx in which the ideals of reason, freedom and justice had been so prominent? As a university student, Habermas, like many of his contemporaries, experienced the intellectual power of Heidegger's *Sein und Zeit* (1927), but he was also deeply affected by Lukács' *History and Class Consciousness* (1922), and especially Horkheimer and Adorno's *Dialectic of Enlightenment* (1944). Before he became Adorno's assistant, Habermas perceived the challenge posed by the *Dialectic of Enlightenment* when in its opening sentence the authors declared:

> In the most general sense of progressive thought, the Enlightenment has always aimed at liberating men from fear and establishing their sovereignty. Yet the fully enlightened earth radiates disaster triumphant.[9]

In the *Dialectic of Enlightenment* the authors relentlessly sought to highlight the "dark side" of the Enlightenment legacy and indeed all of social and cultural modernity – the way in which the Enlightenment gave rise to and promoted a "totalitarian" instrumental rationality that infected every aspect of cultural, social and personal life – even reaching into the inner recesses of the human psyche. In this respect, Horkheimer and Adorno were deepening and extending the concept of reification that Lukács had so brilliantly analyzed in *History and Class Consciousness*. But contrary to Lukács, they categorically rejected the idea that a proletarian revolution would "solve" the problem of reification, or that with development of the proletarian class consciousness, there would be a "final reconciliation" of Subject and Object. Horkheimer and Adorno were at once much closer, and certainly more extreme than, Max Weber – at least the Weber who was read as prophesying that the twentieth century would be the epoch of the triumph of *Zweckrationalität* and bureaucratic normalization creating an "iron cage" from which there is no escape.

Habermas realized that one could not underestimate the growth and spread of instrumental, strategic, and systems rationality in the economic, social, and political structures of the modern world, and their powerful tendencies to reshape and colonize our everyday life-world. But at first, almost instinctively, and later, with increasing theoretical finesse, Habermas argued that this monolithic portrait of the totalitarian character of Enlightenment rationality was overdrawn. It failed to do justice to those philosophic and historical tendencies – also rooted in the Enlightenment – that gave rise to democratic public spaces in which a different type of communal rationality was manifested.[10] At a deeper level there was a failure to do justice to what Habermas first called symbolic interaction (and later called communicative action), and its distinctive type of rationality – the type of action that is oriented to mutual understanding and consensual action rather than to the goals of efficiency and success.

Gradually it became clear to Habermas that a proper response to all those – whether they were associated with the political left or right – who claimed that our modern destiny is one in which there is an ineluctable triumph of instrumental, technological "rationality" (what Heidegger called *Gestell*) is to reopen and rethink the entire problematic of rationality. In this rethinking – this reconstructive project – one needs to draw crucial and categorical distinctions between different types of action, rationality, rationalization processes, and their complex dynamic interrelations. Although Habermas' terminology has shifted and has become more differentiated, he has consistently maintained that there is a categorical distinction between the varieties of instrumental, strategic, systems, and technological rationality *and* communicative, dialogical rationality. Furthermore he has argued that instrumental rationality presupposes and is dependent upon communicative rationality. All attempts to reduce or translate communicative action to monological, teleological, goal-oriented action and rationality fail – or so Habermas argues. Once we make a categorical distinction between communicative and purposive-rational action, we can sharply distinguish what the rationalization of these different action-types means.

"Purposive-rational actions can be regarded under two different aspects – the empirical efficiency of technical means and the consistency of choice between suitable means."[11] "Rationalization" as it pertains to purposive-rational actions means increasing efficiency or the consistency of "rational" choices. This is the type of rationalization that has been privileged by neo-classical economists and those influenced by models of economic rationality.

But "rationalization" of the communicative action has a radically different meaning:

> Rationalization here means extirpating those relations of force that are inconspicuously set in the very structures of communication and that prevent conscious settlement of conflicts .... Rationalization means overcoming such systematically distorted communication in which action supporting consensus concerning the reciprocally raised validity claims ... can be sustained in appearance only, that is counterfactually.[12]

The position expressed in this passage is rich in its consequences. I want to emphasize that Habermas' theoretical reconstructive project of elucidating the universal conditions for communicative action is not merely "theoretical": it has strong practical consequences for orienting our ethical and political activity. It directs us to the normative task of overcoming those material obstacles that prevent or inhibit undistorted and non-coerced communication. Positively stated, it means working toward the cultivation of practices that bring us closer to the ideal of seeking to resolve conflicts through discourses where the only relevant force is the "force of the better argument." Habermas is frequently misread as if he were proposing an ideal form of life in which all conflicts would be settled by rational discussion – an ideal form of life where all violence would disappear. But this is a caricature. Our concrete historical forms of life are always shaped by traditions, social practices and communal bonds that are more concrete and complex than our rational discursive practices. Without these traditions there would be no *substance* to our ethical and political convictions. Violence and distortion may be uneliminable, but they can be diminished. Habermas' limited but all-important thesis is that:

> In action oriented to reaching understanding, validity claims are "always already" implicitly raised. Those universal claims (to the comprehensibility of the symbolic expression, the truth of the propositional content, the truthfulness of the intentional expression, and the rightness of the speech act with respect to existing norms and values) are set in the general structures of possible communication. In these validity claims communicative theory can locate a gentle, but obstinate, a never silent although seldom redeemed claim to reason, a claim that must be recognized *de facto* whenever and wherever there is to be consensual action.[13]

Habermas rejects any philosophy of history that is explicitly or implicitly committed to a grand teleological narrative. Nevertheless he does strongly affirm that, even though the claim to reason – to communicative dialogical reason – is silenced over and over again, it "develops a stubbornly transcending power, because it is renewed with each act of unconstrained understanding, with each moment of living together in solidarity, of successful individuation, and of saving emancipation."[14]

Habermas is a thoroughgoing fallibilist who rejects classical foundationalist and transcendental arguments. One of his criticisms of thinkers like Heidegger, Adorno and Derrida is that they still write in the "shadow of the 'last' philosopher, as did the first generation of Hegelian disciples. They still feel the need to battle against those 'strong' concepts of system, totality, truth, and completed theory which belong to the past."[15] Ironically, much of the *pathos* of their writings gains its force from the specter of the Grand System. "They still think that they have to arouse philosophy from what Derrida calls 'the dream of its heart.' They believe they have to tear philosophy away from the madness of expounding a theory that has the last word."[16] Despite their protests to the contrary, they are still entrapped in the *aporias* and *culs-de-sac* of what Habermas calls "The Philosophy of Subjectivity." Their failure, according to Habermas, is not to realize and fully appreciate that the "fallibilist consciousness of the sciences caught up with philosophy too, a long time ago."[17] When they declare that philosophy or metaphysics is over, their image of philosophy is still that of the Absolute System – the philosophy of "the last word." Each, in his way, wants to keep philosophy or thinking "pure" – pure from any contamination by empirical social scientific research.

Habermas' fallibilism is not incompatible with making universal claims and seeking to redeem them with the strongest arguments we can give. This is the way in which he conceives of his own theory of communicative action. In *this* respect, Habermas sees no epistemological difference between a theory of communicative action and any other scientific theory. For in advancing any theory we are always making universal validity claims which are necessarily open to ongoing criticism and revision.[18]

Throughout his intellectual career, Habermas has relentlessly sought to track down, expose and defeat the varieties of nihilism, relativism, decisionism, historicism and neo-Aristotelian contextualism that have been so fashionable in the twentieth century. Here too his motivations are not exclusively theoretical – they are motivated by his practical concerns. For he argues that the logic of all these "positions," when we think them through, undermines the possibility of critique that is rationally grounded and warranted. He criticizes all forms of totalizing critique, claiming that they lead to performative contradictions. What he says about Nietzsche applies equally to all those who work in his shadow (including Derrida): "Nietzsche's critique consumes the critical impulse itself." "If thought can no longer operate in the realms of truth and validity claims, then analysis and critique lose their meaning." One is left only with the seductions of a "bad" aestheticism that "enthrones *taste*, the 'Yes' and 'No' of the palate ... as the sole organ of knowledge beyond Truth and Falsity, beyond Good and Evil."[19]

Pervading all of Habermas' writings is his strong and unshakeable commitment to democracy. No less than John Dewey, Habermas is the philosopher of democracy. This is one of the reasons why he has been so drawn to the American pragmatic tradition, especially Peirce, Mead, and Dewey. From Peirce he appropriates the idea of an ongoing self-critical community of inquirers always open to criticizing its validity claims. Following Mead, he develops a theory of the genesis of the social self in which democratic individuality, and post-conventional morality are realizable achievements of practical intersubjectivity. With Dewey, Habermas believes in the normative ideal of a democratic society in which all share and participate. Like Dewey, who saw the most urgent problem of our time to be the cultivation of democratic public life, Habermas also believes that democratic participation is compatible with the complexity of advanced technological societies.

Habermas' entire project can be conceived of as a rethinking and rewriting of the *Dialectic of Enlightenment*. Habermas, like his mentors, has been alert to the self-destructive tendencies unleashed by the Enlightenment. But against them he argues that we need a more differentiated analysis of the conflicting tendencies of modernity and the Enlightenment legacy – one that does justice to the powerful tendencies of the growth and spread of systems rationality *and* those fragile practices in which we can still discern the transcending power of communicative rationality. Habermas is far more dialectical than Horkheimer and Adorno. For the overwhelming thrust of the *Dialectic of Enlightenment* is negative – it is a dark narrative of ineluctable self-destruction. But in a more dialectically nuanced manner, Habermas shows that our present situation, and the future possibilities open to us, are systematically ambiguous. Whether we will some day live in the cosmic night of nihilism *or* restore a proper balance between communicative and systems rationality is still an open question. The "colonization of the life world by systems rationality" is the most powerful tendency of advanced technological societies. But this tendency is not the manifestation of a logic of history that is working itself out "behind our backs." The promise of modernity is still an unfinished *project* – a project whose realization is dependent upon our present *praxis*.

Once we get a sense of Habermas' mode of "feeling the whole push," his vision of "the whole drift of life" then many aspects of his thinking and actions fall into place. We can understand why he is so suspicious of the ways in which the talk of "postmodernity" and "post-Enlightenment" slip into "old" variations of counter- or anti-modern themes. We can understand his frequent political and journalistic interventions in a German context. For Habermas is hyper-sensitive to those aspects of the pernicious cultural tendency to separate Germany's "spiritual destiny" from the moral and political achievements of Western democracy. Despite Habermas' acknowledgment that Heidegger – the Heidegger of *Sein und Zeit* – is Germany's greatest twentieth-century philosopher, he is scathing in his exposure and criticism of the ideological biases that infect Heidegger's writings from 1929 on.[20] We can even understand why Habermas is so critical and deeply suspicious of the major tendencies in post-World War II French cultural life. He reads Derrida as little more than a latinized disciple of Heidegger who furthers some of the worst tendencies in the late Heidegger. For he thinks that Derrida seduces us into thinking we can confront contemporary political, ethical and juridical problems by endless deconstruction of texts. Habermas is impatient with anyone who disdains concrete empirical social scientific research – who still wants to keep thinking "pure."

Iris Murdoch once shrewdly remarked "it is always a significant question to ask of any philosopher: what is he afraid of?" The answer for Habermas is clear. It is "irrationalism" whatever guise it takes – whether ugly fascist forms, disguised neo-conservative variations, or the playful antics of those who seek to domesticate Nietzsche. In a time when it has become so fashionable to attack, mock, ridicule the claim to Reason, Habermas is not afraid to appear "old-fashioned" – to insist on "the stubbornness with which philosophy clings to the role of the 'guardian of reason'" – a role that "can hardly be dismissed as an idiosyncrasy of self-absorbed intellectuals, especially in a period in which basic irrationalist undercurrents are transmuted once again into a dubious form of politics."[21]

The elusiveness and threat of otherness

Let me turn abruptly to Derrida. The turn is abrupt because initially it appears to be crossing an unbridgeable chasm. If one can speak of an experience of incommensurability and radical otherness, the turn to Derrida seems to transport us to a different world with few if any points of contact with the problems, theses and concerns that so preoccupy Habermas. I have already suggested that the metaphors of a constellation and force-field are helpful to grasp the agonistic and antagonistic tensions between them. To show this I want to adumbrate a reading of Derrida that brings forth the ethical-political-juridical motifs that run through *all* his writings.[22]

Just as I began my analysis of Habermas by recollecting a formative experience in his intellectual development, I want to juxtapose this with what Derrida himself takes to be a crucial experience of his childhood. Habermas and Derrida are almost exact contemporaries (Habermas was born in 1929, Derrida in 1931). At the time when Habermas was growing up in Nazi Germany, Derrida was experiencing the war as a French Algerian Jew in El-Biar. In the fragments of his autobiography that Derrida weaves into his writings and from some of his interviews, we can gain a glimmer of his childhood experiences – or at least his *memory* of them.

> The war came to Algeria in 1940, and with it, already then, the first concealed rumblings of the Algerian war. As a child, I had the instinctive feeling that the end of the world was at hand, a feeling which at the same time was most natural, and in any case, the only one I ever knew. Even to a child incapable of analyzing things, it was clear that all this would end in fire and blood. No one can escape that violence and fear.[23]

Derrida came from a petit-bourgeois Jewish family which was partially assimilated. He was and was not a Jew. He was and was not an Algerian. As an Algerian Jew he was and was not a Frenchman. By his own testimony his primary experience was a "feeling of non-belonging" – of "otherness."[24] And this continued when he went to France as a student at the age of nineteen. For Derrida has always characterized himself as working at the margins of philosophy and literature. The motifs of alterity, difference, supplementarity, marginality that weave in and out of all of his texts have their *correspondences* in those early experiences. He tells us:

> My central question is: from what site or non-site (*non-lieu*) can philosophy as such appear to itself, so that it can interrogate and reflect upon itself in an original manner? Such a non-site or alterity would be irreducible to philosophy. But the problem is that such a non-site cannot be defined or situated by means of philosophical language.[25]

The experience and obsessive concern with alterity, otherness – or more precisely, the singularity and otherness of the Other – haunt all of Derrida's texts. Furthermore his fascination with otherness (in all its modes) does have powerful ethical-political resonances – as we shall see. Deconstruction cannot be captured or reduced to a formula. Nevertheless, I can think of no more apt description than the one given by Derrida when he says "deconstruction is, in itself, a positive response to an alterity which necessarily calls, summons or motivates it. Deconstruction is therefore a vocation – a response to a call."[26] Deconstruction is "an openness towards the other."[27]

When I say that all the texts signed by Derrida are pervaded by ethical-political-juridical motifs, I do not simply mean that Derrida "has" an ethics and politics. I mean something much stronger. An ethical-political-juridical reading of all his texts is a point of departure for understanding his "mode of feeling the whole push." His ethical-political concerns shape and are shaped by his deconstruction of logocentrism, phonocentrism, phallogocentrism, and especially what he – following Heidegger – calls "the metaphysics of presence."[28]

Derrida is acutely aware that we cannot question or shake traditional ethical and political claims without at the same time also drawing upon these traditional claims. The very dichotomy of "inside–outside" is also deconstructed. We are never simply "inside" or "outside" metaphysics. Derrida has been read – I think seriously misread – as if he were advocating a total rupture with metaphysics, as if some apocalyptic event might occur that would once and for all release us from the metaphysical exigency. But he mocks the very idea of such an apocalyptic happening.[29] He tells us that "the idea that we might be able to get outside of metaphysics has always struck me as naive," and that "we cannot really say that we are 'locked into' or 'condemned to' metaphysics, for we are, strictly speaking, neither inside nor outside."[30]

According to Derrida, memory and promise, repetition and rupture always *come* together.[31] Concerning history and tradition, concerning the complex temporality of past-present-future, Derrida, in a manner that is reminiscent of Benjamin, writes:

> My own conviction is that we must maintain two contradictory affirmations at the same time. On the one hand we affirm the existence of ruptures in history, and on the other we affirm that these ruptures produce gaps or faults (*failles*) in which the most hidden and forgotten archives can emerge and constantly recur and work through history. One must surmount the categorical oppositions of philosophic logic out of fidelity to these conflicting positions of historical discontinuity (rupture) and continuity (repetition), which are neither pure break with the past nor a pure unfolding or explication of it.[32]

There is a another prevalent misreading of Derrida – claiming that he is guilty of some sort of linguistic idealism in his linkage of the history of signification, metaphysics and the "West." The most common criticism of Derrida is that he "reduces" everything to texts (and/or language) and declares that there is nothing beyond the text. But the key question is what does Derrida mean by a "text"? He answers this question in many places, but one of his clearest and most forceful statements occurs in his polemical exchange about apartheid, "Racism's Last Word." He tells us that "text" as he uses the term is not to be confused with the graphisms of a "book."

> No more than writing or trace, it is not limited to the *paper* which you can cover with your graphism. It is precisely for strategic reasons ... that I found it necessary to recast the concept of text by generalizing it almost without any limit that *is*. That's why there is nothing "*beyond* the text." That's why South Africa and *apartheid* are, like you and me, part of this general text, which is not to say that it can be read the way one reads a book. That's why the text is always a field of forces: heterogeneous, differential, open, and so on. That's why deconstructive readings and writings are concerned not only with library books, with discourses, with conceptual and semantic contents. They are not simply analyses of discourse .... They are also effective or active (as one says) interventions that transform contexts without limiting themselves to theoretical or constative utterances even though they must also produce such utterances.[33]

Derrida claims that his "strategic reevaluation of the concept of text allows [him] to bring together in a more consistent fashion, in the most consistent fashion possible, theoretico-philosophical necessities with 'practical,' political and other necessities of what is called deconstruction."[34] He emphatically affirms that "deconstructive practices are also and first of all political and institutional practices."[35]

But what precisely does this mean? How are deconstructive practices "first of all" political and institutional practices? The following passage provides an important clue.

> what is somewhat hastily called deconstruction is not, if it is of any consequence, a specialized set of discursive procedures, even less the rules of a new hermeneutic method, working on texts or utterances in the shelter of a given and stable institution. It is also, at the very least, a way of taking a position, in its work of analysis, concerning the political and institutional structures that make possible and govern our practice, our competences, our performances. Precisely because it is never concerned only with signified content, deconstruction should not be separable from this politico-institutional problematic and should seek a new investigation of responsibility, an investigation which questions the codes inherited from ethics and politics. This means that too political for some, it will seem paralyzing to those who only recognize politics by the most familiar road signs.[36]

Let me step back in order to comment on this dense passage and the controversial claims that Derrida makes here. Derrida is always concerned (obsessed) with the question of the otherness of the Other, with the differences that are presupposed by self-identity. He is always working on the margins, fascinated with the "logic of supplementarity." Metaphors of "exile" and "parasite" weave through his writings. Derrida is not only concerned with the receding limits that are presumably "discovered" or stipulated, he is deeply suspicious of all forms of boundary-fixing – including the boundary-fixing between theoretical and practical-political-institutional "domains." Here too one must be sensitive to Derrida's precise point if we want to grasp what he is "up to." Contrary to what many of his critics (including Habermas) claim, Derrida does *not* seek to deny all distinctions and reduce everything to one confused homogeneous text. He does *not* deny there are important distinctions between philosophy and literature or logic and rhetoric. He scrutinizes the precise "points" where distinctions, dichotomies, dualisms break down and are called into question. His deconstructive practices would not even make sense unless we initially take distinctions, negations, and oppositions "seriously." It is non-reducible heterogeneity and heterology that he makes manifest. He consistently opposes a "logic of apartheid," radical separation into "natural" kinds – whether we understand apartheid "literally" or "figuratively." He sees the *logic* of apartheid at work not only in South Africa but in the "homelands of academic culture." In responding to the critics of his *appeal* concerning apartheid, he concludes with a declaration that has much broader significance:

> in the homelands of academic culture or of "political action" you would favor instead reserved domains, the separate development of each community in the zone assigned to it.
> Not me.[37]

There is no fixed boundary between theoretical and practical domains, between texts and institutional contexts. Willy-nilly, all deconstruction for Derrida is always and also political. But there is a problem here that needs to be squarely confronted. Deconstruction may be "too political for some" but why does it also "seem paralyzing to those who only recognize politics by the most familiar road signs"? We need to probe further.

As a citizen, Derrida has taken strong admirable stands on a variety of political and ethical issues. He has fought against apartheid, written a moving homage to Mandela, actively participated in resisting the French government's attempt to reduce the teaching of philosophy in secondary schools, helped to start a new "open" university in Paris, been an outspoken critic of infringements on human rights, addressed feminist issues, and was even arrested and interrogated on a framed-up charge in Czechoslovakia. He has been an engaged intellectual. But what do these activities have to do with deconstruction? He speaks about this when he was asked: "Can the theoretical radicality of deconstruction be translated into a radical praxis?" He tells us "I must confess that I have never succeeded in directly relating deconstruction to existing political programmes."[38] The key terms here are "directly" and "existing," for Derrida declares "all of our political codes and terminologies still remain fundamentally metaphysical, regardless of whether they originate from the right or the left."[39] But this still leaves open the question whether it is even possible to imagine a "political code" that is not metaphysical – at least in the "objectionable" sense of metaphysical.

Derrida himself is not clear whether this is possible. When asked again whether he thinks this implies inaction and non-commitment, he answers:

> Not at all. But the difficulty is to gesture in opposite directions at the same time: on the one hand to preserve a distance and suspicion with regard to the official political codes governing reality; on the other, to intervene here and now in a practical and *engaged* manner whenever the necessity arises. This position of dual allegiance, in which I personally find myself, is one of perpetual uneasiness. I try where I can to act politically while recognizing that such action remains incommensurate with my intellectual project of deconstruction.[40]

Although this is one of Derrida's most forthright statements on the relation (or non-relation) "between" deconstruction and his politics, it is still open to different and conflicting interpretations. I want to suggest a reading that is consonant with many of his other texts. The danger with any political code is that it can become rigidified or reified – a set of unquestioned formulas that we rely on to direct our actions. More important, no code is ever *sufficient* to justify or legitimate a decision in any specific context. No code can close the gap or diminish the undecidability that confronts us in making an ethical-political decision or choice. "*This particular* undecidable opens the field of decision or of decidability."

> It calls for decision in the order of ethical-political responsibility. It is even its necessary condition. A decision can only come into being in a space that exceeds the calculable program that would destroy all responsibility by transforming it into a programmable effect of determinate causes. There can be no moral or political responsibility without this trial and this passage by way of the undecidable.[41]

Derrida is echoing and reinforcing a point made by many critics of the modern bias that the primary task of moral and political philosophy is to specify and justify the universal rules that ought to govern our decisions and actions. But Derrida is also critical of those who think that an appeal to judgment or *phronēsis* gets us out of this bind.[42] He radicalizes the openness that he takes to be characteristic of responsibility and decision by emphasizing the *experience* of the undecidable. We have to think and act without banisters and barriers – or rather with the realization that it is "we" who construct and deconstruct these barriers. Nevertheless, responsibility, action, and decision "here and now" demand that we at least temporarily suspend constant questioning. (Otherwise we would slip into inaction and non-commitment which are also modes of action and commitment.) This is his point about gesturing "in opposite directions." We cannot escape from the responsibilities and obligations that are thrust upon us – thrust upon us by the Other. Given our radical contingency we can never know or control when we are called upon to respond. We must always be prepared to confront new unpredictable responsibilities.[43] So when Derrida speaks of his "perpetual uneasiness" he is not merely expressing an idiosyncratic subjective state of mind but rather expressing a condition of undecidability which – to speak in a non-Derridean manner – is built into "the human condition."

Derrida has an acute sense that, at least since the "rupture" we call Nietzsche, we can no longer be content with self-satisfied appeals to moral and political foundations, first principles and *archai*. We are compelled to question these. But he is equally acute in his realization that such a questioning doesn't "solve" anything. We cannot assume a permanent frozen stance of *an-archē*. For this is another fixed metaphysical position. We cannot escape responsibility, decision, and choice. They are thrust upon us by the Other. Furthermore, we cannot simply dismiss or ignore those ethical and political principles that are constitutive of our traditions. The problem – and it is a problem for which there cannot be any final or permanent "solution" – is to live this perpetual uneasiness in a way in which we "gesture in opposite directions at the same time," where we keep alive the distance of questioning and are prepared to act decisively "here and now" – where we do not hide in bad faith from the double binds that we always confront.

But still we want to know what sort of politics Derrida does favor. What is its substantive content? Derrida has been extremely tentative and hesitant, although not silent. Considering the subversive quality of all his thinking, and his questioning of all forms of authority (even the authority claimed by "guardians of reason"), it is easier to discern what he is "against" rather than what he is "for." One will not find in his writings a clear and explicit statement of a political program. But I do not think it is fair to say he is entirely negative – that his political views are nothing but a "negative theology" translated into a political register. Derrida himself declares "Deconstruction certainly entails a moment of affirmation. Indeed, I cannot conceive of a radical critique which would not be ultimately motivated by some sort of affirmation, acknowledged or not. Deconstruction always presupposes affirmation...."[44] What then is Derrida affirming?

Let me approach the question of Derrida's normative ethical-political vision in what may seem to be an oblique manner. Already in *Of Grammatology*, Derrida linked phonocentrism, logocentrism, and the metaphysics of presence with phallogocentrism. Phallogocentrism and the question of sexual difference have been persistent iterated motifs throughout his writings – explored with subtle nuances, wit, and sometimes with raucous humor. (Derrida's playfulness – a powerful deconstructive strategy – has infuriated many of his critics and provided ammunition for claiming he is "nonserious".) Derrida's concern with "sexual difference" has been a vehicle for exploring and elaborating what he means by *différance*, even for probing the blindness and insights of Heidegger's all-important notion of "ontological difference." His analyses of "sexual difference" are intended to move us beyond the logic of binary oppositions so characteristic of metaphysics – or more accurately to complicate the logic of binary oppositions in a manner that makes us aware of differences that always elude our conceptual grids. In what may well be one of the most lyrical passages in his writings he dreams about what may be beyond our traditional gendered ways of thinking, acting, and feeling. He sketches the possibility of a different relationship with the other when he writes:

> This double dissymmetry perhaps goes beyond known or coded marks, beyond the grammar and spelling, shall we say (metaphorically) of sexuality. This indeed revives the following question: what if we were to reach, what if we were to approach here (for one does not arrive at this as one would at a determined location) the area of a relationship to the other where the code of sexual marks would no longer be discriminating? The relationship would not be a-sexual, far from it, but would be sexual otherwise: beyond the binary difference that governs the decorum of all codes, beyond the distinction masculine/feminine .... As I dream of saving the chance that his question offers I would like to believe in the multiplicity of sexually marked voices. I would like to believe in the masses, this indeterminable number of blended voices, this mobile of non-identified sexual marks whose choreography can carry, divide, multiply the body of each "individual," whether he be classified as "man" or as "woman" according to the criteria of usage.[45]

The syntactical construction of this passage ("shall we say," "if we were to reach," "I would like to believe," etc.) is itself a sign of Derrida's tentativeness in elaborating what is "beyond the binary difference." But it can be read as an allegory of Derrida's "ethical-political" vision. It also enables one to understand the power of Derrida's thinking for those – whether women, Blacks, or others who have experienced the pain and humiliation of being excluded and silenced. For whether Derrida writes about sexual difference, or the logic of apartheid, or a politics of friendship that is no longer infiltrated by fraternal metaphors, when he calls into question the dichotomy of friend and enemy that Carl Schmitt took to be the defining characteristic of all politics, he is envisioning the possibility of a state of affairs where the violence of discrimination – if not completely eliminated – is at least minimized, where difference is no longer taken to be a threat, but is affirmed and celebrated, difference where there is *both* symmetry and asymmetry, reciprocity and non-reciprocity.[46] He even speaks of this as "a democracy to come" – a democracy not to be identified with any of its existing institutional forms. Here too we can locate Derrida's double gestures. For his tentativeness and hesitancy in elaborating his dream is itself an expression of his conviction that we never quite eliminate violence from our language, institutions, and practices – that it is always a self-deceptive illusion to think this has been achieved – that we can "arrive at this as one would at a determined location." But we can – and Derrida takes this to be a perpetual demanding task to be renewed over and over again –

> try to recognize and analyze [violence] as best we can in its various forms: obvious or disguised, institutional or individual, literal or meta-phoric, candid or hypocritical, in good or guilty conscience. And if, as I believe, violence remains in fact (almost) ineradicable, its analysis and the most refined, ingenious account of its conditions will be the least violent gestures, perhaps even non-violent, and in any case those which contribute most to transforming the legal-ethical-political rules.[47]

The *polemos* of "modernity/postmodernity"

In order to show how "the relational interplay of attractions and aversions" between Habermas and Derrida can be read as an allegory of our "modern/postmodern" condition, I want to consider how they exemplify conflicting strands in the modern/postmodern *Stimmung*. Habermas, as we have seen, is not a naive *Aufklärer*. He is profoundly aware of the ambiguities, conflicts, and treacheries of the Enlightenment legacy. He is not an uncritical champion of modernity. His project has been one of systematically analyzing social and cultural modernity in order to specify and do justice to its conflicting and ambiguous tendencies. The Enlightenment legacy cannot be smoothed out into *either* a grand narrative of the progressive realization of freedom and justice *or* the cosmic night of ineluctable nihilistic self-destruction. With a stubborn persistence, he seeks to keep alive the memory/promise and hope of world in which justice, equality and dialogical rationality are concretely realized in our everyday practices. He staunchly resists all those who claim this hope must be abandoned, that our most cherished dreams of creating and realizing norms of justice must inevitably turn into totalitarian nightmares. He rejects the all too fashionable view that discursive practices are only a meaningless displacement of power/knowledge regimes. He is a "guardian of reason," but the reason he defends is dialogical, intersubjective, communicative. He is a fallibilist, but argues this stance is not only compatible with, but requires a serious attempt to ground critique in universal validity claims, and to engage in political *praxis* directed toward the material achievement of the norms of social critique. For Habermas, we cannot avoid the question, critique "in the name of what?" His quarrel with many so-called "postmodern" thinkers is that they either fail to confront this question, obscure it, or get caught in performative contradictions. One reason why Habermas "speaks" to so many of "us" and is so relevant to the "modern/postmodern" condition is because however feeble and fragile this aspect of the Enlightenment legacy has become, and despite the attacks on this legacy, it nevertheless will not die – the demand for freedom and *claim* to dialogical reasonableness does have a "stubbornly transcending power" – as recent events from South Africa to Eastern Europe so vividly demonstrate.

Derrida, as I have tried to show, is not indifferent to this memory/promise and hope. He even, in his way, calls for a new *Aufklärung*.[48] But his "center" – his mode of "feeling the whole push" is very different from, but not necessarily incompatible with,

Habermas' perspective. What is "central" for Derrida is otherness, alterity, *différance*. His primary concern is with meticulously analyzing and deconstructing the ways in which we consciously or unconsciously exclude, marginalize, suppress, and repress the otherness and singularity of the Other – the Other that refuses to be contained, mastered, domesticated. This is the strand of the "modern/postmodern" mood that Derrida has the genius for exhibiting.

Few contemporary thinkers have been as incisive and nuanced as Derrida in tracking the varieties of otherness, in *showing* how otherness ruptures, disrupts, threatens and eludes our logocentric conceptual grids. He seeks to show us why and how a "logic" of opposition and negation requires to be complicated and supplemented by a "logic" of *différance*. This "logic" is not quite a *logos* that can bind together differences. For Derrida is also stubbornly persistent in analyzing and exposing the difference of difference. The "Other" he speaks about is not a "generalized other" that can be assigned a proper or common name. This is one reason he keeps returning to the question of naming. Translating this into an ethical-political idiom means that when we turn our attention to the singularity of the Other or *différance*, we must focus on the differences that "make" a difference. Derrida avoids the facile "postmodern" temptation to lump together all differences under the general rubric of *the* "Other."

Derrida "speaks to" so many of "us" because the question of otherness (in all its variations) has become a "central" – if not *the* central – theoretical/practical question of our time.[49] How can we hope to be open to, and respond responsibly to the terror of otherness and singularity of the Other? This is primarily an ethical-political question for which there is not and cannot be a "final solution." Derrida is much closer in style and temperament to Adorno and Benjamin than he is to Habermas. Like Adorno, Derrida also seeks to expose the violence of what Adorno called "identity logic" – the multifarious ways that institutionalized forms of rationality and conceptual grids violate singularity. Like Benjamin, Derrida is also obsessed with fragments, detritus, and the fissures that rupture "smooth" historical continuities.

When we place Habermas/Derrida in a new constellation – view them as each other's other – then their strengths and weaknesses come into sharp relief. We can witness their symbiotic "interplay of

220 An Allegory of Modernity/Postmodernity

attractions and aversions." For Habermas, communicative action and rationality are the powerful magnetic poles of his work. Everything he explores emanates from, and is drawn back to these poles. His reading of the philosophic discourse of modernity is that "postmodern" philosophic discourses are caught within the *aporias* of "a philosophy of subjectivity" which is now exhausting itself. These discourses – despite desperate protests to the contrary – have failed to break out of a philosophy of subjectivity or consciousness. They have failed to make the paradigm shift to a model of communicative dialogical action and rationality.[50]

Communicative action – action oriented to mutual reciprocal understanding – never becomes fully thematized in Derrida's writings. But his deconstructive practices bear on it. For Derrida, like Adorno and Benjamin, is far more sensitive to what Habermas acknowledges but does not closely analyze – the multifarious ways in which communication (even under "ideal" conditions) goes awry. He is alert to the ways in which "mutual understanding" so frequently turns into mutual misunderstanding, how appeals to dialogue can and do contain their own hidden violences, how communication – especially in the contemporary world – has become little more than an "economy" of commodity exchange of information bits. He warns us that even appeals to face-to-face spoken communication can repress the heterogeneity and asymmetry of the other.

Abstractly there is something enormously attractive about Habermas' appeal to the "force of the better argument" until we ask ourselves what this means and presupposes. Even under "ideal" conditions where participants are committed to discursive argumentation, there is rarely agreement about what constitutes "the force of the better argument." We philosophers, for example, cannot even agree what are the arguments advanced in any of our canonical texts, whether Plato, Aristotle, Kant or Hegel, etc. – and there is certainly no consensus about who has advanced the better arguments. Furthermore there isn't even any agreement about the *role* the argument does or should play in a philosophic "vocabulary." We should not be innocent about the ways in which "tough minded" appeals to argumentation become ideological weapons for dismissing or excluding philosophical alternatives – for example, when analytic philosophers complain that Continental philosophers (including Habermas) do not argue, or indulge in "sloppy" argumentation. Who decides what is and what is not an argument, by what criteria, and what constitutes the force of the better argument? Who really believes that philosophers can achieve a rational consensus, or even that this is desirable? In raising these issues, I am not suggesting that "anything goes" or that there is never any way of sorting out better or worse arguments. On the contrary, we can and should debate about what constitutes an argument, how forceful it is, and how we are to evaluate competing arguments. But there are rarely (if ever) any algorithms or clear criteria for determining this in non-trivial instances.[51] Think how much more intractable the problems become when we turn to specific ethical and political disputes. Does it even makes sense to think that there might even be a rational consensus about the force of the better argument in the current debates about abortion? Is the very idea of a "rational consensus" in such concrete conflictual contexts even intelligible? Any society must have some procedures for dealing with conflicts that cannot be resolved by argumentation – even when all parties are committed to rational argumentation. But what precisely is the determinate (*bestimmt*) content of declaring one ought to consider only the force of the better argument?

There are friends and foes of Derrida who think that he undermines and ridicules any appeal to rational argument – or that this is a consequence of his deconstructive practices. But this is a slander. It is not what he is doing when he analyzes the complex interplay of logic and rhetoric. He does *not* "reduce" all logic and argumentation to disguised rhetorical tropes.[52] Rather he is showing us just how difficult and complex it is to ferret out argumentation and rhetorical strands even in the most apparently "straightforward" and "serious" speech acts.

Habermas is certainly aware of the pervasiveness of plurality, heterogeneity, and difference. Those who think his insistence on universal validity claims means he has no understanding of contingency and plurality are caricaturing him. He even tells us the "pluralization of diverging universes of discourse belongs to specifically modern experience." There has been a "shattering of naive consensus."[53] For Habermas the primary question is how one is to *respond* to this intensified pluralization. His worry is that the celebration of plurality and difference all too easily degenerates into a self-defeating relativism, contextualism, and "bad" historicism. Habermas does provide an important corrective to those who uncritically celebrate contingency, plurality, difference and otherness. There are manifestations of otherness that we *legitimately* seek to eliminate and destroy – when we are convinced the other we are confronting is evil – like the evil of apartheid and fascism. One of the most obfuscating aspects of "modern/postmodern polemics" is the way in which universality is pitted against plurality and alterity. Even those who celebrate plurality and difference – like Lyotard and Rorty – make an implicit appeal to universality – when, for example, they advocate a world in which there is a *universal* "letting be" where difference is allowed to flourish.

Derrida is not guilty of some of these excesses. He is neither a relativist nor an irrationalist, but he is constantly showing us the treacheries of facile appeals to universals, principles, *archai*. Undecidability for Derrida is not indifference or a mask for nihilism, but rather a constant ethical-political reminder that "a decision can only come into being in a space that exceeds the calculable program that would destroy all responsibility ... [that] there can be no moral or political responsibility without this trial and this passage by way of the undecidable."[54]

Nevertheless, for all Derrida's affirmation that deconstruction intervenes, that it is a way of taking an ethical-political "position," and that it may be "too political" for some, there is a certain "abstractness" in his understanding of politics. Placing Derrida in constellation with Habermas helps to pinpoint this. Deconstruction, he tells us, "should not be separable from [the] politico-institutional problematic and should seek a new investigation of responsibility."[55] Derrida has shown – in a series of perceptive analyses ranging from Kant through Heidegger – how their discourses about the university cannot be separated from their discourses about the institutional structure of the modern university. He has developed a sharp and incisive critique of university institutions and practices. But suppose we step back and ask: what does Derrida mean by a "politico-institutional structure"? Of course, there is no univocal answer to this question. But Derrida never quite rises to the level of *necessary* generality (as he does in telling us what he means by a "text") where we can gain some perspective, some overview of the complex dynamics of institutional structures that shape politics and society in the contemporary world. We will simply *not* find in his writings anything resembling a social and political theory – as we do find in Habermas.

It is an important virtue to be vigilant – as Derrida is – about the ways in which *any* general social and political theory or code can go awry, how it can deconstruct itself. But it is just as important and necessary to seek, in a fallibilistic spirit, for a general understanding and explanation of the institutional dynamics of politics and society. Otherwise the specific ways in which we intervene "here and now" can lack any orientation. Derrida's claims about a "democracy to come" are powerfully evocative. He warns us against identifying this "democracy to come" with any of its present institutional forms. Like Habermas he would insist that it is not the task of the philosopher or theorist – as some sort of "master" intellectual – to lay out blueprints for such a democracy. This can and should be decided by participants. But still it is fair to ask for some determinate content. We want *some* understanding of what kinds of institutions and practices should be developed for "a democracy to come." Or even more minimally, we want some orientation about what changes "here and now" are needed in our present institutional structures. Derrida, thus far, has very little to say about any of this.[56] Consequently there is a danger that, for all the evocative power of the very idea of a "democracy to come," the idea of such a democracy can become an impotent, vague abstraction.

There is another curious lacuna in Derrida's prolific writings. Earlier I indicated Derrida's deep suspicion of "boundary-fixing" and his incisiveness in exposing the precise points where boundaries and limits break down and/or recede. He has consistently maintained that philosophy itself is not a well-defined discipline or *Fach* neatly separable from other disciplines and discourses. But there is one lesson or consequence from this master strategy that he has not drawn – and this is the source of many of the sharpest differences between him and Habermas. Habermas argues that there is no fixed boundary between philosophy and the critical social sciences. There is – and ought to be – a symbiotic relationship between philosophy and the social sciences, although they are not reducible to each other. Pragmatically this means that the philosopher, especially the social and political philosopher, must be responsive and alert to what can be learned from the social disciplines. Whatever our final judgment of ways in which Habermas uses and criticizes Weber,

Durkheim, Parsons, Mead, Piaget, Kohlberg (and many other social scientists), he has consistently sought to develop a subtle dialectical interplay between philosophical speculation and social scientific theoretically oriented empirical research. In this play, this to-and-fro movement between philosophy and the critical social sciences, he has *practiced* what one would think ought to be a consequence of Derrida's own deconstructive analyses.

Although Derrida does deal with what the French take to be the preeminent *sciences humaines* – especially linguistics and psychoanalysis – there are only casual references to the full range of the social disciplines. More important, Derrida's fundamental bias has been to move in one direction only – to show and expose the dubious "philosophic" presuppositions that infect the social disciplines, rather than to ask what, if anything, philosophy might learn from them. He tells us:

> To say to oneself that one is going to study something that is *not* philosophy is to deceive oneself. It is not difficult to show that in political economy, for example, there is a philosophical discourse in operation .... Philosophy, as logocentrism, is present in every scientific discipline and the only justification for transforming philosophy into a specialized discipline is the necessity to render explicit and thematic the philosophical subtext in every discourse. The principal function which the teaching of philosophy serves is to enable people to become "conscious", to become aware of what exactly they are saying, what kind of discourse they are engaged in when they do mathematics, physics, political economy, and so on. There is no system of teaching or transmitting knowledge which can retain its coherence or integrity without, at one moment or another, interrogating itself philosophically, that is, without acknowledging its subtextual premises; and this may even include an interrogation of unspoken political interests or traditional values.[57]

Habermas would agree with everything that is said here, but he would (rightly, I think) ask: should this not be a two-way street? Should we not also ask what philosophy can learn from critical social scientific research?

The issue here is not just metatheoretical. For it conditions the very way in which Derrida deals with social and political themes. When Derrida examines questions of justice, law, violence he does not *primarily* deal with specific institutional practices, but with the written texts, specifically the writings of those who have addressed these issues — Aristotle, Kant, Hegel, Kafka, Benjamin, Levinas, etc. I do not want to denigrate this way — this *methodos*. His analyses are extraordinarily perceptive and rich in their consequences. But surely — as Derrida himself acknowledges — they need to be *supplemented* by the theoretical and empirical study of societal institutions and practices. But this is not what Derrida does. There is nothing in Derrida's writings that seeks to rule out the importance of critical theoretical and empirical research into the structural dynamics of society and politics. On the contrary, such an endeavor is what his own questioning of boundary-fixing demands. Nevertheless, his neglect of dealing more directly and explicitly with political and societal institutions in their historical complexity does have the consequence of making his own understanding of society and politics sound rather "thin."

There are many aspects and problems in the writings of Habermas and Derrida that I have not explored here. But by now I hope the thrust of my argument is clear, and why I believe we can (and should) read them as an *allegory* of the "modern/postmodern" condition. I reiterate what I said earlier. I do not think there is a theoretical perspective from which we can reconcile their differences, their otherness to each other — nor do I think we should smooth out their "aversions and attractions." The nasty questions that they raise about each other's "project" need to be relentlessly pursued. One of the primary lessons of "modernity/postmodernity" is a radical skepticism about the possibility of a reconciliation — an *Aufhebung*, without gaps, fissures, and ruptures. However, *together*, Habermas/Derrida provide us with a force-field that constitutes "the dynamic, transmutational structure of a complex phenomenon" — the phenomenon I have labeled "modernity/postmodernity." *Together* they form a new constellation — a "juxtaposed rather than an integrated cluster of changing elements that resist reduction to a common denominator, essential core, or generative first principle." I have spoken about Habermas/Derrida, but my primary concern here is not simply to focus on their texts — the texts that bear their signatures. The rationale for examining their texts is because, more rigorously and thoroughly than many others (including their "followers"), they *show* the tangled intertwined strands of the "modern/postmodern" *Stimmung*. My reading of Habermas/Derrida is intended to be an allegory of this *Stimmung*. The "logic" of my allegory has been an unstable tensed Both/And rather than a determinate fixed Either/Or. This is what I believe to be – to use an old-fashioned but not outdated expression – the *truth* of the *polemos* of "modernity/postmodernity."

NOTES

1 This passage from Iban Hassan is cited by Albrecht Wellmer, "The Dialectic of Modernity and Post-Modernity," in *Praxis International* 4 (January 1985), p. 338.

2 Jean-François Lyotard, *The Postmodern Condition: A Report on Knowledge*, trans. G. Bennington and B. Massumi, (Minneapolis: University of Minnesota Press, 1984), pp. xxiii–xxiv.

3 I have never been very happy with the term "modernity". Of course, I feel that what is happening in the world today is something unique and singular. As soon, however, as we give it the label of "modernity", we describe it in a certain historical system of evolution or progress (a notion derived from Enlightenment rationalism) which tends to blind us to the fact that what confronts us today is *also* something ancient and hidden in history. I believe that what "happens" in our contemporary world and strikes us as particularly new has in fact an essential connection with something extremely old which has been covered over (*archi-dissumulé*). So that the new is not so much that which occurs for the first time but that "very ancient" dimension which recurs in the "very modern"; and which indeed has been signified repetitively throughout our historical tradition, in Greece and in Rome, in Plato and in Descartes and in Kant, etc. No matter how novel or unprecedented a modern meaning may appear, it is never exclusively *modernist* but is also and at the same time a phenomenon of *repetition*. ("Dialogue with Jacques Derrida," in Richard Kearney, ed., *Dialogues with Contemporary Continental Thinkers* [Manchester: Manchester University Press, 1984], pp. 112–13).

4 Habermas' most sustained discussion of Derrida occurs in *The Philosophical Discourse of Modernity*, trans. F. Lawrence (Cambridge, Mass.: MIT Press, 1987). See chap. 8, "Beyond a Temporalized Philosophy of Origins: Jacques Derrida's Critique of Phonocentrism," and "Excursus on Leveling the Genre Distinction between Philosophy and Literature." Derrida has not systematically discussed Habermas' work. But see his brief and sharp reply to Habermas, p. 156, footnote 9, *Limited Inc.*, ed. Gerald Graff (Evanston: Northwestern University Press, 1988).

5 Martin Jay, *Adorno* (Cambridge, Mass.: Harvard University Press, 1984), p. 14.

6 Ibid., p. 15.

7 William James, *A Pluralistic Universe* (Cambridge, Mass.: Harvard University Press, 1977), pp. 14–15.

8 Jürgen Habermas, "The German Idealism of the Jewish Philosophers," *Philosophical-Political Profiles*, trans. Frederick Lawrence (Cambridge, Mass.: MIT Press, 1983), p. 41.

9 Max Horkheimer and Theodor W. Adorno, *Dialectic of Enlightenment*, trans. John Cumming (New York: Continuum, 1972), p. 3.

10 See Habermas' early book on the public sphere which has recently been translated into English by Thomas Burger and Frederick Lawrence, *The Structural Transformation of the Public Sphere: An Inquiry into a Category of Bourgeois Society.* (Cambridge, Mass.: MIT Press, 1989).

11 Jürgen Habermas, "Historical Materialism and the Development of Normative Structures," in *Communication and the Evolution of Society*, trans. Thomas McCarthy (Boston: Beacon, 1979), p. 117.

12 Ibid., pp. 119–20.

13 Ibid., p. 97.

14 Jürgen Habermas, "A Reply To My Critics," in John B. Thompson and David Held, eds., *Habermas: Critical Debates* (London: MacMillan, 1982), p. 221.

15 Habermas, *The Philosophical Discourse of Modernity*, p. 408.

16 Ibid.

17 Ibid.

18 Habermas does think there is a categorical distinction between the natural sciences and the reconstructive critical social sciences. But both types of sciences are fallibilistic and make universal claims open to ongoing criticism.

19 Jürgen Habermas, "The Entwinement of Myth and Enlightenment: Re-Reading *Dialectic of Enlightenment*," in *New German Critique* 26 (1982), pp. 23, 25, 27.

20 See Jürgen Habermas, "Work and Weltanschauung: The Heidegger Controversy from a German Perspective," *Critical Inquiry* 15 (Winter 1989).

21 Jürgen Habermas, "Questions and Counterquestions," in Richard J. Bernstein, ed., *Habermas and Modernity* (Cambridge, Mass.: MIT Press, 1985), p. 195.

22 Derrida himself frequently uses such hyphenated expressions as "ethical-political-juridical" or "ethical-political." The point of these hyphenated expressions is to mark the inseparability of the issues examined. In this respect Derrida acknowledges the ancient (Greek) tradition in which questions concerning *ēthos*, *polis*, and *nomos* are intertwined. This does not mean that one can ignore important differences between ethics, morality, and politics. For the purposes of this essay I will stress the interrelatedness of these "domains" rather than the crucial differences and distinctions among them.

23 "An Interview with Derrida" in David Wood and Robert Bernasconi,

eds., *Derrida and Différance* (Evanston: Northwestern University Press, 1988), p. 74.

24 Ibid., p. 75.

25 "Dialogue with Jacques Derrida," p. 108.

26 Ibid., p. 118.

27 Ibid., p. 124.

28 See the previous essay, "Serious Play: the Ethical-Political Horizon of Derrida," where I argue that an ethical-political orientation is a point of departure for reading virtually everything Derrida has written. During the past decade the "themes" of violence, justice, law, responsibility have become even more prominent in his writings.

29 See Jacques Derrida, "Of an Apocalyptic Tone Recently Adopted in Philosophy," *Oxford Literary Review* 6 (1984).

30 "Dialogue with Jacques Derrida," p. 111.

31 "I never separate promising from memory," Jacques Derrida, "But beyond ... (Open Letter to Anne McClintock and Rob Nixon)," *Critical Inquiry* 13 (Autumn 1986), p. 160.

32 "Dialogue with Jacques Derrida," p. 113.

33 Derrida, "But beyond ...," pp. 167–8. See also Jacques Derrida, "Racism's Last Word," trans. Peggy Kamuf, *Critical Inquiry* 12 (Autumn 1985).

34 Derrida, "But beyond...," p. 168.

35 Ibid.

36 Jacques Derrida, "The Conflict of Faculties: A *Mochlos*" (forthcoming).

37 Derrida, "But beyond ...," p. 170.

38 "Dialogue with Jacques Derrida," p. 119.

39 Ibid., p. 120.

40 Ibid.

41 Derrida, Afterword, *Limited Inc.*, p. 116.

42 For a critical discussion of recent appropriations of the concept of *phronēsis*, see Richard J. Bernstein, *Beyond Objectivism and Relativism: Science, Hermeneutics and Praxis* (Philadelphia: University of Pennsylvania Press, 1983).

43 Almost every text of Derrida touches on questions of response, responsiveness, and responsibility. In his writings during the past decade the explicit discussion of responsibility has become more and more prominent. See "The Principle of Reason: The University in the Eyes of its Pupils," *Diacritics* 13 (Fall 1983), "The Conflict of Faculties," "Like the Sound of the Sea Deep within a Shell: Paul de Man's War," *Critical Inquiry* 14 (Spring, 1988). Few commentators on the latter essay have noted that it is not only an essay dealing with "Paul de Man's War" but is also a meditation on the question, ambiguities, and double binds of *responsibility*.

44 "Dialogue with Derrida," p. 118.

45 Jacques Derrida, "Choreographics," *Diacritics* 12 (Summer 1982),

pp. 66–7. See also "Voice ii: Jacques Derrida et Verena Andermott Conley," *Boundary 2* 12 (Winter 1984); and *"Geschlecht* – Sexual Difference, Ontological Difference," *Research in Phenomenology* 13 (1983).

46 See Jacques Derrida, "The Politics of Friendship" (unpublished manuscript). See also "Violence and Metaphysics: An Essay on the Thought of Emmanuel Levinas" in *Writing and Difference*, trans. Alan Bass (Chicago: University of Chicago Press, 1978).

47 Derrida, Afterword, *Limited Inc.*, p. 112.

48 See Derrida, "The Principle of Reason."

49 The "problem" of the Other is just as fundamental for Habermas as it is for Derrida. Here too their approaches *supplement* each other. Habermas' primary concern is with the personal Other as it appears in communicative action, i.e., with reciprocal communication in achieving mutual understanding. All communication is dialogical where the *right* of the Other to assent or dissent freely to professed validity claims should prevail as a binding universal norm. Derrida typically focuses on the ways in which the Other eludes understanding and provides a site (non-site) for questioning that which strives to assimilate and master the Other. Whereas Habermas emphasizes reciprocity, symmetry, and mutual recognition, Derrida focuses on non-reciprocity, asymmetry, and the faults in mutual recognition.

50 See Habermas, *The Philosophic Discourse of Modernity*.

51 For a development of this point see my book, *Beyond Objectivism and Relativism*. See also my criticism of Habermas' understanding of his project of reconstructive science of communicative action in "Interpretation and Solidarity: An Interview with Richard Bernstein by Dunja Melcić," *Praxis International* 9, no. 3 (October, 1989).

52 Deconstruction, as I have practiced it, has always been foreign to rhetoricism – which, as its name indicates, can become another form of logocentrism – and this despite or rather because of the interest I have felt obliged to direct at questions of language and at figures of rhetoric. What is all too quickly forgotten is often what is most massively evident, to wit, that deconstruction, that at least to which I refer, *begins* by deconstructing logocentrism, and hence also that which rhetoricism might owe it. Also for the same reason I never assimilated philosophy, science, theory, criticism, law, morality, etc., to literary fictions. (Derrida, Afterword, *Limited Inc.*, p. 156)

53 Habermas, "Questions and Counterquestions," p. 192.

54 Derrida, Afterword, *Limited Inc.*, p. 116.

55 Derrida, "The Conflict of Faculties."

56 See Thomas McCarthy, "The Politics of the Ineffable: Derrida's Deconstructionism," *The Philosophical Forum* 21 (1989–90).

57 "Dialogue with Jacques Derrida," pp. 114–15.

8

One Step Forward, Two Steps Backward
Rorty on Liberal Democracy and Philosophy*

During the last decades of the nineteenth century, John Dewey, who had been strongly influenced by his Vermont Congregationalist upbringing, was in the process of being "radicalized". This was a time of enormous ferment in America, due in part to the effects of rapid industrialization, urbanization, the changing demographic character that resulted from waves of immigration, and the growth of a laissez-faire ideology. Looking back to this period it appears to be a strange mixture of evangelical social zeal, reformist rhetoric, populist sentiment, and fragmented utopian projects. Dewey was caught up in this fervor, as evidenced by his brief encounter with the flamboyant Franklin Ford. Ford, who had been an editor of Wall Street's *Bradstreet's*, turned against the "moneyed classes" and wanted to publish a new socialist-oriented newspaper, *Thought News*, which would spread the gospel of radical social reform. The editor of *Thought News* was to be a young philosophy professor from the University of Michigan, John Dewey. Dewey, who at the time identified himself with philosophical idealism, wrote to his friend William James enthusiastically recommending Ford's writings. In a letter dated June 3, 1891 (when Dewey was thirty-two years old), he wrote:

> What I got out of it is, first, the perception that the true or practical
> bearing of idealism – that philosophy has been the assertion of the

* See Rorty's reply to this critique, "Thugs and Theorists," *Political Theory* 15 (November 1987) pp. 564–80.

unity of intelligence and the external world *in idea* or subjectively, while if true in idea it must finally secure the conditions of its objective expression. And secondly, I believe a tremendous movement is impending, when the intellectual forces which have been gathering since the Renaissance, and the Reformation, shall demand complete free movement, and by getting their physical leverage in the telegraph and printing press, shall through free inquiry in a centralized way, demand the authority of all other so-called authorities.[1]

Dewey's rhetoric, his desire to foster "the true or practical bearing of idealism," even his conviction that journalism might play a leading role in furthering social reform, recall the *esprit* of another young philosophical radical who started as a journalist, Karl Marx. There are even parallels between the role that Feuerbach played for Marx in his movement away from philosophical idealism and the role that Ford played in Dewey's search for the objective expression of the "unity of intelligence and the external world."

Thought News was never published, but this early episode in Dewey's career is indicative of his lifelong desire to reach beyond the university and the academy, to give philosophy a genuinely "practical turn," and to inform philosophic reflection with everyday practical experience. This commitment – this sense of the continuity of reflection and practical engagement – marked Dewey for the rest of his life. It is evidenced in his founding of the Laboratory School of the University of Chicago, his involvement with working-class immigrants at Jane Addams' Hull House, his initiative and support for a variety of progressive social and political causes, his "popular" journalism in such periodicals as *The New Republic* and *The Nation*, and even his willingness to travel to Mexico when he was seventy-eight to serve as chairman of the Commission of Inquiry investigating the charges brought against Trotsky and his son at the infamous Moscow Trials.

Dewey, who was always skeptical of militant revolution, nevertheless advocated radical reform. In *The Public and Its Problems* (1927), *Individualism: Old and New* (1930), *Liberalism and Social Action* (1935), and in many other writings, Dewey returned over and over again to criticize outdated and even pernicious "old" forms of individualism and liberalism, and he sought to articulate and defend his vision of radical communal democracy. Increasingly, Dewey came to believe that the economic, social, and political tendencies at work in American society were distorting and undermining the very conditions that are required for the flourishing of democracy, whose "task is forever that of creation of a freer and more humane experience in which all share and to which all contribute."[2] He wrote about the "eclipse of the public." Democracy, he claimed, is not a set of formal procedures, but a "moral ideal."[3] He even wrote that "Democracy is the very idea of community life itself." In *The Public and Its Problems*, he declared "the invasion of the community by the new and relatively impersonal and mechanical modes of combined human behavior is the outstanding fact of modern life."[4] The one theme that runs throughout all of Dewey's social and educational writings (indeed, it surfaces in virtually all his writings) is the need to reconstruct democratic communal life – a form of life that requires and cultivates civic virtue. Jefferson was always one of Dewey's heroes because Jefferson's own vision of democracy is "moral through and through: in its foundations, its methods, and its ends."[5] For all Dewey's desire to encourage the objective development of democratic communal practices, he was sharply critical of those who claimed that the breakdown of communal life is a *necessary* consequence of modernization, industrialization, and technological development. He never wavered in his conviction of the practical necessity of integrating democratic everyday life with science and technology.

Concerning liberalism, he wrote in 1935:

Liberalism must now become radical, meaning by "radical" perception of the necessity of thorough-going changes in the set-up of institutions and corresponding activity to bring the changes to pass. For the gulf between what the actual situation makes possible and the actual state itself is so great that it cannot be bridged by piecemeal policies undertaken *ad hoc*. The process of producing the changes will be, in any case, a gradual one. But "reforms" that deal now with this abuse and now with that without having a social goal based on an inclusive plan, differ entirely from effort at re-forming, in its literal sense, the institutional scheme of things. The liberals of more than a century ago were denounced in their time as subversive radicals, and only when the new economic order was established did they become apologists for the *status quo*, or else content with social patchwork. If radicalism be defined as perception of the need for radical change, then today any liberalism which is not also radicalism is irrelevant and doomed.[6]

Aestheticism and moral commitment

I have introduced my discussion of Rorty with a brief sketch of Dewey's commitment to radical reform and to democratic communal life for several reasons. When Rorty announced in the opening pages of *Philosophy and the Mirror of Nature* that Dewey (along with Heidegger and Wittgenstein) is one of the "three most important philosophers of the twentieth century,"[7] he shocked many of his readers. Except for a small group of philosophers dedicated to preserving and revitalizing "American pragmatism," most professional Anglo-Amercian and Continental philosophers considered Dewey to be passé, a minor "fuzzy-minded" thinker who, at best, had his heart in the right place, but not his head. Since the publication of *Philosophy and the Mirror of Nature*, Rorty has increasingly identified himself as a "Deweyean pragmatist." Yet, as I hope to show, the disparity between the type of "aestheticized pragmatism" that Rorty advocates and Dewey's primary concerns is becoming greater and greater. But my main aim is not to show that Rorty distorts Dewey's legacy but rather to locate some serious inadequacies in Rorty's emerging "position," especially as it pertains to politics and public life.[8] For despite occasional protests to the contrary, it begins to look as if Rorty's defense of liberalism is little more than an *apologia* for the status quo – the very type of liberalism that Dewey judged to be "irrelevant and doomed."

After Rorty's sustained critique of "professional philosophy" and his attack on the very idea of philosophy (or what he sometimes labels "Philosophy" with a capital "P")[9] as a well-defined *Fach* with its own distinctive foundational problems, he left us in an ambiguous situation about what useful role (if any) the philosopher might still play in the ongoing "conversation of mankind." He suggested that we think of the philosopher (or her successor) as a "kibitzer," a self-consciously amateurish cultural critic.

Roughly speaking, Rorty's kibitzing during the past decade has focused on three interrelated motifs. First there is his continued battle with what he takes to be the legacy of the "bad" foundationalist, ahistorical impulse in philosophy, especially as it is manifested in the preoccupation with the varieties of "realism."

Second, the "aesthetic" strain in Rorty has become more and more pronounced. In one of his early papers, playing on the statement "let a thousand flowers bloom," Rorty advocated the flowering and invention of what he calls different "vocabularies" for "coping". Rorty's own vision of the "good society" is one where we will play, a type of *jouissance* where there is a non-violent tolerant celebration of our capacities for making and self-creation, where we would abandon the "spirit of seriousness" and no longer think it is important to hold positions about "Truth," "Objectivity", "Rationality", and so on. It is a vision where we all become poets who have learned to live with contingency, preferably "strong poets."[10]

The third motif is Rorty's "defense" of pluralistic "postmodern bourgeois liberalism." Against those who think we are living through the cosmic night of a self-destructive nihilism or think we are facing some sort of deep crisis of liberal democracy, Rorty cheerfully thinks that a liberal democracy that embodies and extends the principle of tolerance and encourages the poetic metaphoric impulse of making and self-creation is – if not the best possible world – at least the best possible world achieved by European civilization.

One can also see how these three motifs are interwoven. Sometimes Rorty suggests that if we would only stop worrying about the wrong issues, simply abandon worn out "vocabularies" that have for too long obsessed philosophers, and realize the benefits and moral progress of liberal democracy, then we can all get on with the playful task of poetizing life.

Rorty is sensitive to the charge that his recent writings adopt "the air of light-minded aestheticism ... toward traditional philosophical questions" (p. 271).[11] But although Rorty has expressed his skepticism about the influence of *any* philosophical reflection on the dynamics of society, he defends himself by claiming that "such philosophical superficiality and light-mindedness helps along the disenchantment of the world. It helps make the world's inhabitants more pragmatic, more tolerant, more liberal, more receptive to the appeal of instrumental rationality."

> Moral commitment, after all, does not require taking seriously all the matters which are, for moral reasons, taken seriously by one's fellow-citizens. It may require just the opposite. It may require trying to josh them out of the habit of taking those topics so seriously. There may be serious reasons for so joshing them. More generally, we should not assume that the aesthetic is always the enemy of the moral. I should

argue that in the recent history of liberal societies the willingness to view matters aesthetically ... to be content to indulge in what Schiller called "play" and to discard what Nietzsche called "the spirit of seriousness" has been an important vehicle of moral progress. (p. 272)

For all the attractiveness of Rorty's vision of a world of tolerant liberal play, and his debunking of "the spirit of seriousness," there is something a bit too facile about this vision, or so I want to argue. More important, I want to show how Rorty's rhetoric and the ways in which he structures and poses issues tend to obscure more than they illuminate, and even mask conflicting tendencies in his own thinking. Ironically, although Rorty calls himself a "Deweyean pragmatist," he helps to perpetuate just the sort of fruitless debates that Dewey and the other pragmatists sought to jettison. One reason that the "classical" pragmatism of Peirce, Dewey, Mead, and James went into eclipse is because many thinkers began to feel that the pragmatic attempt to soften and blur all philosophic distinctions had the unfortunate consequence of depriving us of the analytic tools needed for clarifying and getting a grip on important differences that make a difference, and resulted in a bland undifferentiated monotonous holism. Rorty, who has done so much to get philosophers to take pragmatism "seriously" (at least by constantly invoking the names of the pragmatic thinkers), is guilty of a similar tendency of leveling in his light-minded joshing. This tendency comes to the foreground in his recent writings, especially his article "The Priority of Democracy to Philosophy." The very title indicates Rorty's polemical thrust. He seeks to show us that "liberal democracy" is prior to philosophy in the sense that it simply does not stand in need of *any* "philosophical justification."

Rorty's primary intention is to give what he calls a "Deweyean historicist interpretation" of John Rawls' theory of justice, and to defend Rawls against his so-called communitarian critics, in particular, the criticisms advanced by Michael Sandel in *Liberalism and the Limits of Justice*.[12] Rorty confesses that he, along with others, first read Rawls as seeking to provide some sort of foundationalist, quasi-transcendental, ahistorical justification and legitimization for justice as fairness, but he now realizes this was a mistake. Focusing on Rawls' writings since the publication of *A Theory of Justice*, especially "Kantian Constructivism in Moral Theory" and "Justice as Fairness: Political not Metaphysical,"[13] Rorty now sees Rawls as closer to the historicist strain in Hegel and Dewey rather than the transcendental foundationalist, philosophical strain in Kant. According to this interpretation of Rawls' project, we can read *A Theory of Justice* – for all its ambiguity – as elaborating a political "articulation" but *not* a philosophical "justification" of liberal constitutional democracy. Controversial philosophical or metaphysical claims about human nature or the theory of the self are simply irrelevant to articulating the intuitions, settled habits, and shared beliefs of those who identify themselves with the historical community committed to liberal constitutional democracy. Consequently, Rawls disarms his communitarian critics who think that his theory of justice "presupposes" a faulty and objectionable "theory of the self" that needs to be replaced by a better theory of the self. According to Rorty, all of this is beside the point. He concedes that if one feels the urge to elaborate a theory of the self that "comports" with the political institutions that one admires then something like what the communitarians tell us will do, but nothing crucial depends on it.

Emphasizing the principle of tolerance (which for Rorty is close to indifference), we simply do not need "to take a position" on controversial philosophical or metaphysical views just as we do not need to take a position on controversial religious views in order to champion liberal democracy. So Sandel and his fellow communitarian critics are left hanging on a limb that Rawls has deftly sawed off. Liberal democracy does not need any justification at all. Rorty goes even further, for he suggests that to the extent that we elaborate philosophic "theories" they should be adjusted to fit our political intuitions. This is how Rorty understands "Justice as Fairness: Political not Metaphysical."[14]

I want to concentrate on Rorty's claims about liberal democracy and philosophy.[15] In his recent work, Rorty is not primarily interested in arguing against what he takes to be faulty philosophical and metaphysical theories, but he wants to make a more "radical" move – to expose the pointlessness and irrelevance of philosophical and metaphysical vocabularies and debates. In this respect, Rorty exhibits a proto-positivist strain in his thinking that has become more and more blatant. Like the early logical positivists, he seeks to show us that it is pointless to argue about the "truth" or "falsity" of controversial metaphysical "theories." Employing his own terminology, one can say his moral-aesthetic intention is to show us why we should abandon the worn out vocabularies of philosophy and meta-physics. They are no longer useful for coping.

Because I am claiming that Rorty obfuscates more than he illuminates, and that the very way in which he structures issues tends to distract us from questions that really do make a difference, let me locate in a bit more detail the precise point of Rorty's objection to Rawls' communitarian critics. Rorty tells us there are three strands or claims in communitarianism that need to be disentangled. First there is "the empirical prediction that no society can survive which sets aside the idea of ahistorical moral truth in the insouciant way that Dewey recommended" (p. 259). This is the "line" that Rorty claims Horkheimer and Adorno take in *Dialectic of Enlightenment*. "Second, there is the moral judgment that the sort of human being who is produced by liberal institutions and cultures is undesirable" (p. 259). This is the type of judgment that Rorty claims is at the heart of MacIntyre's critique of liberalism. But it is the third claim that Rorty primarily addresses. "Third, there is the claim that political institutions 'presuppose' a doctrine about the nature of human beings, and that such a doctrine must, unlike Enlightenment rationalism, make clear the essentially historical character of the self" (p. 260).

To evaluate this third claim, Rorty poses two questions. "First, whether there is any sense in which liberal democracy 'needs' philosophical justification at all" (p. 260). And, the second question is "whether a conception of the self which, as Taylor says, makes 'the community constitutive of the individual' does in fact comport better with liberal democracy than does the Enlightenment conception of the self" (p. 260). Rorty's answers to these two questions are unequivocal.

> I can preview what is to come by saying that I shall answer "no" to the first question about the communitarians' third claim and "yes" to the second. I shall be arguing that Rawls, following up on Dewey, shows us how liberal democracy can get along without philosophical presuppositions .... But I shall also argue that a conception of the self which makes the community constitutive of the self does comport well with liberal democracy. (p. 261)

We should not think Rorty is conceding very much in his affirmative answer to the second question, for he makes it clear that nothing crucial hangs on fleshing out "our self-image as citizens of such a democracy with a philosophical view of the self" (p. 261).

Democracy without foundations

In order to evaluate Rorty's "arguments," let me first note some striking features of his defense of Rawls. There is scarcely any mention of such themes as the "original position," "the veil of ignorance," "the thin theory of primary goods," or Rawls' understanding of rationality and rational choice. Nor does Rorty pay attention to Rawls' detailed critique of utilitarianism or other versions of liberalism. What is even more surprising is that Rorty never even mentions what – on any interpretation of Rawls – is the heart of his theory, that is, the successive formulations and defense of the two principles of justice. Throughout Rorty simply speaks globally about "liberal democracy" without ever unpacking what it involves or doing justice to the enormous historical controversy about what liberal democracy is or ought to be. Rorty is concerned (one is tempted to say "obsessed") with variations on a single theme – the metatheoretical question of whether Rawls' enterprise is one of "articulation" of common intuitions and shared beliefs or a "justification" of liberal democracy. Is Rawls grounding his theory of justice (whatever its substantive content) on controversial philosophic or metaphysical premises? This is even reflected in Rorty's metaphors. He speaks of "philosophic *foundations*," "philosophic *back-up*," and "philosophic *grounding*." When these metaphors are unpacked or decoded it becomes clear that Rorty's "picture" of justification is simple – perhaps even simplistic. Philosophic justification amounts to deduction from premises that are presumably unassailable.[16] To justify liberal democracy would be to deduce it from such premises – premises about human nature or the self. And if such a deduction fails, then we have failed to legitimize liberal democracy. This is the type of language game that Rorty urges us to abandon. *In this sense* liberal democracy does not need any justification or legitimization.

I do not want to suggest that Rorty is attacking a straw man. There have been philosophers who have endorsed such a "picture" of justification, although I do think that when we "look and see" at the ways in which defenders and critics of the varieties of liberalism actually support their claims, then Rorty's conception of the justificatory process is close to a caricature. Even Rawls does not advocate abandoning "justification" but argues for a more sophisticated and open-textured understanding of justification. Justification is not a matter of deduction from indubitable premises, but rather "a matter of mutual support of many considerations, of everything fitting together into one coherent view."[17]

What I find most objectionable in Rorty's strategy is that it diverts us from the pragmatically important issues that need to be confronted. For there is another sense of "presupposing" that is relevant to controversies about liberalism. "Liberalism" itself is a vague term that embraces many diverse and even incompatible positions. We could not make sense of Dewey's strong critique of older forms of liberalism unless we recognized this. Nor would Rawls' project make much sense unless we appreciate the extent to which he is arguing against what he takes to be mistaken conceptions of liberalism and unsatisfactory justifications of it. For as soon as one attempts to clarify what one means by "liberalism," what one takes to be primary or secondary about liberal democracy, one is caught up in controversy. What for one "liberal" is basic for liberty or freedom is to another "liberal" a mark of coercion. This is illustrated not only in the controversies of political philosophers such as Rawls and Nozick, but is itself manifested in everyday debates about the responsibilities and obligations of the government concerning the range of "welfare rights."

At times Rorty writes as if "we" all have common intuitions about what liberal democracy means or should mean, but this is really ingenuous. It is ironical that Rorty, who in his pragmatic and Wittgensteinian moments argues so effectively against "essentialism," falls into an essentialist mode of speech when he speaks of "liberal democracy" or "political freedom." Sometimes Rorty concedes that there are important differences among the varieties of liberalism, but these differences are *political* not *philosophical*. But Rorty's labeling language game does not really get us very far in clarifying or resolving substantive differences. For he does not clarify what constitutes "the political" or how one is to evaluate critically competing political *arguments*. He writes as if something extremely important depends on labeling controversies about liberalism as "political" rather than "philosophical." This is why I think Rorty is actually perpetuating the sort of fruitless debates that the classical pragmatists sought to dismiss. Furthermore one finds deeply conflicting tendencies in Rorty's own mode of argumentation.

On the one hand, Rorty has relentlessly argued against the very idea that disciplines can be conceived of as "natural kinds" with well-defined domains and methods that demarcate them from different disciplines. (This thesis is "foundational" for his version of "holism.")[18] And in the case of philosophy, Rorty has exposed the ways in which the search for demarcation is little more than a power play, an exclusionary tactic that seeks to rule out the invention of new vocabularies and new modes of description.

But on the other hand, Rorty – especially in his polemics against philosophy and justification – writes as if philosophy is a "natural kind," indeed a noxious weed that should be rooted out and thrown away. And again, he sometimes writes as if labeling a controversy as "political" illuminates the controversy. But "the political" is no less an essentially contested concept than is "the philosophical."

This is why a statement such as the following tells us more about Rorty's rhetorical construction of the issues than it does about how they are to be resolved. In his address to the Eleventh Inter-American Congress of Philosophy, he concludes by stating "briefly and dogmatically a view for which I have argued elsewhere."

> This is that philosophy, even though it is often inspired by politics, should not be thought of as a foundation for politics nor as a weapon of politics .... We should not assume that it is our task as professors of philosophy to be the avant-garde of political movements. We should not ask, say Davidson or Gadamer, for the "political implications" of their view of language, nor spurn their work because of its lack of such implications. We should think of politics as one of the experimental rather than of the theoretical disciplines.

> It may seem foolish to speak of "play" as I have done, in the midst of a political struggle that will decide whether civilization has a future, whether our descendants will have any *chance* to play. But philosophy should try to express our political hopes rather than to ground our political practices. On the view I am suggesting, nothing grounds our practices, nothing legitimizes them, nothing shows them to be in touch with the way things really are. The sense of human languages and practices as the results of experimental self-reflection rather than of an attempt to approximate to a fixed and ahistorical ideal – the

position in which I am claiming the philosophy of our century culminates – makes it less plausible than ever to imagine that a particular theoretical discipline will rescue or redeem us.[19]

We can read this passage sympathetically as a moral-aesthetic plea not to expect more of philosophy than it can deliver, not to judge the "theoretical" discipline of philosophy by inappropriate political standards. But the entire passage is filled with impossible dichotomies that dissolve as soon as we reflect upon them. Once again there is the pervasive contrast between "philosophy" and "politics" as if these labels demarcated "natural kinds." And once again there is the identification of philosophy with seeking "a fixed and ahistorical ideal," with putting us "in touch with the way things really are." (Later I want to examine critically Rorty's claim that this is "the position in which the philosophy of our century culminates.")

When the contrast is made between expressing our political hopes and grounding our political practices, then Rorty's plea has some polemical force. But does it make any sense to speak of expressing political hopes without seeking to evaluate "political practices" critically? Here, too, a hidden ahistorical essentialism creeps into Rorty's rhetoric. For Rorty writes as if we all know what these practices are. Given Rorty's constant appeal to history and historicism, he ignores the *historical fact* that we are confronted with conflicting and incompatible practices – even in so-called liberal democracy. Thus, for example, a number of commentators have argued that to understand American history and political thought we must be sensitive to the tensions and conflicts between a tradition of liberalism with its emphasis on negative liberty and the tradition of civic republicanism that highlights positive participatory freedom. These competing traditions lead to different evaluations of the very practices that are taken to be vital to the flourishing of democracy.[20] We do not settle issues by the appeal to "our political practices" – we need to confront the issues of which practices are to be favored and which are to be modified or eliminated. If we take "seriously" Rorty's claim that politics is an experimental discipline, then don't we need to appeal to some standards or criteria to judge what counts as a "successful" or a "failed" experiment?

Rorty sometimes seems to think that whenever one talks about standards or criteria one is on the slippery slope that leads to "bad" foundationalism. He himself has shown us that this is a myth. But he never faces the hard issue of clarifying what *historical* standards and criteria ought to be employed in evaluating the experimental discipline of politics. Sometimes Rorty writes as if any reference to criteria and standards is irrelevant. We should rather focus on examples and exemplars of what we politically admire. One can be sympathetic with the critique of the modern obsession with rules, principles, criteria, and standards. As Aristotle, Gadamer, and Oakeshott remind us, we should be wary of "bad" rationalism and realize that what is crucial in political and ethical judgment is the application of general principles to particular cases. But we also should not forget the lesson that Socrates teaches us when Euthyphro thinks it is *sufficient* to answer the question "what is piety?" by citing examples. We cannot avoid confronting the question "By virtue of what is a particular example an instance of piety, justice, etc.?"

Rorty's fateful, although shifting, dichotomies – the either/or's that structure his thinking – lead him to all sorts of dubious and double-edged claims. When he distinguishes three responses to the breakdown of the Enlightenment confidence in a universal ahistorical rationality – the absolutist, the pragmatic, and the communitarian, he tells us:

> If we swing to the pragmatist side, and consider talk of "rights" an attempt to enjoy the benefits of metaphysics without assuming the appropriate responsibilities, we shall still need something to distinguish the sort of individual conscience we respect from the sort we condemn as "fanatical." This can only be something relatively "local and ethnocentric" – the tradition of a particular community, the consensus of a particular culture. On this view what counts as rational or as fanatical is relative to the group to which we think it is necessary to justify ourselves – to the body of shared belief which determines the reference of the word "we". (p. 259)[21]

If the *only* alternatives open to us are *either* appealing to what is local and ethnocentric *or* appealing to fixed permanent ahistorical foundations, then Rorty's claim has some bite. But why should we accept this dichotomy? Rorty, of course, knows that there are pernicious and benign forms of ethnocentricism. The standard form of intolerance is one where some group takes itself to be the measure of what is "rational" and excludes some other group whether we speak of "*we* Greeks (versus barbarians)," or "*we* white

South Africans," or "*we* white males." So despite Rorty's manifest plea for extending the principle of tolerance, the latent content of what he says can lead to the worst forms of intolerance *unless* he is prepared to distinguish (even locally and historically) pernicious and benign forms of ethnocentric appeals.

Thus far I have been arguing as if Rorty has nothing to tell us when we turn our attention to substantive disagreements about the type of liberal democracy we ought to endorse. This is not quite accurate. But what he does tell us leads to further *aporias*. According to Rorty, we do not need any "philosophic justification" for liberal democracy, all we need is "reflective equilibrium." Insofar as justice becomes the first virtue of a society

> such a society will get accustomed to the thought that social policy needs no more authority than successful accommodation among individuals, individuals who find themselves heir to the same historical traditions and faced with the same problems. It will be a society which encourages the "end of ideology," that takes reflective equilibrium as the only method needed in discussing social policy. When such a society deliberates, when it collects the principles and intuitions to be brought into equilibrium, it will tend to discard those drawn from philosophical accounts of the self, or of rationality. (p. 264)

The appeal to "reflective equilibrium as the only *method* needed in discussing social policy" is little more than a verbal ornament. Rorty, following Feyerabend, has been a sharp critic of the very idea of "method" – where a method is supposed to lead to some determinate result by well-established procedures. Even if we accept some appeal to reflective equilibrium, it names a problem not a solution. We can agree that in any discussion of political or social alternatives, we begin with "intuitions" or what Dewey called "funded experience." But this is only a *beginning* point because the overwhelming historical fact is that individuals' basic intuitions, even when they reflect upon them, conflict. The problem is rather how are we to resolve these *conflicts* – what sorts of arguments are appropriate in evaluating competing intuitions? I fail to see how Rorty's appeal to "reflective equilibrium" gives us any clue about the resolution of such conflicts.

Here again, Rorty betrays some of his best insights. In philosophic contexts Rorty has criticized those who appeal to the common intuitions that "we" share as a way of resolving philosophic disputes. He has even argued that when realists appeal to "our intuitions" the proper response may be not to deny that we do at times have such intuitions, but that they ought to be abandoned.[22] But it is never clear why he thinks that the appeal to common intuitions in a political context is any more successful in settling controversies than it is in a philosophical debate.

Indeed it begins to look as if Rorty is substituting a "historical myth of the given" for the "epistemological myth of the given" that he has helped to expose. He speaks of "our" practices, "our" tradition, the "consensus" of a particular community as if this were simply a historical given.

He fails to see that he is using a variation on the very type of argument he has sought to discredit. Why is it that liberal democracy needs no philosophic justification or legitimization? Because all the "justification" it needs it gets from the appeal to our common moral and political intuitions, from the consensus of the particular local historical community with which we identify ourselves. But if one is to appeal to a historical consensus or a tradition, then let us be wary of making it into something more solid, harmonious, and coherent than it really is. I agree with MacIntyre when he tells us that a tradition (including the tradition of liberalism) "when vital embodies continuities of conflict" and that when a tradition is "in good order it is always partially constituted by an argument about the goods the pursuit of which gives the tradition its particular point or purpose."[23] If we are serious or playful about politics and liberal democracy, then it is this ongoing *argument* that should be the focus of our attention. Why does Rorty ignore this or seek to dismiss it by telling us that such controversies are political but not philosophical, and that the method of reflective equilibrium is sufficient to resolve disputes about social policy?

In part, this is because he (at times) "presupposes" that all "philosophic justification" and all argument boils down to logical deduction from presumably unassailable premises. But this "presupposition" conflicts with another strain in his thinking. For Rorty, along with many others, has shown us that argumentation in any discipline – whether philosophy, science, or politics – virtually never takes this "canonical" form. But then one would think the task is to enter the fray, to seek to advance stronger substantive arguments – in our historical situation – for the type of liberalism and the vision of democracy that one endorses. Global references to "social practices," "shared beliefs," a "historical consensus" only point to a tangled area of controversy, they do not help us to resolve controversies. But Rorty rarely descends from his metaphilosophical heights to substantive argument. He never ever raises the question (as Dewey did): what is the relation – and tension – between democracy as a moral ideal and liberalism?

He tends to gloss over what appears to be the overwhelming "fact" of contemporary life – the breakdown of moral and political consensus, and the conflicts and incompatibility among competing social practices. Even if Rorty thinks that claims about the breakdown of moral and political consensus are exaggerated, one would expect some *argument* showing why the "crisis mentality" of the twentieth century is mistaken – or, at least a clarification of what are the characteristics of the consensus that he thinks does exist among those who take themselves to be champions of liberal democracy. It is never clear why Rorty, who claims that there is no consensus about competing conceptions of the good life, thinks there is any more consensus about conceptions of justice or liberal democracy.

Rorty also tends to downplay or at least circumscribe what has become a major problem for any internal defense or external critique of liberalism – the disparity between the "ideals" of liberty and equality that liberals profess and the actual state of affairs in so-called liberal societies. Occasionally he writes as if this is simply an "empirical" problem that can be handled by the appeal to social science and piecemeal social engineering. Despite his harsh remarks about Marx and Marxism, I do not see any evidence that Rorty faces up to the *challenge* that Marx poses for us in his critique of ideology, namely, that the structural dynamics of bourgeois society systematically undermine and belie liberal ideals. But one does not need to appeal to Marx to make this point. It is made by Weber – in a different way – when he argues that the spread and institutionalization of *Zweckrationalität*, and the increasing disenchantment of the world (which Rorty favors and wants to further), has the consequence of undermining the very social conditions required for individual autonomy and freedom.[24] And a similar point is made by Dewey when he claims that "the gulf between what the actual situation makes possible and the actual state itself is so great that it cannot be bridged by piecemeal policies undertaken *ad hoc*."[25] Even Rawls seeks to confront this issue in a more forthright way than Rorty does. For *A Theory of Justice* is structured not only to specify and defend the principles of justice, but also to show us how they can be approximated in our "actual state itself." The point can be put simply even if one objects to Marxist claims about the structural conflicts and contradictions of bourgeois capitalist societies.

Since the nineteenth century when the varieties of liberalism have come under heavy attack, there have been those (Marxists, socialists, anarchists, radical reformers, and even Weberians) who have *argued* that when we examine liberalism as it is embodied in concrete modern societies (especially in a capitalist economic order) we discover that it is not a merely accidental contingent fact that liberal ideals of universal freedom and equality are constantly betrayed in bourgeois capitalist societies. There are forces and tendencies at work (e.g., class conflict, social division, patriarchy, racism) that are compatible with liberal political practices but nevertheless foster *real* inequality and limit effective political freedom. At the very least Rorty's "defense" of liberal democracy requires him to show the falsity or speciousness of the claims of the radical critics of liberalism. But Rorty does not argue his case, he simply asserts it. At times he suggests that it is only an "empirical" issue whether or not liberal democracies can and do achieve equality and effective universal liberty. But it is never clear what empirical evidence would justify his claims (or even what he means by labeling this issue "empirical").

It may be objected that I am being unfair to Rorty because he has limited his critique to a single circumscribed issue – whether or not liberal democracy needs a philosophic justification. He is not addressing the question of which version of liberalism we should endorse. But I do not think such a response – this easy way of compartmentalizing issues – is adequate. This is because when we descend from the heights of metaphilosophical discourse to a first-level discussion of competing conceptions of liberalism, then we are forced to face the difficult and controversial reflective issues that Rorty dismisses – whether we label them "political" or "philosophical." This is where competing conceptions of the "self," "liberty," or "political freedom" become pragmatically relevant. This is the sort of issue Dewey was worried about when he said that "any liberalism which is not also radicalism is irrelevant and doomed."

There is another perspective for exposing the dubiousness of Rorty's claims – unpacking what he means by "we." Earlier I cited the passage in which Rorty speaks of "the group to which we think it necessary to justify ourselves – to the body of shared belief which determines the reference of the word 'we'" (p. 259). Rorty frequently speaks of "we" – "we liberals," "we pragmatists," "we inheritors of European civilization." But who precisely constitutes this "we"? Sometimes it seems as if what Rorty means by "we" are "all those who agree with me." On another occasion, Rorty has criticized Foucault for failing to appeal to a "we." It is worthwhile to cite Foucault's reply to Rorty:

> R. Rorty points out ... I do not appeal to any "we" – to any "we's" whose consensus, whose values, whose traditions constitute the framework for a thought and define the conditions in which it can be validated. But the problem is, precisely, to decide if it is in order to assert the principles one recognizes and the values one accepts; or if it is not, rather, necessary to make the future formation of a "we" possible, by elaborating the question. Because it seems to me that the "we" must not be previous to the question; it can only be the result – and the necessary temporary result – of the question as it is posed in new terms in which one formulates it.[26]

At times, as I have already suggested, Rorty seems to be insensitive to the dark side of appealing to "we" when it is used as an exclusionary tactic – as the "rationalization" for fostering intolerance. But Rorty's own appeal to a "we" masks deeper conflicting tendencies in his own thinking. Rorty criticizes those versions of "realism" that appeal to a "fact of the matter" that is presumably independent of my (or our) interpretations. Yet he fails to realize that when he appeals to our shared beliefs and our common historical heritage, he is speaking as if there is at least a historical fact of the matter. This is Rorty's "historical myth of the given," which he substitutes for the "epistemological myth of the given." But Rorty, especially in his Nietzschean and existential moments, subscribes to the thesis that there are "no facts only interpretations." When he defends "strong" readings of texts and traditions, when he emphasizes our capacity for making and self-creation, he comes close to suggesting that "we" are always free to make up what a tradition means for us. There seems to be no genuine resistance, no otherness, nothing corresponding to what Peirce called Secondness to which we must be responsive. Tradition, including the tradition of liberal democracy, does not seem to have any determinate content other than the ways in which we (I) interpret it. And our interpretations, our self-creations, seem to be little more than an expression of our idiosyncratic will to power, our will to self-assertion.

Here it is helpful to contrast Gadamer with Rorty. For Gadamer (and Dewey), we are always already engaged in the "happening" of understanding, interpretation, and appropriation. But for Gadamer, when we are engaged in dialogue, whether it be with another partner, a text, or a tradition, there is always something "other" to which we are being responsive, that speaks to us and constrains us. There is a genuine to-and-fro movement that enables us to constitute a "we" that is more than a projection of my own idiosyncratic desires and beliefs. But for Rorty there never seems to be any effective constraints on *me* and *my* interpretations. This is why Rorty's constant refereces to "we," a common tradition, a shared consensus appear to be hollow – little more than a label for a projected "me."

There is another disturbing feature about Rorty's own "defense" of what he calls "post-modern bourgeois liberalism," and this touches on a larger theme concerning the political significance of recent debates about modernism and postmodernism. When Habermas suggested that the radical credentials of so-called postmodern and poststructuralist thinkers might be questioned, and that there were parallels between postmodern discourse and young conservative counter-Enlightenment discourse, he set off a storm of protest that still has not abated. Peter Dews (in his excellent introduction to a collection of Habermas interviews) pursues this theme when he writes:

> There are some striking parallels between this [Lyotard's] account of postmodernity and the "end of ideology" debate which preoccupied English-speaking political scientists in the late fifties and early sixties. Indeed, it is curious to observe how the conception of ideology developed by American political science during the first Cold War is reduplicated in many of the themes of the "left" Nietzscheanism of Paris during the 1970's. Daniel Bell's definition of a "total ideology" as an "all-inclusive system of comprehensive reality," "a set of beliefs infused with passion" which "seeks to transform the whole of a way of life," captures the burden of this conception, which – independently of any direct Nietzschean influence – is congruent with Nietzsche's fundamental convictions. Nietzsche insists that any comprehensive theoretical or philosophical system must inevitably distort and simplify reality (for Bell, "Ideology makes it unnecessary for people to confront individual issues on their individual merits"), that the energy which enters into the construction of such systems always derives from pre-rational needs and drives (for Bell, "the most important latent function of ideology is to tap emotion"), and that concepts have an

ineliminable pragmatic dimension (for Bell, "not only does ideology transform ideas, it transforms people as well"). Furthermore, like Lyotard, the end-of-ideology theorists portrayed ideological thought as a compensation for the collapse of traditional worldviews, and attributed its decline to the political and social disasters of the twentieth century. Indeed, it is much the same litany of catastrophies, most notably fascism and Stalinism, which is recited in both cases.[27]

Dews' remarks about the parallels between "end of ideology" apologists and champions of postmodernity are even more trenchant when applied to Rorty who explicitly identifies himself with the end-of-ideology movement. Despite Rorty's critique of Lyotard, he basically shares Lyotard's playful celebration and invention of new language games and vocabularies.

Indeed, Rorty's present position is an odd mixture of avant-garde "radical" postmodern playfulness and what looks like old-fashioned cold war liberalism. But just as it became evident that Bell and his fellow travelers were masking a new form of ideology under the slogan of "the end of ideology" so this is true of Rorty. This becomes even more striking when we consider the politics of some of Rorty's new heroes: Sidney Hook, Karl Popper, Michael Oakeshott, and Lezsek Kolakowski. Rorty's thesis of the priority of democracy over philosophy, his celebration of a new tolerant *jouissance* of multiple language games and vocabularies is little more than an ideological *apologia* for an old-fashioned version of cold war liberalism dressed up in fashionable "postmodern" discourse.[28] This is surely one step forward, two steps backward.

The end of philosophy?

Thus far I have only obliquely dealt with Rorty's understanding of philosophy and metaphysics. Because Rorty's ongoing battle against the worn out vocabularies of philosophy and metaphysics is central in all his writings during the past decade, I want to confront his views directly.

Rorty is acutely aware of the self-referential objections that can be brought against his attack on philosophy and metaphysics – that he himself argues against one view of philosophy on the *basis* of another view that he fails to justify. And he nimbly seeks to get around this objection and defuse it. He tell us,

Both "religion" and "philosophy" [one can add metaphysics, RJB] are vague umbrella terms, and both are subject to persuasive redefinition. When these terms are broadly enough defined everybody, even atheists, will be said to have a religious faith (in the Tillichian sense of a symbol of ultimate concern). Everybody, even those who shun metaphysics and epistemology, will be said to have philosophic presuppositions.[29]

In order to prevent any misunderstanding about the way in which we should take his own *philosophic* remarks about the self, he tells us,

If, however, one has a taste for philosophy – if one's vocation, one's private pursuit of happiness entails constructing models of such entities as "the self," "knowledge," "language," "nature," "God," or "history," and then tinkering with them until they mesh with each other – one *will* want a picture of the self. Since my own vocation is of this sort, and the moral identity around which I wish to build such models is that of a citizen of a liberal democratic state, I commend the picture of the self as a centerless and contingent web to those with similar tastes and similar identities. (p. 270)

But is this convincing or hedging? Rorty is not simply constructing a picture of the self that fits with or comports with his convictions as a citizen of a liberal democratic state – where we are "free" to accept it or not according to whether we share or do not share "similar tastes and similar identities." He is *arguing* against all notions of a centered and transcendental self. Whatever his *motivations* in coming up with a picture of "the self as centerless, as historical contingency all the way through," he is arguing that this is a more perspicuous – one is tempted to say a "truer" – understanding of the self. One does not get off the hook by telling us that if one *wants* to play the game of elaborating different "pictures" of the self, that this is a better way to play the game. The game does not make any sense unless one is prepared to show and *argue* – as Rorty claims to do – why one picture is better than its alternatives (regardless of whether or not it comports with one's conception of liberal democracy). And when Rorty tells us that we do not really need to play any of these games at all in order to defend liberal democracy, he once again fails to recognize that as soon as we attempt to *specify* what we mean by liberty or political freedom, to characterize what it is that we are championing, considerations such as those that he takes up in his discussion of alternative "pictures" of the self are implicated. The locus of controversial reflective theories or "pictures" is *not* in grounding political convictions on firm foundations, but in *specifying* and *describing* what precisely we mean by liberalism and liberal democracy.

There is a larger issue looming on the horizon. Why does Rorty think that philosophy (or "Philosophy") amounts to little more than the worn out vocabulary of "bad" foundational discourse? So much of his recent writing falls into the genre of the "God that failed" discourse. There seems to be something almost oedipal – a form of patricide – in Rorty's obsessive attacks on the father figures of philosophy and metaphysics. It is the discourse of a one time "true believer" who has lost his faith.

But I want to bring into the open the narrative of the history of philosophy that informs so much of Rorty's recent work and that is the "straight man" he attacks in his playful "joshing." For Rorty has appropriated a version of the narrative of the history of philosophy that has its most dramatic origins in Nietzsche, has been refined and perpetuated by Heidegger, Derrida, and has been disseminated by many of those who identify themselves as poststructuralist, postmodern, or deconstructionist writers. According to this story, the real villain is Plato – at least the Plato identified (mythologized) by Platonism. Platonism, according to its critics, including Rorty, is like a thousand-headed monster – or better a Proteus – who can take on an indefinite variety of forms. Platonism is the search for "metaphysical comfort," secure ahistorical foundations that will alleviate our deepest anxieties. It is the infatuation with universality, necessity, and *epistēmē*. It is the disdain (even hatred) for radical contingency, particularity, historicity. Platonism has to be slayed wherever it appears whether in Descartes, Kant, Habermas, Peirce, the "new" analytic realists, or in Rawls' communitarian critics. It was Nietzsche who in his brilliant aphorisms first sketched the "history of the West" as the history of Platonism where Christianity becomes Platonism for the masses. Heidegger not only presses these Nietzschean claims but spins a story of the history of the philosophy as the history of the fallenness and forgetfulness of Being. And for Heidegger, Nietzsche is the "last metaphysician." In Heidegger's strong reading of the history of philosophy, the "movement" from Platonism to the nihilistic triumph of *Gestell* (enframing) is the inexorable working out of "prefigured" possibilities. Then along comes Derrida, who in his "exposure" of logocentrism, phono-centrism, phallogocentrism, and metaphysical presence, tells us:

> The entire history of the concept of structure must be thought of as a series of substitutions of center for center, as a linked chain of deter-mination of the center .... The history of metaphysics like the history of the West is the history of those metaphors and metonymies.[30]

And he also seeks to root out the last elements of Heidegger's nos-talgia for Being. Rorty, with a certain amount of self-irony, has noted that there can be indefinite variations on this "game." For Rorty praises Derrida when he is deconstructing the history of philosophy but chides him when he slips into the mode of a "constructive" philo-sopher of language.[31]

There are two dominant strains in this narrative – both of which can be found in Nietzsche. There is the heavy despairing strain about the fate and destiny of the "West," which is expressed in some of Heidegger's gloomiest passages. And there is the laughing, joshing, playful strain in Derrida, which is taken up in Rorty's playfulness.

I do not want to denigrate the power, insight, and provocative quality of this narrative of the history of philosophy and the "history of the West." For it compels us to rethink what philosophy has been, is, and might be. In the best sense there is a Socratic impulse of questioning in this movement – the type of questioning that compels us to face up to our deepest buried judgments and prejudgments.

But I also want to maintain that this narrative is itself rapidly becoming a blinding prejudice that obscures more than it illumi-nates. What was once a stinging critique is becoming a bland, boring cliché. One begins to wonder if there ever was a "foundationist" thinker – at least one who fits the description of what Rorty calls "foundationism." Even Plato – the Plato of the Dialogues – fails to fit this description. I fully agree with Gadamer when he gently chides Heidegger for perpetuating the myth of "Platonism."

> Heidegger interprets the acceptance of the doctrine of ideas as the beginning of that forgetfulness of being that peaks in mere imagin-ings and objectivations and runs along its course in the technolog-ical age as the universal will to power .... But over against this Heideggerian interpretation, the authentic dimension of the Platonic dialectic of ideas has a fundamentally different meaning. The under-

lying principle is a step beyond the simple minded acceptance of ideas, and in the final analysis a counter movement against the metaphysical interpretation of being as the being of existing being [*Sein als das Seins des Seienden*].[32]

My main point here is not simply to oppose one narrative of the history of philosophy with another that stresses the questioning, open character of philosophic thinking. It is rather to call attention to the way in which Rorty's characterization and caricature of the history of philosophy is rapidly running itself into the ground, and to suggest that what is now needed is to demythologize this narrative of the invidious fallenness of Platonism. For it is only to the extent that we still accept some version of Rorty's mythologizing about what philosophy and metaphysics are, and what "philosophic justification" *must* be, that his playful skepticism has any sting. Once we give up this "myth" – once we adopt a more open and playful attitude toward philosophy itself (instead of obsessively trying to kill it off over and over again) – then all the hard issues concerning the defense and critique of liberalism come rushing in. It is time that Rorty himself should appropriate the lesson of Peirce, "Do not block the road to inquiry," and realize that rarified metaphilosophical or metatheoretical discussion can never be a substitute for struggling to articulate, defend, and justify one's vision of a just and good society.

Rorty, who has eloquently called for open conversation, fails to realize how his rhetorical strategies tend to close off serious/playful conversation about liberalism and democracy. The pragmatic legacy (which Rorty constantly invokes) will only be recovered and revitalized when we try to do for our time what Dewey did in his historical context – to articulate, texture, and *justify* a vision of a pragmatically viable ideal of communal democracy.

NOTES

1 Ralph B. Perry, *The Thought and Character of William James* (Boston: Little, Brown, 1935), II, pp. 518–19. For a discussion of Dewey's early involvement with social reform, see Lewis S. Feuer, "John Dewey and the Back-to-the-People Movement in American Thought," *Journal of the History of Ideas* (December 1959), pp. 545–68; and Richard J. Bernstein, *John Dewey* (New York: Washington Square, 1966; reprinted Atascadero, Cal.: Ridgeview, 1981), chap. 3, "The Shaping of a Social Reformer."

2 John Dewey, "Creative Democracy – The Task Before Us," reprinted in M. Fisch, ed., *Classic American Philosophers* (New York: Appleton-Century-Crofts, 1951), p. 394.
3 Ibid.
4 John Dewey, *The Public and Its Problems* (New York: Henry Holt, 1927), p. 98.
5 John Dewey, *Freedom and Culture* (New York: G. P. Putnam, 1939), p. 130.
6 John Dewey, *Liberalism and Social Action* (New York: Capricorn Books, 1935), reprinted in John J. McDermott, ed., *The Philosophy of John Dewey* (New York: G. P. Putnam, 1973), II, pp. 647–8.
7 Richard Rorty, *Philosophy and the Mirror of Nature* (Princeton: Princeton University Press, 1979), p. 5.
8 For a critique of Rorty's relation to pragmatism and his response, see the Symposium on Rorty's "Consequences of Pragmatism," *Transactions of the Charles S. Peirce Society* (Winter 1985), pp. 1–48. See also Gary Brodsky, "Rorty's Interpretation of Pragmatism," *Transactions of the Charles S. Peirce Society* (Fall 1982), pp. 311–37.
9 See Rorty's Introduction to *Consequences of Pragmatism* (Minneapolis: University of Minnesota Press, 1982).
10 See Richard Rorty, "The Contingency of Selfhood," *London Review of Books* 8 (May 1986).
11 Richard Rorty, "The Priority of Democracy to Philosophy," in Robert Vaughan, ed., *The Virginia Statute of Religious Freedom: Two Hundred Years After* (Madison: University of Wisconsin Press, 1988). Page numbers in this essay refer to this article.
12 Rorty labels as communitarians "such theorists as Robert Bellah, Alasdair MacIntyre, Michael Sandel, Charles Taylor, the early Roberto Unger, and many others. These writers share some measure of agreement with a view found in an extreme form, both in Heidegger and in Horkheimer and Adorno's *Dialectic of Enlightenment*" (p. 259). One should be very wary of the label "communitarians," which is now becoming fashionable, not only because it lumps together such diverse thinkers, but because it encompasses thinkers whose views span the political spectrum.

   Furthermore, given Rorty's characterization of "communitarianism" – especially the central claim that "the community is constitutive of the individual," it is difficult to understand the rationale for *not* classifying Dewey as a communitarian. There is no evidence that Dewey thought of himself as elaborating a view of the individual and the self that merely "comports" with his political intuitions about liberal democracy. Ironically, one of the best and most succinct statements of what Dewey meant by community is given by the "communitarian" Michael Sandel when he characterizes the "strong sense" of community and distinguishes it from instrumental and sentimental conceptions of community.

On this strong view, to say that the members of a society are bound by a sense of community is not to say that a great many of them profess communitarian sentiments or pursue communitarian aims, but rather that they conceive their identity – the subject and not just the object of their feelings and aspirations – as defined to some extent by the community of which they are a part. (Michael J. Sandel, *Liberalism and the Limits of Justice* [Cambridge: Cambridge University Press, 1982], p. 147)

13 John Rawls, *A Theory of Justice* (Cambridge, Mass.: Harvard University Press, 1971); "Kantian Constructivism in Moral Theory," *Journal of Philosophy* 77 (1980); "Justice as Fairness: Political not Metaphysical," *Philosophy and Public Affairs* 14 (1985).

14 Because my primary concern in this article is with Rorty's views on liberal democracy and philosophy, I have deliberately avoided the question of the accuracy of Rorty's interpretation of Rawls. I also want to "bracket" the question of whether Rawls in "Justice as Fairness: Political not Metaphysical" is clarifying his original intentions, changing his mind, or rewriting his own history. There are already signs in the secondary literature on Rawls that we are about to witness an outpouring of articles on this topic. I suspect that this will be as unilluminating as the extensive discussion about whether Thomas Kuhn was changing his mind or rewriting his own history when he sought to clarify what he meant in *The Structure of Scientific Revolutions*.

15 There is something curious and asymmetrical about Rorty's interpretation of Rawls and his "communitarian" critics. Although admitting that *A Theory of Justice* is ambiguous, Rorty tends to screen out all those passages where Rawls appears to be making philosophical and metaphysical claims. But when Rorty discusses Sandel and Taylor, he exaggerates their commitment to controversial philosophical and metaphysical theories. Rorty never explores the extent to which the entire debate can be read as a political argument (in his sense of "political") about competing visions of democracy.

16 Rorty writes:

The idea that moral and political controversies should always be "brought back to principles" is reasonable if it means merely that we should seek common ground in the hope of attaining agreement. But it is misleading if it is taken as the claim that there is a natural order of premises from which moral and political conclusions are to be inferred. (p. 269)

17 Rawls, *A Theory of Justice*, pp. 21, 579. See Amy Gutmann's discussion of Rawls' understanding of justification, "Communitarian Critics of Liberalism," *Philosophy and Public Affairs* (Summer 1985), p. 312.

18 See Richard Rorty, "Is Natural Science a Natural Kind?", in Ernan

McMullin, ed., *Construction and Constraint* (South Bend: University of Notre Dame Press, 1988), pp. 49–74.

19   Richard Rorty, "From Logic to Language to Play," *Proceedings and Addresses of the American Philosophical Association* (June 1986), pp. 752–3.

20   See, for example, William Sullivan, *Reconstructing Public Philosophy* (Berkeley: University of California Press, 1982); Hannah Arendt's discussion of the American Revolution and the contribution of Jefferson in *On Revolution* (New York: Viking, 1962); and Dewey, *Freedom and Culture*.

21   Rorty is even more explicit on this point when in his reply to Clifford Geertz's "The Uses at Diversity" he says: "Anti-anti-ethnocentrists, suggest that liberals ... should simply drop the distinction between rational judgment and cultural bias" ("On Ethnocentrism: A Reply to Clifford Geertz," *Michigan Quarterly Review* [Summer 1986], pp. 525–34).

22   See Rorty's discussion of "deep intuitions" in his Introduction to *Consequences of Pragmatism*.

23   Alasdair MacIntyre, *After Virtue* (Notre Dame: University of Notre Dame Press, 1981), p. 206. My criticism that Rorty is substituting a "historical myth of the given" for the "epistemological myth of the given" is closely related to William E. Connolly's claim that Rorty replaces "epistemic foundationalism" with "a species of social foundationalism." I also agree with Connolly that, despite Rorty's critique of what Nietzsche calls "metaphysical comfort," Rorty's portrait of *our* community "comforts and tranquilizes." Consequently, despite Rorty's eloquent plea to keep "the conversation of mankind" open to new "incommensurable vocabularies," he is in effect closing the space for the possibility of a critical, challenging, and disturbing conversation about the "social foundations" of *our* liberal democratic communities. See William E. Connolly, "Mirror of America," *Raritan* (Summer 1983), pp. 124–35.

24   In 1906, Weber wrote:

> It is utterly ridiculous to see any connection between the high capitalism of today ... with democracy or with freedom in any sense of these words. Yet this capitalism is an unavoidable result of our economic development. The question is: how are freedom and democracy in the long run possible under the domination of highly developed capitalism .... The historical origin of modern freedom has had certain unique preconditions which will never repeat themselves. (*Archiv für Sozialwissenschaft und Sozialpolitik*, 12, no. 1, p. 347, cited in H. H. Gerth and C. Wright Mills, eds., *From Max Weber: Essays in Sociology* [New York: Oxford University Press, 1946], p. 71)

In citing Weber, I do not mean to suggest that I endorse his claims, but Weber presents a challenge that Rorty never squarely faces.

25 See note 6.

26 Michel Foucault, "Polemics, Politics, and Problemizations: An Interview," in Paul Rabinow, ed., *The Foucault Reader* (New York: Pantheon, 1984), p. 385.

27 Peter Dews, *Habermas: Autonomy and Solidarity* (London: Verso, 1986), pp. 6–7.

28 There are two points that I want to stress here. Like many anti-communists, Rorty frequently argues as if damning communism and so-called really existing socialism is all one needs to do to defend and "justify" American liberal democracy. Rorty's rhetoric (although not his personal politics) echoes the rhetoric we hear from neo-conservatives. But anti-Stalinism, an opposition to all forms of totalitarianism and a healthy suspicion of the intentions of the Kremlin is not sufficient to justify American liberalism. Some of the best recent analyses and sharpest criticisms of totalitarianism and the Soviet Union have been developed by left thinkers who are also penetrating critics of liberalism – including Jürgen Habermas, Agnes Heller, Ferenc Feher, Claude Lefort, Cornelius Castoriadis, and the Yugoslav *Praxis* group.

Second, although Rorty scorns American neo-conservatism, he fails to note how much he shares with the neo-conservatives that he despises. It is, of course, true that in opposition to the "spirit of seriousness" of neo-conservatives, Rorty advocates light-minded aesthetic playfulness. Nevertheless, Rorty like many neo-conservatives: (1) endorses the "end of ideology" thesis; (2) slides from militant anti-communism to a virtually unqualified endorsement of "really existing democracy" in Western capitalist societies; (3) tends to downplay the significance of imperialistic policies practiced by liberal democracies; (4) never seriously questions the relation between capitalism and liberal democracy; (5) is suspicious of any appeal to universal principles, standards, and criteria; and (6) suggests that it is sufficient in making moral and political judgments to focus exclusively on concrete examples of what "we" admire.

29 This passage appears in the manuscript of "The Priority of Democracy to Philosophy," but is deleted from the published version.

30 Jacques Derrida, "Structure, Sign, and Play in the Discourse of the Human Sciences," *Writing and Difference*, trans. Alan Bass (Chicago: University of Chicago Press, 1978), p. 277.

31 See Richard Rorty, "Philosophy as a Kind of Writing: An Essay on Derrida," in *Consequences of Pragmatism*.

32 Hans-Georg Gadamer, "On the Origin of Philosophical Hermeneutics," in *Philosophical Apprenticeships* (Cambridge, Mass.: MIT Press, 1985), p. 186.

9

Rorty's Liberal Utopia

In 1979, Richard Rorty published his provocative and controversial book, *Philosophy and the Mirror of Nature*. Prior to its publication, Rorty was known primarily as a philosophy professor who had made important contributions to the discussion of such technical professional issues as "the mind–body problem," "incorrigibility," and the epistemological status of "transcendental arguments." But *Philosophy and the Mirror of Nature* is a subversive and ambitious work. Employing his analytic and rhetorical skills, Rorty sought to undermine and deconstruct what he called "the Cartesian-Lockean-Kantian tradition" – a tradition that served as the basis for much of twentieth-century philosophy, including both Anglo-American analytic philosophy and Continental phenomenology. Rorty claims that the three most important philosophers of the twentieth century are Dewey, Heidegger, and Wittgenstein. According to Rorty, "each tried, in his early years, to find a new way of making philosophy 'foundational' – a new way of formulating an ultimate context of thought":

> Each of the three came to see his earlier effort as self-deceptive, as an attempt to retain a certain conception of philosophy after the notions needed to flesh out that conception (the seventeenth-century notions of knowledge and mind) had been discarded. Each of the three, in his later work, broke free of the Kantian conception of philosophy as foundational, and spent his time warning against those very temptations to which he himself once succumbed. Thus their later

work is therapeutic rather than constructive, edifying rather than systematic, designed to make the reader question his own motives for
philosophizing rather than to supply him with a new philosophical
program.[1]

These remarks are self-referential because Rorty viewed his own
earlier efforts as succumbing to the temptation of thinking that philosophy might still serve as a foundational discipline. *Philosophy and the
Mirror of Nature* is the type of book that could have been written only
by an "insider" – someone thoroughly acquainted with the latest
philosophic debates. With wit, irony, and analytic finesse, Rorty uses
the argumentative techniques of analytic philosophers to question
and deflate the pretensions of professional philosophy. The book has
generated an enormous amount of discussion and controversy. Many
analytic philosophers felt it was an act of betrayal. They accused
Rorty of distorting the problems and the positions he discusses, of
winning points by rhetorical tricks rather than by "rigorous"
arguments, and of committing the worst philosophic "sin" – indulging in "sloppy thinking." But many others (philosophers and non-
philosophers) found the book exciting and liberating. Rorty had
effectively exposed the artificiality, narrowness, and arrogant pretensions of analytic philosophy. Rorty had helped to break up the
hegemony of the analytic establishment and opened the way for discussion of important cultural issues long neglected by professional
philosophers. He had even provided a new legitimacy for taking
seriously the writings of Nietzsche, Heidegger, Sartre, Foucault,
Derrida, Gadamer, and Habermas – thinkers who had been
neglected and marginalized by most analytic philosophers.

Rorty himself was much more ambiguous and ambivalent about
what philosophers might do after the demise of epistemology and
foundational philosophy. There were some catchy phrases like "therapy," "edification," and "the conversation of mankind," but no clear
sense of what a successor discipline to traditional philosophy might
even look like. He disclaimed any attempt to come up with a new
"constructive" philosophic program. He suggested opting for a
deliberately amateurish cultural critique – which he ironically called
"kibitzing."

After *Philosophy and the Mirror of Nature*, Rorty turned to the essay
as a literary genre. His essays range over a great variety of contemporary issues and thinkers that cut across traditional disciplines and

philosophic schools. The first fruits of these efforts appear in his collection *Consequences of Pragmatism*.[2] Although these essays were written as occasional pieces, they cluster around three themes. First, he continues his polemical attack on foundational claims and the very idea that philosophy is a well-defined discipline (*Fach*) that addresses perennial philosophic problems. Second, a theme that is barely anticipated in *Philosophy and the Mirror of Nature* begins to come into the foreground – his championing of the virtues and moral achievements of bourgeois liberal democracy. The third theme concerns play, metaphor, and the figure of the poet, who creates herself out of the fabric of her own radical contingencies. These three themes are interrelated. Rorty thinks that once we get over the "hang-ups" of traditional philosophy with Rationality, Truth, Objectivity, and Argumentation, we can get on with the task of creating a postphilosophical liberal culture – where we foster the type of solidarity required to enhance liberal democracy and where we all emulate the poets, who are the new cultural heroes and heroines.

Rhetoric and argument

The antagonism, hostility, and polemical attacks that Rorty has generated during the past decade have increased dramatically. *Philosophy and the Mirror of Nature* is still recognizable as a philosophic book filled with clever and ingenious arguments. But Rorty increasingly ridicules the philosophic obsession with argument. Argument, as he now sees it, is a rhetorical device employed to persuade people to adopt a new "vocabulary" by making it look attractive. By now Rorty has offended and antagonized just about everyone – the political left and right, traditional liberals, feminists, and both analytic and Continental philosophers. His "strong" readings of key figures strike many as idiosyncratic creations of his own fantasies. He has been accused of being "smug," "shallow," "elitist," "priggish," "voyeuristic," "insensitive," and "irresponsible." "Rorty-bashing" is rapidly becoming a new culture industry.

Rorty, who is a master of rhetorical tropes, has sought to parry and blunt the barbs of his critics. He seems to enjoy his ability to josh, offend, and annoy. But there is one line of criticism that Rorty has taken more seriously than most – that he is insensitive to the real pain, suffering, and humiliation of human beings, that the other side of his ironical light-minded joshing is a cruel streak. His new book, *Contingency, Irony and Solidarity*,[3] can be read as an "answer" to this charge. I place "answer" in scare quotes because it is by no means a straightforward reply.

Although there is plenty to criticize in this new book – and I will argue that Rorty's main claims are not only unpersuasive but harbor all sorts of unresolved tensions – nevertheless, it is a disturbingly challenging book. It is all too easy to attack and dismiss it. But it can (and should) be read as raising hard, nasty questions – questions Rorty does not satisfactorily answer – that simply will not go away.

Precisely how is one to read and evaluate this book? We might begin by asking the standard philosophic question: what position(s) does Rorty advocate and what arguments does he present to support his claims? Rorty warns against this approach: "I am not going to offer arguments against the vocabulary I want to replace. Instead I am going to try to make the vocabulary I favor look attractive by showing how it may be used to describe a variety of topics" (p. 9). Rorty reiterates his skepticism about the role of argument in philosophy:

> Any argument to the effect that our familiar use of a familiar term is incoherent, or empty, or confused, or vague, or "merely metaphorical" is bound to be inconclusive and question-begging. For such use is, after all, the paradigm of coherent, meaningful, literal speech. Such arguments are always parasitic upon, and abbreviations for, claims that a better vocabulary is available. Interesting philosophy is rarely an examination of the pros and cons of a thesis. Usually it is, implicitly or explicitly, a contest between an entrenched vocabulary which has become a nuisance and a half-formed new vocabulary which vaguely promises great things. (pp. 8–9)

Rorty *does* argue, but he uses argument for the purpose of redescribing, for trying to get us to see why entrenched vocabularies have become nuisances and why his "half-formed new vocabulary," his new way of thinking, is "better" and "more attractive."

Rorty urges us to replace argument and theory with narratives – narratives that enable us to redescribe our past vocabularies and that show us how we might relate the present to an imagined utopian future. So we might read this book by paying attention to the details of Rorty's narratives. But here too we can be stymied. The "characters" of Rorty's narratives represent his "strong" readings of Hegel, Nietzsche, Foucault, Habermas, Derrida, Dewey, Rawls, Davidson, Freud, Proust, Nabokov, Orwell, and many others. Rorty himself self-ironically characterizes a "strong" reading as a "perverse, egocentric commentary" (p. 160). But many of these readings are so perverse that we can easily get bogged down in sorting out what is illuminating, incisive, and "on target" from what is distortive, misleading, or simply false.

The liberal ironist

To figure out what Rorty is up to I suggest that initially we take him at his word – that his "method" (his quotes) is to create a half-formed new vocabulary in which one redescribes "lots of things in new ways until you have created a pattern of linguistic behavior which will tempt the rising generation to adopt it, thereby causing them to look for appropriate new forms of non-linguistic behavior" (p. 9). This formulation is helpful for understanding what Rorty means by the deliberately vague term "vocabulary." Rorty is freely appropriating Wittgenstein's notion of a language game, or more accurately, a form of life. A vocabulary is a way of describing, evaluating, judging, and even acting. The "method" Rorty advocates

> does not work piece by piece, analyzing concept after concept. Rather it works holistically and pragmatically. It says things like "try thinking of it this way" – or more specifically "try to ignore the apparently futile traditional questions by substituting the following new and possibly interesting questions". (p. 9)

So let us try the imaginative experiment of entering into Rorty's new vocabulary, of adopting his new way of thinking. Rorty begins with a description of the "figure" he wants to sketch and recommend – the "liberal ironist." Borrowing his definition of a "liberal" from Judith Shklar – one that he repeats throughout the book – he tells us "liberals are the people who think that cruelty is the worst thing we do" (p. xv). An "ironist" is

> the sort of person who faces up to the contingency of his or her own most central beliefs and desires – someone sufficiently historicist and nominalist to have abandoned the idea that those central beliefs and desires refer back to something beyond the reach of time and chance.

> Liberal ironists are people who include among these ungroundable desires their own hope that suffering will be diminished, that the humiliation of human beings by other human beings may cease. (p. xv)

This characterization of the "liberal ironist" immediately raises the question, "Why not be cruel?" But Rorty responds (this is the point of joining "liberal" and "ironist"): "For liberal ironists, there is no answer to this question 'Why not be cruel?' – no noncircular theoretical backup for the belief that cruelty is horrible" (p. xv). Those liberals who think we can *rationally* answer this question are what Rorty calls "liberal metaphysicians." The problem with liberal metaphysicians – that is, with most intellectuals and non-intellectuals who think of themselves as liberals – is that they believe it is, or ought to be, possible to give non-question-begging answers to questions like "Why not be cruel?" More generally, they believe that liberalism rests upon, or ought to rest upon, rational foundations.

When Rorty fleshes out what he means by an "ironist" he does so by introducing the notion of a "final vocabulary":

> All human beings carry about a set of words which they employ to justify their actions, their beliefs, and their lives. These are the words in which we formulate praise of our friends and contempt for our enemies, our long-term projects, our deepest self-doubts and our highest hopes. They are words in which we tell, sometimes prospectively and sometimes retrospectively, the story of our lives. I shall call those words a person's "final vocabulary". (p. 73)

He immediately adds:

> It is "final" in the sense that if doubt is cast on the worth of these words, their user has no noncircular argumentative recourse. These words are as far as he can go with language; beyond them there is helpless passivity or resort to force. (p. 73)

With this stipulation of what constitutes a "final vocabulary" Rorty tells us that an "ironist" is someone who fulfills three conditions:

> (1) She has radical and continuing doubts about the final vocabulary she correctly uses, because she has been impressed by other vocabularies, vocabularies taken as final by people or books she has encountered;

(2) She realizes that argument phrased in her present vocabulary can neither underwrite nor dissolve these doubts;

(3) Insofar as she philosophizes about her situation, she does not think her vocabulary is closer to reality than others, that it is in touch with a power not herself. Ironists who are inclined to philosophize see the choice between vocabularies as made neither within a neutral and universal metavocabulary nor by an attempt to fight one's way past appearances to the real, but simply by playing the new off against the old. (p. 73)

Rorty knows that most liberals (past and present) have not been ironists. And those whom Rorty considers to be supreme ironists (e.g., Nietzsche and Heidegger) have been scornful of anything that smacks of liberal democracy. Irony and liberalism appear to be mutually antagonistic – at war with each other. So how can they be reconciled? Isn't the very idea of a "liberal ironist" oxymoronic? If reconciliation means finding some *theoretical* perspective for joining and synthesizing liberalism and irony, then Rorty thinks this is a futile project. He thinks that the desire for reconciliation is part of a larger project that has haunted philosophy since the time of Plato – the attempt to "discover" some theoretical grounding for reconciling the competing and incommensurable claims of our private and public lives. Such a grounding is presumably to be achieved by "discovering" a common human nature or the true character of our "deep selves." But there is no such thing to be "discovered." His major claim – one might say that it is the central thesis of his book – is that the attempt to fuse, synthesize, and reconcile the private and the public is not only a futile project but that it is *unnecessary*. We should recognize that the private and public domains are incommensurable. Nevertheless, each has its own legitimacy and responsibilities. Neither has any priority. Sharply distinguishing public and private questions, "the domain of the liberal from the domain of the ironist ... makes it possible for a single person to be both" (p. 198). We should privatize irony and realize that as public citizens our primary responsibility is to cultivate the type of solidarity required for the flourishing of liberal democracy. Rorty's new vocabulary is intended to persuade us that this can and should be done.

In Rorty's "liberal utopia" we would all recognize that solidarity is not grounded on something that we all share in common. Solidarity is not based upon Reason or Theory. Rather, it is a goal to be achieved by imagination where we become sensitive to the concrete details of the pain and humiliation of our fellow human beings. Journalists, ethnologists, and especially novelists are far more useful in achieving this goal than philosophers or social theorists. The culture of this liberal utopia would be one in which irony is universal. We would no longer even think that we can answer questions like "Why not be cruel?" We would stop searching for theoretical grounding for our "final vocabularies." We would all be historicists and nominalists and look back on the search for essences or a common human nature as quaint. Our heroes and heroines would be poets, self-creators – those lucky enough to create something new out of the contingencies that constitute their lives. Such a liberal utopian culture would no longer be obsessed with Truth, Objectivity, Reality, Rationality, and Argument. It would celebrate play and metaphor.

For all Rorty's ironic playfulness, he is also a passionate moralist (indeed, he wants to show us how a single person can be both). His moral and political concern is in part motivated by what he takes to be "irresponsible" attacks on liberal institutions by *both* radicals and neo-conservatives. In order to make liberalism look attractive (not to ground it), Rorty thinks that "Liberal culture needs an improved self-description rather than a set of foundations" (p. 52):

> We need a redescription of liberalism as the hope that culture as a whole can be "poeticized" rather than as the Enlightenment hope that it can be "rationalized" or "scienticized". (p. 53)

We should "try *not* to want something which stands beyond history and institutions." We should recognize that "a belief can still regulate action, can still be thought worth dying for, among people who are quite aware that this belief is caused by nothing deeper than contingent historical circumstance" (p. 189).

Rorty's project can be seen from a different perspective – by sketching his narrative of what has been happening in the West during the past few centuries, a narrative of intellectual and moral progress. (Throughout his book, he speaks about "progess" but this too has an ironic shading. Progress has nothing to do with teleology. It is the achievement of luck, historical contingencies. It is progress in the sense of being what liberal ironists favor and approve in their "final vocabularies.")

As Rorty sees it, ever since the eighteenth century there has been a growth and spread of liberal institutions and practices in the rich

North Atlantic bourgeois countries. This has occurred *not* because of any philosophic justification or theoretical backing. We only pay ourselves an empty compliment if we think of this as a rational development. There is no necessity or rationale why liberal institutions should have prevailed. Liberal metaphysical *rhetoric* – appeals to "rights," "equality," "liberty" – did play a role in bringing about liberal democracy, but this rhetoric is no longer useful in making liberalism "look good." This is why we now need a redescription of liberalism.

At the same time that liberal societies have made moral progress, Western culture – ever since Hegel – has become increasingly ironic. And when irony is pushed to the extreme it effectively undermines the "seriousness" of those discourses that pretend to provide a theoretical backing for our liberal convictions. So once again the problem for Rorty is how to enhance our liberal convictions, make them "look good," *and* learn the lesson that the culture of irony has taught us, that there is no non-circular argument for justifying our historically contingent beliefs.

Rorty's heroes

Still another way of appreciating what Rorty is up to is to consider his own intellectual predilections, specifically the grouping of his "heroes." On the one hand, he admires Mill, Dewey, Rawls, and Habermas. These are "good guys" as fellow citizens, champions of the type of liberalism that Rorty cherishes. He sharply criticizes them insofar as there are still metaphysical and rationalistic vestiges in their writings, that is, insofar as they tempt us to think that liberal beliefs and practices can be rationally grounded. On the other hand, Rorty also deeply admires Nietzsche, Heidegger, Foucault, and Derrida. They are among the most creative ironists. But he is sharply critical of them insofar as they sometimes succumb to the illusion that they also have a "social mission," that their experiments in irony have relevance for questions of public, political life. Rorty wants us to read Nietzsche, Heidegger, Foucault, and Derrida in the way in which we read Proust. They are all ironic poets (self-creators) who enhance our private lives but have *nothing* to tell us about our public responsibilities. There is no way of reconciling Heidegger and

Habermas, Derrida and Rawls, Nietzsche and Dewey. Their vocabularies are incommensurable with each other. Rorty's happy solution to the tension experienced by anyone who finds both sets of thinkers attractive is apartheid – a rigid separation between private irony and public hope. Although "the existence of these two sides" of our lives "generates dilemmas," neither side has any priority. "Such dilemmas we shall always have with us, but they are never going to be resolved by appeal to some further, higher set of obligations which a philosophical tribunal might discover and apply" (p. 197).

In order to give further specificity to what Rorty is attempting to show us, we need to explore and texture what he means by "contingency," "historicism," and "nominalism." Contingency has always been problematic for philosophy. But typically philosophers, in what Rorty calls the "Plato-Kant" canon, have contrasted contingency with what is universal, necessary, and essential. This is what is behind the variations on the appearance/reality distinction where there has been an implicit or explicit valorization (divinization) of what is presumably essential, universal, and necessary. These concerns have always been the obsession of foundational philosophers. They have sought to discover the "really real," a "truth" that is "out there." But for Rorty, contingency, historicism, and nominalism "go all the way down." There is nothing that is necessary, nothing that escapes time and chance, no essential nature of what we really are. So-called "universal truths" turn out to be the platitudes of entrenched vocabularies. Rorty is acutely aware that in making such categorical assertions he sounds as if he himself is making truth claims and thereby still playing the old game of philosophy. He wants to avoid the trap set by those who will charge him with self-referential inconsistency or "performative contradiction."

> To say that there is no such thing as intrinsic nature is not to say that the intrinsic nature of reality has turned out, surprisingly enough, to be extrinsic. It is to say that the term "intrinsic nature" is one which it would pay us not to use, an expression which has caused more trouble than it has been worth. To say that we should drop the idea of truth as out there waiting to be discovered is not to say that we have discovered that, out there, there is no truth. It is to say that our purposes would be served best by ceasing to see truth as a deep matter, as a topic of philosophical interest, or "true" as a term which repays "analysis". (p. 8)

If we ask what "purposes" are "served best" by this strategy, Rorty's response is that it is "better" for redescribing the liberal utopia that "we" ironic liberals approve. If we ask again why should such a liberal utopia be approved, there is no non-contingent answer to this question. All we can do is to make our new vocabulary look as attractive as possible and play it off old entrenched vocabularies. This may strike many as a "cop-out" – as if Rorty is simply telling us that either one will or will not find such redescription of liberalism attractive, but not giving us any *reasons* for claiming it is "better," "more attractive," "more useful." But Rorty's point (and challenge) is that it is a self-deceptive illusion to think that *anyone* can do more than this. This is the "wisdom" of the ironist.

Rorty's discussion of the contingency of language, selfhood and liberal community (Part I of his book) is packed with all sorts of controversial claims, but the gist of it is something like this: we should give up any belief that philosophers or scientists are the cultural heroes of our time. Rather, we should recognize that the domains of culture that have become important for us are utopian politics and poetry. The poets – in Rorty's broad sense of the term – are the inventors of new metaphors and vocabularies. Proust, Nabokov, Newton, Darwin, Hegel, and Heidegger are poets in this "large generic sense." "Such people are also thought of as rebelling against 'death' – that is, against the failure to have created – more strongly than most of us" (p. 24). A Nietzschean motif runs through Rorty's discussion of contingencies.[4] Rorty sees the history of culture as replacing old gods with new gods. After the demise of theology and metaphysics, philosophers *divinized* rationality, science, and the moral self. Romantic poets *divinized* imagination, poetic genius, and the creative self. There is a deep metaphysical urge to claim that science, morality, or poetry put us in touch with something greater, more real and authentic, than the sheer contingencies that make up our lives. Even Nietzsche and Heidegger are tempted by this desire. But all these projects have failed, all have fallen victim to the ironist's "radical and continuing doubts." But these "failures" need not and should not be the cause for despair. They would lead to despair only if we had some reason for believing that there is something higher or more divine and sublime to be "discovered," something "out there" that redeems our all-too-human strivings. But there is nothing that satisfies *this* desire. We need not "be doomed to spend our conscious lives trying to escape from contingency" (p. 28).

Rather, we should recognize that there is nothing more than contingencies and try to emulate those "strong poets" who seek to create something new out of those contingencies. This is what Harold Bloom (one of Rorty's great heroes) calls "giving birth to oneself."

We can get a more concrete sense of what Rorty means by contingency and self-creation by considering his reading of Freud. Rorty's Freud is not the scientist, rationalist, or discoverer of new "truths" about the unconscious. It is the Freud who shows that "everything to do with our life is chance." "What is new in Freud is the *details* he gives us about the sort of thing which goes into the formation of conscience, his explanation of why certain very concrete situations and persons excite unbearable guilt, intense anxiety, or smoldering rage" (p. 31). Freud helps us to see that there is no core self. We are tissues of contingencies where all distinctions of the higher and lower, the essential and the non-essential, break down. Each of us is engaged in an idiosyncratic moral struggle. Freud "thinks that only if we catch hold of some crucial idiosyncratic contingencies in our past shall we be able to make something worthwhile out of ourselves, to create present selves whom we can respect" (p. 33). Much of what is found in Freud can also be found in Nietzsche. But what makes Freud "more useful and more plausible" is that "Freud's account of unconscious fantasy shows us how to see every human life as a poem – or, more exactly, every human life not so racked by pain as to be unable to learn a language nor so immersed in toil as to have no leisure in which to generate a self-description" (pp. 35–6). Summing up, Rorty tells us that Freud's genius consists in showing us in concrete detail that "poetic, artistic, philosophical, scientific, or political progress results from the accidental coincidence of private obsession with public need" (p. 37).

What does Rorty's celebration of contingency, self-creation, strong poetry, "giving birth to ourselves" have to do with liberal democracy, solidarity, and citizenship? The best short answer is – nothing. Nothing if we think that pursuing our idiosyncractic fantasies and "poeticizing" our lives entails anything about our public responsibilities. Self-creation is a private project. We may begin to feel uneasy and suspicious of this neat apartheid of the private and the public. Rorty, who employs the rhetorical device of anticipating and stating the sharpest objections himself, knows that anyone who denies that there is truth "out there," that there is any "common human nature" or "deep self," and who questions the usefulness of such distinctions as rationality/irrationality or morality/prudence will be suspected of immorality, irrationalism, aestheticism, and a "self-defeating" relativism. Rorty clearly *looks* like a relativist for he is constantly telling us there are no neutral criteria for evaluating competing incommensurable vocabularies.

The evasion of relativism?

Pursuing the way in which Rorty seeks to evade and outflank these charges, especially the accusation of self-defeating relativism, enables us to understand better what he means by playing off a new vocabulary against old entrenched vocabularies that have become nuisances. He tells us that his strategy in responding to the objections of his critics "will be to try to make the vocabulary in which these objections are phrased look bad, thereby changing the subject, rather than granting the objector his choice of weapons and terrain by meeting his criticism head-on" (p. 44). The charge of "relativism" should not be answered but *evaded*. Indeed, once a culture sloughs off the Enlightenment vocabulary in which such criticisms are formulated "it would no longer be haunted by spectres called 'relativism' and 'irrationalism'" (p. 53). They lose their force. This is consonant with Rorty's claim that once we are persuaded to adopt a new vocabulary, the questions and worries that arise in discarded vocabularies do not even arise. So his task is to make the vocabulary of his critics "look bad" and his redescription "look good." But precisely how does he do this – how does he outflank those who accuse him of "bad" relativism? Although Rorty thinks one can use multiple strategies, I want to explore one of his tactics. He considers the standard objection to the views of Isaiah Berlin's defense of negative liberty and Berlin's endorsement of Joseph Schumpeter's claim that "to realize the relative validity of one's convictions and yet stand for them unflinchingly, is what distinguishes a civilized man from a barbarian" (p. 46). Rorty agrees with Berlin's comment "to demand more than this is perhaps a deep incurable metaphysical need; but to allow it to determine one's practice is a symptom of an equally deep, and more dangerous moral and political immaturity."[5] But to speak of "relative validity" opens the way for critics to pounce and ask why the liberal gives a morally privileged status to the value of freedom. This objection is formulated by Michael Sandel when he writes:

> If one's convictions are only relatively valid, why stand for them unflinchingly? In a tragically configured moral universe, such as Berlin assumes, is the ideal of freedom any less subject than competing ideals to the ultimate incommensurability of values? If so, in what can its privileged status consist? And if freedom has no morally privileged status, if it is just one value among many, then what can be said for liberalism?[6]

We can see why it is so important for Rorty to respond – or outflank – these objections. One of his most central claims is that "a belief can still regulate action, can still be thought worth dying for, among people who are quite aware that this belief is caused by nothing deeper than contingent historical circumstance" (p. 189).

Rorty claims that when Sandel poses the above question he is "taking the vocabulary of Enlightenment rationalism for granted" (p. 46). The very notion of "relative validity" only makes sense if it has contrastive force – if we think there are "statements capable of being justified to all those who are uncorrupted – that is, to all those in whom reason, viewed as a built-in truth-seeking faculty, or conscience, viewed as a built-in righteousness detector, is powerful enough to overcome evil passions, vulgar superstitions, and base prejudices" (p. 47). But Rorty calls into question just those Enlightenment distinctions between "relative validity" and "absolute validity," between "reason" and "passion," between "rational convictions" and "convictions caused by contingencies," that are required and presupposed in posing questions like those of Sandel. So Rorty proposes that we simply drop the talk of "relative validity":

> In the jargon I have been developing, Schumpeter's claim that this is the mark of the civilized person translates into the claim that the liberal societies of our century have produced more and more people who are able to recognize the contingency of the vocabulary in which they state their highest hopes – the contingency of their own consciences – and yet have remained faithful to those consciences. (p. 54)

One may object that Rorty is being evasive. He is not meeting the objection: indeed, he is implicitly advocating the sort of ethnocentrism where one simply affirms one's most cherished convictions. Why should we accept Rorty's "final vocabulary" – no matter how passionately he affirms his "prejudices"? Rorty wants to take the sting out of this objection. Of course he is being evasive. But there is nothing wrong with this. The point is to give up the vocabulary of Enlightenment rationalism because it has become a nuisance. If the objector persists and maintains that all Rorty is doing is affirming his own idiosyncratic ethnocentric prejudices, Rorty does not deny this. His response is that, of course, he is being ethnocentric, but some forms of ethnocentrism are better than others, namely, the ethnocentrism of "we" liberal ironists "who have been brought up to distrust ethnocentrism" (p. 198). But why is it better? This is just like asking the question "Why not be cruel?" It is unanswerable if we think we can give any non-circular argument to justify our "final" vocabularies. It may begin to look as if Rorty is moving in a vicious circle – a circle which he breaks by declaring "Here I stand" (full stop). This is the way Rorty looks to someone who hankers after something more basic, more rational than playing off one vocabulary against another. From Rorty's perspective these demands are those of someone who still has the metaphysical urge to expect some sort of non-contingent grounding for our final vocabularies, who fails to grasp the radical contingency of *all* vocabularies, who thinks that there can be a theoretical back-up which is not ethnocentric. But there isn't any such back-up. So the charge of ethnocentrism loses its sting when we realize that it is an illusion to think we can ever "escape" from being ethnocentric. We can only play off good and bad forms of ethnocentrism.

Redescription and humiliation

I said earlier that the one accusation Rorty takes more "seriously" than any other is that, despite his protestations to the contrary, his joshing and debunking have cruel consequences. Rorty has been criticized for being an elitist virtuoso intellectual who is insensitive to the real pain, suffering, and humiliation of his fellow human beings. Rorty knows that ironic redescription often humiliates. "The redescribing ironist, by threatening one's final vocabulary, and thus one's ability to make sense of one's own terms rather then hers, suggests that one's self and one's world are futile, obsolete, powerless. Redescription often humiliates" (p. 90). But redescription is no more closely connected with irony than with metaphysics. "Redescription is a generic trait of the intellectual, not a specific mark of the ironist, so why do ironists arouse special resentment?" (p. 90). Rorty thinks that this is because of the ironist's inability to *empower*, his refusal to acknowledge that any final vocabulary can be rationally justified or grounded. Liberal metaphysicians, on the contrary, speak as if their redescriptions are educating their audiences rather than simply reprogramming them. They speak as if they are "uncovering the interlocutor's true self or the real nature of a common public world which the speaker and the interlocutor share" (p. 90). But this is a self-deceptive illusion because there is no "true self" or "real nature" of a common public world.

Although the liberal ironist maintains that cruelty is the worst thing we do and that we should always try to avoid humiliation, Rorty realizes that such abstract pronouncements don't get us very far. What we take to be cruelty and humiliation will itself be dependent on our historically contingent vocabularies. Even more important, we are frequently unaware of the manifold ways in which we are cruel. The thrust of Rorty's thinking is to direct us away from abstractions, principles, theory, and general pronouncements toward concrete specific descriptions. We need to attend to the details of the springs of cruelty in ourselves and others. The public responsibility of the liberal ironist is to try to become aware of the specific pain and humiliation of others. We should try "to extend our sense of 'we' to people whom we previously thought of as 'they'" (p. 192). It is by this type of imaginative empathy that we can foster solidarity. Who performs this task best? Not philosophers – not even ironic philosophers – or social theorists. Rather it is journalists, ethnologists, and novelists who have the gift for concrete "detailed empirical descriptions" that can be most helpful in performing this task.

Rorty seeks to show this in the last part of his book, "Cruelty and Solidarity," where he gives detailed analyses of two of his favorite novelists, Nabokov and Orwell. For all their differences (Nabokov condemns the sort of novels that Orwell wrote as "topical trash"), Rorty nevertheless tells us that they both wrote novels that help us see "how social practices which we have taken for granted have made us cruel" (p. 141). Nabokov and Orwell had different gifts and different self-images, but "their accomplishment was pretty much the same. Both of them warn the liberal ironist intellectual against the temptations to be cruel" (p. 144). Nabokov exposes what Rorty calls "cruel incuriosity," and "Orwell wanted to be of use to people who were suffering" (p. 170). Even if one agrees with Rorty's claims about the importance of the novel as the medium in a liberal society for making us aware of the details of pain and humiliation, one may wonder just how helpful novels really are in fostering the solidarity that Rorty thinks is so important. At times Rorty himself is tempted to claim that novelists *empower* in ways in which philosophers and social theorists do not. We may begin to feel that Rorty is more concerned with the temptation to be cruel by a small group of intellectuals rather than the suffering of all those who are non-intellectuals. Indeed, we may feel increasingly uneasy with Rorty's master strategy – to separate private irony and public hope. We may think that there is something a bit too facile and cheerful in all this talk of liberal hope, that Rorty is a glib optimist who doesn't really face up to the intractable social and political problems that we confront in our everyday lives. But there is a dark side to what Rorty is saying. The full complexity of his stance comes out only when we pursue this.

Consider his central theme that anything can be made to look good or bad by redescription. Rorty doesn't flinch from the consequences of this claim. It means that what we take to be cruelty and humiliation in one vocabulary may not be described and perceived as such in another vocabulary. For even though Rorty says that pain is non-linguistic, there is no "essence" of cruelty and humiliation. To suggest that the horrors and Holocausts of the twentieth century can be redescribed to "look good" might seem to count as a *reductio ad absurdum* of his position. For Rorty, it is contingently possible that we might some day live in a world of "double-think." He says that this is what Orwell tried to show us in the last third of *1984* where O'Brien becomes the central character. He rejects the interpretation of *1984* by those who say that Orwell is reminding us of some plain moral truths whose obviousness is on a par with "two plus two is four." There are no such moral truths. There aren't any "plain moral facts out there in the world." What Orwell does in the last part of *1984* is to present us with

> an alternative scenario, one which led in the wrong direction. He convinced us that there was a perfectly good chance that the same developments which had made human equality technically possible

might make endless slavery possible. He did so by convincing us that nothing in the nature of truth, or man, or history was going to block that scenario, any more than it was going to underwrite the scenario which liberals had been using between the wars. He convinced us that all the intellectual and poetic gifts which had made Greek philosophy, modern science, and Romantic poetry possible might someday find employment in the Ministry of Truth. (pp. 175–6)

Orwell did not invent O'Brien – the cool cosmopolitan torturer – as a dialectical foil for "sound" liberal convictions but rather "to warn us against him" (p. 176), to show us that he is both *dangerous* and *possible*. Rorty's ironic historicist nominalism is double-edged. We have no *reason* for believing that one vocabulary is better than any other. Furthermore, there is no reason to think that liberal institutions will prevail rather than the scenario where the O'Briens rule the world. There is nothing deep down in us that we can rely on to resist such a scenario. Socialization "goes all the way down." Consequently, we could be socialized so that we become "rational" torturers. Whatever happens in the future – like the rest of history – will be the result of contingencies. This is what gives such urgency to preserving and improving the liberal society Rorty cherishes. He too wants to warn us about the fragility of liberal institutions, and against the illusion that freedom will or must prevail. The scenario where our worst nightmares come to be is just as possible. So the dark side of Rorty's liberal hope is the acute awareness that there is nothing we can rely on to determine which scenario will be our future.

Selfhood

The rhetorical flair, erudition, and scope of Rorty's book are dazzling. His redescriptions and strong readings are always provocative. Yet when we step back and judge what Rorty is saying, then all sorts of unresolved tensions and doubts arise. Rorty hopes that the worries and questions that are rooted in vocabularies which have become a nuisance will disappear. But they don't. They reappear in new forms. Many of these cluster about his logic of apartheid – his rigid separation of the public and the private.

Consider the claims that Rorty makes about the self. On the one hand he criticizes the very idea that there is a common human nature or any deep self to be "discovered." The self, he tells us, is nothing but a contingent weaving and reweaving of desires and beliefs which are themselves the effects of historical contingencies. But on the other hand – despite his statements to the contrary – Rorty seems to be advocating a "theory" of the self. For he also says that we *all* have the capacity for self-creation even though it is only the strong poets who succeed in "giving birth to themselves." Without the notion of self-creation where we can make our lives into works of art, where we can "see every human life as poem" (p. 35), Rorty's redescription of our private lives would not even make sense. Rorty desperately wants to avoid the suggestion that he is playing the old game of philosophy, that his claims about the self should be read as "getting things right." He even declares that "the only argument I could give for the views about language and about selfhood put forward ... was that these views seemed to cohere better with the institutions of a liberal democracy than the available alternatives do" (p. 197). But this remark is disingenuous. For Rorty is not saying that there may well be a common human nature to be discovered but that it is no longer useful to think that there is insofar as we are committed to liberal democracy. This is belied by what he does. In a battery of arguments he shows why the reasons advanced to support the claim that there is a common human nature fail – why they do not justify the belief that there is a truth "out there" to be discovered. If one is to be persuaded that Rorty's vocabulary is "attractive" and the alternatives "look bad," then this will in part depend on his success in *arguing* that these alternative vocabularies fail to accomplish what they claim to prove. This has nothing to do with whether or not we find his description of liberal democracy attractive. Rorty's assertion about the contingency of all vocabularies would be reduced to absurdity if it entailed the consequence that we can believe anything we want to about language and selfhood as long as it coheres with the type of political institutions we find attractive. By his own insistence there is no *reason* why anyone should find one set of political institutions more attractive than another.

Rorty constantly slides from a strong sense of "rational justification" to a weaker and more reasonable sense of justification. When he criticizes our ability to give reasons in support of the central beliefs of our final vocabularies, he means we cannot give any definitive knock-down foundational justifications. But this should not be confused with giving historically contingent fallible reasons to support our beliefs. This is what Rorty himself is constantly doing. We don't need strong foundations in order to assess whether reasons given in specific inquiries are good reasons. One of the major themes in philosophy during the past hundred years – from Peirce through Sellars and Quine to Rorty – has been that it is a mistake to think we can (or need to) give strong foundational justification in any area in human inquiry. But this doesn't mean that we can't distinguish better from worse reasons when we are evaluating a scientific hypothesis or the interpretation of a poem – even if what are to count as "good reasons" are themselves historically conditioned and contestable.

One may also question whether Rorty's redescription of selfhood does "cohere better with the institutions of liberal democracy." Even Rorty's redescription presupposes a minimal sense of human agency. Rorty's liberal ironists are able to do something to avoid or minimize cruelty and to enhance solidarity. Of course no one can know the full consequences of what one does. It is a platitude to say that there are always unexpected contingent consequences of our actions. But at times – in his hyperbolic manner – Rorty so radicalizes his claims about contingency, historicism, and nominalism that one wonders if it even makes sense (in his vocabulary) to speak about human actions, intentions, and projects. If the old idea of "intentional action" were completely abandoned in favor of a thoroughly contingent self, then we would never have any reason to suppose that anything we do would even be likely to have the results we intend. Projects formulated to eliminate cruelty might just as well have the opposite result. For whatever happens is presumably thoroughly contingent. If one really believed this, then what would be the motivation for acting one way rather than another? This also has consequences for Rorty's rhetoric of liberal hope. When Rorty defends ungrounded liberal hope, the target of his polemical attack is the claim that liberalism is doomed, that there are historical tendencies (necessities) at work that prevent the realization of a liberal utopia. But if we accept Rorty's contingency thesis there is no more reason for hope than despair. For there is no *reason* to expect that anything we do is more likely to bring us closer to this utopia than to its opposite.

Universality

Just as Rorty plays fast and loose with the concept of selfhood, he also does this with the concept of universality. His "official" position is to denigrate the search for universals (which he lumps together with essences, intrinsic natures, and necessities). But *his* vocabulary depends on all sorts of controversial universal claims – for example, we *all* have the capacity for self-creation, we should *all* try to avoid cruelty and humiliating others, we should *all* strive to strengthen liberal institutions and increase human solidarity. Rorty might reply that he is not against all forms of universality. Rather, he wants to make us aware of what we are doing when we make such claims. Universals are not "out there" to be discovered. They are only part of the rhetoric of our historically contingent vocabularies. The ironist knows that they cannot be rationally justified. So we should say that the partisan universal claims made within a given vocabulary will be accepted if we find the vocabulary attractive. But even if one goes this far with Rorty, we want to know what makes one vocabulary more attractive than another. If this is interpreted as looking for reasons why a given vocabulary is superior to its alternatives, this is just the move that Rorty wants to block. But is Rorty's strategy here really persuasive? In the final analysis, Rorty has little more to say than that we will or will not find a vocabulary attractive. Whatever our response, it is itself a matter of historical contingencies. The "logic" of Rorty's strategy comes down to making the adoption of a vocabulary a matter of taste about which there can be no rational debate. Rorty's conviction concerning the contingency of all vocabularies begins to look like old-styled vulgar emotivism. For all questions concerning the adoption or rejection of a vocabulary boil down to whether we have a pro or anti attitude toward it. Whatever our attitude, it is itself the contingent effect of historical contingencies. Debates about our basic values and norms are not rational. They are only rhetorical strategies for getting others to adopt our attitudes.

For all of Rorty's advocacy of liberal pluralistic openness, it begins to look as if what he is really recommending is a fideistic absolutism. If none of our central beliefs can be even minimally rationally warranted, if there is no (non-trivial) way of distinguishing relevant and irrelevant considerations for the beliefs we hold, then it looks as if Rorty is telling us that when doubts are raised about one's final vocabulary the only response that is appropriate is "Here I stand (and I hope you will also stand here)."

But what if one doesn't find a given vocabulary attractive, what if – even after Rorty's redescriptions – one finds his portrait of liberal democracy repulsive? Then there is nothing more to be said. This is a strategy that works just as well for those who advocate a world in which cool cosmopolitan torturers should rule. Rorty has cleverly built an unassailable fortress and insulates himself from any criticism, for anyone can enshrine his central convictions in fancy rhetoric, anyone can (if he is imaginative) make his vocabulary "look good" and refuse to give any reasons for holding these beliefs.

This type of fideism makes one question just how successful Rorty is in outflanking and evading the charge of relativism. There are silly versions of relativism where one maintains that any belief is just as good or true as any other. It would be unfair to accuse Rorty of advocating such a vulgar relativism, for he does try to show why his vocabulary is more attractive by redescription. Nevertheless, it isn't clear why in his liberal utopia one would no longer feel the force of the relativist objection. Presumably this is because the liberal ironist has abandoned the distinction between relative and absolute validity. She knows that no final vocabulary can be grounded in something more fundamental, that anything can be made to look good or bad by redescription, that there are no constraints on the invention of new vocabularies. The ironist wants to drop the term "relativism" but – contrary to what Rorty says – she doesn't get rid of a nagging problem, she merely renames it "contingency." For the ironist knows that there are alternative vocabularies which others find attractive – vocabularies that are incompatible and incommensurable with one's final vocabulary. Furthermore she knows there are no rational criteria for adjudicating rival vocabularies. To say, for example, that the vocabulary of Orwell's O'Brien is dangerous is only an elliptical way of saying that *if* one is a liberal then it is dangerous. But from the perspective of O'Brien's world, liberalism is the "real" danger. It is hard to discern any difference that makes a difference between Rorty's claims about the radical contingency of all vocabularies and what from our entrenched vocabularies is called "relativism."

Suppose we follow Rorty and drop the term "relativism" and the distinction between relative and absolute validity. The same point can still be made. For it is Rorty who says that anything can be made to look good and bad by redescription. Any vocabulary can be made to look attractive if one is clever and imaginative enough. There is never a non-trivial *reason* for favoring one vocabulary rather than its incompatible alternatives. But the more Rorty insists upon this the more he shows that such claims can also be made by ironists who detest liberalism and find it repulsive.

Furthermore Rorty himself violates his own stipulative definition of the ironist. The ironist, we recall, "has radical and continuing doubts about the final vocabulary she currently uses." In an abstract way Rorty does have doubts about *his* final vocabulary – at least insofar as he knows it cannot be justified and there are alternative final vocabularies. But such a theoretical skepticism is what Peirce calls "paper" doubt. There is no evidence that Rorty ever really doubts his commitment to liberal democracy. He never really questions it and asks himself whether there are alternatives that should be considered. He has, in effect, insulated his liberal convictions from any doubts. He even tells us "on the *public* side of our lives, *nothing* is less dubious than the worth of those freedoms [the democratic freedoms and relative social equality which some rich lucky societies have, quite recently, come to enjoy]" (p. 197). But why shouldn't this also be subject to "radical and continuing doubts"? What kind of ironist says to herself "I will be ironical only about the private side of my life but not about the public side"?

The primary reason why Rorty never "seriously" questions his liberal convictions is that his entire project depends upon defending "the fundamental premise ... that a belief can still regulate action, can still be thought worth dying for, among people who are quite aware that this belief is caused by nothing deeper than contingent historical circumstance" (p. 189). Without this "fundamental premise" his entire project falls apart.

As with so many of Rorty's hyperbolic claims, one can give a weaker – indeed, a quite reasonable – reading of this "fundamental premise" and a much stronger dubious reading. The reasonable thesis is that once we give up foundationalism or claims to absolute validity, then we must recognize that all our beliefs are always open to criticism and revision. Nevertheless, aware of our own fallibility, we can be passionately committed to the beliefs that regulate our actions. But Rorty is not advocating fallibilism, he is *rejecting* it. For the fallibilist doesn't give up the distinction between good and bad reasons, although she historicizes it. She knows that this distinction is context-dependent and always contestable. When challenged about her fundamental beliefs, she is open to considering why she should modify or abandon them. The fallibilist is open to what Habermas calls the "force of the better argument" and recognizes there can always be disputes about what counts as the better argument. But on the strong reading of what Rorty means by irony, there is no basis for making a distinction between *rational* persuasion and other forms of persuasion. This distinction is completely relative to the vocabulary we adopt. And since there is no reason for adopting a given vocabulary, we are licensed to count as "rational persuasion" whatever "looks good" to us.

One reason why Rorty denies that there is a distinction between rational persuasion and other forms of persuasion (unless we draw the distinction by fiat) is that he relies upon an excessively narrow conception of argument. He writes as if it is appropriate to speak of argument only when there is enough common agreement so that we can all agree on what counts as a better argument. Argument is appropriate when the rules of argumentation are commonly accepted. But it is never clear why we should restrict argument in this narrow way. Whether the domain is science, the interpretation of texts, or politics – when we do argue there is rarely (if ever) complete common agreement about the "rules" for clearly distinguishing better and worse substantive arguments. If there were algorithms for deciding among competing arguments than there would be no need for argument! A computer could "decide" which is the better argument.

Rorty's ironist may in fact think that some beliefs are "worth dying for," but she has nothing to say about why *her* beliefs are worth dying for rather than the strongly held beliefs of the fanatic or the fundamentalist. In the background of Rorty's liberal rhetoric is the cynical conviction that what is really crucial is who has the *power* to enforce his final vocabulary. Before Orwell, Dostoyevsky showed us that the Grand Inquisitor can also be a supreme ironist.

A systematic confusion runs through Rorty's book. Rorty seems to think that the possibility that someday we may live in O'Brien's world, or that when the secret police come knocking on our door to drag us away they are not going to be persuaded by arguments, indicates that there is nothing "out there" or "in ourselves" that we can rely on to prevent such catastrophes. But who denies that the power and sophistication of those who enforce a given vocabulary may be so great that no one is left to oppose them? Who denies that it is possible to live in a world of double-think where no one is left to call it double-think? Who affirms that rational persuasion can stand up against unbounded violence? But what do these all-too-real possibilities have to do with giving the strongest possible historically contingent reasons for the central beliefs we hold and being open to the criticism of those beliefs? The liberal democracy that Rorty so favors depends upon encouraging public debate in which we are open to rational persuasion. Rational persuasion itself requires the belief that we can give and discriminate better and worse arguments rather than simply digging in and declaring that *my* final vocabulary is immune to criticism.

From irony to cynicism

One of Rorty's most seductive and dubious strategies is the way he reduces complex issues to extreme either/or's: *either* liberal ironists *or* liberal metaphysicians; *either* discoverers of truth *or* self-creative makers, etc. But this way of posing issues blocks and obscures nuanced discriminations that need to be made. At times Rorty suggests that we give up the attempt to "justify" our beliefs on the basis of unassailable foundations in favor of what Rawls calls "reflective equilibrium." But if we follow this recommendation we still need to discriminate better and worse, more or less successful attempts to achieve a "reflective equilibrium."

Rorty tells us that we have no reason to think that his liberal utopia will prevail rather than a world of double-think where nobody is left to realize that it is double-think. But he doesn't seem to realize how easily his doctrine about the radical contingency of all vocabularies turns into the opposite of what he intends.

Commenting on "super-relativism" (or, in Rorty's terms, the radical contingency of all vocabularies), Max Horkheimer wrote in 1936:

> With disarming simplicity, the positivists blend relativism with democracy and pacifism, asserting that these have "a natural affinity" with the basic assumptions of relativism .... Mussolini has grasped the situation with more acumen. He has always prided himself on having maintained a relativistic attitude in contrast to socialism and all other political doctrines. His movement never had a straightforward

program. As the situation demanded, it called itself aristocratic or democratic, revolutionary or reactionary, proletarian and anti-proletarian, pacifistic or antipacifistic. [In Rorty's terms, any vocabulary can be made to look good by redescription, RJB] This, according to Mussolini, bears out its claim "to stem directly from the most up-to-date trend of the European mind," namely from the relativistic trend of philosophy. "From the circumstance that one ideology is as good as the next, that is, that all are mere fictions, the modern relativist infers that everybody has the right to create his own ideology [in Rorty's terms, "final vocabulary," RJB] and to get the most out of it with all the energy at his disposal." (Mussolini, "Relativismo e Fascismo," Diuturna, Milan, 1924, pp. 374– 377). Relativism, which is without philosophical justification, is an element of a social dynamic which moves toward authoritarian forms. Indifference to the idea in theory is the precursor of cynicism in practical life.[7]

I don't want to engage in the rhetorical trick of guilt by association. I agree with Rorty that there is no philosophic position that is immune from being used for purposes that are the very opposite of what is intended. Nevertheless, it is hard to see any difference that makes a difference between Rorty's irony and Mussolini's cynicism. My main point is to challenge Rorty's claim that he has given a more attractive redescription of liberalism. On the contrary, Rorty actually *describes* one of the most dangerous and virulent tendencies in liberalism – the conviction that anything can be made to look good by redescription. For this is just the mentality that possessed our political leaders during the Vietnam war and the sordid Watergate affair. What happens to liberal democracy when those who have the power to do so believe that they can make anything look good by redescription and have the power to enforce their vocabulary? Rorty never really faces up to the (contingent) slide from irony to ruthless cynicism – a cynicism which corrupts liberal democracy.

Rorty's politics?

Thus far I have been focusing on tensions and unresolved conflicts that break out in Rorty's *own* vocabulary. But there are further difficulties. For all Rorty's manifest concern with liberal democracy, public responsibilities, and utopian politics, it is curious how little politics one finds in this book. Indeed, despite his battle against abstractions and general principles, he tends to leave us with empty abstractions. We can see this by turning again to his definition of liberals as "people who think that cruelty is the worst thing we do" and "hope that suffering will be diminished, that the humiliation of human beings by other human beings may cease" (p. xv). Contrary to Rorty's reflections on the contingency of all vocabularies, when he writes about pain, suffering, cruelty, and humiliation he comes close to saying that here we touch upon something that is really "out there," something which is non-linguistic and doesn't disappear when we switch vocabularies. But Rorty also affirms that what counts as cruelty and humiliation from the perspective of one vocabulary may not be judged to be cruelty from the perspective of another vocabulary. Even what we now call cruel torture may be redescribed so it is no longer seen as cruelty. So the demand to diminish cruelty is an empty abstraction unless we give a concrete specification of what we take to be examples of cruelty. Not only is the question "Why not be cruel?" unanswerable, but so is the question "Why do you take this to be a concrete instance of cruelty rather than its opposite?" Suppose we accept what looks like Rorty's categorical imperative "Do not be cruel, do not humiliate": how far does this take us in understanding liberalism? It doesn't take much imagination to redescribe many (perhaps most) political issues in a liberal society as conflicts about cruelty. Consider the question of abortion which is so controversial in our liberal society. Those who are "pro-choice" fervently argue that it is cruel to women to forbid them to have control over their bodies. "Pro-lifers" argue that abortion is unmitigated cruelty against the unborn child. So the injunction to diminish cruelty is an abstraction. Rorty might well agree. That's why we need concrete empirical descriptions of cruelty and humiliation. But this move obscures the question of how anyone is to decide what counts as a concrete description of cruelty. Even if one shares Rorty's liberal biases, there is little agreement about what counts as cruelty in liberal societies or what is to be done to diminish cruelty. Rorty also seems to think that there can be no rational argument about what one takes to be examples of cruelty and humiliation. But politics, especially liberal politics, must confront the question of what should be done to deal with serious conflicts about cruelty and humiliation. Rorty never thematizes this question. Rorty's politics seems to be one in which there is *no* public space – the space in which human beings come together to *debate* and *argue* with each other. This is what Dewey (one of Rorty's heroes) called the "eclipse of the public." For public debate presupposes what Rorty seems to want to eliminate – that we can be locked in *argument* with each other.

Rorty hankers after something which can really have "force" in making us aware of cruelty and which can help in diminishing it. He doesn't find this in philosophy or social theory. He thinks that in modern liberal societies, the novel has played such a role – at least for liberal intellectuals. He endorses Milan Kundera's claim "that the precious essence of the European spirit is being held safe as in a treasure chest inside the history of the novel, the wisdom of the novel." For novelists can do something that even ironic philosophers cannot do. They can by imagination make us profoundly aware of the ways in which we are cruel and humiliate others. This is Rorty's rationale for his detailed interpretation of the novels of Nabokov and Orwell. It is the novelists who are the most effective moral educators in a liberal society, not philosophers or social theorists. But Rorty's praise of novelists who educate not by didactism but by imaginative concrete description depends on a dubious presupposition which he never justifies and for which there seems to be little, if any, concrete empirical evidence. Rorty thinks that novels do have "force," they do make a difference in how we act in our everyday lives. This is certainly a cherished belief of many liberal intellectuals. But what is the evidence to support such a claim? No one need deny that *sometimes* some novels can also inspire one to act in different ways – as part of one's moral education. But why privilege the novel rather than any other cultural artifact, especially when one appreciates the ambiguities of the moral stance of novels, and that there seems so little evidence for thinking that even careful readers of novels change the ways that they act in their everyday lives? Again, I don't want to deny that sometimes novels have this effect, but if one is concerned with the type of moral education required for furthering liberal solidarity, then, in a society such as ours where there are fewer and fewer readers of novels, it seems little more than a false nostalgia to think that novels can play the role Rorty so desperately wants them to play. The ironic culture that Rorty finds so attractive undermines his hope for the novel as the vehicle of moral education. One consequence of this ironic culture has been to teach us to be skeptical of the moral "force" of novels.

There is another disturbing consequence of the weight that Rorty places on the novel as a vehicle of moral education in liberal culture.

For Rorty seems to be far more concerned with the cruelties that intellectual liberal ironists may inadvertently commit than with the forms of cruelty and humiliation that pervade our liberal societies. One would think that someone who calls for "Deweyean requests for concrete alternatives and programs" might turn his attention to those scenarios that would diminish institutional forms of cruelty and humiliation that so deeply affect non-intellectuals. But Rorty never quite gets around to this.

Private and public

I want to return to Rorty's logic of apartheid – his rigid separation of the private and the public. For like all apartheid, it has violent consequences.[8] It seems curious that Rorty, who shows us that most distinctions are fuzzy, vague, and subject to historical contingencies, should rely on such a fixed, rigid, ahistorical dichotomy. My objection is not to drawing sharp distinctions. Without doing so, no thinking would be possible. My objection is to the way Rorty uses this *specific* dichotomy, which leads to all sorts of violent consequences.

His readings of Nietzsche, Heidegger, Derrida, and Freud are not simply "strong": they are ruthlessly violent. For he wants to excise all the passages in their works which do bear on our public lives. He would, for example, dismiss all those passages in Heidegger that suggest that we are now living in the age of *Gestell* (enframing) – the essence of technology. He imposes a false grid on Derrida so that the "later" Derrida becomes the supreme ironist who delights in telling "in" jokes. There is no place in Rorty's scheme for the Derrida who is obsessively concerned with ethical and political responsibilities, and who understands deconstruction as intrinsically political. Rorty doesn't even consider what Derrida says, he simply dismisses his ethical-political concerns as lapses of the ironist who thinks he ought to be able to say something important about the public side of our lives, who thinks he has (or ought to have) a "social mission." Rorty fails to even mention how Freud can be interpreted as calling into question Rorty's euphoric description of self-creation. Freud reveals in concrete detail the traps and self-deceptions that confront us in the attempt to create ourselves out of our own historical contingencies. Rorty never pays attention to all the ways in which Freud shows how contingencies undermine and threaten our projects of self-creation. What seems lacking in Rorty's liberal culture of private irony and public liberal hope is any sense of social facticity, stubborn resistance – what Peirce called the brute force of Secondness that smashes our illusions of "giving birth to ourselves" and defeats our most imaginative redescriptions. Rorty's liberal culture seems to be a world in which there is no place for tragedy.

There is another consequence of Rorty's neglect of social facticity, that is, the cruel social realities and the human suffering of the affluent liberal bourgeois societies that Rorty celebrates. Appealing to Rorty's own pragmatic convictions, his own understanding of what is useful, one may wonder whether his aesthetic redescription of liberal democracy is only another diversion leading us away from confronting and ameliorating the concrete social forms of cruelty. C. Wright Mills' acute observations about liberalism are especially relevant to Rorty's description of a liberal utopia. Mills wrote:

> Liberalism, as a set of ideals, is still viable, and even compelling to Western man. That is one reason why it has become a common denominator of American political rhetoric; but there is another reason. The ideals of liberalism have been divorced from any realities of modern social structure that might serve as the means of their realization. Everybody can easily agree on general ends; it is more difficult to agree on means and the relevance of various means to the ends articulated. The detachment of liberalism from the facts of a going society make it an excellent mask for those who do not, cannot, or will not do what would have to be done to realize its ideals ... if the moral force of liberalism is still stimulating, its sociological content is weak; it has no theory of society adequate to its moral aims.[9]

When we turn to Rorty's attempt to privatize irony, to encourage the playing out of private fantasies, it is difficult to understand why anyone who becomes as narcissistic as Rorty advocates would be motivated to assume public responsibilities. This is not just an "abstract" problem. For there is plenty of evidence that a "culture of narcissism" does in fact lead to complete cynicism about public responsibilities. It is little solace to be told that there is no "necessary" connection between private narcissism and public cynicism when we constantly witness this "contingent" joining of attitudes. Sometimes Rorty writes as if the ills of our liberal societies are primarily due to unbridled greed that makes us insensitive to our fellow citizens. But he never "seriously" asks what it is about rich lucky liberal societies that enhances greed and makes us so cynical about political life.

Rorty's challenges

I have argued that Rorty – even on his own turf – leaves us with all sorts of unresolved tensions, conflicts, and instabilities. I have also said that his book is extraordinarily challenging because it raises hard nasty questions that simply will not go away. So I would like to conclude by highlighting Rorty's challenges.

Rorty relentlessly pursues the anti-foundationalist motif that has been gaining momentum during the past 150 years. Once one gives up the conviction that we can rationally ground our most central beliefs on something fixed, permanent, and solid, something that is more basic than contingencies that make up our lives, we *cannot* avoid asking what other forms of justification (if any) or reflective equilibrium are available to us. How are we to warrant those beliefs which we take to be fundamental and which we rely on to guide our actions? Rorty's answer is sharp and disturbing. We cannot give any non-circular argumentative or theoretical back-up to our "final vocabularies." We cannot avoid being ethnocentric. We should stop trying to answer futile "why" questions. All we can do is play off one vocabulary against another and try to make the vocabulary we favor look as attractive as possible by redescribing lots and lots of things and showing how alternative vocabularies look bad. Even if one rejects Rorty's rigid dichotomy of the private and the public, we are still left with the challenge of showing in detail that there is an alternative to Rorty's grand either/or: either strong rational justification or groundless liberal hope. It is Rorty's merit to have put this challenge in such a sharp and inescapable manner. It is as if he is declaring: if you think there is an alternative to this either/or, if you think there is a non-circular way of justifying a final vocabulary, then the burden of proof is on the one who makes such a claim to *show* it – to indicate in detail what forms of justification escape the ironist's "radical and continuing doubts." Rorty has done more than this. He also argues that many of the attempts to show that there is a viable alternative – when we think them through – do not work.

Rorty not only challenges us on the central question of justifying our most central beliefs and desires, he also challenges our political convictions. Rorty believes that the critics of liberal democracy both from the political right and the political left have been guilty of a "failure of nerve." They too frequently retreat into theory and abstractions that have little to do with everyday politics. He is especially hard on those "radicals" who indulge in global rage and fail to turn their attention to working out "concrete scenarios" for how we might do better, how we might improve and strengthen liberal institutions and alleviate human suffering. One may retort that Rorty himself doesn't do much better, that for all his concern with solidarity and diminishing humiliation and cruelty, his own positive suggestions are feeble and abstract. But such a response should not obscure Rorty's challenge. Rorty exposes the tendency of intellectuals who claim to be concerned with real politics but retreat into academic abstractions. Where are those intellectuals today who attempt to do what Dewey did in his historical context or what Gramsci did in his contingent situation?

One reason why Orwell is one of Rorty's heroes is that although he did not answer the question "What is to be done?" he knew that a "useful political description suggests answers" to this question:

> He convinced us that our previous political vocabulary had little relevance to our current political situation, but he did not give us a new one. He sent us back to the drawing board, and we are still there. Nobody has come up with a large framework for relating our large and vague hopes for human equality to the actual distribution of power in the world. The capitalists remain as greedy and shortsighted, and the Communist oligarchs as cynical and corrupt (unless Gorbachev surprises us), [recent events in Eastern Europe reveal contingencies that might even surprise Rorty! RJB] as Orwell said they were. No third force has emerged in the world, and neither neoconservatives nor the post-Marxist left has come up with more than exercises in nostalgia ... nobody has come up with a plausible scenario for actualizing what Orwell called the "technical possibility of human equality."

Rorty himself, despite his advocacy of a liberal utopia, is not sure that it is even possible to come up with such a "plausible scenario," though he poses the question forcefully. Rorty is right in declaring that a useful political description is one which "suggests answers to the question 'What is to be done?'" His political challenge cannot be brushed aside.

Many of the troubling features of Rorty's portrait of the liberal ironist come into sharp focus when we compare it with the figure of O'Brien invented by Orwell. For O'Brien is the *double* of the liberal ironist – a double that haunts Rorty's redescription of liberalism. Rorty tells us "In the view of *1984* I am offering, Orwell has no *answer* to O'Brien, and is not interested in giving one" (p. 176). Rorty himself does not think O'Brien *can* be answered.

> I take Orwell's claim that there is no such thing as *inner* freedom, no such thing as an "autonomous individual," to be the one made by historicist, including Marxist, critics of "liberal individualism." This is that there is nothing deep inside each of us, no common human nature, no built-in human solidarity, to use a moral reference point. There is nothing to people except what has been socialized into them – their ability to use language, and thereby to exchange beliefs and desires with other people. (p. 177)

Compare Rorty's remarks with those of O'Brien when he is about to "break" Winston and thoroughly humiliate him. O'Brien declares, "You believe that reality is something objective, external, existing in its own right. You also believe that the nature of reality is self-evident. When you delude yourself into thinking that you see something, you assume that everyone else sees the same thing as you. But I tell you, Winston, that reality is not external." Or again, "You are imagining that there is something called human nature which will be outraged by what we do and will turn against us. But we create human nature. Men are infinitely malleable."

There is no important difference between Rorty and O'Brien concerning the infinite malleability of human beings and the possibility of socialization "all the way down." O'Brien is the true "disciple" of Rorty who has diabolically mastered the lesson of the contingency of all vocabularies.

What then is the difference that makes a difference between Rorty and O'Brien? Simply put, it is a difference in the "final vocabularies." Rorty is a liberal who thinks that "cruelty is the worst thing we do," O'Brien, the co-author of *The Theory and Practice of Oligarchical Collectivism*, thinks "the object of torture is torture," the point of humiliation is to humiliate.

> O'Brien reminds us that human beings who have been socialized – socialized in any language, any culture – do share a capacity which other animals lack. They can all be given a special kind of pain: They can be humiliated by the forcible tearing down of the particular structures of language and belief in which they were socialized (or which they pride themselves on having formed for themselves. (p. 177)

But let us not forget that for Rorty it makes no sense to claim that one "final vocabulary" is more rational than another (except in a circular sense of "rationality"). It is futile to ask for a justification of a "final vocabulary," or to think there is some standard by which we can objectively judge one "final vocabulary" to be superior to its alternatives. O'Brien would entirely agree with Rorty, and perhaps even mock him for failing to emphasize that the only important issue, the only difference that really makes a difference is who has the intelligence, imagination, sophistication, and *power* to succeed in imposing his vocabulary, to completely socialize human beings in whatever manner he (or the Party) desires.

I have advanced a number of criticisms of Rorty's redescription of liberal democracy and his claim about the radical contingency of all vocabularies. But these criticisms do not blunt Rorty's challenges. Indeed, they may help to show just how provocative they are. In answering the question, "How should one read this book?", I believe it should be read as posing hard nasty questions which cannot be brushed aside – questions that any responsible thinker must confront. There are many ways of evaluating the contribution of a thinker. One of the best is to ask whether he has found a way – invented a vocabulary – that cuts through clichés and the defenses we use to avoid facing sharp challenges. By this criterion, Rorty is eminently successful. Rorty helps to accomplish for our time what that other great ironist, Socrates, did in his historical context. Like Socrates, Rorty also has a knack for annoying, joshing, stinging – being a gadfly to his fellow citizens by forcing them to confront challenges about their *polis* and the "justification" of their basic beliefs. Ironically, Rorty has thereby helped to keep philosophical reflection alive and to fulfill what he once called the "philosophers' moral concern" – " continuing the conversation of the West."

NOTES

1 Richard Rorty, *Philosophy and the Mirror of Nature* (Princeton: Princeton University Press, 1979), p. 5. See my critical discussion of the book, "Philosophy in the Conversation of Mankind," in Richard J. Bernstein, *Philosophical Profiles* (Philadelphia: University of Pennsylvania Press, 1986).

2 Richard Rorty, *Consequences of Pragmatism* (Minneapolis: University of Minnesota Press, 1982).

3 Richard Rorty, *Contingency, Irony and Solidarity* (Cambridge: Cambridge University Press, 1989). All page references in this text refer to this book.

4 One can also see the continuity of Rorty with the American thinker that Nietzsche so admired, Emerson. For a provocative analysis of Emersonian motifs in the American pragmatic tradition, see Cornel West, *The American Evasion of Philosophy: A Genealogy of Pragmatism* (Madison: University of Wisconsin Press, 1989).

5 Isaiah Berlin, *Four Essays on Liberty* (Oxford: Oxford University Press, 1969), p. 134.

6 Michael Sandel, Introduction to *Liberalism and its Critics* (New York: New York University Press, 1984), p. 8.

7 Max Horkheimer, "The Latest Attack on Metaphysics," in *Critical Theory* (New York: Herder and Herder, 1972), p. 165.

8 On the "logic" of apartheid, see Jacques Derrida, "Racism's Last Word," trans. Peggy Kamuf, in *Critical Inquiry* 12 (Autumn 1985). See also Jacques Derrida, "But beyond … (Open Letter to Anne McClintock and Rob Nixon)," *Critical Inquiry* 13 (Autumn 1986).

9 C. Wright Mills, "Liberal Values in the Modern World," in *Power, Politics, and People: The Collected Essays of C. Wright Mills*, ed. Irving Louis Horowitz (New York: Oxford University Press, 1963), p. 189.

10

Reconciliation/Rupture

The most fundamental, powerful – and perhaps seductive – theme in Hegel's philosophy is the promise and fulfillment of reconciliation (*Versöhnung*). From his earliest writings until the end of his life, Hegel keeps returning to the theme of reconciliation – playing out the variations on it. Although it retains quasi-theological overtones, it is ultimately the task and the achievement of philosophy to show how differences, oppositions, ruptures, conflicts and contradictions can and must be reconciled in a dynamic self-identical and self-differentiating totality. In his first published work, Hegel declared that "the need for philosophy arises when the power of unification disappears from the life of men."[1] Hegel experienced a profound sense of the crises of diremption (*Entzweiung*), the painful divisions and splits in every domain of culture, and the wounds that these inflict. He also had an equally profound sense of the healing power of Reason. Like many of his contemporaries Hegel was initially lured by the Hellenic idea – that distinctively German idealization of the Greek *polis* in which there was presumably an unmediated and unselfconscious harmony and unity of human life, a thorough integration of every aspect of culture.[2] But in the modern world this unity and harmony has been fragmented. It has been violently torn asunder. Increasingly, Hegel realized that we cannot return to this idealized unmediated integration, although we are still haunted by it. Hegel's quest is marked by the desire to show that a new mediated integration, a new self-differentiated totality – in which all oppositions are reconciled – is in the process of emerging.

As Habermas notes, "The motives for a philosophy of unification can be traced back to the crisis experiences of the young Hegel. They stand behind the conviction that reason must be brought forward as the reconciling power against the positive elements of an age torn asunder."[3] "By criticizing the philosophic oppositions – nature and spirit, sensibility and understanding, understanding and reason, theoretical and practical reason, judgment and imagination, I and non-I, finite and infinite, knowledge and faith – he wants to respond to the crisis of the diremption of life itself."[4] Life is experienced as a form of "unhappy consciousness," a sense of a divided self that is internally at war with itself.[5] But this "unhappy consciousness" also contains within itself the promise, the possibility and the *necessity* of reconciliation. We can relate the thematics of diremption and reconciliation to the metaphorics of homelessness and homecoming that has dominated so much of Western thought. Although the history of humanity is experienced as a diremptive ruptured homelessness, the reconciliation that it promises means a "re-turn" to humanity's "proper" abode where all estrangement is finally overcome.

What is so acute in Hegel (and so seductively attractive) is his incisive ability to locate and specify the deepest oppositions, conflicts, and contradictions in every domain of culture – philosophy, religion, art, history, ethics, and politics – and to work and think through these antinomies in order to show how they are reconciled, i.e., reconcile themselves in a "higher" synthetic unity. The thematics of self-diremption and reconciliation take on a cosmic significance for Hegel. This is at once the grand historical narrative of Spirit's odyssey *and* the logic (*logos*) of Spirit itself. *Geist* – the absolute reality – is intrinsically active and restless; it continually dirempts itself, it is at war with itself. But *Geist* is always moving beyond these self-engendered internal ruptures, healing its own wounds, seeking and progressively *achieving* reconciliation. This is not an endless meaningless activity – what Hegel calls "the bad infinite" (*schlechte Unendliche*). Rather it is a process of progressive teleological development culminating in the "true infinite" (*wahrhafte Unendliche*) in which the finite and the infinite are themselves reconciled in an all-encompassing self-differentiating totality. In the realm of "objective Spirit" this is the concrete realization of freedom – the *telos* and achievement of History. In the realm of absolute Spirit (which

supersedes objective Spirit) this achievement is Spirit finally knowing itself as it truly is, where, as Hegel says the Concept (*Begriff*)
corresponds with its object and the object corresponds with its Concept. This is the meditated identity of identity and difference, the
mediated identity of thought and Being – the "true" homecoming of
Spirit. This movement is always from the abstract to the concrete,
from partial incomplete "truths" (i.e. falsities) to the whole Truth.
The erotic desire of philosophy itself as the love of wisdom is
directed toward the completed System of Absolute Knowledge.

> The True is the whole. But the whole is nothing other than the
> essence consummating itself through its development. Of the Absol-
> ute it must be said that it is essentially a *result*, that only in the *end* is it
> what it truly is; and that precisely in this consists its nature, viz., to be
> actual, subject, the spontaneous becoming of itself.[6]

Wherever we turn we discover this dialectical logic at work. Thus
the apparent diversity of philosophic systems is not to be understood
as a static series of permanently irreconcilable systems but rather as
necessary "moments" of a single System which is Philosophy itself.
The history of philosophic systems is the "progressive unfolding of
the Truth" (p. 2). Hegel, who is drawn to dynamic, fluid, organic
metaphors, expresses this progressive becoming when he writes:

> The bud disappears in the bursting-forth of the blossom, and one
> might say that the former is refuted by the latter; similarly, when the
> fruit appears, the blossom is shown up in its turn as a false
> manifestation of the plant, and the fruit now emerges as the Truth of
> it instead. These forms are not just distinguished from one another,
> they also supplant one another as mutually incompatible. Yet at the
> same time their fluid nature makes them moments of an organic
> unity in which they not only do not conflict, but in which each is as
> necessary as the other; and this mutual necessity alone constitutes the
> life of the whole. (p. 2)

This "dialectical image" enables us to grasp what initially strikes us
as a fantastic and arrogant claim – that the time has arrived when
philosophy as science (*Wissenschaft*) "can lay aside the title '*love* of
knowing' and be *actual* knowing" (p. 3). Hegel tells us in the Preface
to the *Phenomenology* that this is the task he has set for himself: "to
show that now is the time for philosophy to be raised to the status of

a science would therefore be the only true justification of any effort that has this aim, for to do so would demonstrate the necessity of this aim, would indeed at the same time be the accomplishing of it" (pp. 3–4). Hegel knows full well how grandiose and empty such a claim sounds. He knows that as a statement of intent it is only a "bare assertion." We need to be educated, formed (*gebilt*) and raised to a level where we can experience (*erfahren*) and comprehend (*begreifen*) this as the Truth. And we can comprehend this as the Truth *because* we ourselves (despite our initial incredulity) are manifestations of Spirit – Spirit which is on the verge of fully realizing itself and knowing itself as the systematic totality. The *Phenomenology* can be read as the auto-biography of Spirit where "we" gradually come to realize that the self-formation of *Geist* is "our" self-formation. From the perspective of our limited "natural consciousness" this is a grand inversion where what "natural consciousness" initially takes to be empty, abstract and indeed absurd turns out to be the concrete Truth which is implicit within natural consciousness itself. The *Phenomenology* is a "highway of despair" where we start with the prejudices and certainties of "natural consciousness" only to discover that as our experience unfolds the "truth" that is discovered and experienced is the very opposite of our initial certainty. Each successive and necessary "shape of consciousness" contains the seeds of its own self-destruction which compels us to move to a "higher" more comprehensive and encompassing "shape of consciousness." At each stage – at each station on the way – we think we have achieved fulfillment and completion only to experience apparently irreconcilable internal conflicts and contradictions. In this journey we are constantly deceived into thinking we have achieved a true reconciliation of conflicts and oppositions only to discover that these are *false* unstable reconciliations. Otherness and estrangement are always bursting forth in this restless dialectical movement. There is a tragic moment in *each* of these "shapes of consciousness" – a moment when we experience an irreconcilable antinomy that has been *self*-engendered. But the *Phenomenology* is not only a "highway of despair" where there is an intensification and deepening of unhappy consciousness, it is also a "divine comedy" where the self-inflicted wounds of self-diremption are healed (even when they leave their scars) – where the progressive development of "false" reconciliations culminates in a true reconciliation (the true infinite). We come to realize how each stage of development is a necessary moment in the whole process, the *becoming* of Spirit.

Hegel is not simply concerned with the destiny of philosophy and with demonstrating how it exhibits "the progressive unfolding of truth," he wants to show in detail how the *logos*, Reason itself, is operative and active in every domain of culture. History is not a series of meaningless, purposeless contingencies. There is a grand narrative to be discerned in what initially appear to be the meaningless, violent clash of human passions. When we comprehend these appearances, when we discern *what is* (*Wesen*) and what is fully manifested in them, we discover that through the apparently meaningless clashes and struggles we are witnessing the grand narrative of the concrete realization of universal freedom. This is *not* a narrative grid that we impose upon History for the purpose of ordering what is contingent and chaotic. Hegel is relentless in his critique of all "constructivist" metaphors that suggest that we impose "our" categories on an alien reality. This is the basis of one of his main quarrels with Kant and "Kantian constructivism." On the contrary, Hegel's essential claim is that we *discover* and come to comprehend Reason actively realizing itself in and through History. Or more accurately, Hegel seeks to show that the opposition between "construction" and "discovery" is itself *aufgehoben*. What thought "constructs" and what Being reveals when it becomes fully determinate are identical. There is no "thing in itself" lurking behind "our" categories. If we retain that intuitive sense of "realism" which suggests that there is a world "out there" which we can know, then we must say that Hegel's Idealism is essentially and intrinsically "realistic."

If we consider Hegel's own historical context we witness another variation on the dialectical logic of diremption and reconciliation. For Hegel sought to articulate the conflicts and antinomies of his own age – the modern age – and to show how they can be resolved, reconciled.[7] These antinomies cluster about what Hegel calls the "principle of subjectivity" which is at once the central achievement of modernity and the source of its internal conflicts and discontents. "The principle of the modern world is freedom of subjectivity, the principle that all the essential factors in the intellectual whole are now coming into their right in the course of their development."[8] Habermas gives an apt description of what Hegel means by "subjectivity":

The term "subjectivity" carries primarily four connotations: (a) *individualism*: in the modern world, singularity particularized without limit can make good its pretensions; (b) *the right to criticism*: the principle of the modern world requires that what anyone is to recognize shall reveal itself to him as something entitled to recognition; (c) *autonomy of action*: our responsibility for what we do is characteristic of modern times; (d) finally, *idealistic philosophy* itself: Hegel considers it the work of modern times that philosophy grasps the self-conscious (or self-knowing) Idea.[9]

But each of these four aspects of the "principle of subjectivity" which is the dialectical achievement of modernity harbors its own distinctive dangers and threats. *Individualism* carried to its extreme threatens us with anomic atomism in which all communal (*gestig*) bonds are ruptured. In this respect Hegel anticipates – and indeed states in a more trenchant form – the recurring objection to liberal individualism that has been pressed by "communitarian" critics.[10] The *right* to criticism can itself become self-destructive when it is totalized in a manner where it turns upon itself and undermines the basis for any criticism. The *autonomy of action* can turn into a "fury of destruction" and terror where the demand for *abstract* autonomy, for absolute freedom "ascends the throne of the world without any power being able to resist it" (p. 357). Even *idealistic philosophy* can degenerate into "superficial [*begrifflos*] talk about the identity of Thought and Being" (p. 33).

The antinomies that characterize modernity are themselves exhibited in the Kantian philosophy. Indeed "Hegel sees the essence of the modern world gathered into its focal point in Kantian philosophy."[11] Hegel at once builds upon and criticizes Kant, showing why we must move "beyond" Kant. According to Hegel, Kant leaves us with unstable antinomies that he did not resolve – antinomies which Hegel finds intolerable, and which must be *aufgehoben* and thereby reconciled. Against Kant, Hegel argues that the transcendental dialectic is not a "logic" that reveals the *illusion* of seeking to transcend the limits of the understanding (*Verstand*) but rather – when correctly understood – *shows* the way by which we can comprehend absolute reality as it is in itself. Antinomy and contradiction are not to be avoided, shunned or dissolved by appeal to the specious rigid dichotomy of the phenomenal and the noumenal. In the *Phenomenology*, Hegel emphatically declares, "We have to think pure change, or *think antithesis within the antithesis itself, or contradiction*" (p. 99). And in the *Science of Logic*, where Hegel seeks to show how the Concept in all its manifestations is self-contradictory and therefore inherently antinomic, he tells us "something is therefore alive only insofar as it contains contradiction within it, and moreover is this power to hold and endure the contradiction within it."[12] The Concept (*Begriff*) is "inherently self-contradictory, but it is no less *the contradiction resolved*."[13]

This is Hegel's most difficult and central claim. He knows full well that from the perspectives of "natural consciousness," "common sense," and even Kantian "understanding" such a claim is absurd and abhorrent. But both the *Phenomenology* and the *Science of Logic* – in their educative intent – can be read as works directed toward enabling us to grasp this truth. Hegel knows how much resistance there is to making this transition, how we keep fighting it, falling back into what he calls a finitized understanding of the infinite. But only when we make this transition, only when we break with all finitized attempts to shun the self-contradictory character of the *Concept* will we be able to grasp the speculative nature of the thinking that is essential for the philosophic comprehension of the true infinite.

Hegel then is not only the philosopher of reconciliation, he is also the philosopher of rupture. These are two intrinsic necessary aspects of the same dialectical process. For it is only by violent rupture – self-diremption – that Spirit achieves reconciliation with itself. This is the dialectical power of negativity, the "power to hold and endure the contradiction" within Spirit. This power of negativity which Hegel associates with death is dramatically expressed in the *Phenomenology* when he declares:

> The life of Spirit is not the life that shrinks from death and keeps itself untouched by devastation but rather the life that endures it and maintains itself in it. It wins its truth only when, in utter dismemberment, it finds itself ... Spirit is this power only by looking the negative in the face, and tarrying with it. This tarrying with the negative is the magical power that converts it into being. (p. 19)

To understand what Hegel means here, to grasp the necessary interplay of rupture and reconciliation, we need to comprehend the all-important distinction between *abstract* and *determinate* negation – a distinction closely related to abstract and determinate skepticism (dialectic). Abstract negation is the type of negation wedded to the static binary opposition between the true and the false. From this perspective the true and the false are "eternally" opposed to each other. The abstract negation of the true is the false (just as the abstract negation of the false is the true). This is the form of negation that is entrenched in the common understanding of propositional logic. Abstract skepticism, which employs this notion of abstract negation,

> is just the skepticism which only ever sees pure nothingness in its result and abstracts from the fact that this nothingness is specifically the nothingness of that *from which it results* .... The skepticism that ends up with the bare abstraction of nothingness or emptiness cannot get any further from there, but must wait to see whether something new comes along and what it is, in order to throw it too into the same empty abyss. (p. 51)[4]

Abstract negation is like meaningless (abstract) death that takes death to be only empty nothingness.[15] Abstract negation is the only form of negation available to "natural consciousness," "common sense," and to the Kantian conception of understanding (*Verstand*). But Hegel is always opposing and mocking this notion of abstract negation. Or more accurately, he wants to show its limitations, and that it is *not* the form of negation appropriate to dialectical philosophy and speculative (*begreifende*) thinking. It is not the form of negation that reveals the "power of negativity" by which Spirit ruptures and reconciles itself.

Determinate negation is the form of negation where the result of negation "is conceived as it is in truth," where "a new form has thereby immediately arisen, and in the negation the transition is made through which the progress through the completed series of forms comes about of itself" (p. 51). The logic of Spirit is the logic of determinate negation (dialectic) where a given "moment" is at once negated, affirmed and superseded. Hegel tells us in the *Science of Logic*: "Because the result, the negation, is a specific negation it has a content. It is a fresh concept but higher and richer than its predecessor for it is richer by the negation or opposite of the latter."[16] As we follow the *Phenomenology* and the *Science of Logic* we witness the teleological development of determinate negation. Determinate negation is at once critical and constructive. Steven B. Smith gives a lucid summary of this double character of determinate negation:

The logic of determinate negation has both a critical and constructive aspect. It is critical because it does not accept what a body of thought, a philosophical system, or even an entire culture says about itself, but is concerned to confront that thought, system, or culture with its own internal tensions, incoherences, and anomalies. It is constructive because out of this negation or confrontation we are able to arrive at ever more complete, comprehensive, and coherent bodies of propositions and forms of life. There is, then, a dynamic developmental structure to the Hegelian determinate negation by which human arrangements become progressively more adequate as [a] result of their tensions and contradictions being exposed and brought to light. All science, just like all society, is the result of a cumulative process of negation, whereby both life and thought are tested not against some externally imposed criterion of adequacy, but against their own self-imposed standards of truth. The true system of thought, like the rational form of life, does not stand over and against the others like a "lifeless universal," but grows out of a progressive deepening and enrichment, where nothing is ever lost or wasted but is overcome and preserved in a newer, more comprehensive whole. This is the famous Hegelian *Aufhebung*, in which lesser and more inadequate forms of life are both annulled and preserved in the higher ones.[17]

Smith also shows how the concept of *Aufhebung* – the logic of determinate negation – is the key for understanding reconciliation:

To reconcile means to restore a fractured unity, to heal, to mend or otherwise make whole. The process of restoring harmony involves three states: (a) an initial condition of "immediate" or "undifferentiated" unity; (b) a period of differentiation, division (*Trennung*), or alienation: the first negation; (c) the establishment of a higher differentiated unity or reconciliation: the negation of the negation.[18]

Once again it must be reiterated that this process is not an endless one that never reaches completion and finality. It is a teleological process in which the goal is immanent in the process itself. Hegel makes this point *emphatically* when he discusses the concept of determinate negation in the Introduction to the *Phenomenology*:

But the *goal* is as necessarily fixed for knowledge as the serial progression; it is the point where knowledge finds itself, where [Concept] corresponds to object and object to [Concept]. Hence the progress towards this goal is also unhalting, and short of it no satisfaction is to be found at any of the stations on the way. (p. 51)

Hegel stresses the self-inflicted violence and rupture of this process:

> The consciousness suffers this violence at its own hands: it spoils its
> own limited satisfaction. When consciousness feels this violence, its
> anxiety may well make it retreat from the truth, and strive to hold on
> to what it is in danger of losing. But it can find no peace. If it wishes to
> remain in a state of unthinking inertia, then thought troubles its
> thoughtlessness, and its own unrest disturbs its inertia. (p. 51)

We can begin to understand why despite Hegel's insistence on the
equiprimordialness of diremption (rupture) and reconciliation there
are unstable tensions within his philosophy. We can understand why
soon after Hegel's death his "disciples" split into left and right
Hegelians. For what Hegel desperately seeks to hold together – the
dialectical unity of diremption and reconciliation – has split apart.
His ontological vision of a self-identical and self-differentiating totality has itself been shattered and fragmented. "Left Hegelians" and
Marxist Hegelians have always been suspicious of the appeal to
reconciliation. They are drawn to the potential revolutionary power
of negativity – the contradictions that burst forth and rupture "false"
reconciliations. "Right Hegelians" tend to gravitate toward the healing moment of reconciliation – and especially to our reconciliation to
an estranged world that is achieved by speculative comprehension.
When we grasp all the moments in their internal necessity we
achieve a thinking comprehension. The task of philosophy is *not* to
change the world but to interpret, to comprehend it. Only in this
comprehension do we achieve a true homecoming.

Virtually every thinker since Hegel who has grappled with his
thought has had to struggle with the systematic ambiguities, the
unstable tensions that are the core of his thinking. Nowhere is this
more evident (and consequential) than in confronting the theme of
Recognition (*Anerkennung*) which has captured the imagination of so
many post-Hegelian thinkers. At a crucial stage in the *Phenomenology*
– in the transition (the inversion) from Consciousness (*Bewusstsein*)
to Self-Consciousness (*Selbstbewusstsein*) the Concept of Spirit first
makes its appearance. Hegel tells us:

> What still lies ahead for consciousness is the experience of what Spirit
> is – the absolute substance which is the unity of different independent
> self-consciousnesses which, in their opposition enjoy perfect freedom
> and independence: "I" that is "We" and "We" that is "I". It is in self-

consciousness, in the [Concept] of Spirit that consciousness first finds
its turning-point, where it leaves behind it the colorful show of the
sensuous here-and-now and the nightlike void of the supersensible
beyond and steps out into the spiritual daylight of the present. (p. 110)

Immediately following, Hegel begins his famous discussion of "Lordship and Bondage" with the resonant and provocative statement:

> Self-consciousness exists in and for itself when, and by the fact that, it
> so exists for another; that is, it exists only in being acknowledged. The
> [Concept] of this its unity in its duplication embraces many and
> varied meanings. Its moments, then, must on the one hand be held
> strictly apart, and on the other hand must in this differentiation at
> the same time also be taken and known as not distinct, or in their
> opposite significance. The two-fold significance of the distinct
> moments has in the nature of self-consciousness to be infinite, or
> directly the opposite of the determinateness in which it is posited.
> The detailed exposition of the [Concept] of this spiritual unity in its
> duplication will present us with the process of Recognition. (p. 111)

The dialectic of Lordship and Bondage which begins with the life
and death struggle of *two* individual self-consciousnesses is only the
first stage in this "process of recognition." The rest of the
Phenomenology is the full exposition and articulation of this process. It
becomes clear that Recognition for Hegel is not "mere" recognition,
not simply an abstract cognitive awareness. Recognition comes to
mean encountering and fully experiencing the other itself as a
free, independent being. And this requires that the other self-
consciousnesses that we confront *become* free and independent. We
achieve and recognize our freedom in the fully realized freedom of
other self-consciousnesses. Politically this means that our freedom
is *mutually* bound up with the concrete realization of the freedom of others – indeed with the freedom of all "individual self-
consciousnesses." All projects to achieve individual freedom that do
not foster the universal freedom of all self-consciousnesses are
doomed to failure.

This emancipatory theme of Recognition has inspired and
captured the imagination of many post-Hegelian thinkers, and has
even been used against Hegel in order to break away from and move
beyond Hegel's limited understanding of mutual free recognition.
For we can interpret the Recognition theme as the *practical* demand

for the achievement of reciprocity and symmetry that overcomes all forms of asymmetrical domination and bondage.[19] The lord discovers that in his subjection and domination of the bondsman, he fails to achieve the free recognition that he desires, that the "object in which the Lord has achieved his lordship has in reality turned out to be something quite different from an independent consciousness, but a dependent one ... the *truth* of the independent consciousness is accordingly the servile consciousness of the bondsman" (p. 116). When Hegel analyzes the dialectic of the bondsman who initially takes the lord to be the bondsman's essential reality, the bondsman – through "fear and service" – comes to realize that he has "a mind of one's own," that he is not merely a servile working instrument of the lord whose essential function is to satisfy the lord's desires. The bondsman comes to realize that he is *potentially* a free self-consciousness. This for Hegel is only the *beginning*, the first stage in the process of mutual free Recognition. For the bondsman's freedom "is still enmeshed in servitude."

The dialectic of Lordship and Bondage is radically and systematically ambiguous. The achievement of mutual recognition only makes sense if we *presuppose* (as Hegel does) that there are irreducible differences among self-consciousnesses who confront each other, that there is a genuine plurality among self-consciousnesses. But Hegel at once affirms and denies these differences – this plurality. Recognition comes to mean for Hegel that the differences are *aufgehoben* – that what appears to be other and different from myself is not really other and different, but that "we" are *essentially* the same. Indeed it becomes clear even in the way in which Hegel introduces the struggle of Lord and Bondsman that these are "moments" of diremption within a single Absolute Subject. For self-consciousness must supersede the "otherness of itself for this other is itself" (p. 111).

We can specify this crucial and consequential ambiguity by asking what precisely Hegel means when he speaks of the " 'I' that is 'We' and the 'We' that is 'I'." Is this "We" one where there is real plurality among independent "I"s? Or is this "We" to be understood as ultimately and only a single monological "I" where all differences and plurality are *aufgehoben*? Hegel, we should not forget, has already declared in his Preface that "In my view, which can be justified only by the exposition of the system itself, everything turns on grasping and expressing the true, not only as *substance*, but equally as *Subject*" (pp. 9–10). And this Subject is the single, self-differentiating Absolute Subject.[20] The reason why this systematic ambiguity is so consequential is because we can draw out from Hegel contradictory interpretations of the Recognition theme (which do not lend themselves to a grand reconciliation). On the one hand, we can read the Recognition theme as laying the groundwork for the meaning of dialogue, mutual understanding and reciprocal communication that is so fundamental for Peirce, Dewey, Buber, Gadamer, Apel and Habermas (and many others). But this reading requires a recognition of the irreducible differences among dialogical partners. Otherwise there is no real dialogue, no real *mutual* recognition. For example, we can still hear the echoes of Hegel when Habermas characterizes the "paradoxical achievement of intersubjectivity":

> Subjects who reciprocally recognize each other as such, must consider each other as identical, insofar as they both take up the position of subject; they must at all times subsume themselves and the other under the same category. At the same time, the relation of *reciprocity* of recognition demands the non-identity of one and the other, both must also maintain their absolute difference, for to be a subject implies the claim of individuation.[21]

But we can also read Hegel as being finally ensnared within what Habermas calls "the philosophy of the Subject," where for all his apparent sensitivity to the dynamics of *mutual* reciprocal recognition, there is no place for genuine intersubjectivity, and the "absolute difference" among individual subjects. On this reading we are compelled to say that, despite Hegel's reiterated insistence on the equiprimordialness of sameness and otherness or identity and difference, otherness and difference turn out to be submerged and repressed within the single unified monological Absolute Subject.

It is not only that Hegel is radically ambiguous in a way that allows for the most divergent incompatible readings, but – as I have already suggested – his grand narrative of the realization of Spirit, his Concept of the System and the very Idea of a unified self-differentiating and self-identical totality has been shattered and fragmented for us. When Lyotard begins his polemical and provocative essay, *The Postmodern Condition* with his characterization of the "modern" and the "postmodern" he touched upon a sensitive intellectual nerve that is directly relevant to Hegel. He employs the term "modern" "to designate any science that legitimates itself with reference to a metadiscourse ... making explicit appeal to some grand narrative, such as the dialectics of Spirit." "Postmodern," he characterizes as "incredulity toward metanarratives," toward all grand narratives of legitimation.[22] If this is the way that we understand "postmodern" then the first postmodern thinkers were Nietzsche and Kierkegaard. In different ways they treat the "dialectics of Spirit" with sarcasm and irony. Contrary to Hegel who claims this *is* the Absolute Reality, the Truth revealed by Reason, they criticize his narrative as a grand *myth* to be deconstructed. They mock and ridicule the very idea of the grand narrative of the progressive unfolding of Truth and question the claim that the "truth is the Whole." This incredulity not only towards Hegel's grand narrative but to all such narratives has become a dominant reiterated theme in the twentieth century. Foucault's portrayal of the abrupt displacements of *epistēmēs* and discursive practices is radically anti-Hegelian insofar as he scathingly calls into question Hegel's grand narrative of the progressive realization of Spirit and seeks to root out all appeals to teleological development. Heidegger claims that Hegel succumbs to the ontotheological character of metaphysics which "original thinking" calls into question. Heidegger's own reflections on "ontological difference" are intended to challenge Hegel's *Aufhebung* of identity and difference. Derrida – building on Heidegger – relentlessly attempts to show how the logic of *Aufhebung* deconstructs itself. Derrida, explicitly or implicitly, is always battling Hegel. The "centrality" of *différance* for Derrida is a profoundly anti-Hegelian gesture, for Derrida claims the notion of *différance* "is a non-concept in that it cannot be defined in terms of oppositional predicates; it is neither *this* nor *that*; but rather this *and* that (e.g. the act of differing and of deferring) without being reducible to a dialectical logic of either."[23] Levinas, who reads Hegel as the culmination of Western (Greek) philosophy, claims that Hegel is still caught in the ontological predicament that has haunted philosophy since Parmenides where ontology never gets beyond the problematic of "the Same and the Other" and always seeks to show how the other can be mastered, absorbed, reduced to the same. When Levinas, in his characterization of Ethics as first philosophy, insists upon the asymmetrical and non-reciprocal relation between the "I" and the absolute, exterior Other, he is directly challenging Hegel's understanding of mutual recognition.

Thinkers who are much "closer" to Hegel have resisted Hegel's grand narrative of *Geist*. Habermas, as we have seen, claims that Hegel is ensnared in the *aporias* of "the philosophy of the Subject" and claims that Hegel failed to pursue "the traces of communicative reason that are clearly found in his early writings."[24] Furthermore, Habermas' interpretation and critique of "postmodern" thinkers is that they – despite their protests to the contrary – are still caught within the framework of "the philosophy of the Subject" which is now being exhausted.

Even Gadamer, who is such a brilliant commentator on Hegel and is so close to (and yet distant from) Hegel, characterizes himself in a most anti-Hegelian manner as a Hegelian of the "bad infinite." For against Hegel, Gadamer rejects finality, totality and the very idea of *the* completed system. Experience (*Erfahrung*), especially the hermeneutic experience of understanding, is always and *necessarily* open to further experience; it never completes itself. Adorno whose own "negative dialectics" is parasitic upon Hegelian dialectics is nevertheless "unremittingly hostile to the moment of triumphant reconciliation that traditionally capped a dialectical process."[25]

The "postmodern" celebration of contingency, fragmentation, fissures, singularity, plurality, and ruptures (that defy reconciliation) are profoundly anti-Hegelian gestures; they contribute to reinforcing our incredulity of Hegel's grand narrative – and indeed to all metanarratives. These objections, critiques, and challenges to Hegel are not exclusively internal "philosophic objections" to what now strikes us as the myth of the progressive dialectic of Spirit that culminates in the Absolute System. Many of them are motivated by ethical-political considerations. Anyone experiencing the twentieth century where there has been so much violence, barbarism, genocide can scarcely avoid being incredulous about a narrative of history as the progressive realization of freedom. After Auschwitz and the *Gulag*, one cannot avoid being suspicious and skeptical of achieving reconciliation with reality through speculative comprehension. The entire metaphysics of being "at home" in the world now seems hollow.

And yet, Derrida's insightful remark about Levinas has a much more general application. For he says "Levinas is very close to Hegel, much closer that he admits, and at the very moment when he is apparently opposed to Hegel in the most radical fashion. *This is the situation he must share with all anti-Hegelian thinkers*" (emphasis added).[26]

It is Hegel who teaches us over and over again to be alert to the uncanny ways in which radical gestures of opposition and negation are complicit with, and parasitic upon what they are presumably rejecting. This is just as true for the anti-Hegelian gestures that characterize so much of twentieth-century thinking. We can even detect this in the way in which Hegel's grand narrative has been attacked. It was only with Hegel that the history of philosophy itself came to be understood as a *single* systematic story. This way of understanding the history of philosophy is *not* rejected by those who attack Hegel. It is affirmed with an ironical twist. Whether we speak of the history of philosophy, metaphysics, logocentrism, or, with Heidegger, of the history of Being, there is a subtext in many of the critiques which *presupposes* that Western philosophy from its beginnings to its "end" is indeed a single coherent story or narrative – one which is "now" over, broken, to be overcome. Without this hidden Hegelian presupposition, much of the *pathos* of post-Hegelian critiques of Hegel would lose their power and sting.

To claim that anti-Hegelian thinkers (including Derrida himself) are "very close" to Hegel at the very moment when they take themselves "to be opposed to Hegel in the most radical fashion" does not mean that the multifaceted critiques of Hegel lack validity or that they can be "absorbed" as only another turn within the all-encompassing dialectic of Spirit. I agree with many of the criticisms that have been pressed against Hegel. I am sympathetic – as I have tried to show in some of the previous essays – with those who argue that Hegel fails to do justice to human plurality and singularity; that there is at times a powerful tendency in Hegel to suppress and repress otherness and difference; that Hegel fails to appreciate fully those contingencies that rupture history and which resist the dialectical logic of *Aufhebung*, that Hegel's dream of a "final" reconciliation is not only a failure but can turn into an all too real nightmare; that we need to abandon Hegel's "strong" concepts of theory, truth, and system in favor of a more fallibilistic, open understanding of our historical human finitude. I do think that Hegel at once lays the groundwork for understanding the power of reciprocal, symmetrical recognition so vital for dialogue, communicative rationality and the concrete realization of universal freedom *and* undermines this understanding of intersubjectivity in his triumphant affirmation of the Absolute Subject.

Sometimes what is required is to think with Hegel against Hegel.

This is why I have argued that we should displace Hegel's grand *metaphor* of *Aufhebung* – his master concept for reconciliation and rupture – with the metaphors of constellation and force-field. For these latter metaphors challenge the very idea of a culminating *Aufhebung* that explicitly or implicitly valorizes unity, harmony, integration, wholeness and totality. They call into question the powerful undercurrent of progressive teleology that is always informing and shaping Hegel's thinking. This is why I have characterized "modernity/ postmodernity" itself as a constellation in which there is a "juxtaposed rather than integrated cluster of changing elements that resist reduction to a common denominator, essential core, or generative first principle." Or we can also say that in the *Kraftfeld* of "modernity/postmodernity" there is a dynamic shifting relational interplay of attractions and aversions that resist what Adorno once called "extorted reconciliation." Reconciliation/rupture are themselves irreducible elements of this new constellation – points of attraction and aversion in this new force-field.

To say this means we must seek to do justice to *both* elements, without succumbing to the illusion that they can finally be integrated. In a Hegelian (but also an anti-Hegelian) manner we can characterize this as the logic of "Both/And." For this "Both/And" is itself tensed and unstable – never quite *aufgehoben* or reconciled. Consequently it is too simplistic and misleading to characterize the present *Stimmung* as anti-Hegelian without also seeing how the ghost of Hegel still hovers over us. Let me explain more fully what I mean by referring once again to Hegel's distinctions between abstract negation and determinate negation; abstract skepticism and determinate skepticism.

Employing these distinctions, we can say there has been a strong tendency, an almost irresistible drive in many "postmodern" discourses toward an abstract negation and skepticism. There has been a tendency to slide into an attitude "that ends up with the bare abstraction of nothingness or emptiness [that] cannot get any further from there, but must wait to see whether something new comes along and what it is, in order to throw it too into the same empty abyss" (p. 51). Although I have argued that this is not true of the ways in which Derrida employs deconstructive strategies, it *is* characteristic of some of the "appropriations" of deconstruction. Sometimes it seems that Hegel was prophetic in ways which he could not have realized. According to Hegel this form of skeptical consciousness is only one of the "shapes of consciousness" that Spirit has *already* superseded. But, contrary to Hegel, abstract skepticism seems to be a defining characteristic of our current intellectual situation where there is an ever accelerated drive of destruction and self-destruction, where there is only "restless confusion" – "a confused medley, the dizziness of a perpetually self-engendered disorder." Despite all the professed skepticism about binary oppositions, there has been a tendency in many "postmodern" discourses to reify a new set of fixed oppositions: otherness is pitted against sameness, contingency against necessity, singularity and particularity against universality, fragmentation against wholeness. In each instance it is the former term that is celebrated and valorized while the latter term of these oppositions is damned, marginalized, exiled. But as Heidegger and Derrida tell us (and as Hegel did before them) these reversals and inversions are not really anti-metaphysical gestures. They only reverse our metaphysical valorizations. It is Hegel who teaches us to be wary of such rigid oppositions. It is Hegel who shows us that at the very moment when we desperately seek to damn, exclude and repress one moment of a binary opposition, it has an uncanny (*unheimlich*) way of reasserting itself like the "return of the repressed." So even if we reject – as we have good reason to reject – Hegel's "strong" conception of determinate negation where "the goal is necessarily fixed for knowledge as the serial progression," we can still recognize the *need* to pass beyond endless abstract negation and skepticism to something more determinate.

We can even draw upon Hegel in order to discern a dialectical movement of determinate negation within the discourses of "modernity/postmodernity," especially in regard to ethical-political questions. Initially, what is so striking and manifest in the ruptures of "postmodern" interventions is the moment of abstract negative skepticism. We witness this, for example, in Heidegger's denigration of the traditional philosophic discipline of ethics and in his disparaging remarks about "the particular dictatorship of the public realm." "Ethics," he tells us, only comes to flourish "when original thinking comes to an end." "The thinking that inquires into the truth of Being and so defines man's essential abode from and toward Being is neither ethics nor ontology."[27] Foucault, up until his final writings when he turned to elaborating a new understanding of ethics, expressed his disdain about all forms of ethical and juridical discourse. These were seen as diversionary tactics distorting and screening "power/knowledge regimes." The search for normative foundations is bound up with *normalization* which Foucault takes to be the primary danger of the age of bio-power where the disciplines make our bodies into docile objects. Derrida's early writings seem to bypass ethical-political questions and identify the search for ethical-political principles with the metaphysics of presence. In Rorty's early writings, up to and through *Philosophy and the Mirror of Nature*, he scarcely touched upon ethical-political questions.

It is striking that Foucault, Derrida and Rorty – after their abstract negations – turn in their later writings to struggling with ethical-political questions. And this – as I have argued in previous essays – is not simply a "contingent" fact about the "development" of their thinking, but rather it is an indication of their efforts to face up to the consequences of their *own* thinking. Superficially, we might say that Heidegger's trajectory was the very opposite – that after his disastrous "descent" into the world of real politics in the 1930s, his thinking turned away from politics and ethics. In my essay on Heidegger I have tried to show that this is a superficial and misleading account of the movement of Heidegger's thinking. Furthermore, the most interesting and important consequence of the recent controversy about Heidegger's "politics" is that it compels us to develop a more complex and nuanced understanding of the relations between thinking, philosophy, politics, and ethics.

The point that I am making about the dialectic of "postmodern" interventions – a movement from abstract negation toward a (not-quite) form of Hegelian determinate negation can be stated from a slightly different perspective. When Derrida tells us that the *archai* are trembling, he articulates something extremely important about the "modern/postmodern" *Stimmung*. For he shows what has been deeply and widely experienced in the twentieth century – the lack of certitude, the false "metaphysical comfort" in any and all appeals to a fixed principle, a transcendental signified or Archimedean resting point upon which we can "support" ethical-political convictions. But we cannot avoid asking what happens *after* all the *archai* are made to tremble? What are the consequences of this trembling for "taking" an ethical-political "position"? How are we *now* to answer the classic Socratic question: How one should live. I am not suggesting that philosophy (or any intellectual discipline) can answer this question definitively. Any answer is always open to further questioning. But I am claiming that the question is unavoidable and that we must continue to struggle with it. This is one of the dialectical consequences of the discourses of "modernity/postmodernity" after its experiments with the varieties of abstract negation.

I also think that one of the primary reasons why Lyotard's *The Postmodern Condition* has been a catalyst for the "modern/postmodern" debates is because he focused attention on the question of what sort of ethics and politics "follows from" or is even compatible with a "postmodern" attitude of incredulity toward *all* grand narratives. This is a question that seemed to be excluded or marginalized but which has become more and more dominant. This is also one of the reasons why Levinas' writings are receiving increasing attention. Whatever reservations one has about his claims, he has pushed the question of ethics (and politics too) to the center of philosophy – claiming that ethics as first philosophy has superseded the philosophical concern with ontology – from Parmenides to Heidegger. His characterization of ethics not only challenges the Hegelian emphasis on mutual, reciprocal, symmetrical recognition, but relates ethics to that theme which has dominated so much of twentieth-century Continental philosophy – the otherness of the Other that resists any and all reduction to the Same.

I am claiming that the dialectic of the discourses of "modernity/postmodernity" show the *traces* of the Hegelian movement from abstract to determinate negation – even though we must be wary of the promise of an *Aufhebung* that will mediate and reconcile all ruptures and contingencies.

Hegel's ghost hovers over us in still another way. I have spoken of the promise and need for reconciliation as *one* of the irreducible elements of a new constellation. But I have also affirmed that it is an illusion to think or expect that there can be a final reconciliation that integrates all ruptures and differences. One cannot ignore the extent to which "modern/postmodern" emphases on plurality, otherness, *différance*, alterity and fragmentation are themselves expressions and reflections of what has become a fact of "modern/postmodern" forms of life. For our everyday experience is one of a fractured totality. This is expressed by Lyotard when he declares

We have paid a high enough price for the nostalgia of the whole and one, for the reconciliation of the concept and the sensible, of the transparent and the communicable experience. Under the general demand for slackening and for appeasement, we can hear the mutterings of the desire for a return of terror, for the realization of the fantasy to seize reality. The answer is: Let us wage war on totality, let us be witnesses of the unpresentable, let us activate the differences.[28]

"Let us activate the differences" – this might be taken as the banner in the "war" being waged by so many "postmodern" thinkers. Ironically (even though this war is being waged against Hegel – among others), Hegel would have no difficulty endorsing such a slogan. Hegel would go further and maintain that differences will always willy-nilly activate themselves and thereby rupture and destroy false and abstract reconciliations. But the need for critical reconciliation is not therefore to be abandoned. For an uncritical celebration and valorization of plurality, differences, and otherness harbors its own dangers. What is too frequently obscured is the need to make critical discriminations and judgments. Not all forms of otherness and difference are to be celebrated. For example, there is something dis-ingenuous in Lyotard's and Rorty's reiterated celebration of contingency and a plurality of forms of life. They presumably oppose all forms of universality and are suspicious of the reconciliation of differences. Yet they both advocate a type of plurality and contingency in which there is *universal* non-violent play. The type of "reconciliation" they advocate is one in which we learn to live in peace with incommensurable vocabularies and forms of life. But they never thematize this legitimate *universal* regulative ideal.

Habermas – who is one of the targets of Lyotard's (and Rorty's) polemic – makes this point when he acknowledges that the "pluralization of diverging universes of discourses belongs to specifically modern experience" and that "individuals, groups, and nations have drifted far apart in their backgrounds of biographical and social-cultural experience."[29] As Habermas notes, the rupturing and "the shattering of naive consensus is the impetus for what Hegel calls the 'experience of reflection'."[30] This experience of reflection is the demand that we *seek* for a type of reconciliation of pluralization and differences without ignoring or repressing the otherness of the Other. Otherwise we are threatened by a new form of tribalism in which difference and otherness are reified, and where there is a fail-ure to seek out communalities and solidarities. So rather than interpreting the *Stimmung* of "modernity/postmodernity" as essentially anti-Hegelian, I am arguing that we are experiencing a new constellation which is at once Hegelian and anti-Hegelian, which is "Both/And" – in which there are attractions and repulsions between reconciliation and rupture.[31]

Finally, I want to turn to the question of critique which has been at the center of philosophy ever since Kant and which has become so problematic for us today.[32] It is with Kant's critical philosophy that the concept of critique was thrust into the foreground of philosophy. Critique for Kant is both negative and positive. The task of the *Critique of Pure Reason* is to demonstrate – once and for all – what the limits of experience and knowledge are. This is to be accomplished by specifying the transcendental conditions for the possibility of knowledge. According to Kant he had to "deny" knowledge (of the transcendent) not only to make "room" for faith but for the possibility of human freedom, autonomy, and morality. The need and rationale for critique is poignantly expressed by Kant in the Preface of the *Critique of Pure Reason*:

> Human reason has this peculiar fate that in one species of its knowledge it is burdened by questions which, as prescribed by the very nature of reason itself, it is not able to ignore, but which, as transcending all its powers, it is also not able to answer.
>
> The perplexity into which it thus falls is not due to any fault of its own. It begins with principles which it has no option save to employ in the course of experience, and which this experience at the same time abundantly justifies in using. Rising with their aid (since it is determined to this also by its own nature) to ever higher, ever more remote, conditions, it soon becomes aware that in this way – the questions never ceasing – its work must always remain incomplete: and it therefore finds itself compelled to resort to principles which overstep all possible empirical employment, and which yet seem so unobjectionable that even ordinary consciousness readily accepts them. But by this procedure human reason precipitates itself into darkness and contradictions.[33]

This crisis of darkness and contradiction is the occasion for a critical philosophy that shows us the way out of this darkness by enabling us to resolve the contradictions, the antinomies generated by reason itself.

But Hegel, as we know, found Kant's "solution" to the contradictions generated by "human reason" to be unstable and unsatisfactory – precisely because Kant failed to realize "contradiction is the root of all movement and vitality; it is only insofar as something has contradiction within it that it moves, has an urge and actuality."[34] Speculative thinking does not abhor contradictions. On the contrary it sharpens contradictions, recognizes the "positive side of contradiction" and shows how these contradictions are reconciled in an absolute totality. Hegel engages in a critique of Kantian critique. He even ridicules the very idea that by a self-reflexive act of reflection we can critically examine knowing itself as an "instrument." With Hegel a new style of critique comes into play – *immanent critique* which does not import or presuppose alien "standards." Rather it accepts the standard (*Massstab*) immanent within a "shape of consciousness" and then shows how the "shape of consciousness" falls prey to contradiction. It exposes the discrepancy, the clash, the contradictions that are implicit in the "shape of consciousness" – how it fails in light of its own *internal* standards. This is the activity that compels us to move on to a new more comprehensive "shape of consciousness." This is the dialectical process of determinate negation that fulfills itself only when the Concept is adequate to the object and the object is adequate to the Concept. And in this dialectical process there is a development, a necessary transformation of the standards immanent in the process itself. We come to realize that *Spirit* itself "contains" its own standards of critique.

Immanent critique has been one of the most powerful and richest forms of critique practiced not only by Hegel but by Marx and those thinkers shaped by the Hegelian-Marxist tradition – including the members of the Frankfurt School of Critical Theory.[35] Marx turns immanent critique against Hegel himself. This is especially true in Marx's early writings where he seeks to show that, contrary to Hegel's claims, Hegel himself fails to achieve a genuine reconciliation. According to Marx, Hegel's concept of Reason – when relentlessly criticized and exposed – turns out to be a form of "rationalization" that masks and distorts the "real" contradictions and ruptures immanent in society and revealed by the critique of political economy.

Not only does the movement from Kant through Hegel to Marx represent a series of transformations in the understanding and practice of critique but also a transformation in the object and scope of critique. Foucault in his essay "What is Enlightenment?" suggests that Kant initiated a new critical way of thinking about philosophy

and its relation to its historical present. Kant "is not seeking to
understand the present on the basis of a totality or a future achievement. He is looking for a difference; what difference does today
introduce with respect to yesterday?"[36] Whether or not one agrees
with Foucault's claim, there is no doubt that this becomes a primary
concern for Hegel. For Hegel's immanent critique is not only
directed toward the categories of philosophic thinking but to History
itself. His critique of History is intended to bring forth what is distinctive and different about the historical present. Marx, building
upon and going "beyond" Hegel, criticizes him for substituting a
mythic History of *Geist* for the "real history" of the struggles and
conflicts of human beings.

For all the consequential differences among Kant, Hegel, and
Marx, they share a common perspective. For all three are convinced
not only that a critical project is viable but that critique itself can be
properly *grounded*. Kant never seriously doubts that Reason can self-
reflexively critically examine itself and determine the transcendental conditions for the possibility of knowledge. Hegel does not doubt
that the *telos* of philosophy is *Wissenschaft* – the Absolute System
which internally "justifies" its own standards of critique. Marx does
not doubt that there is a sharp categorical distinction between science and ideology, and that a true scientific knowledge of political
economy is the rational basis for the critique of ideology.

It is this confidence in the rational grounding of critique that has
been shaken for us. Once again we can say that Nietzsche plays a
decisive role in calling into question the "supposed" rational foundations of critique. His scathing barbs about Enlightenment, his genealogical experiments, his "laughter" are directed toward that "will to
knowledge" that deludes itself into thinking it can rationally "justify" the foundations for critique. Nietzsche's rupture, his radical
skepticism, his smashing of illusions, his philosophizing with a ham-
mer, his calling into question the rational pretensions of philosophy
itself hovers over and haunts the twentieth century. His decisive
influence on Heidegger, Foucault and Derrida is all too evident
(although each of them reads Nietzsche differently). But here
we touch upon an *aporia* that resounds throughout "modern/
postmodern" debates. On the one hand Nietzsche himself engages in
radical critique. But on the other hand he appears to call into question any and all attempts to "justify" critique – to secure some
grounding for critique. This *aporia* can be generalized. For there is an

ironical twist to Kant's claim about *his* age: "Our age, is in especial degree, the age of criticism, and to criticism everything must submit." As I have indicated, Kant never seriously doubted that there are rational standards for critique and that the task of philosophy is to show how critique can be grounded. But for us – in our "modern/postmodern" age, this is precisely what has been subject to radical critique itself.

There are those like Habermas who argue that "Nietzsche's critique consumes the critical impulse itself." Habermas thinks this is just as true for all those "postmodern" thinkers who work in Nietzsche's shadow. He claims that "if thought can no longer operate in the realms of truth and validity claims, then analysis and critique lose their meaning."[37] Those who engage in a totalizing critique – where critique turns upon and undermines itself – are caught within a "performative contradiction" where they at once seek to practice critique and at the same time undermine the very possibility of critique. They consume "the critical impulse." Habermas' theory of communicative action and his discourse ethics are intended to show how the project of critique can and must be rationally grounded without an appeal to metaphysical foundations. Whatever judgment we make about the success and adequacy of his ambitious project of grounding critique, Habermas persistently and relentlessly compels us to confront the unavoidable question – critique in the name of what? What is it that we are implicitly or explicitly affirming when we engage in critique? Furthermore how can we "justify" or warrant what we affirm – the norms and standards for engaging in critique? How are we to avoid lapsing into a "performative contradiction"?

For all their differences (and speaking past each other) Derrida does *not* disagree with Habermas on the symbiotic relation between critique and affirmation. He forthrightly declares "I cannot conceive of a radical critique which would not be ultimately motivated by some sort of affirmation, acknowledged or not."[38] He also says "every culture and society requires an internal critique as an essential part of its development .... Every culture needs an element of self-interrogation and of distance from itself, if it is to transform itself."[39] The question that Derrida compels us to confront when he speaks of affirmation is: what precisely are we affirming and why?

There are some who think that posing the issue as I have done – asking the question "critique in the name of what?" or what are we

affirming and why are we affirming it when we engage in critique? –
is itself a misleading formulation. For these questions invite
(seduce) us into thinking that there is or can be some universal or
global answer. But this is itself an illusion. All effective critique is
local and specific – dependent on local contexts. In my essay on
Foucault, we encountered one version of this objection.[40] But the
objection itself is an evasion of the central issue. One need not sub-
scribe to the illusion that the philosopher or the "universal intellectual" has the task of "grounding" universal standards of critique
before anyone can legitimately engage in critique. One need not
claim there are fixed universal ahistorical rational standards of
critique. There is something grotesque and absurd about the very
idea of the philosopher first "discovering" or laying down standards
of critique before anyone can "legitimately" engage in critique. One
can agree with Bernard Williams that "there are many styles of
critique, and the most potent of them rely, as they always have, not
so much on philosophical arguments as on showing up those
attitudes as resting on myths, falsehoods about what people are
like."[41] But a focus on context, specificity and locality does not mean
we can avoid facing up to our affirmations – especially when they are
challenged. For even if one maintains all effective critique must be
local and specific, we still have to face up to what we are affirming
when we engage in critique.

There are those like Rorty who tell us there is simply nothing
more to be said when our "final vocabularies" are called into question. "These words are as far as [we] can go with language; beyond
them there is helpless passivity or resort to force."[42] But I have
already argued that such a response is not only unsatisfactory but
that Rorty's irony slides into cynicism.

I think we must honestly confront the instability of any project of
critique. We must recognize that there cannot be any critique without some sort of affirmation, that we cannot avoid asking the question, "critique in the name of what?" And we must be prepared to
defend our affirmations and standards of critique when they are
challenged. We can never fully anticipate those contingencies which
will rupture our affirmations. We need to maintain a vigilant *double*
attitude where we are at once aware of the need for affirmation and
that any affirmation can be called into question. Although a defense
of our affirmations secreted by the practice of critique can never be
final and conclusive, we use a variety of "strategies" in defending

or criticizing them – argumentation, narrative, imagining new possibilities, articulating visions of what we take to be desirable. Such a bricolage will not satisfy those who hanker after something more solid, foundational, and secure – those who dream of some sort of conclusive "grounding." But as Hannah Arendt once remarked, we have to learn to think without banisters. We have to learn to exorcize the quest for certainty and certitude.

One of the primary lessons of the new constellation is that we engage in critique as second person *participants* and not as third person neutral observers. As participants our critiques and affirmations are always tentative, fallible, open to further questioning. Returning to Kafka's parable which I discussed in my first essay, "Philosophy, History, and Critique," "He" (as a participant) is never able "to jump out of the fighting line" (which is the *topos* of critique) and assume the position of a neutral umpire. Kant, Hegel, and Marx did (at least some of the time) think such neutrality was a real possibility. They did think there could be a definitive grounding for critique. But what has haunted thinkers ever since Nietzsche is that this dream of a conclusive grounding is an illusion. And this has led to the anxiety that the "critical impulse will consume itself." But like "He" in Kafka's parable we cannot "jump out of the fighting line." "He" must be vigilant in defending his affirmations without any final security. "He" can neither give up the need and desire for reconciliation nor his openness to new, unexpected, contingent ruptures. Reconciliation/Rupture is the space in-between the new constellation – the space that is the *topos* in which critique thrives.

NOTES

1 G. W. F. Hegel, *Werke in Zwanzig Bänden*, eds. E. Moldenhauer and K. M. Michel (Frankfurt, Suhrkamp, 1971) 2, p. 22.
2 See J. Glenn Gray, *Hegel's Hellenic Ideal* (New York: King's Crown Press, 1941).
3 Jürgen Habermas, *The Philosophical Discourse of Modernity* (Cambridge, Mass.: MIT Press, 1987), pp. 21–2.
4 Ibid., p. 21.
5 Jean Hyppolite argues that "unhappy consciousness" is the dominant theme of Hegel's *Phenomenology of Spirit*. See *Genesis and Structure of Hegel's Phenomenology of Spirit* (Evanston: Northwestern University Press, 1974). See also Steven B. Smith's discussion of the "divided self" in

Hegel, *Hegel's Critique of Liberalism* (Chicago: University of Chicago Press, 1989), pp. 17ff.

6   G. W. F. Hegel, *The Phenomenology of Spirit*, trans. A. V. Miller (New York: Oxford University Press, 1977), p. 11. Page numbers in the text refer to this work.

7   See "Part I: The Claims of Speculative Reason" of Charles Taylor, *Hegel* (Cambridge: Cambridge University Press, 1975), where Taylor relates Hegel's itinerary to the conflicts of his age. See also Smith's discussion of "The Origins of the Hegelian Project" in *Hegel's Critique of Liberalism*.

8   G. W. F. Hegel, *Philosophy of Right*, trans. T. M. Knox (Oxford: Clarendon Press, 1952), p. 286.

9   Habermas, *The Philosophical Discourse of Modernity*, p. 17.

10 Smith perceptively demonstrates this in *Hegel's Critique of Liberalism*.

11 Habermas, *The Philosophical Discourse of Modernity*, p. 42.

12 *Science of Logic*, trans. A. V. Miller (New York: Humanities Press, 1969), p. 440.

13 Ibid., p. 442.

14 Hegel's understanding of ancient and modern skepticism, and the way in which he relates dialectic to skepticism, is complex and subtle. See Smith, *Hegel's Critique of Liberalism*, pp. 180ff; and Michael N. Forster, *Hegel and Skepticism* (Chicago: University of Chicago Press, 1989).

15 In "Lordship and Bondage" Hegel characterizes the life and death struggle as an act of "abstract negation, not the negation coming from consciousness, which supersedes in such a way as to preserve and maintain what is superseded, and consequently survives its own supersession." *The Phenomenology of Spirit*, pp. 114–15.

16 *Science of Logic*, p. 54.

17 Smith, *Hegel's Critique of Liberalism*, p. 189.

18 Ibid., p. 191.

19 One must be careful not be "reduce" the Recognition theme to only its political and social meanings. For it keeps reappearing in a variety of meanings throughout Hegel's writings. See H. S. Harris, "The Concept of Recognition," *Hegel-Studien, Beiheft* 20 (1980); L. Siep, *Anerkennung als Prinzip der praktischen Philosophie*; Elliot Jurist, "Hegel's Concept of Recognition: Its Origins, Development and Significance," unpublished Ph.D. Dissertation, Columbia University, 1983.

20 The radical systematic ambiguity of the Recognition theme crops up over and over again. For example, consider the following passage which occurs just before Hegel makes the transition to Religion in *The Phenomenology of Spirit*:

> The reconciling Yea, in which the two "I"s let go their antithetical *existence*, is the *existence* of the "I" which has expanded into a duality, and therein remains identical with itself, and, in its complete externalization and opposite, possesses the certainty of itself: it is God manifested in the

midst of those who know themselves in the form of pure knowledge. (p. 409)

21 Jürgen Habermas, "Sprachspiel, Intention und Bedeutung. Zu Motiven bei Sellars und Wittgenstein," in R. W. Wiggerhaus, ed., *Sprachanalyse und Soziologie* (Frankfurt: Suhrkamp, 1972), p. 334. See also Vittorio Hösle's comprehensive and provocative analysis of intersubjectivity in *Hegels System: Der Idealismus der Subjectivität und das Problem der Intersubjectivität* (Hamburg: Felix Meiner, 1987).
22 Jean-François Lyotard, *The Postmodern Condition: A Report on Knowledge*, trans. G. Bennington and B. Massumi (Minneapolis: University of Minnesota Press, 1984), pp. xxiii–xxiv.
23 "Dialogue with Jacques Derrida" in Richard Kearney, ed., *Dialogues with Contemporary Continental Thinkers* (Manchester: Manchester University Press, 1984), p. 110.
24 *The Philosophical Discourse of Modernity*, p. 31. See also "Labor and Interaction: Remarks on Hegel's Jena Philosophy of Mind" in *Theory and Practice*, trans. John Viertel (Boston: Beacon, 1973).
25 Martin Jay, *Adorno* (Cambridge, Mass.: Harvard University Press, 1984), p. 15.
26 Jacques Derrida, "Violence and Metaphysics: An Essay on the Thought of Emmanuel Levinas" in *Writing and Difference*, trans. Alan Bass (Chicago: University of Chicago Press, 1978), p. 99.
27 Martin Heidegger, "Letter on Humanism," in *Martin Heidegger: Basic Writings*, ed. and trans. David F. Krell (New York: Harper and Row, 1977), p. 195.
28 *The Postmodern Condition*, pp. 81–2.
29 Jürgen Habermas, "Questions and Counterquestions," in Richard J. Bernstein, ed., *Habermas and Modernity* (Cambridge, Mass.: MIT Press, 1985), p. 182.
30 Ibid.
31 This is what I have characterized as an "engaged fallibilistic pluralism." See "Pragmatism, Pluralism, and the Healing of Wounds," p. 336.
32 See Reinhart Koselleck, *Critique and Crisis* (Cambridge, Mass.: MIT Press, 1988).
33 Immanuel Kant, *Critique of Pure Reason*, trans. Norman Kemp Smith (New York: St Martin's Press, 1968), p. 7.
34 *Science of Logic*, p. 439.
35 For a subtle analysis of the development and transformations of the concept of critique from Kant to Habermas, see Seyla Benhabib, *Critique, Norm, and Utopia* (New York: Columbia University Press, 1986).
36 Michel Foucault, "What is Enlightenment?", in Paul Rabinow, ed., *The Foucault Reader* (New York: Pantheon, 1984), p. 34.

37 Jürgen Habermas, "The Entwinement of Myth and Enlightenment: Re-Reading *Dialectic of Enlightenment*," *New German Critique* 26 (1982), p. 25.

38 "Dialogue with Jacques Derrida," p. 118.

39 Ibid.

40 See pp. 159–61.

41 Bernard Williams, *Ethics and the Limits of Philosophy* (Cambridge, Mass.: Harvard University Press, 1985), p. 71.

42 Richard Rorty, *Contingency, Irony and Solidarity* (Cambridge: Cambridge University Press, 1989), p. 73.

Appendix: Pragmatism, Pluralism, and the Healing of Wounds

Presidential Address delivered before the Eighty-fourth Annual Eastern Division Meeting of the American Philosophical Association in Washington, DC, December 29, 1988.

Several years ago, Hans-Georg Gadamer visited my college and gave an eloquent lecture on hermeneutics. After the lecture, several of us took him out to dinner to a local Chinese restaurant. We concluded the meal by reading the messages of our fortune cookies. The art of writing a good fortune message is to be sufficiently vague and ambiguous so when it is read it seems to have specific and unique relevance. But in this instance, Gadamer's fortune message was especially apt. For it summed up his lecture and epitomized his philosophy. When his turn came his "fortune" read: "Sometimes to understand the present, one needs to study the past." When I was preparing this address that message kept intruding itself. For I want to try to understand and gain a critical perspective on our present situation in philosophy. To do so one must study the past – the traditions that have shaped and still are shaping us. For I agree with Gadamer that we belong to traditions before they belong to, and are appropriated by, us: but as soon as one speaks in this manner, treacherous problems come pouring in. Not the least of which is, who is this "we"? Even if one limits oneself to philosophy in America, or more specifically, to philosophy in the United States, we are an extremely heterogeneous bunch, perhaps more so today than at any time in our past. And "we" have been shaped by conflicting rival traditions.

Alasdair MacIntyre has given one of the best succinct characterizations of a tradition when he tells us that a tradition "not only embodies the narrative of an argument, but is only recovered by an argumentative retelling of that narrative which will itself be in conflict with other argumentative retellings."[1] Today I want to sketch an argumentative retelling of the pragmatic tradition. Although it is only one of the traditions to which we belong, it is nevertheless one of the richest traditions that has shaped philosophy in America. I want to draw upon this tradition because it enables us to gain a critical perspective on our present situation in philosophy. It will become clear that I think this tradition is very much alive and that pragmatic themes weave through diverse contemporary orientations of many philosophers who do not think of themselves as belonging to this tradition. Indeed, the pragmatic thinkers were ahead of their times. Recently there has been a good deal of loose talk about our "postmodern condition." Yet if we pay close attention to the characteristic themes and challenges of the "postmodern" discourses, we will see how they were anticipated by the pragmatists. What is even more impressive and important is that the pragmatists were concerned with the question of how to *respond* to these challenges. The dialectic of many contemporary trends in philosophy leads us back to pragmatic insights.

It is that pragmatic *ēthos* that I hope to elicit by focusing on some of the dominant interrelated motifs characteristic of this style of thinking. I do not think of pragmatism as a set of doctrines or even as a method. Any close student of Peirce, James, Dewey, Mead, and Royce in his late pragmatic writings is immediately struck by their clashing philosophic temperaments, and by the different problems that preoccupied them. We can best appreciate the vitality and diversity of this tradition when we approach it as an ongoing engaged conversation consisting of distinctive – sometimes competing – voices.

Before turning to highlighting themes running through this tradition that are relevant to our present situation, let me remind you of some of the striking features of the outburst and flourishing of philosophy in the latter part of the nineteenth century. We must not forget that the institution of the graduate school and the "professionalization" of academic philosophy as we know it today did not exist in the post-Civil War period in the United States. Philosophically, Peirce and James were autodidacts. They were not "formally" trained as philosophers. Peirce was a practicing experimental scientist and thought of himself as a logician. James was trained as a medical doctor, and his philosophic speculations grew out of his psychological investigations. Dewey was among the first to receive a Ph.D. in philosophy at the newly founded graduate school at Johns Hopkins. When they turned to philosophy, they drew upon diverse sources and traditions. Peirce's early philosophic work began with reflections on the Kantian categories. He even claimed to know the *Critique of Pure Reason* "almost by heart." At a time when there was scarcely any knowledge or appreciation of the intricacies of scholastic philosophy, Peirce identified himself as a "Scotistic realist." James' deepest philosophic affinities were with the tradition of British empiricism, although he was also a sharp critic of what he took to be the artificial, thin, emasculated conception of experience in this tradition. In his later years, he recognized his affinities (and differences) with Bergson. Dewey, as a graduate student, was profoundly influenced by Hegelianism. Each drew upon diverse European philosophic traditions, reshaping and criticizing them in distinctive ways. The very idea of an Anglo-American/Continental split in philosophy would have made no sense during this creative formative stage of the pragmatic *ēthos*.

We should also remember the fluidity of academic disciplines at this time. There was no sense of sharp boundaries or that philosophy was a well-defined *Fach* or discipline to be rigorously demarcated from other types of inquiry. The pragmatic thinkers moved freely over the range of different areas of inquiry and experience. This fluidity and openness deeply marked their philosophic approach to problems. For the pragmatic thinkers were skeptical and critical of the metaphysical and epistemological dichotomies that had dominated so much of traditional and modern philosophy. Finally, we must remember that while they all resisted scientism – the conviction that science and science alone is the standard for determining what counts as legitimate knowledge and for determining what is "real" – they were equally strong in their conviction that any responsible philosophic reflection must be responsive to scientific developments and practices. Collectively the classical pragmatic thinkers drew upon a variety of philosophic traditions, were deeply suspicious of hard and fixed boundaries, and grappled with new scientific developments, especially those brought into the foreground by the Darwinian revolution.

With an eye to the present, let me turn to five interrelated substantive themes that enable us to characterize the pragmatic *ēthos*:

(1) "Anti-foundationalism" is not an expression that the pragmatists used. They certainly did not mean what is sometimes meant today when "anti-foundationalism" is polemically used to attack the very idea of philosophy. Yet I do not think there is an important argument in the anti-foundational arsenal that was not anticipated (and sometimes stated in a much more trenchant form) in the remarkable series of articles that Peirce published in 1868.[2] Peirce presents a battery of arguments directed against the idea that knowledge rests upon fixed foundations, and that we possess a special faculty of insight or intuition by which we can know these foundations. Peirce was exposing what has come to be called "the metaphysics of presence." Peirce realized that in criticizing foundationalism he was attacking many of the most cherished doctrines and dogmas that constituted modern philosophy. He makes this clear when he contrasts Cartesianism with the scholasticism that it displaced. He begins his article "Some Consequences of Four Incapacities" by declaring:

> Descartes is the father of modern philosophy, and the spirit of Cartesianism – that which principally distinguishes it from the scholasticism which it displaced – may be compendiously stated as follows:
>
> 1 It teaches that philosophy must begin with universal doubt, whereas scholasticism had never questioned fundamentals.
>
> 2 It teaches that the ultimate test of certainty is to be found in individual consciousness; whereas scholasticism had rested on the testimony of sages and of the Catholic Church.
>
> 3 The multiform argumentation of the Middle Ages is replaced by a single thread of inference depending often on inconspicuous premises.
>
> 4 Scholasticism had its mysteries of faith, but undertook to explain all created things. But there are many facts which Cartesianism not only does not explain but renders absolutely inexplicable, unless to say "God makes them so" is regarded as an explanation.
>
> In some, or all these respects, most modern philosophers have been, in effect, Cartesians. Now without wishing to return to scholasticism, it seems to me that modern science and modern logic require us to stand upon a very different platform from this.[3]

Peirce realized that his critique of Cartesianism, his elaboration of a different platform that is required by modern science and logic, required a rethinking of every major philosophic problem. For in one fell swoop he sought to demolish the idea that there are or can be any absolute beginnings or endings in philosophy. He sought to exorcize what Dewey later called "the quest for certainty" and the "spectator theory of knowledge." He called into question the privileged status of subjectivity and consciousness that had dominated so much of modern philosophy. He elaborated a theory of signs where interpretants are always and necessarily open to further interpretation, determination, and critical correction.

We find variations on these themes in all the pragmatic thinkers. We can see how subsequent philosophers have continued to refine the anti-foundational arguments adumbrated by Peirce. They are developed further in Quine's own distinctive version of pragmatism and in Wilfrid Sellars' work when he criticizes "the myth of the given" and declares that "empirical knowledge, like its sophisticated extension science, is rational, not because it has a foundation, but because it is a self-correcting enterprise which can put any claim in jeopardy, though not *all* at once."[4]

(2) But if we abandon foundationalism and the craving for absolutes, then what is the alternative? There are many who have thought that to give up foundationalism can lead only to some version of skepticism or relativism. But this was not the response of Peirce and the pragmatists. Their alternative to foundationalism was to elaborate a thoroughgoing fallibilism where we realize that although we must begin any inquiry with prejudgments and can never call everything into question at once, nevertheless there is no belief or thesis – no matter how fundamental – that is not open to further interpretation and criticism. Peirce advocated that we displace the "foundation" metaphor with the metaphor of a "cable." In philosophy, as in the sciences, we ought to "trust rather to the multitude and variety of its arguments than to the conclusiveness of any one. Its reasoning should not form a chain which is no stronger than its weakest link, but a cable whose fibers may be ever so slender, provided they are sufficiently numerous and intimately connected."[5] The pragmatists argued not only that fallibilism is characteristic of the experimental habit of mind but that philosophy itself is intrinsically fallibilistic. Philosophy is interpretive, tentative, always subject to correction.

(3)   It is this fallibilism that brings me to the next theme that is so vital for the pragmatists – the social character of the self and the need to nurture a critical community of inquirers. If we are fallible and always limited in our perspectives then "we individually cannot reasonably hope to attain the ultimate philosophy which we pursue; we can only seek it, therefore, for the *community* of philosophers. Hence, if disciplined and candid minds carefully examine a theory and refuse to accept it, this ought to create doubts in the mind of the author of the theory himself."[6] The theme of the social character of the self and of community is played out in many variations by the pragmatic thinkers. The very idea of an individual consciousness that is independent of shared social practices is criticized. In this respect, the pragmatists sought to dismantle and deconstruct the philosophy of consciousness and the philosophy of subjectivity. What has come to be called the decentering of the subject is integral to the pragmatic project. Peirce appeals to the regulative ideal of a critical community of inquirers. Royce sought to extend this ideal to a universal community of interpreters. Dewey explored the social and political consequences of the idea of community for understanding the moral ideal of democracy. Mead was a pioneer in developing a theory of the social-psychological genesis of the social self – a theory of "practical intersubjectivity."[7]

Today there are many who have raised doubts about the Peircian conviction that – in the long run – there will be a convergence of inquiry. But doubts about an ideal convergence do not undermine the necessity of always appealing to a critical community. On the contrary, they heighten its importance. For it is only by submitting our hypotheses to public critical discussion that we become aware of what is valid in our claims and what fails to withstand critical scrutiny. It is only by the serious encounter with what is other, different, and alien that we can hope to determine what is idiosyncratic, limited, and partial.

(4)   Anti-foundationalism, fallibilism, and the nurturing of critical communities leads to the fourth theme running through the pragmatic tradition – the awareness and sensitivity to radical contingency and chance that mark the universe, our inquiries, our lives. Contingency and chance have always been problematic for philosophy. In the concern with universality and necessity, there has been a deep desire to master, contain and repress contingency – to assign

it to its "proper" restricted place. For the pragmatists, contingency and chance are not merely signs of human ignorance, they are ineradicable and pervasive features of the universe. Long before the rise of quantum physics, Peirce developed a variety of arguments against the doctrine of mechanical necessity. He speculatively advanced a theory of cosmic evolution where there is a continuous interplay between evolving laws – habits of nature – and chance. But the insistence on the inescapability of chance and contingency – on what Dewey called "the precariousness of existence" where the "world is a scene of risk" and is "uncannily unstable"[8] – conditioned their understanding of experience and philosophy itself. We can never hope to "master" unforeseen and unexpected contingencies. We live in an "open universe" which is always at once threatening and a source of tragedy and opportunity. This is why the pragmatists placed so much emphasis on how we are to respond to contingencies – on developing the complex of dispositions and critical habits that Dewey called "reflective intelligence."

(5) I come finally to the theme of plurality. We can see how it pervades the other themes that I have sketched. There can be no escape from plurality – a plurality of traditions, perspectives, philosophic orientations. Later I will try to clarify what the pragmatists did and did not mean by pluralism and how it is relevant for understanding our present situation in philosophy. James described his own pluralistic orientation as follows:

> It is curious how little countenance radical pluralism has ever had from philosophers. Whether materialistically or spiritualistically minded, philosophers have always aimed at cleaning up the litter with which the world apparently is filled. They have substituted economical and orderly conceptions for the first sensible tangle; whether these were morally elevated or only intellectually neat, they were at any rate always aesthetically pure and definite, and aimed at ascribing to the world something clean and intellectual in the way of inner structure. As compared with all these rationalizing pictures, the pluralistic empiricism which I profess offers but a sorry appearance. It is a turbid, muddled, gothic sort of affair without a sweeping outline and with little pictorial nobility.[9]

I have sketched some of the interrelated themes of the pragmatic style of thinking – the pragmatic *ēthos*. These themes are intended to

330 Pragmatism, Pluralism, the Healing of Wounds

serve as reminders because the richness and diversity of this tradition consists in the ways in which they have been explored and refined. But what has happened to this pragmatic legacy? I have already indicated that these themes keep resurfacing – even in the works of those who are not directly indebted to the pragmatists. But there has also been a forgetfulness of this tradition. By the mid-twentieth century, many philosophers in America thought of pragmatism as a movement that had exhausted itself. Other agendas had much greater appeal for our burgeoning profession. No one can underestimate the ways in which the émigré philosophers from Europe – Reichenbach, Carnap, Feigl, Tarski, Hempel (and many others) – were reshaping philosophy in America. There were, of course, transitional figures like C. I. Lewis and Ernest Nagel who had a grounding in the pragmatic tradition, but their interests in logic and the philosophy of science helped to foster an ambience for the receptivity of logical positivism and logical empiricism. Logical positivism in the militant form of the Vienna Circle or in its polemical form advocated by A. J. Ayer did not take deep root in America.[10] But a positivistic temper, and the legacy of logical empiricism, did flourish. During the period following the Second World War, when there was an enormous growth of academic philosophy, there was virtually a scurrying to refashion graduate schools so that they would become respectable analytic departments. This was a time of great confidence among professional philosophers. It was felt by the growing analytic community that "we" philosophers had "finally" discovered the conceptual tools and techniques to make progress in solving or dissolving philosophic problems. This was also the time when the Anglo-American/Continental split became an almost unbridgeable chasm. What was going on in European "philosophy" was taken to be pretentious, obscure, woolly, and muddled. By the new standards of what constituted "doing philosophy," Continental philosophy no longer counted as "serious" philosophy. Of course, there were pockets of resistance to the new analytic styles of "doing philosophy." There were those who defended and practiced speculative metaphysics in the manner of Whitehead; there were those who saw greater promise in phenomenology and existentialism, there were those who sought to keep the pragmatic tradition alive; there were those who still believed that a careful study of the history of philosophy was relevant for contemporary philosophizing. But philosophers who had not taken the analytic "linguistic turn" were clearly on the defensive. Richard Rorty captures the mood of this time when he writes:

> In 1951, a graduate student who (like myself) was in the process of learning about, or being converted to, analytic philosophy could still believe that there were a finite number of distinct specifiable problems to be resolved – problems which any serious analytic philosopher would agree to be *the* outstanding problems. For example, there was the problem of the counterfactual conditional, the problem of whether an "emotive" analysis of ethical terms was satisfactory, Quine's problem about the nature of analyticity, and a few more. These were problems which fitted nicely into the vocabulary of the positivists. They could be seen as the final, proper formulation of problems which had been seen, as in a glass darkly, by Leibniz, Hume, and Kant. Further, there was agreement on what a solution to a philosophic problem looked like – e.g. Russell on definite descriptions, Frege on meaning and reference, Tarski on truth. In those days, when my generation was young, all of the conditions for a Kuhnian "normal" problem-solving discipline were fulfilled.[11]

There were other influences shaping the character of analytic philosophy. In the post-Second World War period, there was also a receptivity to the type of "ordinary language philosophy" or "conceptual analysis" that was so fashionable at Oxford. Ryle, Austin and the later Wittgenstein (as filtered and domesticated through Anglo-American spectacles) rivaled the more formalistic methods favored by logical empiricists. But whether one's allegiances were to the more formal or informal methods of analysis, there was a growing conviction that philosophers could now make genuine progress in solving well-formulated problems. Soon a new generation of philosophers were trained in America who not only mastered analytic techniques, but whose contributions surpassed the work of their teachers. Quine was a new hero, for he represented a figure who had assimilated what was taken to be most enduring in the pragmatic tradition but whose style of argumentation and logical finesse owed more to Carnap and Tarski than to Peirce, James, or Dewey. With the increased sophistication of analytic philosophy, there was also a growing internal complexity. Whereas with an earlier generation of logical positivists and empiricists, the consequences of their claims for other fields of inquiry could be clearly discerned – even if they were provocative and controversial – it was difficult for many outsiders (or even insiders to philosophy who were not tuned in to the latest debates in the professional journals) to figure out the significance of the problems that analytic philosophers took to be so central. It looked as if philosophers were perfecting a jargon that was barely intelligible to others. But for insiders this is what was to be properly expected as philosophy became more rigorous and sophisticated. Looking back at the development of analytic philosophy a generation after its initial triumph, Rorty continues his sketch:

> To recite this list of problems and paradigms is to evoke memories of a simple, brighter, vanished world. In the interlocking "central" areas of analytic philosophy – epistemology, philosophy of language, and metaphysics – there are now as many paradigms as there are major philosophy departments .... Any problem that enjoys a simultaneous vogue in ten of the hundred or so "analytic" philosophy departments in America is doing exceptionally well. The field these days is a jungle of competing research programs, programs which seem to have a shorter and shorter half-life as the years go by .... The best hope for an American philosopher is Andy Warhol's promise that we shall *all* be superstars, for approximately fifteen minutes apiece.[12]

Rorty's portrait may seem to be a caricature, but it is nevertheless a revealing one. It does not do justice to what has been achieved by analytic styles of philosophizing, nor does it mention what has always been characteristic of philosophy in America – its sheer heterogeneity and plurality. For even when the analytic *ēthos* had its greatest influence, it never completely dominated the American scene. It is important to distinguish the many impressive achievements of analytic work from the arrogant ideology that surrounded it during the first wave of its flourishing in America. For it is this ideology – the frequently unspoken belief that it was the *only* serious and proper way of doing philosophy – that is now breaking up. I do not think we should be naive, for there are still many analytic philosophers who believe in their hearts that there is no serious alternative, and are hostile and disdainful of other philosophic orientations. But such an ideology, which is still a source of intellectual violence and wounds in our profession, is becoming increasingly archaic and quaint.

Suppose we ask how this breakup of ideology has come about – and what its consequences are. Here we need to focus on both external and internal factors, although they have been intertwined. By external factors, I mean what has been happening in the world outside of academic philosophy. For at the very time when analytic philosophy seemed to be consolidating during the decades of the 1950s and 1960s, many philosophers resisted the constraints imposed by analytic philosophy on what counted as serious philosophizing. Both James and Dewey had warned us about the dangers of a growing professionalism and specialization of the "problems of philosophy." Dewey spoke of the need to address the "problems of men" – the problems of human beings. In the turmoil taking place in the outside world, many philosophers in America turned their attention to other philosophic orientations – to phenomenology, hermeneutics, critical theory, the varieties of structuralism and poststructuralism which they believed provided more powerfully illuminating ways of philosophizing. There was also a rebellion against the ahistorical and anti-historical biases of the analytic ideology. In the past few decades there has been a flourishing of historical studies with a systematic intent. This growing interest in the history of philosophy is itself an expression of the impulse to enlarge the scope of philosophic reflection. New voices also demanded to be heard – as evidenced by feminist and minority concerns. And as the philosophy curriculum in many prestigious analytic graduate departments began to shrink – excluding or marginalizing philosophers who were no longer to be taken "seriously" – our colleagues in departments of religion and literature began teaching Hegel, Nietzsche, Kierkegaard, and Heidegger.

"We" philosophers have all sorts of defense mechanisms and techniques for deflating or ignoring the criticisms of "outsiders." But "we" are much more sensitive to the criticisms of "insiders." During the past two decades, it is the criticisms of insiders that have shaken us up and stirred so much controversy and resentment. Consider the controversies generated by the writings of three former presidents of our division, Richard Rorty, Alasdair MacIntyre, and Hilary Putnam. No one could fault them for being ignorant of analytic styles of philosophizing. Each had made major contributions to the ongoing debates that have been at the cutting edge of analytic philosophy. But in different ways each has severely criticized the exclusionary biases of the analytic ideology. Each has helped to open up and expand what Rorty calls the conversation of philosophy. Each has questioned the boundary-fixing tendency of the ideological phase of analytic philosophy. Indeed, we are beginning to see how silly and unfruitful it is to think in terms of an Anglo-American/Continental split. If we "look and see," we find elaborate crisscrossings taking place, and discover how similar issues crop up in what were once taken to be radically different philosophic vocabularies. Kuhn comes to recognize the affinities of his work with hermeneutics. The French discover Austin and Wittgenstein. Habermas appropriates speech act theory in his theory of communicative action. Apel's transcendental pragmatics builds on the pioneering work of Peirce.

But something else has been happening – especially among younger members of our profession – which is perhaps even more important. For what James wrote in 1904 seems especially relevant in our situation:

> It is difficult not to notice a curious unrest in the philosophic atmosphere of the time, a loosening of old landmarks, a softening of oppositions, a mutual borrowing from one another on the part of systems anciently closed, and an interest in new suggestions, however vague, as if the one thing sure was the inadequacy of the extant school-solutions. The dissatisfaction with these seems due for the most part to a feeling that they are too abstract and academic. Life is confused and superabundant, and what the younger generation appears to crave is more of the temperament of life in its philosophy, even though it were at some cost of logical rigor and formal purity.[13]

One of the most hopeful signs for philosophy in America today is this "unrest in the philosophic atmosphere," this "loosening of old landmarks." The ideological battles of my generation are beginning to seem remote and irrelevant. Scars from the wounds of these battles still remain, but there are encouraging signs of the emergence of a new *ēthos* – one which bears strong affinities with the *ēthos* characteristic of the formative stages of the pragmatic movement. There are all sorts of crisscrossings and interweavings. One may discover the ways in which deconstruction shows affinities with pragmatism or with the investigations of the later Wittgenstein. One may realize that Hegel's distinction between *Moralität* and *Sichlichkeit* is relevant for understanding contemporary moral and ethical theory. One may realize that Popper and Foucault are relevant for untangling the complexities of historicism. These interweavings extend to the interplay of disciplines which not so long ago were taken to be quite distinct – philosophy and law, philosophy and literature, philosophy and the social disciplines, philosophy and medicine, and so forth.

Indeed, there is another emerging phenomenon that exhibits a new intellectual mood of fluidity and breaking down of boundaries. Throughout the country in our universities and colleges there has been an explosion of study and discussion groups that cluster about new constellations of texts and themes that cut across disciplines. What distinguishes these groups from older models of "interdisciplinary" discussions is that there is no longer the presumption of a distinctive disciplinary approach to a given problem – as if there were a unique philosophic, literary or anthropological point of view. The intermingling and overlapping is much more radical where pursuing issues in one's own field necessitates drawing upon the ways in which issues are explored in other fields of inquiry. It is almost as if there is a "counter-disciplinary" movement developing which no longer finds the disciplinary matrices that have shaped our academic departments helpful in dealing with intellectual problems. Some of us are beginning to discover that we share more intellectually with colleagues trained in different disciplines than with our own departmental philosophic colleagues.

What then is our situation in philosophy today? Perhaps the simplest and most direct answer is Babel, a confusion of tongues. But Babel itself is not so simple. We cannot escape the fact that there has been a decentering of philosophy itself. There has been a radical pluralization of different vocabularies, research programs, voices demanding to be heard. I sometimes think that a primary reason why there has been so much concern with problems of incommensurability and relativism is because this is the condition that we find ourselves in as philosophers, where we speak such radically different tongues that we are unable to understand what even our closest neighbors are saying – as if we were becoming like windowless monads. There are dangers and challenges in this situation.

Here I want to return to the theme of pluralism, or rather to the question of how one is to respond to this extreme pluralization. For pluralism itself is open to many interpretations and we need to make some important distinctions. For there is a danger of a *fragmenting* pluralism where the centrifugal forces become so strong that we are only able to communicate with the small group that already shares our own biases, and no longer even experience the need to talk with others outside of this circle. There is a *flabby* pluralism where our borrowings from different orientations are little more than glib superficial poaching. There is *polemical* pluralism where the appeal to pluralism doesn't signify a genuine willingness to listen and learn from others, but becomes rather an ideological weapon to advance one's own orientation. There is *defensive* pluralism, a form of tokenism, where we pay lip service to others "doing their own thing" but are already convinced that there is nothing important to be learned from them.

The type of pluralism that represents what is best in our pragmatic tradition is an *engaged fallibilistic pluralism*. Such a pluralistic *ēthos* places new responsibilities upon each of us. For it means taking our own fallibility seriously – resolving that however much we are committed to our own styles of thinking, we are willing to listen to others without denying or suppressing the otherness of the other. It means being vigilant against the dual temptations of simply dismissing what others are saying by falling back on one of those standard defensive ploys where we condemn it as obscure, woolly, or trivial, or thinking we can always easily translate what is alien into our own entrenched vocabularies. Sometimes understanding rival traditions requires what Alasdair MacIntyre characterizes as learning a second first language where we come to recognize the ways in which rival traditions are and are not translatable.[14] What makes this task so difficult and unstable is the growing realization that there are no uncontested rules or procedures "which will tell us how rational agreement can be reached on what would settle the issue on every point where statements seem to conflict."[15] But this doesn't mean that we have to fall back to some version of what Popper called the "myth of the framework" where we are prisoners caught in the framework of our theories – our expectations, our past experiences, our language – "and that we are so imprisoned into these frameworks that we cannot even communicate with those imprisoned in radically different frameworks."[16] Or rather, to the extent that this does happen, it is, I believe, primarily an *ethical* failure rather than a cognitive or linguistic one. Ultimately the appeal to the regulative ideal of a community of inquirers or interpreters is – as the pragmatists emphasized – an ethical or normative ideal.

Whether one draws upon Davidsonian or Habermasian arguments, we can question the very idea of conceptual schemes that are so self-enclosed that there is no possibility of reciprocal translation, understanding, and argumentation. But because there are no uncontested decision procedures for adjudicating the claims of rival philosophic orientations, it is always a *task* to seek out commonalities and points of difference and conflict. The *achievement* of a "we" –

where "we" are locked in argument with others – is a fragile and temporary achievement that can always be ruptured by unexpected contingencies. Conflict and disagreement are unavoidable in our pluralistic situation. There is little reason to believe that "we" philosophers will ever achieve any substantive permanent consensus, and there are many good reasons for questioning the desirability of such a consensus. What matters, however, is how we respond to conflict. The response that the pragmatists call for is a dialogical response where we genuinely seek to achieve a mutual reciprocal understanding – an understanding that does not preclude disagreement.

One of the consequences of the analytic movement has been to encourage the "adversarial" or "confrontational" style of argumentation. According to this style, when one is confronted with a claim or thesis that one takes to be mistaken one relentlessly "goes after it." The other is viewed as an opponent, and the aim is to locate specifically what is wrong in the opponent's position, to expose its weaknesses. The practice of this style of argumentation requires attention to details, working through specific claims and arguments in order to show up their falsity and sometimes to expose their triviality. There are great advantages to this style of argumentation. It is never satisfied with vague claims, it helps to pinpoint issues in dispute, and it can expose difficulties that need to be confronted. But there are also dangers in this style of argumentation when carried to extremes. For in being primarily concerned with exposing weaknesses, with showing the absurdities in what is taken to be mistaken, we can be blind to what the other is saying and to the truth that the other is contributing to the discussion.

The adversarial confrontational style can be contrasted with a model of dialogical encounter. Here one begins with the assumption that the other has something to say to us and to contribute to our understanding. The initial task is to grasp the other's position in the *strongest* possible light. One must always attempt to be responsive to what the other is saying and showing. This requires imagination, sensitivity and perfecting hermeneutical skills. There is a play, a to-and-fro movement in dialogical encounters, a seeking for a common ground in which we can understand our differences. The other is not an adversary or an opponent, but a conversational partner. Conflict is just as important in dialogical encounters, because understanding does not entail agreement. On the contrary, it is the way to clarify our disagreements. Gadamer states the point succinctly when he writes: "One does not seek to score a point by exploiting the other's weaknesses; rather, one seeks to strengthen the other's argument as much as possible so as to render it plausible. Such an effort seems to me to be constitutive for any communication."[17] An engaged fallibilistic pluralism that is true to what is best in the pragmatic tradition requires a delicate balance between these different styles of argumentation and encounter. Unfortunately, during the past few decades, "we" philosophers have not only perfected our adversarial skills but have carried them to excess. In this respect, our practices reflect what is occurring throughout society. "We" need to counterbalance these practices with cultivating dialogical encounters. Such encounters require what Rorty calls the Socratic virtues, "the willingness to talk, to listen to other people, to weigh the consequences of our actions upon other people."[18] Perhaps "we" philosophers might even play a modest role in encouraging the type of civility that is becoming so rare in our social practices.

I began by seeking to elicit the pragmatic *ēthos* by adumbrating the themes of anti-foundationalism, fallibilism, the social character of the self and the regulative ideal of a critical community, contingency, and pluralism. I did this in order to gain a critical perspective on our present situation in philosophy. But in speaking about the present I have slipped into making an *appeal* – with a future reference. An appeal presupposes a sense of disparity between what presently exists and what one hopes will prevail. Because "we" philosophers are human-all-too-human, it is perhaps utopian to think that we will ever completely escape from ideological contentiousness. Nevertheless, we can aspire to displace ideological labeling with reasonable philosophic engagement.

The time has come to realize that there has been an ideological cultural lag in our profession – to realize that the ideological battles characteristic of the first wave of the reception of analytic philosophy in America no longer make much sense. The time has come to heal the wounds of these ideological battles. The time has come to realize how unilluminating and unfruitful it is to think in terms of an Anglo-American/Continental split. The philosophic interminglings that are now taking place defy any such simplistic dichotomy. Philosophy has been decentered. There is no single paradigm, research program, or orientation that dominates philosophy. The fact is that our situation is pluralistic. But the question becomes how we are to *respond* to this pluralism. There are powerful centrifugal tendencies toward fragmentation. But there are also counter-tendencies – not toward convergence, consensus, and harmony – but toward breaking down of boundaries, "a loosening of old landmarks" and dialogical encounters where we reasonably explore our differences and conflicts. In this situation, the pragmatic legacy is especially relevant, in particular the call to nurture the type of community and solidarity where there is an engaged fallibilistic pluralism – one that is based upon mutual respect, where we are willing to risk our own prejudgments, are open to listening and learning from others, and we respond to others with responsiveness and responsibility.

I conclude with a citation from John Courtney Murray, who eloquently expressed the *ēthos* of an engaged fallibilistic pluralism.

Barbarism ... threatens when men cease to talk together according to reasonable laws. There are laws of argument, the observance of which is imperative if discourse is to be civilized. Argument ceases to be civil when it is dominated by passion and prejudice; when its vocabulary becomes solipsist, premised on the theory that my insight is mine alone and cannot be shared; when dialogue gives way to a series of monologues; when the parties to the conversation cease to listen to one another, or hear only what they want to hear, or see the other's argument only through the screen of their own categories .... When things like this happen, men cannot be locked together in argument. Conversation becomes merely quarrelsome or querulous. Civility dies with the death of dialogue.[19]

NOTES

1 Alasdair MacIntyre, "Epistemological Crises, Dramatic Narrative and the Philosophy of Science," *Monist* 60 (1977), p. 461.
2 Charles Sanders Peirce, "Questions Concerning Certain Faculties Claimed for Man," "Some Consequences of Four Incapacities," and "Grounds of Validity on the Laws of Logic." These papers are included in vol. 5 of Charles S. Peirce's *Collected Papers*, ed. Charles Hartshorne and Paul Weiss (Cambridge, Mass.: Harvard University Press, 1932 – 5).
3 Charles S. Peirce, *Collected Papers*, 5.264.
4 Wilfrid Sellars, "Empiricism and the Philosophy of Mind," in *Minnesota Studies in the Philosophy of Science*, 1, ed. Herbert Feigl and Michael Scriven (Minneapolis: University of Minnesota Press, 1956), p. 300.
5 Peirce, *Collected Papers*, 5.265.
6 Ibid.

7   See Hans Joas, *G. H. Mead: A Contemporary Re-examination of His Thought* (Cambridge, Mass.: MIT Press, 1985).

8   John Dewey, *Experience and Nature, The Later Works 1925–1953*, 1, ed. Jo Ann Boydston (Carbondale: Southern Illinois University Press, 1981), p. 43.

9   William James, A *Pluralistic Universe* (Cambridge, Mass.: Harvard University Press, 1977), p. 26.

10   The following paragraphs are adapted from the introduction of my book, *Philosophical Profiles* (Philadelphia: University of Pennsylvania Press, 1986), pp. 2–5.

11   Richard Rorty, "Philosophy in America Today," in his *Consequences of Pragmatism* (Minneapolis: University of Minnesota Press, 1982), p. 215.

12   Ibid.

13   William James, "A World of Pure Experience," *Journal of Philosophy, Psychology and Scientific Methods*, I (1904), p. 533.

14   Alasdair MacIntyre, *Whose Justice? Which Rationality?* (Notre Dame: University of Notre Dame Press, 1988). See especially chap. 19, "Tradition and Translation."

15   Richard Rorty, *Philosophy and the Mirror of Nature* (Princeton: Princeton University Press, 1979), p. 316.

16   Karl Popper, "Normal Science and Its Dangers," in Imre Lakatos and Alan Musgrave, eds., *Criticism and the Growth of Knowledge* (Cambridge: Cambridge University Press, 1970), p. 56.

17   Hans-Georg Gadamer, *Text und Interpretation* (Munich: Finh, 1984). The English translation is from Fred R. Dallmayr, "Hermeneutics and Deconstruction," in *Critical Encounters* (Notre Dame: University of Notre Dame Press, 1987), p. 135.

18   Richard Rorty, "Pragmatism, Relativism, and Irrationalism," *Proceedings and Addresses of the American Philosophical Association* 53 (1980), p. 736.

19   John Courtney Murray, SJ, *We Hold These Truths* (New York: Sheed and Ward, 1960), p. 14.

Index of Subjects

Index of Names